Votes for Women

VOTES FOR WOMEN

The Story of a Struggle

by

ROGER FULFORD

WHITE LION PUBLISHERS LIMITED
London, New York, Sydney and Toronto

First published in Great Britain by
Faber and Faber 1957
© Rodger Fulford 1957

White Lion Edition 1976

ISBN 085617 969 8

Made and printed in Great Britain
for White Lion Publishers Limited
138 Park Lane, London W1Y 3DD
by Latimer Trend & Co. Ltd. Plymouth

'What will the Future make of the Present?'

C. F. G. MASTERMAN: *Condition of England.* 1909

Contents

I. 'WOMEN OF ENGLAND, AWAKE'   *page* 19

II. REFORM FOR MEN ONLY   32

III. 'HE WANTS GIRLS IN PARLIAMENT'   41

IV. LYDIA BECKER FROM MANCHESTER   54

V. MRS. MAXWELL VOTES   63

VI. 'THIS MAD, WICKED FOLLY OF WOMEN'S RIGHTS'   73

VII. DEATH OF MISS BECKER   77

VIII. SWAYING FORTUNES AT WESTMINSTER   82

IX. APPLAUSES FROM THE LADIES GALLERY   91

X. LABOUR TO THE RESCUE   97

XI. RICHARD AND EMMELINE PANKHURST   109

XII. W.S.P.U. IS BORN   119

XIII. A CHALLENGING QUESTION TO CHURCHILL   125

XIV. THE ASSAULT ON LONDON   132

XV. THE TWO EMMELINES AND MRS. DESPARD   145

XVI. KEEP THE LIBERAL OUT   156

XVII. A SPLIT—THE LEAGUE IS FORMED   164

XVIII. CLINGING TO THEIR CHAINS   172

XIX. PAGEANTRY ON THE STREETS OF LONDON   179

XX. INSIDE BOW STREET POLICE COURT   185

XXI. 'THE WOMEN OF ENGLAND ARE CLAMOURING OUTSIDE'   193

XXII. THE HUNGER STRIKE   201

9

Contents

XXIII. Lady Constance in Disguise   *page* 209

XXIV. Conciliation and King Edward's Death   215

XXV. From Prison to Citizenship   235

XXVI. 'War is Declared on Women'   242

XXVII. Smashing the Windows   245

XXVIII. The Emmelines Part Company   255

XXIX. An Obscene Letter to 'The Times'   260

XXX. The Constitutionalists Progress   165

XXXI. Strange Colours at Balmoral   269

XXXII. 'Burning to Vote'   280

XXXIII. 'I Don't Know What We Are Coming To' 287

XXXIV. The Vote at Last   298

Appendix I. Biographical Index   308

II. Dates of Enfranchisement of Women   328
      Abroad

Index   331

Illustrations

1. Meeting in Hanover Square Rooms about 1870; Rhoda Garrett speaking; Mrs. Mark Pattison talking to Mrs. Fawcett; Miss Becker is in the centre   *facing page* 32
Reproduction by courtesy of Picture Post Library

2a. Frances Power Cobbe   33
Reproduced by courtesy of Picture Post Library

2b. Lydia Ernestine Becker   33
This photograph is taken from Miss Helen Blackburn's 'History of Women's Suffrage' (by kind permission of Williams & Norgate)

2c. Mrs. Pankhurst   33
Reproduced by permission of the Trustees of the London Museum

2d. Mrs. Despard   33
Reproduced by permission of the Trustees of the London Museum

3. Trafalgar Square, October 1908; Mrs. Pankhurst speaking, 'General' Drummond in the background   48
Reproduced by permission of the Trustess of the London Museum

4. Mrs. Pankhurst and Miss Christabel Pankhurst in their prison clothes   49
Reproduced by courtesy of Picture Post Library

5. W.S.P.U. Leaders and their motor-car; seated, Mrs. Pankhurst and Miss Anne Kenney; standing, Mrs. Pethick-Lawrence   112
Reproduced by permission of the Trustees of the London Museum

6. Lady Constance Lytton at Newcastle, about to throw her stone   113
This photograph is taken from Miss Sylvia Pankhurst's 'The Suffragette Movemen't 1931 (by kind permission of Longmans, Green)

7a. Jane Warton   128
Reproduced by permission of the Trustees of the London Museum

7b. Mrs. Pankhurst   128
Reproduced by permission of the Trustees of the London Museum

Illustrations

8*a*. Sylvia Pankhurst in the East End: a post-war celebration breakfast *facing page* 129
Reproduced by courtesy of Picture Post Library

8*b*. On the door-step; 'the General' picketing Sir Edward Carson's house in Eaton Place 129
Reproduced by courtesy of Picture Post Library

9. 'Cat and Mouse'—a W.S.P.U. impression of McKenna's Act 176
Reproduced by permission of the Trustees of the London Museum

10. 'The Modern Inquisition'—a W.S.P.U. impression of forcible feeding 177
Reproduced by permission of the Trustees of the London Museum

11. Funeral of Emily Wilding Davison; the cortege crossing Piccadilly Circus 192
Reproduced by courtesy of Picture Post Library

12. Funeral of Emily Wilding Davison; the coffin at Victoria Station 193
Reproduced by courtesy of Picture Post Library

13. Mrs. Despard in Downing Street: a group of sympathizers 240
Reproduced by courtesy of Picture Post Library

14. Mounted Police clearing Trafalgar Square after a Suffragette meeting—May 1913 241
Reproduced by courtesy of Picture Post Library

15. Attempt to enter Buckingham Palace: Mrs. Pankhurst being removed by a police inspector 256
Reproduced by courtesy of Picture Post Library

16. Attempt on Buckingham Palace: an arrest 257
Reproduced by courtesy of Picture Post Library

Introduction

From the vantage-ground reached by human beings in the middle of the twentieth century, with the sky stormy and the path arduous, the years before 1914 seem to lie in the background, like a golden valley, where all is order and contentment. Travellers still with us, who knew that happy land, attempting to recall some scene or anecdote from that vanished world, often preface their tale with some such words as 'It was before '14'. The listener almost seems to catch the anguish in their tone—to sense from that plaintive cry something of what is implied for them in the shift from certainty to disorder. Talleyrand, who was no mere *laudator temporis acti*, said of the world before the French Revolution that only those who had lived then could know the sweetness of life. Similarly in the seventeenth century in England people, contrasting the dire events of the middle of that century—the catastrophes and bitterness of civil war—with the serenity and elegance of earlier decades, looked backwards with sorrow. This particular point has been expressed with all his characteristic feeling and perception by Lord David Cecil in his book *Two Quiet Lives* when he observes that even if the dwellers in seventeenth-century England could escape the full shock of the storm of those injurious years 'its rumour reverberated always in the distance, its shadow brooded darkly over the landscape. An uneasy sadness pervaded the spirit'. So might it be said of human beings in mid-twentieth-century England.

Yet it is possible that in reality the years before 1914 were neither quite so golden nor quite so prosaic as they appear to-day. For the war created no changes and reforms; it merely accelerated those which already existed. However peaceful and languid the landscape may seem from the century's maturity, those looking at it closely could not possibly challenge the verdict of Sir Robert Ensor, the great chronicler of those times, that it was seething and teeming with immense ferment and restless fertility. In politics this was conspicuously the case. The political Labour movement, the safeguarding by the State of those who through misfortune or immaturity had no place in the thriving throng of wage-earners, and the claims of women to equality were all established by 1914. But if the last was established it was certainly not generally accepted. Rich old ladies with a train of companions, nurses and 'maids', devoted daughters of professional families and stray spinsters from working-class homes looking after fading relatives were only too sadly obvious. Their crotchets and pathos are enshrined for posterity in Sir Osbert Sitwell's *Before the Bombardment*. Yet in women of all classes—as is proved by the story of the struggle for the vote—there was a stir, it assailed all the ranks of femininity, the stir of adventure and new ideas, comparable with the agitation which may be noted in a flock of migrants impelled by the lure of new worlds.

This book tries to tell the story of a single aspect of that wide movement, to concentrate on the struggle for political enfranchisement, and to disentangle it from the general march of women towards emancipation. In 1914 not a single woman might record her vote at a general election in Great Britain. Four years later— at the General Election of 1918—every woman (with a few trifling exceptions) over 30 was allowed to vote. The generally accepted cliché is that women won the vote because of their war-service. How far such an argument could be sustained is a matter of opinion. The curtain falls on my story in 1914, and I have not attempted to draw it back and show off my actors and actresses after the battle was won, still less to declaim to the audience that votes for women have proved good or bad, or that women Members of Parliament have been a success or a failure. I have merely sought to set out the facts, and to catch something of the hopes and enthusiasm which lent those facts their life and fascination for posterity.

A distinguished writer, Mr. V. S. Pritchett, lately pointed out that the long-drawn campaign for the emancipation of women has been more notable for its ricochets than for its bulls-eyes. No one glancing through the books on the subject could fail to endorse this emphatic comment. And if the partisans on each side have been somewhat wild in their shooting, the great masters of history have tended to view the efforts of feminists with too much indifference and amusement. How often must the enquiring reader on turning to his books have shared the disappointment expressed by Virginia Woolf in *A Room of One's Own*, 'I went to the shelf where the histories stand . . . I looked up "Women", found "wife beating"!' There is a considerable output of books on the enfranchisement of women and anyone, who has read in them, would agree that there is much enjoyment and information there, but both have to be disengaged from a certain masculine condescension from the one sex and an almost apostolic fervour from the other. These characteristics are more apparent in the nineteenth-century writers than those of the twentieth century.

The literature on the political and social position of women between 1850 and 1914 has recently been the subject of a masterly analysis by Mr. O. R. McGregor: his bibliography was first published in the *British Journal of Sociology* in March 1955. To his industry and perception I pay my modest tribute: and I acknowledge my indebtedness to his work which I have borne with me, as it were a compass, through libraries and reading-rooms, up to attics and down to basements where it has never failed to comfort me by the constancy with which it points to what is salient.

I express here the very deep sense of my obligation to Miss Sylvia Pankhurst for her two books on which I have unashamedly drawn for an understanding of the exciting (though at times confusing) story of militancy. The first, written while the battle, with all its subtle changes of fortune, was at its height was published in 1912 and is called *The Suffragette*: the second, which is ampler and more detached, was published in 1931 and is called *The Suffragette Movement*. I have also drawn freely on a book, generously documented, written by A. E. Metcalfe and published by Basil Blackwell in 1917. This is called *Woman's Effort—A Chronicle of 50 Years Struggle for Citizenship*, and when Mr. Asquith read it he noted that it was 'a curious book'. The interest of this book, and the explanation for Mr. Asquith's comment, lies in its attempt to give an intellectual justification for militant tactics. On the nineteenth century Miss Helen Blackburn's book—*Record of Women's Suffrage*, which was published in 1902, gives an indispensable account of those formative years. Mrs. Oliver Strachey, in her book *The Cause: A Short History of the Women's Movement in Great Britain*, which was published in 1929, describes the struggle as it appeared to those who were outside militancy and to one who belonged to a family which will ever be honoured for the intellectual stimulus which it gave to the movement. These are the corner-stones on which I have arranged my structure and I acknowledge, with abiding gratitude, my feeling of security. I have excluded from the book any list of authorities partly because such a list would seem to err on the side of ostentation and chiefly because Mr. McGregor's bibliography makes it unnecessary.

I have been fortunate in being given access to two important collections. The Suffragette Fellowship, which came into existence after the vote was won and after most of the societies, formed to fight for it, had been disbanded, gathered together various records and emblems of militancy which were presented to the London Museum. To the Trustees of that Museum, and to Mr. Hayes, the assistant keeper in charge of the documents, I am deeply grateful for permission to examine them. The John Rylands Library at Manchester possesses a set of newspaper-cutting files originally formed by the National Union of Societies for Equal Citizenship: they are pasted up by a lady with that accuracy and neatness which captivate the admiration of the opposite sex, and they proved an invaluable quarry—a rather unexpected find among the bibliographical treasures of that great library. I sincerely thank the Keeper of Printed Books, Mr. Ronald Hall, for all his help.

I have not deliberately sought manuscript material, because there seemed to me sufficient information for my purpose in printed sources and in the ephemerae of the time. For a different reason I have not attempted to gather recollections of those who still survive from those famous days. There were inevitably shades of difference—and at times open discord—among the ladies of the suffrage movement: it seemed to me, in all the circumstances, fairer to eschew the recollections of those who chanced to survive and form my own conclusions from the ample records available. I am, however, very grateful to Mrs. Billington Greig, whose association with the movement goes back to the earliest days of militancy in Manchester in 1905, for allowing me to call on her and for giving me valuable recollections of Mrs. Despard. Miss Stella Newsome, the honorary secretary of the Suffragette Fellowship, has helped me in countless ways.

I record my appreciation of the assistance given to me by Mr. Maywood, of the editorial staff of *The Times*, for providing me with facts about Mrs. Despard: by Mrs. F. W. Hirst for information about her aunt, Miss Jane Cobden: by Mrs. Hannah Mitchell, formerly a distinguished member of the Manchester City Council, for advice about Mrs. Despard: by the Editor of the *Wigan Observer* for letting me see the files of his newspaper: by the City Librarian, Salford for information about a former Mayor: by the City Librarian, Sheffield for information about an early suffrage society: by Mr. J. F. E. Stephenson for an account of his eminent forbear—Mr. Edward Pleydell-Bouverie: by Mr. Donald Read for useful information about comments in the Manchester press on the emancipation of women in the nineteenth century: by the staff of the Manchester Reference Library for much help and courtesy, and by the Under-Treasurer at Lincoln's Inn for some facts about Mr. Richard Pankhurst.

Miss Vera Douie, the Librarian of the Woman's Service League, which must possess easily the finest collection of printed books on the women's cause, has been tireless in helping and advising me—not least with her own matchless knowledge of the contents of her library. And if I leave to the last the London Library it is only that I may the more particularly express my thanks to the staff, and record my gratitude for that atmosphere of detachment and learning which its members know so well, and which not even the acrimonious wrangles of the rights of women can disperse.

At the end of the book will be found a brief biographical index of every woman mentioned in the text. Too few of them have found their niches in the Dictionary of National Biography and scarcely any were included, in their lifetimes, in conventional books of reference. The index is not intended as more than a means of identification—though where information was easily obtainable, such as the addresses of a few of the militants at the time, I have included it. While conscious that such a compilation must include mistakes, I hope that it may prove useful, before too many of the lives, thus briefly noted, are lost in the mists of yesterday. I thank my wife for making the index.

Throughout I have striven to avoid diminishing the dignity of the women's cause and of those who fought for it. I have not referred loosely to militants or the others, in the fashionable habit of to-day, by their Christian names except here and there, to avoid constant repetition of a surname. Naturally it has not been possible to recall the names of all the women who, in Victorian times suffered ridicule, or in the twentieth century, to the number of more than one thousand, endured imprisonment for a cause which is now a familiar part of our political lives. Their courage will, without undue emphasis in these pages, never be far from the mind of the reader.

ROGER FULFORD

August 1956

18

I

'Women of England, Awake'

The story of the struggle for woman's suffrage, whose closing chapters were to be marked by confusion and turbulence, began quietly and unobtrusively. In fact so modest and almost furtive was the start that the history is not easily traced back to its forgotten genesis, nor easily disentangled from wider agitations—such as those for the admission of women to the professions or to the intellectual dignity of a degree at the University. Throughout the nineteenth century this battle for emancipation was fought on the widest front, and inevitably any ground won on one sector was a stimulus to those struggling in some other part of the field. For it could certainly be argued that when Florence Nightingale organized a nursing service, when Girton College at Cambridge sprang to life or when Elizabeth Garrett Anderson opened her dispensary at Marylebone, the idea of a woman voting seemed less ridiculous and fantastic than it had previously done. The entire movement, as it advanced, opened up a part of the human mind where prejudice and convention had formerly reigned in darkness. Yet the franchise struggle, though helped forward by developments over the whole field, remained a complete episode—its problems political and its history distinctive.

In particular it differed from all the other agitations because those in the van of the franchise fight saw themselves battling for the restoration of rights which women were believed to have enjoyed in earlier times. They were not, as in the case of women clamouring to be doctors or professors, asking for new rights to which they were entitled through the progress of civilization.

Votes for women was a Paradise which women had once possessed, had now lost and must regain.

Support for the theory that women had certain ancient political rights was not unimpressive. A woman could reign: women, in their own right, could succeed to peerages. Were not these the last fruits from that Garden of Eden where men and women enjoyed an equality of political power?

Rummaging among the practices of our very remote ancestors the supporters of the women's vote were also able to call in aid two curious points. The first was that abbesses had, at one time, received summonses to attend the earliest Parliaments. The Abbesses of Shaftesbury, Barking, Wilton and St. Mary of Winchester were undoubtedly parliamentarians: these formidable ladies come to mind, swathed in their ample robes, with heavy faces and tightly closed lips, their quick-seeing eyes burdened with all the sorrows of humanity, jogging along to take their places in some primitive Witenagemot. But the invitation to these august devotees did not persist, and they ceased to attend the medieval parliaments. This exclusion from political honour seems to have been accompanied by a widely held feeling that women were better suited for domestic life, and that even the intellectual and artistic elegances of monastic life spoiled them for the home where their position was natural, their talents appropriate. This point of view was forcibly expressed by the first Lord Pembroke in Tudor times: as he watched the nuns, when monastic houses were being dissolved, streaming out of Wilton and leaving for ever the life which they had known of learning and culture, he called out to them with the coarse, good sense of his family, 'Go spin, you jades, go spin.'

The second argument, which emerged from the mists of antiquity, was that some women who were large landowners had always been able to control elections, and the most effective example was Anne, Countess of Dorset. This illustrious lady, who lived in the seventeenth century, owned huge tracts of northern England including a string of castles from Skipton to Appleby. In the latter town her parliamentary influence decided elections, and in the reign of Charles II one of the Secretaries of State wrote to urge her to use her influence in favour of a particular candidate.

She replied, 'I have been bullied by an usurper [Cromwell]. I have been ill-treated by a court [Charles II] but I won't be dictated to by a subject. Your man shall not stand.'

This reply delighted Horace Walpole, when he came across it a century afterwards, and although its authenticity may be doubtful it is characteristic of one who always showed the spirit of a militant.

In addition to these precedents, the legality for excluding women from a vote was not without its ambiguity. In the seventeenth century when interest in antiquarian matters was developing strongly, especially among lawyers, there was some discussion about the right of women to vote. In a case in the reign of James I, which is still familiar to constitutional lawyers because it laid down that a clergyman could not vote, it was stated that a spinster, who is a freeholder 'can vote for a parliament man'. But twenty years later, at the time of the election of the Long Parliament, the eminent antiquary Sir Simonds D'Ewes, who was high sheriff for Suffolk, and therefore in some measure responsible for the conduct of elections in his county, was horrified to find that, owing to the ignorance of the clerks, some women had voted and he decreed that to make use of such votes was 'verie unworthie of any gentleman and most dishonourable'.

But it was not until 1733 that the right of women to vote was closely examined by lawyers, and virtually determined by a case in that year. This concerned the election of a sexton at one of the City churches—St. Bartolph Without Bishopsgate. Sarah Bly had stood and received 169 male votes and 40 votes from women householders. Her male opponent had received 174 male votes and only 22 from women householders. Sarah Bly had been duly elected and her defeated opponent brought the case to invalidate her election, on the grounds that the women voters should have been excluded. The dispute was tried by four judges including the Lord Chief Justice—Lee, who was a learned student of past times, and displayed on the Bench all the robustness of the Augustan Age typified by his remark that a merry, honest wife was the best medicine a man could have. With him was Page, the judge familiar to readers of Tom Jones, who greeted a man tried for stealing a horse with the words, 'thou didst not only find a horse, but a halter too, I promise'. But on this occasion the alarming man said, 'I see no disability in a woman from voting for a Parliament-man'. One of the other judges differed from Page because 'Such a choice requires an improved understanding which women are not supposed to have'. Lee twice deferred judgment and evidently ransacked the authorities since he stated that the *obiter dicta* of the judge in the case in James I's time, which has already been mentioned, created difficulty. He finally said 'What inclines me to think that they may be admitted to vote in the particular instance is, that the sexton's duty seems to be in the nature of a private trust, he having only the custody of the *Bona Parochianorum*, etc., and it does not seem a thing of public consideration in which I incline to think women have not a right of voting, though they are not positively excluded'. Lee meant that there was no law positively forbidding women to vote or confining the franchise to men. And in the twentieth century when the fury and rancour of Party have invaded local elections, the reader may smile at his dogmatic and innocent judgment that parochial elections were not matters of 'public consideration.' But the distinction which he drew is of some consequence because it was partly the explanation why women were given the right to vote at local elections half a century before they could vote at parliamentary elections.

In early times, as far back as the days of Queen Elizabeth and the Stuarts, the duty of voting was regarded as an inconvenient imposition not greatly different from the obligation to pay taxes. Throughout the eighteenth century this point of view began to change, and people saw the vote as something worth having; the outward and visible sign that a human being had reached political maturity. But the idea that women could be included in any such category was not seriously entertained. Lord Chesterfield, who set out in his letters to his son the views which should guide the existence of every man of birth and intelligence, wrote that women were 'only children of a larger growth: they have an entertaining tattle and sometimes wit; but for solid, reasoning, good sense I never in my life knew one that had it: they love mightily to be dabbling in business (which by the way they always spoil)'.

The Age of Reason, as the eighteenth century is often proudly acclaimed, would seem to have been an Eden in which Adam strolled with all the comfortable assurance of a sultan. Although Lord Chesterfield was not a conspicuous Christian, he would undoubtedly have applauded that Early Father who wrote, 'Adam was beguiled by Eve, not Eve by Adam. It is just that woman should take as her ruler him whom she incited to sin, that he may not fall a second time through female levity.'

A more reasonable case for excluding women from voting is to be found in a House of Commons debate in 1797—apparently the first occasion on which the matter was discussed there. The distinguished statesman, Grey, had raised the question of parliamentary reform, and in the course of debate Fox asked the rhetorical question why it had never been imagined that women should have the right to vote. He answered this by saying that both the law of nations and the law of nature had made 'that sex dependent on ours', and that therefore 'their voices would be governed by the relations in which they stand to society'. He is here using an argument (much beloved by opponents of female franchise throughout the nineteenth century) that if women were given the vote they would merely use it as directed by husband or father, and Fox added that this was why 'in all the theories of the most absurd speculation, it has never been suggested that it would be advisable to extend the elective franchise to the other sex.'

One of the 'absurd theorists' whom Fox had in mind was undoubtedly Mary Godwin or 'the Hyena in petticoats' as she was less politely called by Horace Walpole. After experiencing the miseries of spinster existence as a governess, this writer, before her marriage to Godwin and when she was still Mary Wollstonecraft, set out the wrongs of her fellow women in a book called *A Vindication of the Rights of Women* which had been published a few years before this debate. She derived the title and some parts of her book from the revolutionary outpourings of Tom Paine called *The Rights of Man*, and it was this revolutionary taint which compelled Walpole to 'excommunicate it outside the pale of my Library'. Other readers, despite their broad Augustan minds, were shocked at the outspokenness of certain passages, in which the authoress developed her theme that women, by education, should lift themselves out of the terrestial horrors of being man's plaything into the celestial glories of being his companion. With the question of votes Mary Wollstonecraft was scarcely concerned, and it was no doubt on this account that Thompson, the first real exponent of female suffrage, curtly dimissed her as 'having narrow views'.

This first exponent of the principle of 'Votes for Women' was a strange philosopher called William Thompson, and it was not till thirty years after Mary Godwin that he carried her story to its inevitable appendix with the plea that women should no longer be excluded from political power. The true beginning of the movement for women's suffrage dates from 1825—the year in which Thompson's important book was given to the public. Even the most fervent suffragettes and suffragists seem to have been scarcely aware of the name of their pioneer—the first fighter for their cause, for the tremendous processions in favour of votes for women, which delicately wound their way through the streets of central London before 1914, with banners recalling a diversity of famous women and the names of illustrious men in Parliament and outside who had supported the cause invariably omitted one name—the most important. Admittedly the omission could be excused since William Thompson was never widely known in his life-time, which spanned the years from 1785 to 1833; nor even after death when it seemed that oblivion was to be his lot. From this fate he was delivered by the sudden realization that this forgotten Anglo-Irishman was in reality the teacher and inspiration of Karl Marx.

When the *Dictionary of National Biography*, that gigantic and successful attempt to record the achievement of every memorable British man and woman, was completed in 1900, and adorned the libraries of discriminating readers with all the majesty of its sixty-three volumes, a sketch of William Thompson was not included. Space was found for fabulous characters like King Arthur, Didymus Mountain, and Mother Shipton, but not for 'Philosopher' Thompson. Then in 1901 three more volumes of the dictionary were published to cover those eminent persons who had died during the fifteen years when the *Dictionary* was in the course of publication. In this supplement an article on Thompson is included, although he had died seventy years previously. The explanation for his inclusion is that in 1900 Leslie Stephen, on whose industry and genius the dictionary is based, for he was its first editor, wrote a book on the English Utilitarians, which pointed to Thompson as the founder of scientific socialism, and Stephen evidently persuaded his colleagues on the dictionary to include Thompson in the supplement as a sop for his exclusion from the main work. Rediscovered by posterity for his socialism, he was also seen to have been the pioneer of votes for women.

Thompson was one of those ardent spirits, who outstrip both the opinions and the imagination of their contemporaries, and whose real worth can be only faintly perceived through the mists of ridicule and obloquy which they seem to create. He was a wealthy man, his father was a merchant in Cork, his mother a relation of Lord Bantry, and he inherited a considerable estate near Glandore, some fifty miles westward along the coast from Cork, on the fringe of the country which was to form the background against which the merry wit of Somerville and Ross was to flash and sparkle in a stream of brilliance. But the mind of Thompson bounded forward far beyond the limits of County Cork, and after starting a form of communal farming on his estates, he travelled to London in the early 1820's to study the distribution of wealth. There he quickly gravitated to the society of advanced political thinkers, staying with Bentham, and regularly attending the debates of the Co-operative Society in Chancery Lane, which are fully described in John Stuart Mill's *Autobiography*. Indeed Mill clearly recalled him, and refers to him as 'a very estimable man'. This was during the 1820's when the misery and horror which followed the disastrous financial crisis of 1825 seemed to lend reality to even the wildest speculations of these philosophers and radicals. However, about this time 'the very estimable man' formed an unorthodox connection with a strange lady called Mrs. Wheeler, who deserves to be remembered both on account of her influence over the philosopher, and as an ancestress of militancy, being the great-grandmother of Lady Constance Lytton.

Like much that was best and most potent in the Women's Suffrage Movement Mrs. Wheeler came from Ireland, the daughter of a highly respected archdeacon. She married a typical Irish squire who, possibly irritated by her opinions, took to the hunting field and the bottle. Her daughter who married Bulwer Lytton, the novelist, wrote 'my mother's figure (though on a larger scale than I admire) was as faultless as her face'. But the faultless face and faultless figure began to pine for an ampler life than that derived from the sodden rudeness of an Irish squire. She bolted from Ireland and threw herself on the protection of an uncle, who was governor of Guernsey; Mr. Michael Sadleir, in his stimulating book on Bulwer Lytton, says that, 'dukes, diamonds and dinner parties captured her shallow and suburban mind'. How she came to exchange the pomps and vanities of these flashing soirées for the charms of Philosopher Thompson, history does not relate, and possibly the suggestion that she was graced with a suburban mind is hardly just for her daughter's biographer tells us in nervous undertones, 'Mrs. Wheeler had democratic and levelling principles', and then in a shocked aside 'and she was not a Christian'. The reason for this accusation was that, in her condescending, possessive fashion she used to refer to Jesus Christ as 'our eastern philosopher'. Disraeli, who once met her at dinner, described her as 'something between Jeremy Bentham and Meg Merrilies, very clever but awfully revolutionary'. The conjuction of these two remarkable minds, the philosopher's and the injured wife's, led to their discussion of political theories, unfettered by either convention or tradition. Their meeting roughly coincided with the publication of the sixth edition of the *Encyclopædia Britannica*.

The twentieth-century reader, familiar with contemporary editions of the Encyclopædia, ample, staid and glossy, may find it difficult to imagine that there was once a time when the new Britannica was a best seller, eagerly awaited by political thinkers for support and inspiration for their opinions. This particular edition was published in 1823 and contained the resounding article on government by James Mill, which has often been reprinted, and was to serve as a bible for the philosphic radicals, and a venerable authority to which Liberals and enlightened thinkers were to turn throughout the nineteenth century.

Unluckily Mill slipped into his article this sentence—'one thing is pretty clear, that all those individuals whose interests are indisputably included in those of other individuals may be struck off from political rights without inconvenience. In this light may be viewed all children up to a certain age, whose interests are involved in those of their parents. In this light also women may be regarded, the interest of almost all of whom is involved in that of their fathers or in that of their husbands.'

The feelings of Mrs. Wheeler—a lady of powerful, volatile but injured spirit, can be imagined, as she read those fatal lines. The memory of all her wrongs must have come flooding back, the child-bride of fifteen, the succession of dead babies, the grey remorseless rain of Ballywire, County Limerick, with her husband Francis Massey Wheeler roaring in the background, She, the goddaughter of the great Grattan, to depend for her political rights on the roistering squire of Ballywire! She poured her tribulation into the receptive ear of Philosopher Thompson and together they concocted an answer to Mill; they would crush his article with a book. They enlisted the help of the famous publishing house of Longman, and in 1825 was launched the first real statement of the case for women's suffrage.

The title judged by modern standards was hardly calculated to help the sales of the book; it ran, *An appeal of one half the human race, Women against the pretentions of the other half, Men, to retain them in political, and thence in civil and domestic slavery: In reply to a paragraph of Mr. Mill's celebrated Article on Government.* This was followed by two lines which summed up the theme of Thompson's book:

> '*Tis all stern duty on the female side*
> *On man's, mere sensual lust and surly pride.*

Unfortunately Longman's printed 'Gust' instead of 'Lust', a variation which somewhat twisted Thompson's intention.

Although the book is described as 'by Wm. Thompson', the joint authorship is evidenced by the inclusion of a handsome portrait of Mrs. Wheeler as a frontispiece and an introductory letter to her which read 'Honoured with your acquaintance, ambitious of your friendship, I have endeavoured to arrange the expression of those feelings, sentiments and reasonings, which have emanated from your mind . . . though not to me is that "divine inspiration given" which can clothe in the grace and eloquence of your unpremeditated effusions the calm stream of argument . . . to you am I indebted for those bolder and more comprehensive views which perhaps can only be elicited by concentration of the mind on one darling though terrific theme. To separate your thoughts from mine were now to me impossible, so amalgamated are they with my own.'

Here one curious point deserves to be noticed. Forty years on, James Mill's son, John Stuart Mill, was to publish his book on *The Subjection of Women* and to attribute all the credit for it (as indeed he attributed all the credit for most of his economic doctrines) to Mrs. Mill. The 'surly pride' of some of Mill's masculine admirers has led them to doubt the truth of this, and perhaps the devotion of Philosopher Thompson made him also magnify the tricklings of a 'suburban mind' into the 'calm stream of argument'. But both Mill and Thompson believed that they were merely the amanuenses for ladies gifted with minds of singular intellectual force. Be that as it may, 'The Appeal to one half of the human race' is forthright, powerfully argued and splendidly written. On sexual matters there are no feeble beatings about the bush but the author plunges straight in, forcing the reader's attention over and over again to the horrors and dangers of what he calls 'the shared pillow'. Marriage is merely a superstition called in aid by men when they wish to admit women to the high honour of becoming their 'involuntary breeding machines and household slaves'.

He held a somewhat weird belief that conception was much more likely if the marriage act was followed by a period of rest. He thought that the more promiscuous habits of Scotland and the north of England were not followed by conception because the women were not 'the drowsy slaves of their respective masters'.

The recurring theme of his book was that married women were slaves. 'Home is the eternal prison-house of the wife,' he wrote, 'the husband paints it as the abode of calm bliss, but takes care to find out of doors, for his own use, a species of bliss not quite so calm. . . . The house is his house with everything in it, and of all fixtures the most abjectly his is his breeding machine, the wife.'

In the next decade one of Thompson's disciples published a curious tribute to him along the lines of Landor's *Imaginary*

'Women of England, Awake'

Conversations called *Hampden in the Nineteenth Century* and one of the characters is made to say in reference to Thompson's book, 'I have been restrained by the style of certain portions of the volume from putting it into the hands of some of my female friends.' But in spite of this stimulating suggestion of obscenity, Thompson's sales were meagre and the book is scarce.

Yet in the history of woman's suffrage Thompson's *Appeal* is a cardinal document, because like the board in chess, it prescribed the field of battle for the disputants. The arguments for and against are set out and defined. Since they were based on the essential characteristics of human beings, those arguments were not materially changed by the economic or political developments of the nineteenth century. What Thompson wrote Mrs. Pankhurst was to say a century afterwards.

He agreed with James Mill that there was in human beings a boundless and instinctive demand for power which had to be reduced by checks. Only by political equality could women escape from the tyranny of men which reduced them to 'the condition of negroes in the West Indies'. Their demand was for complete equality: 'They ask every facility of access to every art, occupation, profession, from the highest to the lowest. They ask the removal of all restraints and exclusions not applicable to men of equal capacities.' The preliminary for satisfying these demands was political equality. He further argued that, by itself, political equality would lead to a vast expansion of the female mind and to a surge of benevolent feelings in ladies. He dealt firmly with the argument, which originated in Roman times and was to last in Great Britain until 1917, that since women could not defend the country their exclusion from the franchise was just. In the exercise of political functions what kind of courage is needed? asked Thompson. 'Is it the warrior's or the nurse's qualities?' And then he answers, 'It is not the activity which will lift much, run much, or slay much, but which will watch much and with never-ceasing patience endure much.' He closes with a passage of almost lyrical splendour and magnificence, 'Women of England! Women in whatever country ye breathe, degraded—Awake. Awake to the contemplation of the happiness that awaits you when all your faculties of mind and body shall be fully cultivated and developed:

29

when every path in which you can exercise those improved faculties shall be laid open and rendered delightful to you, even as to them who now ignorantly enslave and degrade you. As your bondage has chained down man to the ignorance and vices of despotism, so will your liberation reward him with knowledge, with freedom and with happiness.'

But the women of England did not wake. Perhaps disappointed, the Philosopher and his Irish lady set out to rouse the more impressionable people of France. They met with only a small measure of success, for the French contrived to cover them with ridicule, and laughed at them as merely the exponents and advocates of free love. A later though eminent French disciple of Thompson, the political thinker Proudhon, summed up what was perhaps the instinctive reaction of the Latin races to such matters—'The day on which my wife is given the vote will be the day of my divorce.'

And then unhappily disaster overtook Thompson. He was to linger in the minds of his fellow men not as the estimable feminist, not as the beneficient landlord, not as the pioneer communist but as the victim of a comical funeral. He died at his home near Glandore, where he had made himself conspicuous by walking about with a tricolour flag tied to his walking-stick. After Thompson had died, Lord Bantry insisted on having him buried according to the rites of the Established Church, but the service was greatly interrupted by the wailing of Irish peasants lamenting that an infidel was being allowed to lie with their own beloved dead. Lord Bantry bought silence with a guinea but the cries were justified. After the funeral, as was the custom in those times, the will was opened, and it contained the embarrassing provision that no priest—Christian, Mohammedan, or Hindu—'is to meddle with my remains'. Moreover he left his body to be publicly carved up by a lecturer in anatomy, and the bones were then to be strung together and exhibited in a museum. One hundred pounds a year was bequeathed to Mrs. Wheeler, and the rest of his fortune was to be used to found communal societies. The embarrassment of family and executors was not diminished by the news that an equally unorthodox socialist, Pierre Baume, had sailed for Ireland to claim the cranium for a series of phrenological lectures. After many years the will was upset as running counter to public morality, but the Irish always believed that the full horror had been kept from them. They believed that Thompson had really said that his skeleton was to be shipped to England, the bones tipped with silver, and that the resulting object was to be placed in Mrs. Wheeler's drawing-room as an affecting Souvenir d'Amour.

Thompson's career illustrates one feature which was to mark the lives of all those who were to agitate for the political enfranchisement of women, the fatal ease with which these people stumbled from the sublime to the ridiculous. There have never existed such receptive targets for the heavy shafts of the male jester. We see these men and women, high principled, high minded, clever and argumentative, suddenly brought low, tumbled and mocked as their theories lead them into the strange territory of sexual relations. They are like people walking soberly about their business who are abruptly brought face to face with a distorting mirror. The observer is tempted to laugh, but some mortals realizing the deadly earnestness, the passionate feelings and the deep sense of injustice of those ridiculed, are conscious, behind the laughter, of the pity of it all. For Thompson died an abject failure. Not only were his books unread, but the arrangements that he made for keeping them in print and for spreading his doctrines after his death, were disrupted by the dispute over his will. So it was that when in the 1850's and 1860's there was a revival of interest in the question of women's political rights, those concerned were not able to get out their Thompson and argue their case on a rational foundation of economics and philosophy.[1]

[1] William Thompson was the subject of a sympathetic study published in 1954 by Miss Sylvia Pankhurst's son, Dr. Richard Pankhurst.

II

Reform for Men Only

These varied but almost imperceptible beginnings—the practices of antiquity, the gentle eloquence of injured spinsterhood, and the strident arguments of Thompson, might have contributed to form a respectable stream of opinion if such had not been effectively dammed by the Reform Bill of 1832. That famous measure, sweeping away a multiplicity of abuses in one direction, surprisingly established a fresh injustice by enacting that the vote in the new boroughs, created by the bill to take the place of the Rotten Boroughs, was to be confined to 'male persons'. The reader will recall that Lord Chief Justice Lee, in his judgment, had made a particular point that he was inclined to think that women had no right to vote but that they were not 'positively excluded', meaning that there was no legal case or statute which specifically forbade it. That positive exclusion, so far as the new boroughs went, was introduced for the first time in English history by the Reform Bill. There is no indication in the long-drawn debates on the bill why this was done, and the most likely explanation is that the draughtsman of the act, conscious that there had been legal ambiguities on the point, slipped in the word male to avoid uncertainty in the future.

Long afterwards, those searching for some new argument in this ancient battle maintained that this was an insulting innovation, a characteristic attempt by men to keep the field to themselves, to act in the spirit of the family motto of one, who in the twentieth century was to prove a doughty antagonist of female suffrage, 'Let Curzon holde what Curzon helde'. The debates on the Reform Bill show that any such intention was completely absent from the

1. Meeting in Hanover Square Rooms about 1870; Rhoda Garrett speaking; Mrs. Mark Pattison talking to Mrs. Fawcett; Miss Becker is in the centre

2*a*. Frances Power Cobbe

2*b*. Lydia Ernestine Becker

.2*c*. Mrs. Pankhurst

2*d*. Mrs. Despard

minds of those earnest Whig and Tory debaters. They were concerned with constitutional doctrines, enlivened here and there with temper and a whiff of revolution, but from the disordered dress of the Tory spokesman, Wetherell, to the white hat of the Radical, Hunt, all was masculine. There was no subtle intention to deprive women of their just rights because it never crossed the minds of these parliamentarians that such rights existed. Even the celebrated Black Book, which immortalized all the Radical fury of those times, and which enshrines in its pages the faintest whimper of any scandal, ranging from a clerical pluralist to a family placeman, said that universal suffrage (which was of course advocated even in the 1830's by a handful of extremists) would have to include females as well as males. Such an unlimited scheme of franchise could not be seriously entertained, the book argues, and then it continues, 'If asked why disfranchise women in preference to men we confess, in answer, to these enquiries we can only give one reply, namely, that expediency, not strict justice, dictates their exclusion.' This shows how even as late as 1832 the political mind was closed to the Rights of Women.

No sooner was the Reform Bill passed than there was a trifling development which deserves to be recalled from the shadows of oblivion, because it was the first occasion on which female suffrage was seriously advocated in Parliament and because it enshrined an argument which, in the end, was to swell into one of the most powerful contributory streams which was to sweep away the obstruction to the rights of women to vote. On 3rd August 1832 'Orator' Hunt, perhaps the most advanced Radical in the House of Commons at that time, whose butcher-like visage and loud flowing oratory had dominated the field at Peterloo, presented a petition to Parliament that 'every unmarried female, possessing the necessary pecuniary qualification, should be allowed to vote'.[1] Hunt was chosen to present the petition because he was an advocate of universal suffrage and, as the Black Book had correctly stated, if universal suffrage was granted, the admission of women to the vote was an inevitable corollary of it. As well as being the first occasion on which the matter was urged in Parliament, this

---

[1] The Borough franchise was householders rated at £10: the County franchise was £10 copyholders, £50 leaseholders and 40s. freeholders.

was the first petition for female suffrage laid before the House of Commons, a method of agitation which was to prove a formidable weapon on behalf of women over the next half century.[1]

The author of the petition had little enough in common with Hunt the Radical: she was Miss Mary Smith, a lady of enormous wealth, who lived tucked away in one of the Ridings of Yorkshire. Miss Smith's petition emphasizes one line of argument (namely that if a woman, by the ownership of property, is qualified to vote then she should be allowed to use her vote) which is a strong and constant element in the controversy. It is virtually unanswerable. Although it was caught up in the main torrent of the female suffrage case, it is distinct from the case by decided shades of difference easily detected by the observer. Fundamentally this particular claim rests on property and not on sex. 'Our property is tarnished because it lacks the lustre of a vote' they could have argued. A lady once asked Richard Cobden if she could transfer some property to an enlightened male so that the vote on that property should not be lost to the Liberal cause. These *Femmes Soles*, fatherless and husbandless but owning riches, clearly fell outside James Mill's definition of individuals whose interests were 'indisputably included in those of other individuals'. They had no husband whom they could bully or wheedle into voting as they wished: the injustice of excluding them from the ballot was palpable.

As the industrial prosperity of the country advanced, these wealthy spinsters and widows were a class which increased both in numbers and in influence. Their fortunes firmly based on busy mills and factories in the north, they lived their comfortable lives quaffing the waters of Malvern, limping and stumping through conservatories at Torquay, tittle-tattling in splendid houses at Brighton or bowing to Colonels in Cheltenham: ever at their heels followed an obsequious rag, tag, and bobtail of clergymen and medical men. They devoted themselves to such worthy objects as the building of churches and chapels, the relief of cholera victims and the conversion of blacks: but just a handful, possibly more

[1] The presentation of petitions to either House of Parliament was the traditiona way of airing a grievance before Questions to Ministers were established. The petition was ordered to lie on the table of the House, and there was very often a debate following the presentation.

clever than some of their sisters and possibly a little dubious about
the paradise awaiting them in the world to come, dedicated themselves to the attainment of political power. Though inclined to be
capricious supporters they provided the wealth and leisure which,
during the nineteenth century, animated the woman's suffrage
agitation. The courage of these ladies deserves to be applauded.
While it is easy enough to write a large cheque for the building of
a church, or the education of the Reverend Quiverfull's prodigious
family, it is more difficult to stand up and espouse an unpopular
cause, which, in that age of modesty, was regarded as almost
immoral: nor was a generation which liked sly little jokes about
the 'Sex' calculated to find this particular topic anything but funny.
These points are all clearly brought out when Hunt presented his
petition on 3rd August 1832, and the courage of Miss Mary Smith,
the pioneer and prototype of scores of forgotten names, can be
acclaimed across the years.

Mr. Hunt began by saying that he had a petition 'which might
be a subject of mirth to some Hon. Gentlemen . . .'. He continued,
'It came from a lady of rank and fortune—Mary Smith of Stanmore
in the County of York. The petitioner stated that she paid taxes, and
therefore did not see why she should not have a share in the election of a Representative.' The petition continued with the argument that since women were liable for all punishments of the law,
they should be given the chance of making laws and acting as
jurors.

According to Hansard, who in those days was less precise in
reporting the proceedings in Parliament than he has since become,
the petitioner was understood to express 'her indignation against
those vile wretches who would not marry and yet would exclude
females from a share in the legislation.'

As soon as Orator Hunt had finished speaking, Sir Frederick
Trench, a military man, who was responsible for the original idea
of the Thames Embankment, asked if it might not be 'rather
queer' if a jury, composed of men and women, had to be locked up
together for a night. Hunt was not the kind of man to be curbed
by any feelings of delicacy, and he shouted back that he well knew
that the Hon. and gallant Member was frequently in the company
of ladies for whole nights and that he did not know that any mis-

chief resulted from the circumstance. Perhaps nothing in the whole history of the battle for the political recognition of women was more galling to them than the repeated ribaldry with which the subject was treated in Parliament. The reader can easily picture how Miss Smith's friends and acquaintances would whisper behind her back that she was the cause of some dreadful things being said by those gentlemen in the House of Commons. Such were the penalties of being unorthodox.

'Orthodoxy', observed the learned eighteenth-century Bishop Warburton, 'is my doxy: heterodoxy is the other people's doxy.' In the two decades immediately following Miss Smith's petition there was a development which contributed towards lifting this question of women's rights out of other people's doxy into channels which were more respectable and orthodox.

The remarkable creation of wealth in the country, steadily developing as the nineteenth century advanced, led to a great improvement in the general well-being of all sections of English people, and, in this material up-lift women shared. The philanthropist Wilberforce especially noticed how the condition of unmarried women had improved in his life-time. This in turn was reflected in a blossoming of literary talent; not just the great names 'roses that down the alleys shine afar' but a general profusion, possibly belonging more to the world of journalism than to the realms of genius, but not wholly forgotten even to-day. There was a voluminous Mrs. Ellis who wrote, *The Women of England*, *The Wives of England*, the *Daughters of England* and the *Mothers of England*. Although it could be argued that she was not strictly speaking in sympathy with the political claims of women since she wrote, 'it is unquestionably the inalienable right of all men, whether ill or well, rich or poor, wise or foolish, to be treated with deference, and made much of in their own homes', she nevertheless drew attention to the talents of women both through her own skill as a writer and by the subject matter of her books. People began to see that there was something wrong in the old methods which, as Sydney Smith said, 'kept women with nimble fingers and vacant understandings'. Miss Harriet Martineau from the seclusion of the Lake District (where the frugal Wordsworth had advised her not to offer her visitors more than tea, unless they offered to pay) poured out an astonishing stream of books and articles in expounding the beliefs and doctrines of the Philosophic Radicals. Then there was Mrs. Jameson, unhappily married, and seeking independence by her pen, but even to this day a reliable guide on some matters of art, who wrote voluminously on all social questions, and showed characteristic devotion to her craft by dying from a cold caught in the Reading Room of the British Museum. There was also Lady Morgan, an Irish lady, with an obstetric surgeon for a husband, who revelled in fashionable society and came nearer perhaps to sharing the feminist views of her compatriot Thompson than any of these other ladies. She had a racy but flamboyant style, and in her book *Woman and her Master* which was published in 1840, she wrote, that woman is 'denounced as a thing unsexed, a *Lusus naturae* if she diverts her thoughts to pursuits which aspire to serve, and which never fail to elevate. Educating her for the Harem, but calling on her for the practises of the Portico, man expects from his odalisque[1] the firmness of the stoic, and demands from his servant the exercise of those virtues which, placing the Elite of his own sex at the head of its muster-roll, give immortality to the Master.' Her meaning is cloudy, but its general direction can be followed.

While these developments were making themselves felt, and women were beginning to take a recognized position in the intellectual life of the country, and thereby to throw up in slightly comic relief that characteristically male attitude towards women, which is typified by Keats's remark, 'God she's like a milk white lamb that bleats for man's protection', there was one small but constant section of the community which was not without influence in the struggle. From their earliest origins in seventeenth-century England the Quakers had set women on an equality with men in the organization of their society, and for them it was a natural step that women should take their place in the wider world of affairs. In 1847 the first leaflet ever issued on women's suffrage was published by an ancient Quaker lady, Miss Anne Knight, who discharged her thunderbolt from the peaceful seclusion of Quiet House, Chelmsford. Though the arguments in this document were in no way original, and its circulation was no doubt appropri-

[1] This means a concubine in the harem of a Turkish sultan.

37

ately modest, they were a clear call for the removal of the sex disability in the franchise and they mark an important moment in the controversy. After the excitements of the Reform Bill were over, they were followed by the inevitable sense of disappointment which always seems to travel in the wake of change. These frustrations were all caught up in the agitations in the late 1830's for the Charter; the principal aim of the Charter was to give the vote to the working classes, who were almost entirely excluded from it by the property qualifications which prevailed in nearly all constituencies. Universal suffrage was the foundation of the Charter, and in its early stages it specifically included the franchise for women. Throughout the 1840's the Chartists, with their extravagant reforms, which were greatly in advance of public opinion, monopolized the public interest in voting reforms, but by the end of the 1840's the force behind the Chartist agitation was spent, and Miss Knight's pamphlet was discharged at a propitious moment, when through all the frothy agitation, the Chartist tide was seen to be on the ebb.

In the same decade, which saw the publication of Miss Knight's pamphlet, women were directly linked with political agitation through the Corn Law League where, under the leadership of Cobden and Bright, Quaker influences were also strong. Women were especially prominent in Manchester: in 1841 they organized a vast tea party in the Corn Exchange, Manchester; although the ladies did not speak, a lady presided at each of the tea tables. The famous French Economist, Bastiat, who was closely bound up with the free trade agitation in England, expressed with typical Gallic vividness the part which women could play in this struggle, which he and his associates always looked at as a moral struggle quite as much as a narrowly political one. 'Oh, if only woman would but cast on political abjectness that poignant contempt with which she formerly withered military cowardness: if she had for him who traffics in a vote, for him who betrays a trust, for him who deserts the cause of truth, and justice, some of that moral irony, with which in other times, she would have overwhelmed the felon knight who had abandoned the lists, or purchased his life at the expense of his honour, our conflict could not offer that spectacle of demoralization and baseness which saddens elevated hearts.'

Although women will ever look to Manchester as the source from which they drew much of the idealism and inspiration, which was to form the mainspring of their struggle, they should not overlook the fact that the great Yorkshire city of Sheffield is rightly proud of the part which it played in these shadowy beginnings.

On 26th February 1851 the Sheffield Association for Female Franchise, which had been stirred into life by the indefatigable Anne Knight, held its first meeting at the Democratic Temperance Hotel in Sheffield. From this fusty background the Association issued a trumpet call to all the women of England beginning 'Beloved Sisters'. The appeal began by emphasizing the injustice of excluding women from all share in politics and correctly asked 'What is liberty if the claims of women be disregarded?' The object of the society was described as the entire political enfranchisement of women: it ended with an appeal to 'our sisters of England' to help with what it solemnly called 'this holy work'. They were also successful in persuading the 7th Lord Carlisle, a former Viceroy of Ireland, nephew of the bachelor Duke of Devonshire and endowed with very advanced and enlightened opinions, to present a petition to the House of Lords. This petition was described as coming from the female inhabitants of the Borough of Sheffield in the County of York and it prayed their lordships 'to take into their serious consideration the propriety of enacting an Electoral Law which will include adult females'. It was ordered to lie on the table as the petition of Mrs. Abiah Higginbottom who was in the chair at the meeting and was the only person to sign the petition. Of this meeting of devoted ladies, of Mrs. Abiah Higginbottom all trace has unhappily vanished, except that she was the corresponding secretary of the Sheffield Association. Her christian name was taken from one of the interminable lists of the issue of the patriarchs at the sight of which even the most intrepid biblical student is known to blanch, and, with her surname, made an interesting combination. Lord Carlisle, who was a frequent lecturer in the industrial towns on such topics as sanitation and popular education, may have heard of her when lecturing in the north, or her fame may have travelled to Chatsworth across the plateau of the Peak; it is difficult to suppose that she or the leaders of the Sheffield Society would have petitioned the Lords without Carlisle's guidance.

Yet there was nothing which could be called a movement, nothing to give cohesion to the sporadic and unrelated expression of opinion from Manchester, Sheffield and Chelmsford. Indifferent to these stimulating suggestions, the great mass of Victorian womanhood remained busy and contented in their homes. The fortunate ones married and bred, the less fortunate, meek and wan, took posts as governesses or companions and all rested on a vast, brawny and unheeding army which cooked, dusted and scoured. From the bright world outside they were shielded by the shadow of man: the ideals and problems of the world only reached them as they were retailed by their lords and masters. 'He wished for her to have come to him out of an egg-shell, somewhat more astonished at things than a chicken, but as completely enclosed, before he tapped the shell.' Such a point of view, enshrined for us in the pages of *The Egoist* by Meredith, was general in mid-Victorian times. Against this background of Victorian womanhood, contented, bustling and humdrum, the tiny handful of rebels stands out in relief so conspicuous and startling, that they seem odd and almost ridiculous, till time sets them in their true place not as freaks but as leaders in the van of an irresistible march.

III

'He Wants Girls in Parliament'

Throughout the 1850's, there was a decided and perceptible change in the Victorian outlook on women. So far as a single individual can achieve a revolution that had been done by Florence Nightingale in the Crimean War, who, in a single spectacular flash, was able to lighten a dark corner of the human mind. Taking advantage of her achievement other women were able to illumine the road which led away from kitchen and scullery, from needle and wash tub towards a professional life. At the end of this decade the *Englishwoman's Journal*, which afterwards became the *Englishwoman's Review*, was started; in this venture the most prominent name was Mrs. Bodichon, the original of George Eliot's Romola and later to be one of the founders of Girton; with her were Jessie Boucherette, the head of a Lincolnshire county family, Bessie Parkes, the formidable mother of Hilaire Belloc and of Mrs. Belloc Lowndes, and Adelaide Proctor, whose poems in that epoch were second only in popularity to those of Tennyson.

The objective of these ladies and of the journal was not the vote but a career: their exertions did however widen the outlook of their readers, making the political enfranchisement of women seem less revolutionary and less impossible.

Considering how the Victorians loved organizing themselves, how they enjoyed a meeting, how they stilled any uneasiness of conscience by sitting through a committee on a hard chair, the reader may reasonably be surprised that a woman's suffrage society was not founded before the late 1860's. Perhaps the explanation for the delay, and it is at once impossible to exaggerate the force of convention or for the twentieth century to apprehend

41

the dead-weight of inertia which it caused, is to be found in the restrictions of family life. 'Never be conspicuous', 'Don't get yourself talked about'. Those words of command rolling off the tongues of Victorian mothers established the rules as effectively as did the width of the croquet hoop, in the fashionable past-times of those days. Even in fiction, when Victorian writers wished to portray unorthodox women, they generally did so by removing them from a normal background of home life. Jane Eyre, Dorothea in *Middlemarch*, and Lady Eustace in *The Eustace Diamonds* are examples of this. Not only did the conventions of home life keep women's minds static, but even when the women were convinced of the need for a break away, the strength of those conventions restrained their ardour. One of a famous family of literary and philanthropic sisters, Emily Winkworth, writing to her sister at the end of 1840, of a friend she had met said, 'I have had one regular, good, hard talk, two or three hours long. She is a decided "Rights of Woman" personage but has her aristocratic education to thank for a very strong dislike for all improprieties and oddnesses.' But the truth was that women had no hope of advancing their rights without seeming slightly improper and decidedly odd.

In this dilemma they found unexpected succour from man. As was to happen throughout the history of the suffrage movement a debate in Parliament, or even a change of feeling in the House of Commons, was like the application of the whip to a sensitive horse: over and over again what happened in Parliament was to set off a burst of activity in these high-spirited persons, eager to show their paces in public affairs, but condemned by their sex to exclusion.

Nothing proved this more clearly than the events of 1866, when the deliberations of men in the House of Commons gave a sharp impetus to the latent demand for the woman's vote. In that year almost the entire thinking political strength of the English people was concentrated on the single issue of parliamentary reform. In that summer Prussia assumed the mastery of Germany following the resounding defeat of Austria, but this pregnant event passed almost unheeded in England where people were engrossed by delicate conundrums about the value of borough franchises. The explanation for all this ferment was that in 1866 Reform meant giving the vote to a section of working men: for the first time in history a slice of political power was being given to the working classes. In the history of women's franchise 1866 is a year of importance partly because, in the general agitation, people's minds were open to innovation, and chiefly because the efforts to influence opinion in the House of Commons made by those in favour of a wider male franchise, were to form a well-trimmed path along which supporters of the women's franchise were to tread. The broad outline of what happened in 1866 is almost essential for an understanding of the later stages in the struggle for votes for women.

Ever since the Reform Bill of 1832 there had been sporadic outbursts of popular feeling in favour of a further measure of reform. The Whig and Liberal parties had throughout the confused party politics of the 1850's and 1860's voiced this sentiment and had (possibly without any burning convictions on the subject) brought forward proposals both in the Cabinet and in the House of Commons. But two events in particular brought the question to the front and made 1866 a likely year for an advance beyond the ground won in 1832. The Prime Minister, Lord Palmerston, who was suspected of being lukewarm in support of reform, died at the close of 1865 and was succeeded by Lord John Russell, a strong reformer, but by this time sitting in the House of Lords as Earl Russell. The General Election, held shortly before Palmerston's death, had given the Liberal Party a majority computed at seventy. (Ninety years ago the limits of party loyalty were far less clearly defined than they are to-day and the precise figure was not known.) With at any rate a reasonable majority, with Russell and Gladstone, who was leading the Government in the Commons, convinced that reform was inescapable, the Cabinet felt that they would be shirking their responsibilities if they put reform on the shelf. The session of 1866 opened brilliantly—graced by the presence of Queen Victoria and made memorable by the fact that this was the first time that she had appeared at any such ceremony since the death of the Prince Consort. The Government seemed setting sail on a long and prosperous voyage: brave would have been the man to foretell that it was doomed to shipwreck on the rocks of reform before four months were out.

The Government Reform Bill was laid before Parliament in March and it reduced the value of the property qualification in counties from £50 to £14 and in boroughs from £10 to £7. Anyone with £50 in the Savings Bank, for two consecutive years, and certain classes of lodgers were also give the vote. These proposals were accompanied by a considerable measure of re-distribution of seats by which the industrial constituencies were enabled to return an increased number of members. Gladstone estimated that roughly 400,000 new men would be given the vote and that, of these, about 200,000 would be working-class voters, but he poured scorn on the idea that the working men would vote *en bloc* as a class.

The supporters of the Government were, however, restive as had been shown before ever the details of this bill were known. A Liberal, who was perhaps more illustrious as a highly successful whist player than politician—James Clay, member of Parliament for Hull—proposed that before any man might vote he should have to pass an examination in reading, writing, spelling and the four rules of arithmetic. The examination was to be conducted by the Civil Service Commissioners who, in those days of diminutive Government Departments, had abundant leisure. The proposal was seconded by William Gregory—a member of the Liberal Party who managed to combine attachment to that respectable body with a somewhat wild career on the turf. This idea of a voters examination was strongly supported by the Conservatives. Such were the happy fancies of that tranquil time.

Yet the punter and the whist player truly reflected the consternation of a large section of the Liberal Party. For in Gladstone's proposals, many Liberal members saw revolution (not necessarily with the bloodshed and barricades of France) but carrying with it an irrevocable transfer of political power to a new force. These malcontents were described with brilliant effect by John Bright, a strong supporter of the measure, as Adullamites. In that period when an educated public followed every syllable of the Parliamentary debates with the same concentrated attention with which they read their Bibles, the reference to David feigning madness in the Cave of Adullam where 'everyone that was discontented gathered themselves unto him' was a bull's-eye which all could applaud. The Adullamites were led by Robert Lowe—a statesman of academic distinction and wit, who was to attack the proposals of his former Liberal associates with devastating effect. When Gladstone argued that the new working-class voters were 'flesh and blood' like anyone else, Lowe replied that if that were to be the test for the franchise the country could look forward to a Parliament of Beasts. Gladstone's tremendous powers of eloquence, exerted to the full when in winding up on the Second Reading he spoke of the great social forces 'moving on in their might and majesty' being marshalled on the Liberal side, were used in vain. The Liberal majority on the Second Reading of the Bill was only five, and after a precarious existence till the middle of June the Government fell.

The Conservative Government which followed, carried through a Reform Bill, eventually passed in 1867, which did not greatly differ from that of the Liberals. How far the conversion of the Conservatives was accelerated by a spontaneous explosion of popular feeling is a matter of opinion: that it had some influence on the House of Commons is indisputable. And this unmistakable expression of the people's wishes was constantly invoked as a precedent by each side in the long-drawn struggle for the right of women to vote. For in later times opponents of woman's suffrage were to repeat as one of their stock arguments that if women really wanted the vote they should demonstrate as the men had done on 23rd July 1866. And the programme of that exciting day was to stimulate the minds of women to a realization of the triumphs of scuffling with policemen and of the tempting glories of violence.

A public meeting had been planned and advertised for the evening of July 23rd in Hyde Park. To-day it would have been called 'a rally' or 'a demonstration': in the simpler but not less expressive language of our forbears it was called 'a monster meeting'. A summer evening in Hyde Park in Victorian times set off to advantage the carriages and horses of prosperous London: they perambulated along the Row, they trotted round the Park—a perfect *concours d'élégance* which would have been rudely shattered by the oratory of a 'monster' meeting. The police announced that as they disapproved of a place of recreation being put to such a purpose they would close the park-gates against the meeting. As the afternoon merged into evening the Chief Commissioner of Police, Sir Richard Mayne (who had been prominent in the London Police since their start thirty-seven years earlier) took up his stand at the head of 1,600 police inside the park, round the Marble Arch. On this sensitive point the demonstrators marched from all parts of London. At the head of the marchers moved comfortably a small array of growlers, and seated in the first was Mr. Edmund Beales. This ornament of Eton and Cambridge was by profession a conveyancer in Lincoln's Inn. After a tiring day, dealing with trusts, mortgages, tenants-for-life, and delving into mysteries of the legal estate and roping in elusive remaindermen, this gentleman loved nothing better than to be seen in the company of all kinds of toughs and blackguards, marching beneath the ample folds of the red flag. After a colloquy with Sir Richard Mayne he moved off and drove away past the Houses of Parliament to Trafalgar Square where he proposed to hold the forbidden meeting. A section of the crowd followed their leader—but not all. Those that remained, moving down Park Lane, entered the park at a variety of points by pulling down the railings, for the defence of which the police were not sufficient. At 8 o'clock the Guards marched in, but the crowd was in possession of the ground. Speakers leapt on to improvised platforms. Amid the confusion of roughs mobbing the police and soldiers deploying, and rendered shadowy by the fast-falling dusk, Miss Harriet Laws sprang to her feet and poured out a fervent torrent of words on the rights of the people. Like some terrible jack-in-the-box, Miss Laws bursts into history and then disappears for ever. Yet she deserves her sprig of rosemary for she spoke through the noise and dust of battle: her eloquence was discharged literally at the point of the bayonet. This whole episode—strange and fierce and alarming—was burned vividly into the public mind, and was an undoubted influence in persuading the Conservative Government of Derby and Disraeli to pass their surprisingly sweeping Reform Bill in 1867. But for the women July 23rd was a challenge, just the faintest whisper of a taunt from the past—'That was what the men did when they wanted the vote.'

Yet it is curious that although throughout this year the public mind was seething with reform, receptive to all kinds of weird arguments and new ideas, the proposal to extend the vote to the outlawed half of the human race received scant attention in Parliament. But it was at this juncture that service of inestimable advantage to the women's cause was given by John Stuart Mill— the son of that James Mill whose famous article had dealt a deadly blow to the aspirations of women. If it is true, as the Old Testament warns us, that the Almighty will punish the children for the iniquity of the fathers, John Stuart Mill acted with characteristic wisdom and reasonableness in forestalling any possible retribution for the wrong-doing of his father, by placing himself at the head of the feminist movement. But possibly the true explanation of his enthusiasm for the women's cause was that he was influenced, much as Thompson had been, by a woman of force and genius, whom he subsequently married: to this lady, who was the widow of his friend (an intellectual druggist) called John Taylor, and her daughter, Miss Helen Taylor, Mill has attributed the thoughts which inspired his writings on philosophic and economic matters. About Mill's nature there hung something faintly monastic, some instinct of celibacy, for did he not believe that the economic evils of the world came through the failure of man to control his passions? Mill was no lady's man—his knowledge of women was particular not general—and it could be argued that he made the mistake of supposing that all women—from the simpering Victorian Miss with pointed toe and fluttering fan down to the struggling mother in a slum—were blessed with the capabilities of Mrs. Taylor and her daughter Helen. On this particular subject of women's rights Mill, whose views were otherwise logically based on reason and reflection, allowed himself to be swayed by anger. In 1854 he chanced to be in the London Library, in St. James's Square, and picked up *Bleak House* which had been published in the previous year. This contained the portrait of Mrs. Jellyby whose interests principally lay, it will be remembered, in Borrioboola-Ga: her daughter, Caddy, said 'I have tidied over and over again: but it's useless, Ma and Africa, together, upset the whole house directly'. To his wife Mill wrote, 'That creature Dickens whose last story, *Bleak House*, I found accidentally at the London Library the other day . . . has the vulgar impudence in this thing to ridicule rights of women. It is done in the very vulgarest way—just the style in which vulgar men used to ridicule "learned ladies".' Four years later Mill's wife died, and Mill became thenceforward attached to the women's cause by ties that were sacred. At the General Election of 1865 he was invited to stand for Westminster: this he agreed to do provided he was not expected to canvass or to show the slightest interest in local affairs. He agreed to address a very few meetings and at one of them in reply to the question, 'Did you once say in writing that the working-class were generally liars?' he answered, 'I did'. This model candidate was duly elected, and his success must be acclaimed as a triumph of unpopularity. Among other quirks and fancies he included in his election address the statement that he favoured votes for women. Hearing of this champion the intrepid Madame Bodichon hired a carriage and covering it with placards drove through the streets of Westminster in company with Madame Belloc, Miss Emily Davies, afterwards Mistress of Girton, and Isa Craig, a poetess of moderate talent. Peeping out from their 'fly' these weirdly assorted ladies found little to encourage them among the stern-visaged electors of Westminster, and they had to be content with hearing that their candidate had been described as 'the man who wants girls in Parliament'. Yet girls or no he was elected and from that moment the cry of votes for women was lifted from the drawing-room into the House of Commons.

With their champion safely on the Government benches, for Mill was elected as a Liberal supporter of the Whig Cabinet, the ladies received totally unexpected support from the opposition. In the course of his speech in the eight-day debate on reform in April 1866 Disraeli said, 'I say that in a country governed by a woman—where you allow women to form part of the other estate of the realm—peeresses in their own right for example—where you allow a woman not only to hold land, but to be a lady of the manor and hold legal courts—where a woman by law may be a churchwarden and overseer of the poor—I do not see, when she has so much to do with the state and Church, on what reasons, if you come to right, she has not a right to vote.'

With logic and without affectation Disraeli stated a case whose force thus clearly explained seems to-day impossible to rebut.

3. Trafalgar Square, October 1908; Mrs. Pankhurst speaking, 'General' Drummond in the background

4. Mrs. Pankhurst and Miss Christabel Pankhurst in their prison clothes

Indeed can we blame those eager ladies because they felt, as did Gideon and his diminutive force centuries before them, that they had only to make a noise, and only to hold up the lamp of truth on high, for their opponents to flee from a position which was incapable of defence? But Disraeli's words did not by any means fall comfortably on the ears of his aristocratic followers nor did they meet with any real response across the floor of the House among the representatives of commerce and the professions crowded behind Mr. Gladstone. But they fell with electric effect on those ladies who had perambulated through the streets of Westminster in support of Mill. These worthies came together on the following morning and at once drafted a petition which their champion could present to the House of Commons. The work of organizing the petition fell to the hands of Madame Bodichon, Miss Boucherette and Miss Rosamond Hill—the sister of Octavia Hill, the eminent housing reformer. These ladies met in the house of Elizabeth Garrett, who was flushed with triumph at having just passed the examination of the Society of Apothecaries and, what was more to the point, having discovered that the Society could not strip her of her honours merely because she was a woman. In the formal language needed for a parliamentary petition, those responsible for the draft stated that property was the basis for the vote, and that it was 'an evident anomaly' that a certain class of property holders were excluded from the franchise; they then adopted Disraeli's point that the admission of women to political rights was constitutional and parallel with their rights and duties in other spheres of national life. By the beginning of June 1866 they had almost 1,500 signatures (all women). When June 7th dawned Madame Bodichon, perhaps flagging under her exertions and the excitement, was ill and it fell to Miss Emily Davies, and Miss Elizabeth Garrett to escort the great scroll to Westminster—travelling once again in a cab—but this time 'a growler' without the gay embellishments of posters. At Westminster Hall, where they sent in a message for Mill, panic assailed them. In those days the legal business of the nation was still conducted in the courts off the Hall, and the building was thronged with barristers, barristers' clerks and solicitors—lawyers and their attendants have always been a slightly merciless section of the community eager for any quip or joke to take their minds off business. The two young ladies, seriously preoccupied with their scroll, would have been obvious targets for wit, and to escape this they asked a friendly seller of apples to hide their document under her stall. There is a certain irony in picturing the petition—the battering ram with which these spirited ladies hoped to overturn the defences of the male sex—lying among those fruits by which man, through the guile of a woman, was supposed to have damned himself. When Mill arrived in Westminster Hall the scroll was drawn from its hiding place, and giving way to one of those rare flashes of his lighter manner Mill said, 'Ah! this I can brandish with effect.'

Massive as the petiton may have been it was not 'bright with names that men remember'. The shining names of mid-Victorian times were absent. Florence Nightingale did not sign: the best-selling novelists, Mrs. Henry Wood, Miss Braddon or Miss Yonge were not there; the great worlds of fashion and the arts were not represented. The signatories were not uniform and they fall into no precise class but they drew their strength from women of considerable intellectual attainments but moderate fame; the reader can call them up from the past, widows and spinsters, in their dark clothes and steel spectacles, seated at their Davenports before a large ink-well and a quill pen, with a distant look in their tired eyes, recalling a life of hardship and achievement but cheered and inspired by distant visions of freedom and progress, and the confidant hope that women of the future might escape from the tribulations which they had known. Their writings lie deeply buried in the learned but ephemeral publications of Victorian days: their books, with the sermons of their fathers, brothers and cousins fill the cheapest trays of the booksellers. But yet they draw our sympathy and attention—twinkling but constant they shine out from the inert, conventional mass of Victorian womanhood bravely illumining some dark corner of Bath, Torquay, Budleigh Salterton, Malvern or St. Leonards. Among them were Frances Power Cobbe, an Irish lady of ample proportions, whose interests ranged from ragged schools to friendless girls, from American philosophy to anti-vivisection: she edited the *Zoophilist* and preached in Unitarian chapels: Amelia Edwards, the eminent

Egyptologist and successful novelist, who lived at The Larches,
Westbury-on-Trym; Matilda Betham Edwards, who in 1917 was
to celebrate the diamond jubilee of her literary life and had behind
her a lengthy string of novels based on life in Suffolk and spiced
with anti-clericalism; Annie Keary whose novel *Clemency Francklin*
was published in the year of the petition; Harriet Martineau, who
from her comfortable retreat at Clappersgate in Westmorland,
had just finished a connection which had lasted for fourteen years
with the *Daily News* during which she had written at least three
articles a week; Mary Somerville, who was to give her name to the
college at Oxford and who, although she was eighty-six at the
time of the petition, had just completed a book on *Molecular and
Microscopic Science*; Anna Swanwick, a highly accomplished German
and classical scholar, a Unitarian and the friend of Tennyson,
Browning and Gladstone; Mrs. Augusta Webster, the daughter of
the Chief Constable of Cambridge, who was able, by the chances
of propinquity, to indulge in some of the forbidden fruits of university learning and to marry a Fellow of Trinity and who, in
later life, was to write plays, novels and poems by way of change
from representing Chelsea on the London School Board; and
Susannah Winkworth who, from the conventional background of
Clifton, published a batch of more or less unreadable German
theological translations, and founded the Jacob's Well housing
scheme at Bristol. Their very christian names—Susannah, Augusta,
Anna, Mary, Harriet, Annie, Matilda, Amelia, Frances—they
seem to bring to mind those virtues of patience and resignation
which lie at the heart of Victorian womanhood. But instead of
accepting their lot these writing ladies fought it. Almost all their
books are marked by a tilting against the proprieties, and their
blows—though they were gentle ones—for the most part, fell on
a place where they hurt—the clergy and conventions of the
Established Church.

The signatures of the literary ladies were supported by those
who had had experience of affairs—Martha Merrington, the first
woman Poor Law Guardian; Florence Davenport-Hill, member
of a family renowned for its work in reformatories and industrial
schools; Mrs. William Grey, who was to found the Girls Public
Day School Company and is perhaps yet remembered as the

author, many years after the signing of the petition, of *Last Words to Girls on Life in School, and after School*; her sister Miss Shirreff, who in 1870 was to be Mistress of Girton; Mrs. Lucas, the sister of John Bright, a conspicuous temperance reformer, and Josephine Butler, who was to be largely responsible for the repeal of the Contagious Diseases Act in 1886—a monstrous measure by which women leading immoral lives in garrison towns could be placed under police supervision.

Also included among the signatories was an assortment of ladies who were pre-eminently political: they called themselves 'the suffrage leaders'. For the most part their fathers or husbands had played a stormy part in left-wing politics, worshipping the names of Cobden and Bright in preference to more conventional deities. Here were Mrs. P. A. Taylor, wife of the famous anti-clerical Radical who had roused the House of Commons by his attacks on the Home Secretary for reading Massini's private correspondence, Miss Lilian Ashworth, daughter of Cobden's intimate—Henry Ashworth, a member of the Society of Friends who betrayed a most un-Quakerly passion for grouse shooting, and Mrs. Pease Nichol, wife of the famous but rationalist Scottish astronomer. Almost all the signatories of the Petition seem to have shared strong Quaker or Unitarian principles: the great Church names of English life are missing from the list. This was noticed at the time by one of their opponents—Mrs. Samuel Carter Hall, an Irish lady of some literary standing who wrote, 'I believe that the originators and a large majority of the sustainers of this monstrous project are not members of any Christian Church. A woman without an altar is even more degraded than a woman without a hearth'.

Although to-day the name of McLaren conjures up a vista of gorgeous rhododendrons blooming in one of the most spectacular gardens in Great Britain, the real fame of this family lies less in Rhododendron Aberconway or Rhododendron Bodnant than in their valuable and undeviating attachment to the cause of women's franchise. The founder of the House, Mr. Duncan McLaren, a man of great energy and understanding who was popularly known in the House of Commons as 'the member for Scotland' was represented in the list of names by his third wife, who was

Bright's sister, and by one of his daughters. Also on this list were the names of Lady Anna Gore-Langton, heiress of the great political tradition of the Dukes of Buckingham (which in default of male heirs had descended to her) who felt not unreasonably aggrieved because, as a woman, she could exercise no part of her political inheritance, and Lady Amberley, daughter-in-law of Lord John Russell and mother of an illustrious son still living, who had the quick-silver mind of her family—the Stanleys of Alderley.

Readers may be forgiven for smiling as they picture the austere figure of Mill, moving away from Westminster Hall with the great scroll of these and hundreds of other names which had been rapidly but earnestly collected. This champion of the ladies was no Sir Lancelot—vibrating with masculine vigour as he thundered into battle: he was—as is clear from the famous portrait of him by Watts—ascetic and somewhat ethereal—an inconspicuous man whom the Lancelots of this world would dismiss with a snort of contempt. He presented the petition without disturbance and his task was now to bend the will of men along the paths laid down by these pioneer women. For on that summer morning in June 1866 a movement had been born.

IV

Lydia Becker from Manchester

In those carefree times there was no autumn session of Parliament and, when both houses were prorogued on August 10th for the rest of 1866, there was an inevitable subsidence in the public excitement over reform. This somewhat diminished the activity of those agitating for woman's suffrage but the ladies who had organized the petition seem to have remained together as an informal committee. And at this point the story goes northwards to Manchester, which throughout the history of this question was again and again to revivify the flagging spirit of London. That autumn, a curious though not unimportant body called the National Association for the Advancement of Social Science was holding its annual meeting in Manchester. This organization owed its existence in large part to the wide but too swiftly flowing mind of Lord Brougham, who was eighty-eight at this time and spoke at this meeting with his powers trembling on the edge of senility; although some of the preoccupations of the Association were rather perverse, it served as a useful trial ground for many ideas which were valuable and which have become now an established part of British institutions. Madame Bodichon had travelled from London to attend the meetings: she read a paper on woman's suffrage which, though it was not reported in the published transactions of the Society, was of much consequence in the fortunes of the movement. Madame Bodichon's paper attracted considerable notice and a large audience which included Lydia Ernestine Becker. Though other names since her day may have engrossed public notice among those fighting for woman's suffrage, and though her personality was formidable rather than attractive, Miss

Becker's name demands the devotion of women and will receive the applauses of posterity. The development of suffragette militancy in the early twentieth century might be described as a revolt against Becker, which in some degree explains the eclipse of her fame, but the perceptive reader will not forget that it was as courageous in the 1860's for a woman to make a speech in public as it was in 1912 for a woman to hurl a stone. Lydia Becker was the daughter of a German gentleman, Hannibal Becker, and a Lancashire mother. The steadfastness of purpose of the German coupled with the spirit of a Lancashire lass produced in the daughter a rare temper—unflagging, ingenious and cool. Her interests were scientific, and readers of Darwin will recognize her as his friend and valued correspondent on botanical researches. When she was in her middle thirties she moved into Manchester with her father and started one of those pathetic little Societies with which, like the graves of Victorian children in our churchyards, the intellectual cities of Great Britain are freely and sadly sprinkled. Miss Becker's Literary and Scientific Society died its premature death. Shortly after this misfortune Madame Bodichon's lecture was given, and the words of the lecturer fell on Lydia Becker's ears like a shower on a parched garden. The effect was instant. Her conversion, unlike that of St. Paul, was not from the ranks of opposition: it was rather a conversion from ignorance —of one who had failed to appreciate the movement which was developing: but like St. Paul she was convinced that her task was to turn the unconvinced from darkness to light.

The Association meeting was in October 1866, and by the following January Miss Becker had formed the Manchester Women's Suffrage Committee—a provisional committee but the first body of its kind in the United Kingdom.[1] This met in the house of Dr. Louis Borchardt, and in addition to the Doctor and Miss Becker, five people attended—the Reverend S. A. Steinthal, who was under Mr. Gaskell minister at the Cross Street Chapel, Manchester, Mrs. Gloyne, Mr. Max Kyllman, Miss Wolstenholme and Mr. Jacob Bright. Miss Wolstenholme was the daughter of a

---

[1] A Committee had been formed in London in the previous year, but it was formed for the specific purpose of organizing the appeal to Parliament, and was disbanded after the Petition had been presented by Mill, though it met informally.

Methodist minister at Eccles, roughly contemporary with Miss Becker in age and as Mrs. Wolstenholme Elmy lived to be a prominent personality among twentieth-century suffragettes, carrying into Edwardian times the ringlets of her early Victorian youth. Jacob Bright—younger brother of John Bright—was Member of Parliament for Manchester and a valuable mouthpiece of the women's claims in the House of Commons. In February Miss Becker was appointed Secretary of this Manchester Committee.

Although this Manchester body is properly acclaimed as the first established woman's suffrage committee, Londoners were not inactive, and a provisional committee was formed there for the particular purpose of organizing further petitions to Parliament at about the same time as the gathering in Dr. Borchardt's house. Originators of new ideas, founders of new movements, organizers and secretaries love few things better than the sentence, 'A strong committee was formed'. Those 'strong' or 'representative' committees come to mind, full of ardour and eagerness, with their unanimity, their absence of quarrels, their well-filled rows of chairs not yet afflicted with the murrain of 'apologies for absence' and 'pressure of other commitments'. But although they were distinguished by unity and devotion to the cause, these early suffrage committees were hardly strong because they were too narrowly recruited. But the provisional London Committee, in addition to the familiar names, successfully attracted some people from a rather wider field. Mrs. Hensleigh Wedgwood, wife of an eminent authority on language belonging to the family of potters, Lady Goldsmid, wife of the head of one of the leading Jewish political families, Miss Anne Manning, a prolific writer who invented diaries of historical personages which had a somewhat unhealthy vogue in the 1850's and 1860's, and Professor Cairnes—a learned and singularly agreeable professor of political economy at University College, London, were conspicuous among the fresh names. But the crowning triumph was the inclusion on the committee of the Dean of Canterbury. Dean Alford, the Cambridge friend of Tennyson, Arthur Hallam, Spedding and Christopher Wordsworth, was a man of astonishing versatility and force whose interests ranged from Biblical scholarship to wood carving and

church music. Perhaps it would not be fanciful to suggest that this
writer of a famous hymn allowed his mind to stretch forward to
the time when the women's movement would attract myriads of
supporters and would, in his own words, consist of

> *Ten thousand times ten thousand,*
> *In sparkling raiment bright.*

Those days lay far ahead, and for the present the movement could
be rightly satisfied with the inclusion of a Dean in an era when
men's minds were dominated by church concerns, and when these
suffrage societies were decidedly over-weighted by anti-clerical
influences. In March and April 1867 a number of petitions in
favour of the women's vote, was presented to Parliament—some
signed exclusively by women and others by men and women
jointly. All this was leading up to the great day, when Mill was to
raise the question in the House of Commons, and followed the
procedure laid down by the Parliamentary Reformers forty years
earlier, who softened the ground before debate with a shower of
petitions.

On 20th May 1867 Mill rose to move an amendment to the
Representation of the People Bill which had been introduced by
the Conservative Government and which (as has been said)
broadly adopted the proposals of the Liberal Government in
1866. This bill reduced the value of the franchise in the counties
from £10 to £5 for copyholders and leaseholders, and from £50 to
£12 for occupiers. In boroughs all occupiers of dwelling-houses
rated for poor rate, and all occupiers of lodgings of £10 a year
unfurnished rent were given the vote. In addition there was a
wide measure of re-distribution of seats which gave an increased
number of seats to the industrial areas. Now Mill's amendment
was carefully aimed at a rather complicated but weak point in the
phrasing of the Bill. The reader will remember that the Reform
Bill of 1832 had for the first time specifically excluded women and
confined the vote to men by slipping in the words 'male persons':
this limitation only applied to the new constituencies created by
the 1832 Bill. The Bill of 1867 did not follow the Bill of 1832 in
using 'male persons' but used the word 'man'. Although the
matter is somewhat ambiguous, male person is a more narrowly

masculine term than man, which was generally interpreted in its broadest sense of mankind and was taken to include women. This interpretation was given statutory force by an Act of Parliament, passed in 1850, generally called Lord Romilly's Act, which laid down that in all Acts of Parliament, words imputing the masculine gender should be taken to include females unless it was clearly stated otherwise. Probably, on a strictly legal interpretation, the wording of the 1867 Act, because it used 'man' and not 'male persons', did not exclude women from the vote, but in view of the prevailing custom against their voting, it would have needed something more specific to enfranchise them. A few weeks before Mill spoke, Mr. George Denman, an accomplished lawyer, afterwards a judge of the High Court, who then sat for Tiverton, drew Disraeli's attention to this wording of the Bill and asked if it was the intention of the Government to enfranchise women. Disraeli scored a cheap laugh, and infuriated Denman, by saying that the Gentlemen of the Long Robe, that is to say the lawyers, might be consulted on the point. On a subsequent occasion Denman gave it as his opinion that if the Court of Queen's Bench was asked to decide on the construction of these clauses they would have held that they gave women the right to vote. To this sensitive point Mill directed his attack, moving that the word person should be substituted for man. This would, of course, have resolved any ambiguity and enfranchised the ladies.

Mill began his speech by saying that his proposal could excite no party or class feeling and, in reference to the prevailing apprehensions about enfranchising working-men added 'it cannot afflict the timid with revolutionary terrors'. He then argued that the exclusion of women was in a totally different category from any other franchise exclusion for it was 'absolute'. He meant by this that the other excluded classes—lunatics on recovering their reason, children on coming of age or paupers on acquiring sufficient income—could emerge from exclusion. Not so women. He spoke very moderately and carefully, including in his remarks an assessment of the altered position of women. 'We talk of political revolutions, but we do not sufficiently attend to the fact that there has taken place around us a silent domestic revolution: women and men are, for the first time in history, really each other's companions . . . they had been separate in their amusements and in their serious occupations . . . the man no longer gives his spare hours to violent outdoor exercises and boisterous conviviality with male associates . . . when men and women are really companions, if women are frivolous men will be frivolous . . . the two sexes must rise or sink together.'

No doubt it could be held that Mill was arguing too much from his own particular experience, that he saw all women as Mrs. Mill, spending a domestic evening in the shared delights of a blue book. A reading of the novels of Trollope and a consideration of the married life of the Parson of Framly, written during this decade, scarcely reinforce what Mill was saying. No doubt there was respectable historic authority for the belief that the old type of Regency buck—with his pugilism, his four-in-hand, and his steeplechasing—had lost his following in Queen Victoria's reign, and there was also some foundation for Mill's feeling that in intelligent, middle-class circles the wife was more of a companion to her husband than had been the case in the days of George IV. But a robust Conservative, the Member of Parliament for Colchester, who followed Mill said that there had been too much political economy in his speech and too little sense.

Samuel Laing, traveller, imperialist, Chairman of the London and Brighton Railway and somewhat unexpectedly a Liberal, who sat for Orkney and Shetland, stated that Mill's proposals would reduce England to the Court of Dahomey—the negro state which called in aid an army of Amazons. Mill was also reminded of his divergence of view from his father when a member quoted a remark made on a former occasion by F. H. F. Berkeley, a noted amateur boxer who devoted his political life to carrying a measure for introducing the secret ballot, who had said that James Mill—if he had been living—would say to his son, 'John, stick to the ballot, and leave the women alone.'

But Mill was unconscious of such gibes: for him the occasion was almost sacred and, as he was calling up visions of revolutionary change, based on intellectual companionship of husband and wife, he must have seen the shadow of his own wife, who had died nine years previously; to her commanding intelligence he had submitted not only his intellectual life but every detail of his existence down to the kind of braces he should wear when he went to see the doctor. This no doubt is the explanation of a curious and rather pathetic episode. Lady Amberley recalls how she and a few active supporters were in the Gallery to hear the debate, and to their horror after Mill had been speaking for a short time he came to a dead stop. She described the scene 'he stood silent for near two minutes or more: he seemed quite lost, only his eyebrows worked fearfully'. But the emotional strain of the day had one abundant consolation—seventy-three Members of Parliament voted in the Aye lobby, on the side for which Mill and Mr. Russell Gurney acted as tellers. One hundred and ninety-four members voted against the amendment.

In the majority opposed to votes for women, were the expected names of those solid, unreflecting mortals—valuable checks and balances—who steady politicians from rushing headlong down the helter-skelter. But among them were surprises—the names of Acland, Buxton, Pease and Cecil and the towering Gladstone. The minority included Lord Amberley, John Bright, the author and Christian Socialist Tom Hughes, who sat for Lambeth, Henry Labouchere, about to win undying fame as a journalist, P. A. Taylor, and Laurence Oliphant, a truly romantic Victorian who almost immediately after voting joined an unorthodox religious community at Salem-on-Erie, and The O'Donoghue. But the minority was by no means composed of Radicals and eccentrics— Sir Samuel Peto, the great contractor voted with them, and ortho- dox conservatism was represented by Lady Anna's husband— Mr. Gore-Langton, by Lord John and Lord William Hay and by Mr. Percy Wyndham, the member for Cockermouth. While election statistical men of a later age might have succeeded in analysing the voters into groups and categories, and in tracing trends and tendencies, it is sufficient to say that the minority was representative and respectable. The blind and highly accomplished Henry Fawcett, who had lately married Millicent Garrett, followed Mill in debate and said that he had brought the question out of the region of ridicule. The size of the minority drove home this truth. Mill called it 'unexpectedly large' adding that it must give 'an immense impulse to the question'.

As is perhaps often the case in politics, the impulse was to the converted rather than to the heathen. Miss Becker was quickly off the mark and, unperturbed by dead seasons, she formed the first permanent suffrage society in August 1867 in Manchester. The previous committees in both Manchester and London had been provisional. She was followed by London, and by Mrs. Duncan McLaren in Edinburgh. Though these societies all main tained their independence, a central body was also formed in London—the National Society for Women's Suffrage. But how narrowly these bodies were recruited is illustrated by the fact that Florence Nightingale refused to join (though she did so later) on the grounds that other grievances than the vote pressed more heavily on women. A flourishing society was formed in Bristol at the beginning of 1868—that famous political city which had showed its fervour for male suffrage by riot and bloodshed in the 1830's. But here again the reader may suppose that the Society sprang less from the zeal of the Bristol Burghers than from the proximity of Lady Anna Gore-Langton and her husband, who lived at Newton Park, just outside the city. In Bristol itself—unlike the other centres—the preliminaries for forming the committee were undertaken by a man—Matthew Davenport Hill—an extreme Radical, enlightened law reformer and bankruptcy commissioner who claimed the distinction of being the first Birmingham man called to the Bar. His daughters Florence and Rosamund were prominent in the feminist movement. But how difficult it then was, even in an enlightened family, for daughters to take the lead is illustrated by the form in which certain selected Bristolians were circularized. The statement was headed 'Provisional Suffrage Societies—Bristol Committee' and it ran: 'With a view to forming such a society, if possible, Mr. Commissioner Hill, who is now at 3 Mall, Clifton, permits his daughter to invite so many as his drawing-room will hold, to meet there on 24th January 1868 at 3 p.m. for a friendly consultation on this public question, although from the narrowness of space the meeting cannot be public.' The Secretary chosen for the Bristol Committee was F. W. Newman too often loosely dismissed as 'The Cardinal's Brother' but deserving on his own account a not inconspicuous niche in history. His domestic circle was possibly not in open sympathy with the women's movement since his wife, who was a Plymouth Sister, once jumped out of the window rather than meet Harriet Martineau. But he himself was in the van of every advanced and unorthodox movement—a vegetarian, a strong temperance advocate, a member of no church though Dean Stanley bravely asserted that his book on *The Soul* would live long after everything his brother, the Cardinal, wrote had been forgotten. This wayward, gentle character lived for thirty years after the inaugural meeting and was throughout life and far beyond the confines of Bristol a penetrating supporter of the political rights of women. At the meeting Commissioner Hill stated that the cause 'unlike that of all other great causes will require your support for a very short time.'

In 1871 the *Manchester Guardian* made the same point, when a leader writer said that the admission of women to the franchise was only a question of time, and that the time was likely to be short. The writer was C. P. Scott, not then Editor, who had changed the policy of the paper from hostility to friendliness towards the women's claims.

V

Mrs. Maxwell Votes

For these feelings of confidence there were two foundations.
The first was the certainty that, in that epoch when reason
seemed firmly enthroned in the mind of man, the case for including women in the political structure of the nation was not only
overwhelming but unanswerable. When for example F. W. Newman wrote that the English law towards women was more unjust
than that of the great historically despotic nations, and even than
Turkey with its sultanas and seraglios, the average reader was
startled into agreeing with his inevitable conclusion that the female
franchise is essential to justice. But if readers for Newman's close-
knit writings were somewhat few and far between, there was
always the second foundation for confidence—namely that the
legal position was so ambiguous that women had only to assert
their desire to vote to find their wish fulfilled.

On this particular point—the confused state of the law—the
supporters of the women's vote concentrated throughout 1868.
Its full possibilities were brought home to shrewd observers by a
picturesque episode in Manchester during a by-election at the end
of 1867. By a strange but not unknown mistake the authorities
admitted the name of Mrs. Lily Maxwell to the list of voters. She
was an independent woman who kept a little shop where she sold
kitchen crockery. As she was a ratepayer on her own account, it
can be seen how easily the mistake could occur. The indefatigable
Miss Becker spotted what had happened, hurried round to Mrs.
Maxwell and asked if she would vote for Jacob Bright—the
Liberal candidate. She received an answer which would warm the
heart of any political canvasser, 'If I'd twenty votes I would give

them all to Jacob Bright.' On the following day the brave Becker escorted her prize to Bright's Committee Rooms. Accompanied by a group of Liberal gentlemen the ladies made their progress to the polling booth. Here it is necessary to interrupt the account of what happened with a reminder of a stock but persistent argument against women voting—namely that there was something indelicate about a lady going into a polling booth. The argument was to drift ponderously across the field of battle for forty years till Lord Quickswood put it out of its misery with shafts of coruscating ridicule. But in the 1860's, when voting by ballot was still in the future, even those who believed in women voting thought there was something improper about a woman taking part in the public proceedings inside a polling booth, and one of Mill's influential supporters in the debate, Sir George Bowyer—a distinguished lawyer and Roman Catholic who was later to be expelled from the Reform Club for illiberal opinions—had said that women would have to vote with ballot papers because it would be 'manifestly indecorous' for them to attend the booth. In 1867 voting was more in the nature of testifying at a revivalist meeting —the voter publicly stated his wishes and was jeered or cheered according to the fancy of the motley crowd assembled in the booth. For this reason protective man thought there were risks for a woman in the polling booth, and this anxiety to avoid any unpleasantness was the explanation why the two ladies were attended by a posse of men from the Liberal Committee rooms. Confronted with Mrs. Maxwell's name on the list of electors, the Returning Officer had no alternative but to accept her vote. When she had voted, all the occupants of the booth, whether Jacob Bright's supporters or drawn from the ranks of Tuscany, joined in three hearty cheers for Mrs. Maxwell—heroine and pioneer. The *Englishwoman's Journal* in recounting the scene said that they had been informed by a lady, who was present, that there was less inconvenience than is often experienced 'at a public concert or fashionable chapel'. Certainly it was a brilliant stroke to compare the polling booth, with its loungers all supposedly eager for the nameless horrors of hustling and leering, with the God-fearing crowd flocking to hear the Reverend Charles Honeyman at Lady Whittlesea's Chapel.

Unluckily for the supporters of the women's vote, the remarkable achievement of Mrs. Maxwell was eclipsed by another event which had happened in Manchester three days previously—the public execution, with all the panoply of a draped scaffold and the muttered incantations of Irish priests, of the three Fenians who had murdered a Manchester policeman. The mill girls, who if the world, as John Stuart Mill hoped, had been animated by reason should have been lining the streets to cheer Mrs. Maxwell were in fact part of the massed crowd which filled the approaches to Salford and even as far as the respectable length of Deansgate in an attempt to see the execution. As was to happen for the next forty-five years political issues of the greatest excitement were to push the women's suffrage on to the shelf. How could Miss Becker and Mrs. Maxwell hope to draw attention which was comparable to the thrill of the crowd as the hangman placed the white cap over the faces of Gould, Allen and Larkin?

Yet if the public was lukewarm, the enthusiasts were encouraged. The case of Lily Maxwell proved that once women were on the register there was nothing to prevent them from voting. If the belief was well founded in law that there was no legal provision against women being placed on the register except in those new constituencies created by the 1832 Bill, the point of attack must be concentrated on the right of women to be admitted to the Register as the law then stood. This issue was brought to public notice by Thomas Chisholm Anstey—a barrister and erstwhile Member of Parliament whose career had been distinguished by the display of ideas inspired by the weirdest assortment of quirks and crotchets. He had made an effort to impeach Lord Palmerston in the 1840's and he had been (not unjustly) described as 'a malcontent of the highest bore-power'. But whatever his drawbacks, he marshalled all the legal arguments on female franchise with the skill and clarity of the trained advocate. F. W. Newman justly observed that as Mill was the champion of woman's suffrage in Parliament so Anstey was its champion in law. He was ably abetted by a youthful and equally ardent barrister from Manchester, Richard Pankhurst. The name of Pankhurst was to proliferate in the early twentieth century with spectacular brilliance, and that fact has tended to obscure the career and gifts of the founder of the family. He was a Manchester man with a pride in his native city and a contempt for the refinements and affectations of the south—a point of view more common then than now. His mind was of razor-like penetration, and it must have led him to the pinnacles of his profession if all had not been spoiled and blunted by a fatal inability to hold his tongue. Mr. Philip Snowden, who remembered him, recalled that he spoke in a high-pitched voice which, on occasions, caused him to be mistaken for a woman. There has always been a type of Radical—and Richard Pankhurst was one of them—whose method has been to convince and convert by shock tactics. Men of this type seem to regard public opinion rather as an elderly lady in bonnet, shawl and mittens against whom they aim their shafts: they are completely satisfied with their day's work if the poor thing lets out a little scream of anguish or terror. In the eyes of these choice spirits the more venerable an institution or the more tenderly cherished an opinion the more obvious it is for their flouts and jeers. For Richard Pankhurst nothing was too outrageous. The House of Lords was a 'public abattoir' which existed only to butcher the liberties of mankind. Manchester Cathedral was an 'obsolete medieval residuum' and the clergy 'a portentous beadledom'. In company with Joseph Chamberlain in Birmingham, Sir Charles Dilke in Newcastle and Bradlaugh he sprang to the attack of the Royal Family. As the dark shadow of widowhood obscured the popularity of the Monarchy, Richard Pankhurst presided at the formation of the Manchester Republican Club. He became in the familiar saying 'his own worst enemy' or in the bourgeois slang of those days 'a holy terror'. Perhaps it was not chance that his Christian names—Richard Marsden—recalled a famous north country Chartist, for he had been born in 1836 while the rather furtive deeds of Marsden and his associates were winning some support outside conventional English political parties. He was the son of a Manchester auctioneer, and was educated at Manchester University, when it was Owen's College, and before it assumed the name, which he would have particularly disliked, of The Victoria University. He was also at London University, of which place of learning he was gold medallist and Doctor of Laws: he started his professional life as a solicitor but he was called to the

Bar by Lincoln's Inn in 1867, and it is immediately afterwards that he breaks into the story of woman's suffrage with all the zeal and energy of his character. In the autumn of 1868 he wrote an important article, using his exceptional knowledge of the law and of legal history, to show that women could vote under the Act of 1867. This was published in the *Fortnightly*—a periodical which was rapidly gaining distinction under the able editorship of John Morley. The opinion of Pankhurst and other lawyers, coupled with the exertions of Anstey, encouraged the leaders of the suffrage movement to test the ground by an action at law.

Here the energy and ingenuity of Lydia Becker were seen to advantage. A great number of women householders—5,000 in the City of Manchester alone and several hundreds in the adjoining constituencies, and also a few throughout the country as a whole, applied for inclusion on the Parliamentary Register, which was being prepared for the General Election of 1868. The claims came before the overseers of the Register (they were the representatives of the local authority), and a few of these officials, on their own decision, struck out the women but the majority of them left the matter to the revising court, presided over by a member of the Bar. Most of the revising barristers struck off the women, but a few of these learned men decided that they only had the power to strike people out where an objection had been raised. Therefore, where no objection was raised by the representatives of the political parties, the women remained. Mankind could hardly have reduced a simple issue to a more formidable tangle. *The Times* described the situation as 'decidedly an odd one' and referred to 'the glorious uncertainty of the law'.

There was a right of appeal to the High Court from the revising barristers' courts, and the suffrage pioneers selected four cases for appeal. The first which was a case known as *Chorlton* v. *Lings*—was heard in the Court of Common Pleas on 7th November 1868. This virtually settled the question, for with the brusque finality of English justice any rights which women claimed from ancient times were decided to be non-existent. Those pleasant antiquarian fields with abbesses setting off to Westminster and ladies of the manor nominating their representative for the Commons were as effectively barred as once had been the Garden of Eden. Sir John

Coleridge, Q.C., afterwards Lord Chief Justice, appeared for the women with Richard Pankhurst as his junior, and the case was presented, doubtless owing to Pankhurst's researches, with great judicial scholarship and learning. But it was in vain—Sir William Bovill, a Conservative, the Chief Justice of the Common Pleas and a splendid judge, decided emphatically against them and was supported by his three brethren on the Bench: Willes, Keating and Byles. Both Byles and Willes, who rather fancied themselves in the world of literature, saw fit to indulge in somewhat strange *obiter dicta*. Byles trusted that 'our unanimous decision will for ever exorcise and lay this ghost of a doubt which ought never to have made its appearance.' Willes went further and hoped that nobody would imagine that their decision was based on 'any underrating of the sex, either in point of intellect or in worth. That would be quite inconsistent with one of the glories of our civilization—the respect and honour in which women are held.' He then invoked the support of the great lawyer Selden for the argument that 'the exemption from voting was founded upon motives of decorum and was a privilege of the sex (*honestatis privilegium*)'.

While the judges were happily mouthing out these historic rotundities of phrase they were perhaps unaware of the figure of Lydia Becker intently listening to their judgment. As soon as the case was over, she slipped out to the nearest telegraph office and sent off a telegram with the cryptic words of command 'Post your letters'. Immediately afterwards the 800 candidates for the General Election, then being fought, received a letter from Miss Becker asking if they would support a bill giving women the vote. When the election came Miss Becker had a busy day driving round Manchester in a carriage and pair of greys roping in the thirteen ladies—orphans of the storm, who had survived the objections of the revising barristers and were consequently able to vote. The election was generally favourable to the Liberal Party, and the supporters of woman's suffrage increased by about a dozen, but there was one deadly blow—the defeat of Mill for Westminster. He had had a majority of 700 in 1865 and this was twisted into a majority of 1,400 for his Conservative opponent—W. H. Smith—the newspaper distributor. Commenting on the very corrupt campaign in Westminster, *The Times* said that Smith had probably won the seat by his riches and saved himself from being unseated by his character—a somewhat oblique tribute but one which sheds a curious side-light on the Victorian respect for wealth. But though withdrawn from the lists, Mill was not inactive, and he published in the following year his famous book on *The Subjection of Women*, which he had written eight years previously, after the death of his wife but based on talks with her and enriched by the co-operation of his step-daughter—Helen Taylor. The book was designed to show the hardships of women under the existing laws of marriage and property. He described an English married woman as merely 'the personal body-servant of a despot' and he thought that as in the case of any other servant, the natural sequel of her position would be that she should change her place again and again till she found a good master. There was always a certain naïvety about Mill and the reader may well smile when he comes to the passage about women's brains, 'It is within my knowledge that a man who had weighed many human brains said that the heaviest he knew of, heavier even than Cuvier[1] was that of a woman.' But the main argument is as keenly knit and tersely expressed as ever, leading up to a great swelling climax about 'the moral regeneration of mankind only really commencing, when the most fundamental of the social relations is placed under the rule of equal justice'.

Going back in imagination to the 1860's and lulled by the eloquence of Mill's sentences till we almost fancy we can hear the mighty waters rolling evermore we could be forgiven for amazement that his plea was virtually unheeded. Admittedly there were pockets of enlightenment and enthusiasm over the country, which were in entire agreement with Mill's thesis, but indifference reigned supreme in that quarter where opinion is formed and the pathway for legislation prepared—the political-social life of the capital. 'I hear much of women's rights' blandly observed a famous duchess 'but I only know that I have no wrongs.' And from Park Lane through the airy respectability of Bloomsbury to the chaotic life of East London there was a feeling that things like the rights of women were best left alone, that they were merely the whimperings of those who had failed to a get a real prize in life—a man, or

[1] The eminent French naturalist.

as it was expressed in the conventional Victorian witticism 'Women's Rights are Men's Lefts'. The majority felt that there was something faintly uncomfortable about it: that it produced feelings akin to those experienced by the congregation when the clergyman forgets to bowdlerize some of the braver passages in the Bible. People were a trifle uneasy, a shade embarrassed. Nor were these feelings by any means diminished when Lord Amberley, who with his wife, was a very strong supporter of women's rights took the chair at a meeting of the London Dialectical Society, when the subject of birth control was discussed, in the summer of 1868. The whole question of feminism partly because people were a little afraid of it—partly because it had met with unexpected success was ripe for ridicule.

The weak point in the case for female suffrage lay in the limited class which was to be enfranchised. All married women were excluded because, on marriage, their property passed to their husbands and they therefore could not be ratepayers. The class was conseqently limited to widows and to affluent spinsters. Therefore even as far back as 1866 Mill's proposals, though they were advanced and progressive in principle, were not democratic. The movement in fact was always bourgeois and intellectual rather than popular. *The Times*, which was a worthy and enduring adversary of the women's vote, drew attention to the weakness of this limited suffrage in a leading article at the time of Mill's amendment in 1867. 'It is not very easy to speak with perfect gravity—the paper stated—of a scheme which perpetuating the disenfranchisement of married ladies who are not separated from their husbands, and of young ladies who are not orphans, admits to the polling booth a mixed multitude of widows and those whom, for want of a more respectful term, we must needs call old maids.' Some years later the weekly journal *Truth* was to sharpen the point by asserting that votes were to be showered on courtesans but withheld from respectably married women: the proposal 'grants to Hagar what it denies to Sarah'.

There was a further aspect of the matter which invited attack. Although in those days social life rested on the now vanished etiquette of calling, with all the subtleties of the precise number of cards to be left, the significance of an up-turned corner and the beauty of the copper-plate engraving of the name, the conventions encouraged a lady to say that she was not at home if a single gentleman came to call on her. To the Victorian mind the idea of a lady being canvassed by a political tout for her vote was scarcely distinguishable from subjecting her to an indelicate advance. 'What does voting imply? It implies solicitation and dunning, reproaching, humbugging and cajoling. Why are respectable women, because they happen to be widows or spinsters and live in houses of their own, to be exposed to the impertinent intrusion of agents, canvassers and candidates—to be beseiged alternately by the adulation of fools and by the insolence of bullies?'

These words were published, a fortnight after Mill had presented his petition, in the *Saturday Review*. That journal, which was perhaps the most influential of all the Victorian periodicals, was to direct a fierce jet of scorn and ridicule against the claims of women. Its editor, J. D. Cook, collected a highly accomplished and spirited team of writers who could claim—whatever their subsequent failure and shortcomings—that to have fought under Cook (like those who fought under Harry of England) was to have made their names a household word. Among this team was an extraordinary writer—Mrs. Lynn Linton, and it is perhaps an indication of Cook's intrepid character that he once shook his fist in the face of this alarming lady. During the later 1860's Mrs. Lynn Linton poured out an arresting torrent of articles in the *Saturday Review* on her own sex which included 'The Girl of The Period'—a severe commentary on the decorum and morality of the young ladies who, under the lead of fashion, were just emerging from the restrictions of the crinoline. To Mrs. Lynn Linton, whose idea of the ideal woman seems to have been bounded by the lifeless, malleable doll beloved by Dickens, women who advocated the vote for their own sex were completely anathema: she called them by turns The Epicene Sex or The Shrieking Sisterhood. Her rabid fustian is only worth recalling because here and there she makes a point which was effective, and which struck response in the hearts of those opposed to votes for women. She could be quite as absurd as the American theologian who could solemnly write in 1869 that if women were given the vote they would become 'thinner, sharp-featured, lank and dry', or as Lord Leighton's sister, a clever and enlightened lady, wrote in the nineteenth century, if women were ever to be emancipated 'not only the power of love in women, but for either sex its possibility will have passed away'. But Mrs. Linton's silliness was sometimes redeemed by sense. For example in her article on The Shrieking Sisterhood she wrote, 'While the shrieking sisterhood remains to the front, the world will stop its ears'. That was precisely what happened: the very success that Miss Becker and her associates had achieved stirred up the most violent antagonism.

VI

'This Mad, Wicked Folly of Women's Rights'

These antagonisms seem to have been touched off by the sight of women stepping on to a public platform and speaking. The first public meeting ever held in support of the female franchise was on 14th April 1868—in Manchester—at the Assembly Room of the Free Trade Hall. The chair was taken by the enlightened Mayor of Salford, Davis Pochin. The first resolution and it was a model invariably followed throughout the rest of the nineteenth century—stated that the exclusion of women from voting was 'unjust in principle and inexpedient in practice' and that the vote ought to be granted to them on the same terms 'as it is or may be granted to men'. There was a powerful team of speakers—the Archdeacon of Coventry—a learned and Liberal member of the Sandford family—F. B. Potter, the member for Rochdale, Richard Pankhurst, Anstey, Mill, Jacob Bright and F. W. H. Myers—a poet and man of the rarest intellectual gifts. But what marked the meeting, what shocked observers outside, was the news that the resolution had been moved in a speech by Lydia Becker. With a cackle of asinine laughter, the joke spread that human beings were now of three sexes—masculine, feminine and Miss Becker.

The first public meeting in London was held a year after the Manchester meeting, in the premises of the Architectural Society in Conduit Street on 17th July 1869. The team of male speakers was varied and accomplished. It consisted of Thomas Hare—the eminent law reporter and the father of Proportional Representation—Boyd Kinnear—a Scottish advocate who sat for East Fife until he was defeated by Mr. Asquith—Mill, Charles Kingsley, Professor Fawcett—the blind, Radical Member of Parliament for Brighton—Lord Houghton, John Morley, Sir Charles Dilke, who in spite of having some rather fierce bees buzzing in his bonnet sat as Member of Parliament for Chelsea, P. A. Taylor and Professor Masson the outstanding Milton scholar. Slipped in among this diversity of male orations was a short speech from Mrs. Fawcett. She was twenty-two at the time and she was to survive until after the General Election of 1929 when men and women were included on the parliamentary register for the first time in an absolute equality. Her youth, her obvious sincerity and her charm of manner commanded respect, and she was not confronted by the outcry which had assailed Miss Becker's appearance as a speaker.

The next London meeting, which was held in the Hanover Square Rooms in March 1870 was more criticized possibly because women were more in evidence. Mrs. P. A. Taylor took the chair and was unluckily inaudible because of a sore throat. Mill's stepdaughter, Helen Taylor, was 'fashionably dressed in slight mourning' but was thought 'really eloquent'. Mrs. Fawcett was less successful than on the first occasion but Mrs. Grote, the wife of the historian, made a characteristically rattling speech in which she said that she had never been engaged in any controversy in which her feelings were more completely seconded by her reason. There was a considerable outcry after these female pipings in Hanover Square and Lady Russell—the former Prime Minister's wife and a broad-minded custodian of the Whig tradition—wrote to her son, Lord Amberley, 'Good-bye dear boy and I congratulate your wife on not having made a speech.' But the wise old lady spoke too soon. For after many heart-searchings Lady Amberley decided to read a paper on female suffrage at the Mechanics Institute in Stroud. In this town where Conservative strength and Radical doctrines have always been nicely balanced, Lady Amberley drew an audience which was more respectable than 'cloth-capped'. Sir John Dorington of Lyppiat Park took the chair and among the audience was the Chairman of the Great Western Railway perhaps better known—for such are the injustices of memory—as the father of Mrs. Sidney Webb. Lady Amberley spoke with all the force and distinction of her character, and the meeting (at the thought of which she had been highly nervous) passed off peacefully and successfully. But the peace of Stroud was rudely shattered by a storm of abuse which rumbled out of Fleet Street for many days. Almost the only glint of brightness to reach Lady Amberley was a letter from Helen Taylor who wrote that she would rather members of west end clubs 'called one a strong-minded woman than that they told scandalous stories about one'. There was, however, no great danger of Helen Taylor figuring in a scandalous story: she was not likely (even in slight mourning) to be the toast of White's.

But even worse than the flashes and cavernous roarings of Fleet Street were the horrified comments of that august personality withdrawn behind the walls of Windsor, but faithfully reflecting the sensibilities of the typical middle-class mind. In a letter to Theodore Martin, deep in his biography of the Prince Consort, Queen Victoria wrote:

'The Queen is most anxious to enlist everyone who can speak or write or join in checking this mad, wicked folly of "Woman's Rights" with all its attendant horrors, on which her poor feeble sex is bent, forgetting every sense of womanly feeling and propriety. Lady Amberley ought to get a *good whipping*.'

Those words, which were only made public forty years later, and even then Lady Amberley's name was concealed, were perhaps less balanced and more forthright than others of Queen Victoria's *obiter dicta*, but they reflect a point of view to which she clung with passionate tenacity. Nor will it be overlooked that in those days there was probably a majority of British women who, though they may have lacked the expressive vocabulary of the Queen, shared to the full her feelings on the enfranchisement of women. Against that almost emotional opposition the movement was brought to a standstill. For the next thirty-five years there was virtually no progress whatever. Like some huge vehicle which has advanced steadily towards the summit of a hill the cause of female suffrage was halted. In vain the enthusiasts crowded round to push, to advise or to suggest alterations of strategy but the only result of their efforts was a shudder, a scuffling of dust, a sense of disturbance. There was no forward movement. Worse still, minor measures affecting women such as the Married Women's Property Act, the Contagious Diseases Act, or even, after a chequered career, the Deceased Wife's Sister Bill sped past the crippled machine and shot out of sight over the brow of the hill. The great vehicle which had started forward so bravely and gaily in the middle 1860's lay motionless for all the remaining years of the nineteenth century.

VII

Death of Miss Becker

No advantage would be gained from detailing the debates and arguments which sprang from the topic of woman's suffrage during the last thirty years of the nineteenth century: the case for or against showed no change from 1867. Lord Morley in his biography of Gladstone, writing of another issue, has well described the static waters of argument in which the political voyager can only too easily become becalmed—'The case had been argued to the dregs, the conclusion was fixed, and all interest was centred in the play of forces, the working of high motives and low, the balance of parties, the secret ambitions and antagonism of persons.' In the case of Votes for Women the play of forces on the side of the opponents was in reality the deployment of prejudice. The salient events which marked the movement during the last thirty years of the nineteenth century showed how surprisingly effective this powerful weapon was in blocking any advance, and how it was used from quarters where greater sense might have been expected.

For example in their impasse the supporters of woman's suffrage could reasonably have expected some help from the scientists in undermining these deep-rooted prejudices. This was not forthcoming. Huxley, for example, could write, 'In every excellent character, whether mental or physical, the average woman is inferior to the average man, in the sense of having that character less in quantity and lower in quality. . . . Even in physical beauty man is superior.' Darwin, though more guarded was hardly less offensive; he wrote, 'It is generally admitted that with women the powers of intuition, or rapid perception, and perhaps of imitation,

77

are more strongly marked than in man: but some at least of these faculties are characteristic of the lower races, and therefore of a past and lower state of civilization.' Nor were the philosophers really more helpful than the scientists. Herbert Spencer, over a cup of tea with Lady Amberley, told her that unless women could fight they should not vote. This was of course a weightier and more sensible argument than many that were used, and it was to remain the constant rallying cry of those opposed to female franchise. In fact it could be maintained that the enfranchisement of women was impossible until that particular argument was repudiated by the facts of the first war.

In trying to account for the failure of the movement to advance, observers will pay heed to the ingrained prejudices of mankind on this question—and will note how they were derived in some degree from the teaching of the churches. 'If the Bible and Religion stood in the way of women's rights then the Bible and Religion must go.' Such were the brave words of Annie Besant in her socialist and atheistical youth before she bowed the knee to the strange mysteries of theosophy. But people were not likely to be shaken out of ancient prejudices by exaggerated and violent argument: the only hope was to wean them away from natural instincts by patience and reason.

These were the pre-eminent qualities of Lydia Becker, and for more than twenty years she carried on the struggle, rewarded by no progress, but confident that an advance would come later but inexorably.

> *Others I doubt not if not we*
> *The outcome of our work shall see,*
> *And children gather as their own*
> *The harvest which the dead have sown.*

The history of the decades from 1860 to 1890—so far as women's suffrage is concerned—is the history of Miss Becker. In addition to her routine activities—organizing the Manchester society, travelling to London to guide the National Society and supervising all parliamentary work together with an unrelenting programme of lectures and speeches—she started in 1870 and conducted for twenty years, till her death in 1890, the *Women's*

Suffrage Journal. This is an astonishingly careful record—interrupted neither by explosive arguments nor by bitter asides—of every speech in and out of Parliament and every development which seemed to favour the women getting the vote. The tidiness and neatness of the feminine mind is apparent in every paragraph. Speeches of all male supporters of woman's franchise were fully reported, and a nice distinction was drawn between speeches by Members of Parliament and speeches by gentlemen, which always appeared under different headings. Critics could certainly complain that she was a little humourless in what she said: a well-filled drawing-room meeting in London was generally called 'a fine display of public feeling', and if the folding-doors were thrown open and the back drawing-room was called into use then the meeting tended to become 'a national demonstration'. Her materials were often meagre, and she did not hesitate to dress her window with obvious trifles—such as the news that Mrs. Joicey had been elected churchwarden of her parish church near Newcastle. With backsliders she was severe, and she generally published her correspondence with them. In 1870 she wrote to the member for Caernarvonshire, who rejoiced in the name of Love Jones Parry, to point out that his name appeared among those voting against a proposal for enfranchising women, although during his candidature he had promised to vote the other way. The question was an awkward one, and it was adroitly handled. The erring member wrote:

Dear Madam,   House of Commons, 17th May, 1870.

In the county I represent (Caernarvonshire) the women are all Liberal in politics and Nonconformists in religion—that is the vast majority of them: and this may be said of all North Wales. On the other hand in England, and particularly in boroughs such as Bath, women are Conservative under great clerical influence, which always tends to fetter freedom of thought.

I reluctantly, for these reasons, voted (against my own interests) to prevent women being made capable of doing what I consider political wrong in many places, i.e. voting against the Liberal Party.

Yours faithfully,

LOVE JONES PARRY.

Sir Wilfrid Lawson, the humorous and progressive member for Cockermouth, described this apostacy as an example of Breach of Promise.

The observer will also notice that it was during these disheartening decades that the solidarity of those women fighting for the vote becomes noticeable, with slightly exaggerated (and possibly unhealthy) feelings of personal devotion and loyalty to their leaders. This is how Miss Becker described a meeting, largely filled with working-class women, in Manchester at the end of the 1870's, 'How they listened—how they cheered. . . . If my eyes had been shut I should have fancied it was men who were cheering and clapping: the applause was as hearty and strong as at a men's meeting. I can't tell you how my heart went out to those women: and to see them look at me—oh, it was really sacred—awful: it was as if I received a baptism. It has been a new life to me to know and feel the strength there is in those women. . . .' The inherent danger within the movement was that it might develop into a crusade, not so much for the vote as against the male sex, with its members bound to each other by the mystical fidelity of warrior knights. That was to be a development—unwelcome and perhaps inevitable—in the twentieth century, but Miss Becker was not spared to see it for she died in middle life. Her services to the cause are perhaps most vividly illustrated by the fact that with her death the *Women's Suffrage Journal* ceased. She had started it, conducted it for twenty years and it died with her. The volume which was put together after news of her death in Switzerland was received, contained this paragraph: 'To all Readers. For twenty years and four months this *Journal* has received the impress of one hand and one mind, so that its long row of volumes forms one continuous work, and now when that careful hand is laid low and the energies of that far-seeing mind are carried beyond our mortal ken, it would seem the most fitting course to close these pages where Miss Becker left them.'

Miss Becker was spared the tinsel of a pompous obituary, and it would have delighted her cool and critical mind to know that her character was to be analysed in the last number of her *Journal* by Leonard Courtney—at that time Deputy Speaker of the House of Commons and justly described as carrying out his duties with impartial unfairness to both sides. This critical spirit did not desert him in his writings and, after alluding to variations of temper in the women's movement, he stated that Miss Becker 'sometimes failed in following the most difficult of all the Apostle's social precepts'. He presumably had in mind that verse in the Epistle to the Romans where St. Paul writes: 'If it be possible, as much as lieth in you, live peaceably with all men.' Here no Act of Parliament was needed to construe men as including women. But if Miss Becker was, by nature, quarrelsome and impatient of rivalry such shadows across her character fade into insignificance in contrast with her qualities. Severely dressed, with thick hair plaited and placed on the top of her head and wearing narrow, metal spectacles she looked somewhat grim, and the public, encouraged by *Punch*, occasionally flocked to her meetings to enjoy the inane pleasure of sniggering at the speaker. All this she endured superbly—perhaps comforted by the reflection that it was better to face this transitory ridicule than to live surrounded by what Horace Walpole called 'giggledom' as a governess, or to undergo the melancholy grumbles of old ladies as a companion. There were virtually no other employments for the Victorian spinster. In those days mankind could not believe that a woman, whose only preoccupation was meetings, official statistics and agitations could be anything but monstrous, a thing unsexed so that it is agreeable to record that Miss Becker was not only an adept at a pudding, and an excellent needlewoman but 'danced the hop-waltz beautifully'.

VIII

Swaying Fortunes at Westminster

The whole of Miss Becker's strategy was concentrated on the House of Commons. There she felt that the battle had to be fought and could be won. Without taking away from the devoted service of many men in the House of Commons, historians will agree that Miss Becker was the general who mustered her forces in the House, deployed them for attack and provided them with their ammunition.

Under her management a woman's suffrage bill was brought in and debated every year in the 1870's except 1874. The voting figures are curious. In 1870 there was a majority of 33 in favour of woman's suffrage: this was turned into a minority of 69 in 1871, and into minorities of 79 in 1872, of 67 in 1873, of 35 in 1875, of 87 in 1876. The bill in 1877 was talked out and, the majority in 1878 was 80 against, and in 1879 it was 114 against. The explanation of these figures seems to be that at first the proposal was treated lightly, but from the middle of the 1870's the opponents took it more seriously and organized themselves effectively. During the 1880's the matter only came to a division once—in 1886—when there was a small majority in favour. This happened also in the 1890's when there was one striking success, in 1897, the majority in favour being seventy-one.

There would be little point in recalling the speeches which were made in these debates for (as has been emphasized on a previous page), the serious arguments were laid down in the debate of 1867, and they never greatly varied. It is not only familiarity with the position of women accepted by twentieth-century standards—nor even partiality—which makes anyone reading these debates conscious that the weight of argument fell heavily on the side of enfranchising women. The battle was between reason and prejudice.

And the names of those—not perhaps greatly prominent in national history—who struggled to uphold what was reasonable, in spite of the mockery and threadbare arguments of those who fought to exclude women from the vote, deserves to be rescued from the dusty pages of Hansard.

After Mill the conspicuous name among the champions of woman's suffrage in the House of Commons was Jacob Bright. He has been inevitably eclipsed by his famous elder brother, and as in private life he was a shade more worldly so in politics he was somewhat more practical. The young Quaker, Jacob Bright, who once slightly shocked John Bright by staying to watch a dance, and even by organizing a picnic party on First Day had perhaps a shrewder understanding of human beings than his more cloistered brother. He gained experience of life through a long term of managing the family mill at Rochdale and, in those days when courage was needed to espouse the women's cause, he spoke with all the incisive forthrightness of a business man who knows his own mind. In 1870 he made a speech in Edinburgh which rallied his more timid followers and stung his opponents to anger: 'I know', he said, 'of no reason for the electoral disabilities of women. I know some reasons, which if there are to be electoral disabilities, would lead me to begin elsewhere than with women. Women are less criminal than men: they are more temperate than men— the distinction is not small, it is broad and conspicuous; women are less vicious in their habits than men; they are more thrifty, more provident: they give more to the family, and take less to themselves.'

Professor G. M. Trevelyan in contrasting the two brothers has pointed out that Jacob Bright had all his brother's fearless and unyielding temper, together with a greater measure of intellectual daring and suppleness. Speaking with all the authority of Member of Parliament for the potent City of Manchester he seemed to bring to these discussions on the franchise something of the thrust and foresight which had brought riches to the area of England which he represented. But the politics of Manchester were less constant than the hum of their machines, and Bright was twice defeated there before he finally resigned in 1895. In consequence, and especially as his health began to fail, he withdrew from the lead of the agitation for the franchise in the House of Commons after the General Election of 1874.

His place was then taken by William Forsyth—a learned and literary Q.C.—who sat as a Conservative for Marylebone. Jacob Bright was again returned at a by-election in 1876 and, with Leonard Courtney, he was prominent again. In the 1880's the lead was assumed by Mr. Hugh Mason, Member for Ashton-under-Lyne, William Woodall the china manufacturer from Burslem who sat for Stoke-on-Trent and Baron de Worms—a character greatly beloved by *Punch*—who sat as a Conservative for Greenwich. In the 1890's the leaders were Lord Wolmer, afterwards Lord Selborne and High Commissioner for South Africa, Mr. George Wyndham, Conservative Member for Dover, and Ferdinand Faithful Begg, a Conservative stock-broker, who sat for the St. Rollox Division of Glasgow. The achievement of Mr. Walter Beach, a greatly respected Conservative country member, who voted in every division from 1867 till his death in 1901, in favour of woman's suffrage, deserves to be recalled and applauded.

On the other side an organization was formed, at the end of the 1860's, of Members of Parliament and Peers to maintain 'the integrity of the franchise'. This was an influential body drawing its support from well-to-do Liberals and Conservative back benchers. The power behind this opposition was a delightful old Whig, Edward Fleydell-Bouverie who managed to combine a number of reactionary views, including a detestation for Mr. Gladstone, while sitting for the great Radical fortress of Kilmarnock, where he had no difficulty in defeating Sir Edwin Chadwick who believed in new-fangled things like drainage for the poor, and who stood against him as a Liberal. An Harrovian and a Cambridge man, he was a neat classical scholar and his accomplishment in this respect invites the suggestion that many of the most redoubtable opponents of woman's suffrage were those most deeply grounded in the ancient civilizations of Greece and Rome. Certainly the home of these studies—the universities of Oxford and

Cambridge—were conspicuous for their opposition to the claims of women.

Too often in these debates the spokesman on behalf of the women had no case to answer, since the debate tended to drivel away in a series of jests—a few of which reached the heights of wit but most of which sank to the depths of facetiousness. One stock argument, deployed every year, was that women had all the political power they needed through their influence over their male relations. In the debate of 1870 Jacob Bright dealt with this assertion and pointed out that legislation moved in the following order—first to deal with those who were dangerous, secondly with those who could exercise pressure at the polling booth but always lastly for those who were voteless. He instanced how he had seen Members of the House of Commons sitting up through-out the night to defeat the bill which would enable married women to keep their own property instead of having to hand it over to their lords and masters. Some fears had also been raised lest women should swamp men at the booths but as the proposal was to enfranchise *femmes soles* he showed that this was impossible. Bath, its terraces and crescents saturated with rich, old ladies, was the nearest point of danger when there would have been one woman voter to every 3·8 male voters: in the industrial town of Walsall there would have been 22·9 men to every one woman and the average in all constituencies would have been one woman to seven or eight men.

Jacob Bright found it possible to give these figures because of a great and unexpected triumph which he won immediately after the General Election of 1868. In the course of the Queen's speech at the opening of the new Parliament in February 1869 some references were made to municipal elections and the prevailing corruption which accompanied those contests. A select committee was appointed to enquire into these abuses, and this was followed by a Bill to give the vote to every male occupier of a house in a borough who had lived there for a year. Jacob Bright persuaded the sponsor of the Bill, who was his neighbour John Hibbert, the member for Oldham, to agree to an amendment leaving out the word male. This was accepted by the then Liberal Government and became law. There was some tooting on the antiquarian trumpet from the supporters of the woman's vote who acclaimed this measure as 'The Restoration of the Municipal Franchise'. But although the twentieth century has magnified gas and water politics into something positively respectable and worthy of battle, our Victorian forbears took a different view and they were not greatly concerned if out of the cloudy trickle of local politics the public secured a chandler or a haberdasher to act as an overseer of the poor. But still it was a step forward that women could share in these matters, and it gave pleasure to a handful of them (including Miss Becker) to serve their community on the local school board or as a Poor Law Guardian. How little it meant in reality is illustrated by what happened twenty years later.

The first elections in the London boroughs after the creation of the London County Council was in 1889 and Lady Sandhurst, an intrepid Liberal and the widow of a distinguished general, put up for Brixton, which returned two members. With Sir Edmund Verney she was elected, defeating one of her Conservative opponents by 300 votes and the other by 600 votes. By chance the first of these opponents was the son of Beresford Hope one of the leaders of the opposition to female suffrage in the House of Commons. He, supported by the Conservative who was bottom and who was not inappropriately named Smallman, immediately the counting of votes was over, objected to Lady Sandhurst's election on the ground that she was a woman.[1] The Returning Officer, with some show of spirit, overruled the objection. Beresford Hope then brought an action against Lady Sandhurst. The case came before Baron Huddleston, a clever, witty judge, a survivor of the Court of Exchequer as it was before the Judicature Acts of the 1870's, who called himself 'The Last of the Barons'. He decided that Lady Sandhurst could not sit, and that her votes were 'thrown away'. Lady Sandhurst appealed, and the case came before Coleridge, now Lord Chief Justice, who had appeared with Richard Pankhurst in *Chorlton* v. *Lings*; whatever his private sympathies he decided that although women unquestionably had the right to vote, there was nothing in the Municipal Corporation Acts of 1869 and 1882 or of the London County Council Act of 1888, that

---

[1] Miss Jane Cobden was elected for Bromley and Bow, but also could not take her seat.

gave women the right to sit. He stated that the right of anyone to sit for the London County Council could only be found 'within the four corners of the statute creating that body'.

The dignity of the franchise and how, if it were shared between the male sex and women, it might lead to the elevation of humanity, was a favourite theme of Mill's. But the participation in municipal voting, though rightly acclaimed by Jacob Bright, did little to advance that ideal. Far from meaning that women would take up the burden of citizenship with patient dignity, the municipal polling booth too often resembled a pot house, too often gave those who used it an excuse for a Saturnalia. In shocked tones Pleydell-Bouverie described to the House of Commons what a municipal election was like in Manchester. 'Staggering women, supported by staggering men—not their husbands—were seen going up to vote, both sexes boisterous and obscene in their language.' And then the pious old Whig, genuinely horrified by the picture he so graphically described, added 'There was a Book far more esteemed by his countrywomen than the writings of Mr. Mill', and it said, 'Thy desire shall be to thy husband, and he shall rule over thee.'[1]

His sentiments were echoed some years later in hallowed tones, by Edward Knatchbull-Hugessen who spoke with all the authority of a great nephew of Jane Austen, 'When I speak of the women of England, I have in my mind those young, pure-minded girls, who are the light and life of their homes: who develop into the wives and mothers of England: who bring up England's children in the fear of God, and in the love of all that is pure and good: who shed a hallowing influence over the families among whom their lot is cast, and bless the homes of which they are the pride and comfort.' He was arguing that it was unfair to deny to these angels what was given to the grumbling widows in Bath and still worse to the reeling hussies of the Manchester municipal booth.

With a strange disregard for the principles of logic, some opponents of votes for women argued that these influential personages in the state—as soon as they were invested with the vote —would fall entirely under the influence of men—particularly the clergy. Priests would whisper dreadful things into delicate ears.

[1] Genesis Ch. iii.

The head of the great Warwickshire family of Newdegate assured the House of Commons in 1876 that Roman Catholic priests were secretly working for woman's suffrage so that they could establish a priestly despotism in England. Strangely enough John Bright had always gone a long way to meet this particular terror, which was especially insulting to the intelligence of Englishwomen. As early as 1871 he was writing to a friend that the enfranchisement of women must inevitably lead to an increase in the power of priest-craft in all three kingdoms. But he had voted in favour of women's suffrage in 1867, and Mill in his *Autobiography* says that Bright was converted while listening to the debate. During the debate in 1876 Bright said that Mill was 'entirely mistaken. I voted under extreme doubt and far more from sympathy with him.' He then went on to explain why he was going to change his opinion and vote against the women, principally because he had been gradually convinced that the grievances of women in this particular had been exaggerated. He was afraid that women voters would be plied with drink, adding that at a municipal election women had certainly been served with what was not 'wholesome' for them. But he emphasised what was the principal reason for his opposition to the Bill—his fear that it could only lead to an increase in the political power of 'priests and parsons'. The ladies, anxiously listening from the Gallery, thought that the apostate looked pale, and that his hands trembled—but an impartial observer[1] records that his speech was successful, and that he was loudly cheered; an examination of the Division List shows that the Noes increased by forty-two.

The debate of 1876 was conducted with some acrimony throughout, but it was left to the bachelor Member for Cambridge Town, Mr. Patrick Boyle Smollett to sink below the level of good taste by drawing attention to the ludicrous names of the ladies behind the campaign. With facetious emphasis he read them over to the House of Commons—Miss Becker, Miss Babb, Miss Biggs, Mrs. Hoggan, Miss Beedy, M.A.,[2] Miss Garrett, Mrs. McLaren and Miss Tod. He referred to them as the Beedys and the Beckers of this worthless agitation. 'I did expect', he said, 'to see ladies of

---

[1] The Annual Register.
[2] She possessed an American university degree.

greater social eminence than these heading the movement.' *Punch* made the following effective comment on Smollett—'We understand Mr. Smollett is descended from the novelist. We hope he will not descend any lower.' In the debate during the previous year Sir Henry James, the eminent lawyer, had referred to votes for women as 'the crotchet' of a few 'social failures'. This stung the sponsor of the Bill into a retort which serves as an answer to the gibes of Smollett: 'Petitions have been presented in favour of this Bill signed by the Dowager Countess of Buchan, Viscountess Combermere, Lady Julia Lockwood, Lady Helen Stewart, the Honourable Miss Canning and Miss Florence Nightingale.' And the reader can almost catch the scandalized tone in this Member of Parliament's voice, reflecting the veneration of the true Victorian for ladies of high degree, as he asked, 'Are they social failures?'

Inevitably, over this long range of debates, some foolish things were said but the arguments, which filled supporters of the women with despair, were those directed to the glorification of man. A characteristic example of this was the speech in 1873 of Lord Percy, in all the youthful plumage of hereditary honours— he was afterwards the 7th Duke of Northumberland—who spoke of the agitation being based on the 'delusion of equality' which he described as a 'will-o'-the-wisp reserved for us in the nineteenth century'. He went on to demolish the idea that there could be any equality between the sexes—'the real fact is that man in the beginning was ordained to rule over the woman, and this is an eternal decree which we have no right and no power to alter'. Twenty years later Lord Percy was to be matched by an imperial trumpeter of grandiloquent proportions, who pointed to the vast weight of the great British Empire resting on man. This was the member for the respectable cathedral city of Hereford, Radcliffe Cooke. In the course of his speech he asked who founded the glorious British Empire. In ringing tones he answered 'Man'. He quoted Daniel Webster, the American statesman, about the morning drum beat which 'encircles the earth with the unbroken strain of the martial airs of England', and again he answered that the drum was beaten by man. 'Who safeguarded us in our sea-girt isle? Man.' And then he rose to his mighty climax—'What is the outcome of all these unceasing and ever-increasing labours of man?' And before he could make his answer the penetrating voice of Mr. William Allan—the Radical Member for Gateshead—shouted, 'children'.

Perhaps the most effective, because it was the most light-hearted, means of exposing male pomposities on the women's vote resided in humour, and a good example of this is to be found in an anonymous article published in the 1870's in *Fraser's Magazine*. The writer gives an imaginary sketch of conditions in the planet Venus, with whom contact has been established through space-travel. It was found that although the sovereign at the time happened to be a king, the political business of the planet was wholly discharged by women. A bill had lately been introduced to the Venus Parliament, composed exclusively of ladies, to admit men. 'The notion of admitting young cornets, cricketers and fops of the Dundreary pattern to a share in the legislature, the prospect of Parliamentary benches recruited from the racecourse, the hunting-field and the billiard-room was a picture that proved too much for the gravity of the Commons.' The leader of the Opposition, whose attractions were strongly emphasized, replied to the debate and pointed out the superiority of woman to man. 'With finer natural perceptions than man, less ungovernable in her emotions, quicker and clearer in intellect, physically better fitted for sedentary life, more inclined to study and thought, everything seems to qualify her especially for legislation. . . . It is a false mistake to try to turn men into women, to shut them up indoors, and set them to study blue-books and reports in their intervals of business, to enforce on them an amount of thought, seclusion and inaction so manifestly uncongenial to their physical constitution, which points so plainly to the field, the deck, the workshop. . . .' To-day, if the twentieth century reader turns back to the speeches in Parliament of those opposed to the claims of woman, the arguments seem hardly less fanciful than those imagined by the fertile brain of this writer. And Parliament, throughout those closing decades of the nineteenth-century, could perhaps be criticized because the weakness of the opponents case was not reflected in the voting lobby. The strong arguments of Mill, Jacob Bright and Fawcett were not followed by strength in the Division List; time after time they sent the pointer soaring to the greatest heights but the bell was not rung, the penny was not returned.

IX

Applause from the Ladies Gallery

Now one of the reasons for the disappointing results of the debates has perhaps never been adequately explained, and was certainly never understood by the women. This reason was the effect of female franchise on party politics. If there had been universal male suffrage it might have been easy to graft on to it universal female suffrage, thereby not upsetting party calculations, but universal suffrage was throughout the nineteenth century an ill-defined dream of a handful of Radicals. Property was still the qualification for a vote, and it cannot be too often emphasised that, when they are examined, the proposals of all these Victorian feminists would have only given the vote to a handful of propertied women. Moreover the majority of this handful was elderly because they were either widows or spinsters, and in those days most spinsters had no possessions during the life of their parents so that propertied spinsters tended to be middle-aged or elderly. As the historian Acton expressed it in a letter to Gladstone's daughter, 'Girls and widows are Tories, and channels of clerical influence.' The Liberal Party would certainly have been more whole-heartedly behind votes for women if they had not sensed that it would mean enfranchising a section of the population, which was drawn both by possessions and age towards conservatism. Gladstone's own opinions on the question were curiously indecisive, and were not unfairly described by one of his most fastidious supporters (Lord Arthur Russell) after the 1871 debate as follows: 'Gladstone spoke in favour, said he would vote against and ran away finally.' We may assume that he was unconsciously influenced by the fear of women's innate conservatism for he also touched on this point during the debate of 1871; he said that for the House of Commons, in voting on the female franchise, to be influenced by considerations of party was 'a sin against first principles'. No doubt he was right and it was a sin, but an examination of any Act of Parliament affecting elections would show that such acts were in fact always drawn forward by a nicely balanced pair of horses—Principle and Party.

The Reform Bill of 1884 proves the point tolerably clearly. The Act of 1867 had brought democracy to the towns: the Act of 1884 brought it to the countryside, by giving every householder, which of course included the agricultural labourer, the vote. Party considerations—in this case the determination of the Liberals to strike at the political power of the landed aristocracy—was an obvious element in the measure. A large number of these new voters could neither read nor write and at the first election after their enfranchisement, Liberal meetings in the rural areas were enlivened by chalk and blackboard showing the new men where they should place their cross on the voting paper. Could the women and their supporters feel anything but discouraged when the prize, which some of them so ardently desired, was lightheartedly tossed to a partly illiterate class merely because they had been born men?

Naturally enough the case of the women was brought forward energetically by their supporters in the House of Commons during the time that the measure of 1884 was under consideration. Seventy-nine Liberal members memorialized Mr. Gladstone asking that the Bill should recognize the claim of woman householders. In his reply Mr. Gladstone emphasized a point which was to be of great importance in the turbulent days of the twentieth century but which was never properly grasped by the ladies; though the language may be a little elaborate, round-about and Gladstonian the meaning is tolerably clear. He said, 'the question with what subjects, viewing the actual state of business and of parties, we can afford to deal in and by the Franchise Bill is a question in regard to which the undivided responsibility rests with the Government, and cannot be devolved by them upon any section, however respected, of the House of Commons. They have introduced into the Bill as much as, in their opinion, it can safely carry.' He added that additional burdens must endanger the measure, and would therefore be a breach of the Government's duty 'to the Bill and the nation'. Anyone with experience of parliamentary business will recognize the difficulty, even for a strongly entrenched Government, of passing controversial measures into law. When those measures affect electoral matters, the difficulties become immense and, as Gladstone's own experience in 1866 reminds us, they can strain to breaking point even a large ministerial majority. To people outside, passionately desiring a measure to become law, respect for such fine points as the balance of parties in the House of Commons and the available time for Government measures seems merely faint-heartedness, tactics or indulgence in the pat ball of the party game. But that is a total misreading of the picture; and this blindness to the pitfalls confronting suffrage legislation was to give rise in the twentieth century to abundant mischief.

In the meantime the Act of 1884 seemed to usher in a period when the women's claims lapsed into oblivion. Eight years later Mr. Asquith, in a characteristally delightful shaft, said in the House of Commons that the great mass of women were watching the struggle for the emancipation of their sex 'with languid and imperturbable indifference'. Everything looked hopeless, and the 1884 Act had still further emphasized the ostracism of women from their constitutional rights. This point was made in a letter to *The Times* by Sophia Jex-Blake, the courageous pioneer for the admission of women to medicine, and Adeline Pauline Irby who is rather unexpectedly described in the pompous pages of Burke's peerage as 'Friend of Servia and Bosnia', where in fact she did much valuable educational work. In their letter these ladies, who explained that they had previously taken little part in the agitation for the vote, pointed out that the consequences of the Reform Act of 1884 were to accentuate the insult to women by enlarging the male electorate. Women had become 'conspicuously isolated'.

There were two other reasons which made the years following the Act of 1884 ones of especial difficulty. The first was the formation of the Primrose League in 1885 and of the Women's Liberal Federation two years later.

The women Liberals derived their cohesion from that Society—

the Quakers—which throughout history has worked for the women's cause. As early as 1880 sporadic women's Liberal Societies were formed in the Friends strongholds of York, Darlington and Bristol: these were closely linked with the Peace propaganda of the Society. The central body—the Women's Liberal Federation—was founded in 1886 at Mrs. Theodore Fry's house in Queen Anne's Gate. The Quaker influence was also emphasized in the rule that no candidate, whose moral character would not bear investigation, should be supported.

The Primrose League was less particular, possibly because it was always under masculine control; in its organization it seemed to derive inspiration from Freemasonry and that strange underworld of Buffaloes, Rechabites and Oddfellows. The Women's Liberal Federation was severely feminine, and was more distinctly inclined to the cause of woman's suffrage than was the Primrose League. But the point was that both these organizations, by employing women as canvassers during elections and as auxiliaries in the party fight, did something to distract attention from the suffrage issue and to make women feel that they were not altogether outcasts from the pale of the constitution.

The other reason which was to make the years after 1884 of special difficulty was the emergence of the Home Rule issue, which stirred violent passions and made it difficult for partisans of Mr. Gladstone to be even civil to those in the other camp. The various suffrage committees included Conservatives and Liberals, Home Rulers and anti-Home Rulers. If a gentlemanly establishment like Brooks's was riven by these animosities, the women were not likely to escape and, partly for this reason partly for others the London National Society split into two parts.

But although looking below the surface the reader can see that some of the spring of the movement had gone, it managed to keep its old parliamentary phalanx and to inspire much of the old terrors in the breasts of its opponents. Mrs. Lynn Linton, twenty years older than when she wrote of The 'Shrieking Sisterhood', greeted the Primrose League and the Women's Liberal Federation with a characteristic burst of artillery in the *National Review* in 1889 'Now we have the two hostile camps in full activity of guerrilla warfare, with worse to follow when their guns are charged with ball instead of blank cartridges, when they have the vote instead of the right of mere talk. . . . Think of our imperial policy directly influenced by the local genteel spinsters and small shop-keepers whose mental range reaches as high as the curate and as far as the school feast.'

The 1890's saw a satisfactory position in the House of Commons where in 1892 those in favour of women's suffrage were only beaten by twenty-three. Following this the women's societies organized a monster petition for which they obtained a quarter of a million signatures. These were certainly achievements—they were the fruits of Miss Becker's policy of patience, but people began to wonder whether these triumphs were really moving the great machine forward. Could not something spectacular be done to jolt mankind out of his complacency?

In 1895 a strange ally stepped forward to help the ladies. John Macdona was a progressive Conservative whose interests varied from female suffrage to the restoration of the ancient rights of Thames lightermen. He had for some years been a Cheshire rector but, resigning his orders, he persuaded the strongly Radical electors of Rotherhithe to vote for him, and duly won that seat. He secured a place in the ballot for woman's suffrage and supported by rather unorthodox elements in the movement he prepared to move his Bill. The wise Miss Becker could have told him that he was badly placed because there was ample opportunity for the opponents to talk out time on the previous bill, a measure dealing with corrupt practices at elections. He and his coterie of supporters decided to impress the House of Commons with the struggle of opinion behind the Bill. Accordingly on that May afternoon fashionably dressed ladies pressed into the House of Commons. The parliamentary correspondent of the *Manchester Guardian* described the scene and said, 'The Central Hall was as bright as a flower garden with gay colours, and the sweet odours of fashionable scents'. Macdona ushered these political blooms to the Ladies Gallery. Here they were treated to the particular form of torture which the recognized leaders of their movement could have described to them with precision—Labouchere talking brilliant rubbish on the Bill before Macdona's so as to leave no time for any speeches or voting on the dreaded subject of Votes for Women. 'Labby's' view on the franchise of women are difficult to explain. Sitting with Bradlaugh for the two-membered seat of Northampton he was on the very tip of the extreme left of the Liberal Party and he had in fact voted with Mill, in the original debate of 1867, in favour of votes for women. As a younger man he was popularly supposed to have lived with a circus lady, and he certainly married an actress. Whether these experiences encouraged him to think that women were best kept for man's entertainment is unknown, but he suddenly opposed their political cause with all the ferocity of his nature. The shapely familiar head, adorned with the trim beard, has been handed down to us by countless Victorian caricaturists and we are so accustomed to think of him puncturing some conceit or anachronism with his impish wit that it is rather a surprise to see him, bringing his light but deadly artillery, into play on the side of reaction. Hour after hour Macdona's ladies sat in the gallery—their colours somewhat drooping, their scents a trifle faded. Labouchere rose and began his speech by saying that he came down with an open mind on the Bill—that is the Corrupt Practices Bill. He went on, 'I have not read it. I thought it was one of those minor bills, about which there would be some trifling discussion, and that the House would speedily get to that most interesting subject the Suffrage of Women'. Hansard then records: 'Applause in the Ladies Gallery: Cries of order and laughter.' Every member swung round to look up at the Gallery whence came this unpardonable interruption. A little flushed but assuming airs of indifference and bravery sat the band of gaily dressed ladies. They were a portent.

X

Labour to the Rescue

The ladies, light-heartedly applauding from the Gallery in the House of Commons, were however something more than bright harbingers of militancy: they reflected an alteration in the English character which was perceptible and important. The *gravitas* of Miss Becker's generation was yielding to something more flippant and less mindful of authority. Moreover this gaiety was general, and by no means confined to women, for as the nineteenth century drew towards its ending, a shadowy but perceptible change moved across the face of the English character. Something of the old sternness of demeanour, something of the old austerities of a commercial people, something of those unrelenting virtues expounded by the simple but eloquent voices of Christian preachers gave way: they weakened under the pressure of riches: they were adulterated by the excitements of imperial glory. The 1890's may have been naughty, the youths and maidens of that famous epoch may have been daring but such things were not fundamental: they were symptoms. The cardinal change was a sliding away from principle to self-interest, a flight from morality in the direction of ease. And this sliding away from the grim heights of rectitude infected politics, bringing with it important changes in the women's struggle.

In the nineteenth century the Houses of Parliament had been broadly concerned with the application of political principle to the issues—at home and abroad—by which public men were confronted. However by the end of that century and increasingly throughout the twentieth century Parliament became engrossed with satisfying the claims or patching the grievances of groups and classes. The difference is illustrated by a saying of Lord Palmerston, whose views, though enlightened, were those of the old school of parliamentarians: he gave it as his opinion that, if working men were elected to the House of Commons, Members of Parliament would have to give time to pettifogging matters: he thought that the House of Commons would be preoccupied with such things as 'the grievances of journeymen bakers'. And when in 1892 Keir Hardie, backed by a majority of over 1,000 in West Ham, adorned with his cloth cap, was played into the sacred precints of Westminster by a rowdy brass band[1] he marks the change. To combat this new development the Conservative Party subtly adapted itself: like the lizard, which sheds its skin in pieces, the Party was able to shed much of its old church and country character in favour of new men, with all the sleekness and prosperity of business and finance. These matters together with questions of labour began to absorb much parliamentary time, and by a strange paradox although they stirred much feeling and temper they did not arouse the interest of the public as had the old political issues of the heyday of Victorianism.

And with this change came the need for new methods in politics. The excitement of an election subsided somewhat, the reports of meetings and of parliamentary debates were less ample and the instinctive draw of a political speech was less keenly felt. Although elections may have been more civilly conducted than in the days of Eatanswill, the appeal for votes was coarsened. The vulgar flamboyancy of the khaki election of 1900, when Liberals were dubbed 'traitors' by a leading Conservative cabinet minister, and a Liberal-Unionist candidate in Bradford could blithely proclaim that a vote for the Liberals was a vote for the Boers, marks the progress of this new tempo in British politics. Six years later the Liberals showed that they had learned some tricks from their opponents when they accused the Conservatives of having re-introduced slavery by the employment of Chinese labour in the goldfields of South Africa, and when they stooped to the illustrated argument that under the Conservatives there would be a small loaf and under the Liberals a big one. To

---

[1] G. D. H. Cole in 'British Working Class Politics' (1946) is doubtless correct in hinting that the band in fact consisted of a single but enthusiastic cornetist.

grip the interest of the public politics had to be at once simpler and more vivid.

And in this glittering setting what chance had the annual Woman's Suffrage Bill, with its threadbare arguments and its antique air, of enlisting support and commanding attention? The minds of shallow patriots were filled with the bright colours of imperial glory, with vague ideas about the power of Her Majesty's Navy and with a sense of confidence on seeing the cheerful uniforms of Tommy Atkins: the far-sighted and thoughtful were preoccupied by the contrast between the fantastic luxury of London and the south, and the harsh squalor of those who worked in mine and mill to provide the wealth which was gaily spent in Piccadilly. The rights of women were admitted, but they could well wait till important and immediate questions were solved. Thus men argued.

But even during these difficult days of the 1890's, when people were preoccupied with other matters, the faithful women who carried on Miss Becker's work could point to little gleams of light. The jubilee year of 1897 saw a majority in the House of Commons of seventy-one in favour of woman's suffrage: the Conservative Leader of the House of Commons, Arthur Balfour, who had in private life a taste for the company of clever women, and who has been happily described by H. G. Wells as having about him 'an odour of intelligence which made his Conservative associates uncomfortable' admitted that any further parliamentary reform would have to include female suffrage: in 1894 a quarter of a million women signed a petition for the vote,which was exhibited in Westminster Hall.

And in 1900 there were two developments—trifling in themselves but historically important because they mark the first occasion on which women decisively intervened in a General Election. Two fashionable but forceful ladies—Mrs. Josceline Bagot in South Westmorland and Lady Dickson-Poynder in Wiltshire—wrote and signed the election addresses of their husbands who were at the Front in South Africa.

Also during the 1890's the suffrage cause was strengthened by the successes won for women in other fields, and by the realization of those fighting there that they were severely handicapped by the political impotence of women. Mrs Josephine Butler, who had seen the triumph of her cause in the repeal of the Contagious Diseases Act in 1886 said: 'there was one thing which made our battle harder than it would have been. We have had to fight outside the Constitution.' And turning from the handicap to their achievement they could point to the spread of the higher education of women all over the world, their admission to the medical profession and (in America) to the legal and clerical professions, their hard-won right to sit on School Boards and as Guardians of the Poor, and their rights under the Married Women Property Acts. Miss Cobbe happily compared these successes with the incoming tide, each separate wave of which carried forward the whole.

But these comforting portents—reminiscent of the earlier if smaller triumphs of the 1860's—could not be interpreted by even the keenest listener as the distant trumpets of victory. And who, looking back, could doubt that in the bright, noisy world, which came in with King Edward, the cause of political women would have to rely less on passages from philosophic economists and more on high spirits, less on demureness and more on heroics? And as soon as the Labour movement, thrilling with youth and vitality, touched the suffrage issue high spirits and heroics sparked upwards in a shower of dazzling intensity.

Up to this time, that is to say up to the end of the nineteenth century, the women's movement had been well-to-do and respectable: if it is necessary to describe it by a less agreeable, but more precise, term it could be called 'middle-class'; though it was saved from the hated description of 'bourgeois' by always attracting to its ranks a sprinkling of aristocratic ladies and a steady stream of highly gifted women who virtually formed a feminine intelligentsia. But as Parliament remained unconvinced by appeals to reason and justice, the shrewdest minds began to see that pressure would have to be exerted by the inarticulate but powerful mass of women working in industry—especially in the textile trade of the north-west, where female labour was powerfully concentrated. The later Victorians were acutely conscious of the growing power of the working classes and a speaker in the House of Commons could openly refer to them as 'our masters'. Might not the toiling women, if properly informed and properly led, make an appeal which Parliament could only ignore at its peril? Labouchere thought that working men would always prefer what he called 'angels of the hearth' to their opposites which he characterized as 'political Boadiceas': yet it was these working women, like the fierce, proud queen and her daughters of ancient times, who had it in their power to end an oppression which was intolerable. But even fifty years ago, as the nineteenth century dissolved into the twentieth, the women workers were almost unconscious of their strength because they were virtually unorganized.

The struggle for the recognition of women's rights in industry resembled in many respects the larger struggle for political freedom. From the 1860's onwards there was agitation for women to have their own unions—a development which came about in the 1870's with the formation of the Women Trades Union League. This was inspired by a number of distinguished philanthropists— principally clergy of the Church of England: it had for its first secretary a remarkable and accomplished woman—Mrs. Emma Paterson. She had been, for a short time, secretary of the Women's Suffrage Association but a visit to America, where she had seen the parasol and umbrella female workers managing a flourishing union, diverted her enthusiasm from the vote to union work. Throughout the 1870's and 1880's, and under the inspiration of Mrs. Paterson, many women's trades unions were formed, but in some cases, particularly in the textile trade, the existing unions admitted both men and women. As the women were paid a considerably lower wage than the men, they paid a smaller contribution than men, and were in consequence excluded from any share in the management of these mixed unions. Although eminent historians of the Labour and trade union movements have preferred to scuttle hurriedly across this dangerous ground, the women's battle in the unions was with the men rather than with the employers—with the domestic not the economic boss. A stalwart trade unionist, glorying in manhood,[1] said at one of the Trades Union Congresses in the 1870's: 'They (the men) had the future of their country and children to consider, and it was their duty as men and husbands to use their utmost efforts to bring

[1] This was Henry Broadhurst, afterwards Liberal Member of Parliament for Leicester, and it is fair to add that his opinions were much disliked by Labour pioneers.

about a condition of things, where their wives would be in their proper sphere at home, instead of being dragged into competition for livelihood against the great and strong men of the world.' But by degrees these great, strong men of the world began to see that their strength (at least their economic strength) would be enhanced by blending their interests with those of women, and by the end of the nineteenth century the independent women's unions were perishing since women were, by that time, generally admitted on just terms to the men's unions. Women tended to be somewhat unstable in their attachments to trades unions, but in Lancashire they were well organized and an important force.

Although Mrs. Paterson and many of the philanthropists, who encouraged the organization of female labour into unions, were strong supporters of female suffrage the pioneer women's unions had no other sympathy or affinity with the agitation for the vote, except the personal sympathies of their leaders. The battle against male intransigence was really the same—whether it happened to be fought in the Trades Union Congress or in the House of Commons—but the fight remained in fields which were strictly separate. An effort to bring the two together developed among the cotton workers of the north-west at the end of the 1890's, and it was a development of the first importance in the Suffrage Movement's history.

The credit for this belongs to two forgotten but devoted ladies —Miss Esther Roper and Miss Eva Gore-Booth. When Esther Roper died in 1938 there were just a few lines in the faithful mouthpiece of Liberal opinion in the north, but the event was otherwise unnoticed. Never a militant and, if such things need be recorded, always a dull speaker Esther Roper (if we calculate by achievement rather than by noise) emerges in retrospect in the vanguard of the leaders. She was, at the turn of the century, the secretary of the Lancashire and Cheshire Women's Suffrage Society and she came to live in Manchester accompanied by her friend—one of the rarest and most romantic spirits ever attracted to the women's movement. This friend was Eva Gore-Booth, the second daughter of a well-connected Irish baronet: her girlhood and youth were spent at Lissadell, a property which was beautiful both in name and in fact and was bounded by the waves of the

Atlantic Ocean, on the southern shore of Donegal Bay. With her elder sister, Constance, afterwards the Countess Markievicz and the first woman elected to the House of Commons, she led an unconventional existence caring little for the customs or exponents of aristocratic life but devoted to Ireland, its people and its wrongs. 'Your sister and yourself, two beautiful figures among the trees at Lissadell are among the dear memories of my youth', wrote W. B. Yeats to her in later years. She brought to the suffrage movement something of the recklessness, which was to lead her sister to the edge of the gallows for her part in the Dublin rising of 1916, but above all something of the burning sense of injustice which excuses much of the extravagances of both sisters and which was entirely new in the humdrum round of British suffrage societies—bounded as they were by committees, learned papers, protests and petitions. Yet it is fair to add that when the point about the dullness of those nineteenth-century pioneers has been made, it remains true that the justice of their cause shone through methods of propagating it which were conventional. At the end of her wayward life the Countess in a speech in the Irish Dail said: 'My first realization of tyranny came from some chance words spoken in favour of women's suffrage.' And the impact of these rebellious minds from Ireland on the British suffrage movement was momentous. Something of the quality of the sisters can be deduced from the lines which Eva addressed 'To Con' during one of the Countess's frequently recurring terms of imprisonment:

> *The wind is our confederate,*
> *The night has left her doors ajar,*
> *We meet beyond earth's barred gate,*
> *Where all the world's wild rebels are.*

And while those circles, to which she belonged by birth, were shouting themselves hoarse with joy at the Diamond Jubilee of Queen Victoria, Eva Gore-Booth unnoticed and unheralded arrived in Manchester where she was to remain until 1913, when she and Esther Roper settled in Hampstead.

The reader would however be mistaken in supposing that Eva Gore-Booth showed any particular wildness or rebelliousness during her long sojourn in Manchester. Her importance in the movement derives from the fact that she was able to fire the imagination not only of the working women in the unions, but of the more respectable, well-to-do supporters of the women's vote in that area.

She and her helpers used an effective pamphlet, which asked two questions. First—why are working women paid 5s. a week, and working men 25s.? Secondly why do working women live on bread and margarine while working men eat beefsteak and butter? The answer was of course that it was because women had no votes.

Within the space of eight years she and her associates were able to point to three considerable triumphs. In 1901 and 1902 they were able to organize petitions to Parliament, for votes for women, signed in all by 67,000 workers in the textile trades. Then in 1902 the sitting Liberal Member of Parliament for Clitheroe was made a peer, and it was arranged, with the somewhat grudging consent of the Liberals, to run a Labour candidate, David Shackleton, at the ensuing by-election. The decision to run this Labour candidate and to pay his salary was taken by ballot inside the unions in which the women greatly outnumbered the men. As soon as Shackleton was elected to Parliament—he was returned unopposed—the women sent him a gentle reminder of his debt to them in the shape of a petition signed by 5,500 of his women constituents urging him to press the political claims of women.

Encouraged by their success at Clitheroe these ladies, with their high spirits but diminutive organization, decided to carry the case a logical step further and to run a male candidate of their own, basing his appeal to the electorate on the cry of 'Votes for Women'. For this purpose they chose the rather unpromising seat of Wigan. That town—in reality so much more attractive than it is made to appear from the jokes of Lancashire comedians—was unpromising because it is predominantly a mining area and the textile trades were less strongly represented there than in other parts of the north-west. But politically the ladies showed great judgment. Wigan, for some unaccountable reason, had returned a Conservative member for years. He was Sir Francis Powell who had been before the electors since the far distant days of Palmerston and Lord John Russell in 1852. The Liberals were ill-organized with a candidate who rather unexpectedly was both Mayor of Wigan and a cavalry colonel. As the General Election of 1906 grew near the prospects for an unorthodox candidate did not seem hopeless.

The ladies chose a local man, a monumental mason called Thorley Smith. He was one of those sterling characters, simple but sensible and virtuous, his politics closely intertwined with religion, who were perhaps the only attraction to converts, which the Labour Movement had to offer in the 1890's, and who shine down the years to us with a compelling charm.[1] The election got under way just before Christmas 1905 and Thorley Smith was immediately handicapped by a characteristically and disgracefully unenlightened decision of the miners. On their motion and through their votes it was decided at a meeting of the Wigan and District Trades Council to withhold support from Thorley Smith, although the opposite course was strongly urged by the railwaymen —Wigan was an important railway centre with two stations on the North-Western and Lancashire and Yorkshire railways. The significance of this decision, which did not of course prevent individual trades unionists from supporting Thorley Smith, was that he could not look to official trades union sources for financial support. This probably explains why almost all his meetings—despite the fact that it was mid-winter—were held in the open-air, his organizers no doubt feeling that they could not afford the expense of hiring halls. Woman's suffrage was in the front of his programme, which also included the conventional Radical-Labour policies of old age pensions, good houses for the working man, work for the unemployed and the protection of trades union funds. But if Thorley Smith displayed a few tempting gew-gaws to catch the fancy of the casual voter, there was no effort to conceal the main part of his programme. At his opening meeting, apparently the only one held indoors, he was supported by six women who included Esther Roper, Eva Gore-Booth and 'Mrs. Pankhurst of Manchester'—as she was described in the local papers. At this meeting it was stated that there were 96,000 women trades unionists in Lancashire without any political power whatever, and that thousands of women were living on wages of as little as 6s. to 10s. a week. The women speakers spoke at no less than

[1] He died in 1940.

eighty outdoor meetings during the election, and on polling day
Thorley Smith drove through the town in a large and gaily
decorated barouche, drawn by four horses and preceded by two
outriders, sitting encompassed by his six political Amazons. The
local reporters thought that he did not entirely relish his escort, but
he carried it off bravely and the result was extremely gratifying—

Sir F. S. Powell, Bt.	Conservative	3,573
Thorley Smith	Women's Candidate and Ind. Lab.	2,205
Colonel W. Woods	Liberal	1,900

No doubt the remarkable result at Wigan could be in part explained by the fact that Thorley Smith's vote was more Labour
than female suffrage. But yet it was the money and enthusiasm of
the women which enabled him to go to the poll in defiance of the
craven vote of the miners. After the election Miss Gore-Booth
explained 'we appealed from the parties and organizations to the
men at the mills and factories and workshops and mines and football fields. . . . Our appeal is from the Government to the nation,
from the House of Commons to the electors, from the rich to the
poor. . . . The Government says "We have nothing to do with
you, you can bring no pressure to bear on us", but the nation
says, "we feel the pressure of your poverty".'

The feat of these ladies in harnessing working-class opinion—
even in the narrow sphere of the north-west—behind the suffrage
movement was considerable, when it is appreciated that the
working man had scant natural sympathy for the rights of women.
His attitude was well epitomized by a drawing of Bernard Part-
ridge in *Punch* (throughout the twentieth century a doughty
champion of the women's cause) which shows a working man in
all the Edwardian insignia of his class, heavy boots, corduroy
trousers, a thick leather belt, many-buttoned coat, neckerchief
and cap: this individual, with drooping moustache, and beer
written all over his face, turns on the steps of the polling booth to
say to a young lady: 'Ah, you may pay rates and taxes, an' you
may 'ave responserbilities an' all; but when it comes to *votin'*, you
must leave it to *us* men.' The same point of view was betrayed by
the working man who when he was asked whether he thought
that his wife should go out to work answered: 'No. Let her stay at
home and wash my moleskin trousers.' (These garments, which

were greatly favoured by the working man in the early years of the twentieth century, looked like moleskin but were in fact made of fustian.) But whatever the force of ingrained prejudice who can doubt that these ladies in Lancashire were speeding forward the women's suffrage case along a road which was bound to lead to success? For nearly forty years their appeal had lain unheeded before Parliament and before the well-to-do classes. Now was the psychological moment to lay the case before the people—to appeal in Eva Gore-Booth's words 'from the Government to the nation'.

For this in reality was the strength of the Labour Movement in the days of its infancy: it brought its wares to the homes of the people. For while the leading statesman of the day—Joseph Chamberlain, Rosebery, Arthur Balfour or Asquith, moved up and down the country drawing packed meetings to Corn Exchanges, Town Halls and provincial theatres—speaking with no artificial aids and glad (certainly in the case of Rosebery) to catch an interruption and hurl back a witticism at the head of a heckler, the day of those great political rallies was drawing to its evening. They depended less on the eloquence of the speaker than on the instructed appreciation of the vast audience, for as these intelligent artisans followed the speaker's points with something of the specialized knowledge of a football crowd they laughed and cheered in all the right places. Such meetings were a superb intellectual entertainment. But as something of the seriousness of the nineteenth century gave way to the lighter mood of the twentieth, those meetings proved less alluring to the working man. And here lay the timely good fortune of the pioneers of the Labour Movement. Through chapels, through clubs, through concert parties, through primitive bicycle clubs they drove their doctrines home to the people. As Mr. Cole expresses it—the people 'entered into a new fellowship in which a common belief in Socialism formed the basis for having a high old time'. The well-to-do classes, confused in their minds as to what was happening, suddenly woke up to the terrors of socialism and revolution. This feeling is caught in retrospect with unerring skill by Miss Sackville West when, in *The Edwardians* she makes a young lady say of Socialism, 'Aunt Clemmie explained it to me. Everything we believe in would go by the board. All decencies. All principles.' And the virtuous Horatio Bottomley could seriously write of Socialism: 'So in future it will not be my wife or your wife but our wife.' But it was not in fact Socialism which caused those frightened squawks from the last strongholds of privilege: it was the feeling that the working classes, rather like an infinite number of particles of mercury, had rushed together in a solid mass, under the influence of Socialism. All the skill of an election analyst would be needed to say how many of the thousands of votes given to Labour candidates at the Election of 1906 were given because the voter understood and believed Socialism or because he thought it was the best way of having a 'shy at the toff'. Commonsense suggests that for every one of the former there were five of the latter. In earlier times the revolutionary iconoclasts—those who wished to hurl down and destroy—were outside the charmed circle of the constitution. The men who smashed the Duke of Wellington's windows at the time of the Reform Bill, the alarming crowds of Chartists in Kennington Common or even the Hyde Park mob in 1866 were not composed of voters. Now with the twentieth century their sons and grandsons were almost all voters, and they brought to elections and parliamentary business a faint whiff of revolution. This was something new, and men were uncertain how this strange portent would behave: they felt like a group experimenting in a science laboratory and vaguely wondering if the professor might not be blown sky high at the end of it all. In the then brilliant pages of the *Daily Chronicle* the return of Labour men to Parliament was described as 'the first crest of the wave which is rising from the dim depths of popular life'. The little group of ladies in the northwest were surely wise and far-sighted to try to harness to their struggle this new force in politics? Might not the knowledge that working-class opinion was behind the suffrage agitation force the established political parties to take it seriously? The election at Wigan was certainly the most encouraging sign since the events of the 1860's. But to explain why a development which promised so fair had in fact only promise and no fruition it is necessary for readers to turn their attention to Dr. Pankhurst and his family.

XI

Richard and Emmeline Pankhurst

Since Richard Pankhurst appeared on behalf of the women voters in the case of *Chorlton* v. *Lings* in 1868, his reputation had grown but his fortunes had not prospered. His practice on the northern circuit was important rather than lucrative, he specialized in public questions especially local Government work. His interests outside his work are shown from his being a member of the Council of the National Association for the promotion of Social Science, a fellow of the Royal Statistical Society and a life member of the Association for the Reform and Codification of the Laws of Nations. In politics he remained sturdily to the left—the harbinger of a great diversity of unpopular causes. He stood as a Radical candidate for Manchester at a by-election in 1883, and as a Liberal candidate for Rotherhithe in 1885. He failed decisively in both elections. His opponent at Rotherhithe said to one of the Liberals after the election: 'Next time you bring out a candidate, bring out a gentleman, and not a slum politician.' His wife, who was helping him, noticed that at Rotherhithe the Irish vote went absolutely against him although he was supporting Gladstone's Home Rule Bill. He told her that this strange example of Irish logic was perfectly sound because by hitting the Government indiscriminately, whether they happened to be friend or foe, a minority could always advertise its grievance. Those chance words were remembered.

When the Independent Labour Party was formed in 1893 Pankhurst was one of its early members. He was likewise a member of the Fabian Society, which was formed in the 1880's; this last body, sometimes mistakenly regarded as a political party, was in reality a recruiting ground for quick-witted, political eccentrics like Shaw and H. G. Wells, who formed with the Webbs and other serious-minded members a body which existed to guide legislation. To the Fabians, Socialism was not a revolutionary doctrine but merely the best means of increasing the efficiency of the nation; it seemed to them to offer the most sensible way of taking advantage of the enormous strides in economic knowledge made throughout the nineteenth century. In this climate Richard Pankhurst was perfectly at ease, and it is not difficult to suppose that his expert knowledge of municipal matters was of much service to the Society. At the General Election of 1895 these new loyalties encouraged him to put himself forward as Labour candidate or (speaking strictly) as an Independent Labour Party man for the Gorton Division of Manchester. As he emphasized his attachment to Home Rule he was not opposed by the Liberals and, though he was defeated, his poll was respectable. For the early Labour Party —perhaps somewhat overloaded with high ideals and moderate talents—the support in Parliament of a man of Pankhurst's trained capacity would have been of incalculable advantage. This was not to be: he died suddenly in Manchester in the summer of 1898 when he was still in the prime of life.

Under the influence of ardent Labour men (and presumably with the encouragement of the family) Dr. Pankhurst's funeral assumed the character of a demonstration. Even a splash of pageantry made itself felt. The conventional trappings of grief or the lugubrious intonings of clergyman had no place in Richard Pankhurst's life or at his death: the doctor moved towards the grave, as he had lived his life, a conspicuous man and, to the last, intolerant of humbug. The gay procession started from his home in Victoria Park, Manchester on a Saturday afternoon for the Brookwood cemetery, a few miles outside the city. It was accompanied by a deputation of members of the I.L.P. and escorted by a contingent of the Clarion Cycling Club all wearing white rosettes. The coffin was borne on an open carriage, and given the place of honour, arresting the attention of every casual sightseer, was a gigantic wreath, a blaze of revolution: for it was composed of double scarlet geraniums, with red carnations in the middle— not perhaps a very good advertisement for the florist's sense of combining colours, but unusual in the funerals of those days when all was arum lilies and tuberoses. But the undertaker was giving literal interpretation to the familiar line of Gray:

> *E'en in our ashes live their wonted fires.*

As soon as the cavalcade reached the cemetery the coffin, without more ado, was put in the ground and at the open grave a succession of Labour pioneers stepped forward and orated. There was one lady speaker, Mrs. Cliff Scatcherd, who correctly emphasized that there was no aspect of the women's movement in which Pankhurst had not take a noble part. The most powerful speech came from Bruce Glasier—then at the height of his powers —perhaps the simplest but finest character among the pioneers of English Socialism, who owed his Socialism not to the economic ponderosities of Marx but to the long and important tradition of English Radicalism; he said that Richard Pankhurst was 'one of the most beautiful figures of our time, and will fill one of the rarest pages in history.' To the observer, looking back, these political funerals, much beloved by early supporters of the Labour Party, are among the more pathetic manifestations of Radical mankind. Deprived of a celestial crown the unfortunate deceased is promised the no less elusive laurels of history; but the Labour Party, in the days of its success, has always been dominated by a weird reluctance to eulogize its leaders, dead or alive, and in fact no laurels have sprouted on those long-forgotten brows. Pankhurst with a host of other men who helped to found the Party have never received their due from history except perhaps in the devoted pages of G. D. H. Cole.

The untimely death of Richard Pankhurst left his family in difficult circumstances. He was survived by his widow, a son and three daughters. His wife Emmeline Pankhurst was a true Mancunian. Her father, Robert Goulden, was a prominent cotton spinner at Salford. She was nurtured in the great city, throve on the rather unorthodox opinions of her father and his friends, and showed her loyalty to the City by being married in a brown velvet dress from Kendal Milne. (Readers will have no difficulty in realizing how intensely Dr. Pankhurst would have disliked anything in the nature of a 'white wedding'.) But on those strictly

Manchester foundations was imposed a Parisian education during the turmoil of the 1870's so that Emmeline Pankhurst's mind ranged along hardly more conventional flights than that of her husband. But in her case the harshness of a rebellious spirit was softened by great good looks and by an endearing sympathy of manner.

Her life after marriage was not easy. Her family was increasing and her husband's earnings were meagre. The Rotherhithe election, in which, it will be remembered, the Doctor fought and lost as a Liberal in 1885, marked a serious fall in their fortunes. During the election Pankhurst's opponents had made considerable capital out of a statement which he was supposed to have made in Manchester Town Hall. This was couched in an arresting form, which merits the description of a tactless man's confession of faith: 'Let me tell you I am in a position to say to-night if there be a God. And I say there is no God. I defy God. If there is a devil I am in a position to defy the devil.' Not unnaturally echoes of this remarkable testimony found their way to Rotherhithe and in the rough, electioneering habits of those times the Conservatives blazoned those words on bills, printed in the Liberal colours, on the door of churches and chapels. After the election Dr. Pankhurst brought an action for libel against the *Manchester Courier* which had originally published the words. Unfortunately this case came before Mr. Justice Grantham, a jovial Tory squire with a detestation of Liberals, who was placed on the Bench by his political friends. In giving judgment he said that he thought Pankhurst's proper course would have been to write to the paper, asking the editor to publish a denial. Instead of that—Grantham went on—'he only gave notice of an action. This is not the course the Legislature expected a gentleman to pursue. . . .'

Pankhurst brought a number of further actions none of them successful, but all of them serving to advertise what he was supposed to have said.

For the Pankhursts the serious thing about this election and the subsequent actions was that they combined to make it very unlikely that Pankhurst would ever again be accepted as candidate by a Liberal Association. The taint of agnosticism was a very formidable objection to an aspirant for adoption by a constituency—

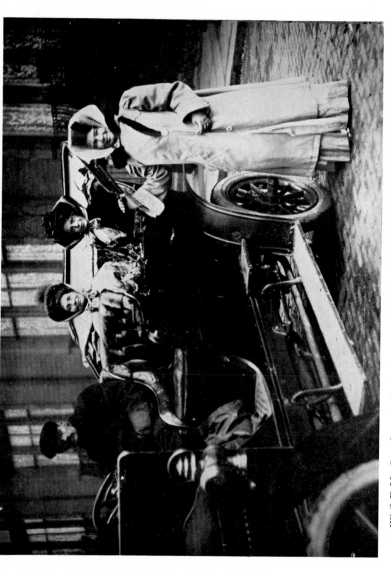

5. W.S.P.U. Leaders and their motor-car; seated, Mrs. Pankhurst and Miss Anne Kenney; standing, Mrs. Pethick-Lawrence

6. Lady Constance Lytton at Newcastle, about to throw her stone

perhaps insuperable except in a rare constituency such as North-
ampton. After the hearing of the action, the family settled in
London, and formed a suffrage society called The Women's
Franchise League which existed for a few precarious years. Mrs.
Pankhurst tried to supplement their fortunes by opening a shop for
gay furnishings called Emmerson and Company, while the
Doctor worked on occasional briefs in London and Manchester.
During this time they lived in a house in Russell Square; the house
was large and it served as a meeting place for the Women's Franchise League. These meetings ranged freely over wider subjects
than Women's Franchise, and were attended by a strange assortment of drifting idealists including the famous munshi, who was
teaching Queen Victoria Hindustani. The Royal Family disliked
this oriental inmate of the British Court almost as much as they
had disliked John Brown, and if they had known of these jaunts
to Russell Square they might have been able to shake the Queen's
confidence in the Indian. Also these meetings in Russell Square
were marked by songs from Antoinette Sterling—the great
American contralto who never wore a corset; another of her
characteristics was that she never drank tea—a feat of self-denial
which she imposed on herself as a perpetual reminder of the
Boston Tea Party. She had made her name singing 'The Lost
Chord'.

But London was not wholly a success for the Pankhursts:
though it planted in the children a taste for public questions: at an
age when other children demanded a pretty doll or a lollipop,
their only cry was, 'Take me to a meeting'. The shop never throve,
and in the course of the 1890's the family came back to Manchester.
Immediately after her husband's death Mrs. Pankhurst took work
with the Registrar of Births, Deaths and Marriages in Manchester,
but as the nineteenth century merged into the twentieth she became increasingly active in working for the Independent Labour
Party in Manchester, and her family being older she gave up her
paid work. However she seems quickly to have realized that the
Labour Party was really no sounder on the suffrage issue than
were the Liberals or the Conservatives. Although some Labour
men, and in particular Keir Hardie, were unswerving supporters
of the woman's suffrage cause the majority was not enthusiastic—

merely looking ahead to the time when the woman's vote would follow naturally as part of universal adult suffrage. After some months of work in Manchester with leading Labour men, Mrs. Pankhurst decided, in 1903, to form a Labour Party women's organization along the lines of the Women's Liberal Federation. This was to have been called the Women's Labour Representation Committee—the Labour Representation Committee being the name given at that time to the body co-ordinating the Independent Labour Party and the Trade Unions—but Mrs. Pankhurst being increasingly dissatisfied with the attitude of her political comrades, hesitated. At that moment her eldest daughter, Christabel, who was twenty-three and had inherited many of her mother's gifts combined with a beautiful speaking voice and a highly effective *raillerie*, insisted successfully that the name should be changed to Women's Social and Political Union. That body, which, during the next ten years, was to combine some of the highest ideals in the women's movement with tactics which would seem to have been inspired by the gym mistress at Roedean, and was to throw a fitful shadow across the gay Edwardian scene, was formed on 10th October 1903. That critical autumn month has often been chosen by male revolutionaries, and the word Octobrist seems to bring to mind a far-off picture of palisades and antique bombs. Nor did the initials by which the organization was always known—W.S.P.U.—wholly dispel the idea of swinging cloaks, rattling daggers and secret orders. Yet the choice of the word 'Social' was curious and would not appear to have been anywhere adequately explained. A Social Union, in the sense of a glorified Women's Institute with cocoa and bath buns on Friday, was never a characteristic of W.S.P.U. and can hardly have been the intention of its founders. Conviviality and 'good cheer' were never in their compass: we should as soon expect to find such things in a committee meeting of Jesuits presided over by Ignatios Loyola. On the other hand the word might have been chosen to suggest comfortable comradely feelings, the fraternity of earlier revolutionaries—'O happy band of sisters'—but if this were so the word was not exactly happily used. The most likely explanation is that 'Social' was used to imply Socialism but to conceal it: to attract the vague idealist but to avoid a dangerous and possibly repellant title—a kind of hazy suggestion of millennia without the precise significance of a 'Clarion' call. The truth was that although the Women's Social and Political Union had its origins deeply in the early history of the Labour Movement, it struck out on an independent course of its own—not unlike a courageous duckling on escaping from the security of its shell. The explanation for this may perhaps be found in a chance remark of Mrs. Bruce Glasier, who with her husband, lived not far from Manchester at Chapel-en-le-Frith and, like her husband, infused distinction and idealism into the early Labour movement; she said, 'Since her daughters have grown up, Mrs. Pankhurst is no longer sweet and gentle as of old.'[1]

The personalities and characters of Mrs. Pankhurst's two daughters Christabel and Sylvia were destined to play their part in influencing the battle for women's suffrage with, all its subtly balanced and swaying fortunes, which was about to start on its decisive phase. At this time they were on the border between girl-hood and womanhood—Christabel studying law at Manchester and Sylvia studying art in the same city, and later at the Royal College of Art, South Kensington. While it is not necessary to endorse Mrs. Bruce Glasier's conclusion that Mrs. Pankhurst's character hardened under the influence of her daughters, it is indisputable that they (and especially Christabel) did in certain respects guide and influence their mother. From their entry into the suffrage agitation in Manchester they were immediately associated with Esther Roper and Eva Gore-Booth: the latter with Christabel Pankhurst and other helpers formed the Manchester and Salford Women's Trade Council at the same time as Mrs. Pankhurst formed the Women's Social and Political Union. The consequence of the friendship between Mrs. Pankhurst's daughters and Eva Gore-Booth is an important contributory stream to the broad story of militancy. Eva Gore-Booth herself was certainly no militant: she had neither the figure nor the physique of an Amazon. We can see her in the pages of Miss Sylvia Pankhurst's book: 'Tall and excessively slender . . . be-

---

[1] Most of the facts about the early days of the Women's Social and Political Union are taken from the valuable account in Miss Sylvia Pankhurst's book, who, although still in her teens, was in the thick of all these events.

spectacled, bending forward, short of breath with high-pitched voice and gasping speech'—the incarnation of a spinster lady out of Scarborough, 'Before the Bombardment'. But then Miss Pankhurst adds these words: 'she was nevertheless a personality of great charm.' And there can be no doubt that this rebellious spirit spurning convention and courting suffering, planted ideas in the minds of the sisters—ideas which luxuriated in the brooding calm of Lissadell but were not likely to be found on the more conventional pavements of Bloomsbury or Victoria Park, Manchester. History suggests that revolutionary movements often draw their most dangerous doctrines and sometimes the most fiery exponents of such doctrines from the lavish, reckless and iconoclastic ideas to be found in a sophisticated upper-class. So it was in this case. There is some evidence that Mrs. Pankhurst disapproved of her daughters' close association with Eva Gore-Booth, but it is possible that this disapproval merely sprang from the feeling that such a friendship was drawing them away from the conventional doctrines of the Labour Party.

These events inside the Pankhurst family are symptoms of a more general development, which was to give impetus to the militant movement—the growing independence of young women. The old Victorian idea that women had either to marry or go out as governesses was fast dissolving. Not only could they be trained for certain professions but the universities, the arts and even business were all opening before them. Lady typists for instance were first seen in the City of London at the end of the 1890's. The general spread of riches during this period meant that, in addition to these young women working outside the swaddling bands of home, there was a considerable class of unmarried young women living in varying degrees of independence on allowances or investments. No doubt for many of them this liberty merely meant games of golf at Felixstowe and a tendency to speak of 'the mater', a study of Italian paintings at Florence or leisurely contests in diabolo with the vicar's wife. But for a few it meant something more—the realization that the old-established world was creaking to its end and that wisdom, as in the familiar story of the virgins, lay in preparing the human spirit for what was about to happen. In her excellent book *Three Guineas*, which largely deals with the influence

of women on politics, Virginia Woolf points out that amidst all
the great political hostesses of history the unmarried daughter of
a man of education is not to be found. She then correctly decides
that influence divorced from wealth is ineffective in politics. But
with the twentieth century came the new phenomenon of a
generation of young women, armed with a modicum of wealth,
who began to make some impact on politics. Although successful
novels of Edwardian times seem to the modern palate almost as
thin and watery as the social intelligence of the *Morning Post*, these
independent-minded young ladies provided a recurring theme for
the writers at that time.

Indeed with the twentieth century, and with gathering mo-
mentum, there came the first mutterings of revolt by the young
against the conventions of their elders—against the insipidities of
home life. And it could be maintained that this was only part of a
more general movement by the younger generation to escape
from the artificialities of well-to-do life into the realities of existence. A formerly widely read writer, Stephen Reynolds, has drawn
attention to this contrast in his book *A Poor Man's House* which
was published in 1909. He describes a visit to a hotel on Dartmoor
where the conversation never rises higher than such banal questions as, 'Isn't it a pity that there is no char-à-banc service to Yes
Tor? Is the society here quite as good as it might be? What do you
think of the *table d'hôte*?' This he contrasts with a visit to a fisher-
man's family when the question asked was 'Shall us hae money to
go through the winter?' Reynolds goes on to comment: 'Here they
skate over a dead sea upon the ice of convention: but there they
swim in the salted waters, swallow great gulps, and nevertheless
strike out manfully, knowing no more than anyone else exactly
where the shore lies, yet possessing I think an instinct of direction.
Here comfort is at stake: there existence.' Certainly it would be
unjust to the intelligent and generous-minded young women,
nurtured in many middle-class homes, to imply that they were
content with the cloying comforts of home: they must have often
longed to test those wider waters, where existence was at stake.
But such longings were apt to be extinguished by their parents
who, like the Suitor in the nursery rhyme, dangled before their
daughters the prospects of a life of picturesque ease.

Goldilocks, Goldilocks, wilt thou be mine?
Thou shalt neither wash dishes nor yet feed the swine.
But sit on a cushion and sew a fine seam,
And feed upon strawberries, sugar and cream.

This spread of independence was helped by one other small but important innovation—the growth of the tea-shop. A few expensive restaurants existed but apart from these there were no places for a quick meal other than the formality of the large damask table-cloth and the best silver at home, or the brisk clatter of the bar parlour. The tea-shop gave the young—perhaps in revolt against the stiffness of family afternoon tea—an ideal meeting place: it was an integral part of the women's liberation movement.[1]

[1] See the *Manchester Guardian* for January 24 1955.

XII

W.S.P.U. is Born

So it was that the Women's Social and Political Union embodied and caught into an organization both the rebellious spirit of youth and the more fundamental political discontents of the Labour Party. At the inaugural meeting of the Union, which was held in Mrs. Pankhurst's house 62 Nelson Street, Manchester, on 10th October 1903, the foundress defined the objective of the Union with two words 'immediate enfranchisement'. She then added these significant words: 'we shall work not by means of any outworn missionary methods but by political action.'

For the next two years the Union concentrated on propaganda work in Lancashire, within the broad framework of the Labour movement. The women were asked to speak at meetings of Labour Party branches, Clarion Clubs and Trades Unions: they also undertook on their own account a number of open-air meetings, especially on the Sunday before the opening of Wakes Week in the various cotton towns, when the citizens strolled forth to see the preparations for all the fun of the fair. As Mrs. Pankhurst expressed it: 'We soon rivalled in popularity the Salvation Army and even the tooth-drawers and patent-medicine pedlars.'

Mrs. Pankhurst, with her two daughters, was the abiding force in the speaking team; and she was assisted by her youngest daughter Adela occasionally, and by her schoolboy son Harry as a valued species of A.D.C. They were helped by stalwarts of the Women's Movement like Esther Roper and Eva Gore-Booth, and they attracted two fresh personalities of considerable importance. The first was Theresa Billington,[1] a school teacher in Manchester,

---

[1] Now Mrs. Billington-Greig.

119

who had run away from home in her teens: she was the first
woman national organizer appointed by the I.L.P. To the eloquent, rather uncontrolled but not ineffective oratory of the
Pankhursts she brought the discipline of a trained mind and the
concise logic of an intellectual. The second recruit was almost
the exact opposite of Miss Billington—an impulsive and attractive
mill-hand, Annie Kenney, who was completely converted after a
meeting at Oldham. Annie Kenney was a contemporary of the
Pankhurst sisters and, being a working-class girl, she brought to
the movement something new—together with a true understanding of working-class opinion. She was courageous and original,
and it was her idea, for example, to mingle with the pill vendors and
tooth-drawers on the Wakes grounds.

But although there was much bustle (and some fun) during
these early months of the Union in Manchester, there was no substantial advance. In fact as the General Election of 1906 came
nearer the work grew depressingly difficult: the Labour Party,
reasonably enough, concentrated on getting the support of existing voters and lost interest in questions of abstract justice which
could only muster (as it seemed to them) a rabble of political in-
effectives who differed only in morality from the camp followers
of an army.

Nevertheless Mrs. Pankhurst had certainly carried out her
declared intention of 'political action', and the question now was
—how would these trumpetings which sounded bravely through
the humid mists of Lancashire strike the ears of the more experienced and possibly wiser Londoner? In that city there were no
excitements to match those in Manchester. The routine work of
Miss Becker in securing publicity and working among Members
of Parliament was carried on by Miss Helen Blackburn, who was
a disciple of Miss Becker and published an extremely valuable
account of the whole struggle in the nineteenth century. Of her,
Lady Frances Balfour (who was possibly blessed with a trifle too
much of Scotch frankness) recorded that 'the countenance of a
great soul shone through the plainness of her face'. But 'the great
soul' was quite unable to shift the suffrage issue onwards and,
when she died in 1903, matters were broadly as they had stood in
Miss Becker's time.

There was an important debate in Parliament in 1904, when the partisans of female suffrage were able to point in triumph to Australia where (with the exception of Victoria) every woman had been lately given a vote for the state legislature, and also to the events in Lancashire, where the clearly expressed interest of working-class women seemed to dispose of the old argument that women's suffrage was merely a fad of a few wealthy and leisured ladies. Labouchere answered these points with the tale, reputed to come from a north country town, of a man who was found, in compromising circumstances, visiting another man's wife: he defended himself on the grounds that he was canvassing her vote since he contemplated becoming a town councillor. 'I do not know', continued Labouchere, 'how domestic bliss is to be continued if a man is perpetually leaving his own wife and visiting another man's wife on the plea that he wanted to be a town councillor.' He argued that the danger would be increased a hundred-fold if women were given the parliamentary vote. But the House of Commons was not impressed by the dangers to domestic bliss from these amorous burgesses, and passed the Bill by 182 votes to 68. (Both Mr. Lloyd George and Mr. Winston Churchill were among the majority.) The victory was satisfactory but bore no fruits since, like its many predecessors, the measure was carried no further.

There is no evidence that Mrs. Pankhurst or the Women's Social and Political Union were prominent in the House of Commons during this debate, but after it Mrs. Pankhurst would seem to have conceived the idea of lobbying Members of Parliament during the course of a debate on woman's suffrage. In the February following this debate Mrs. Pankhurst wrote to Mrs. Dora Montefiore, who had been prominent in the fight for the women's vote in New South Wales, was active in the early days of the Union and was afterwards to win some fame as an extremist of the Left, 'the old-fashioned and official gang will never undertake the work of lobbying. I have no confidence in them.' Certainly the official gang had no idea what an alarming ally was speeding to their aid from Manchester. A few weeks revealed the truth more plainly.

On 12th May 1905 there was enacted one of those scenes in

Parliament which almost seem to justify the eruption of some Cromwell or a Hitler into the tranquil mysteries of parliamentary procedure. A Bill, which simply stated that in all acts concerning the qualifications for voting, words of the masculine gender should be held to include women, was the second on the list for that day. The preceding question was a Bill to provide that carts should carry a rear light at night—a consequence of the increasing development of motor traffic. On this pettifogging topic all the ingenuity of those opposed to the women's franchise was lavished, in order to take time from the second motion for the day. Conspicuous in this performance was Sir Frederick Banbury, with his silk hat, starched appearance and starched mind—an extraordinary but respected survival of the ancient Tory tradition, who was in the 1920's to lie stranded, like some object from the ocean, attracting the envious glances of those ruder specimens of Tory humanity who crowded the Commons in the degenerate days of Lloyd George's coalition. He was able to waste at least half an hour by arguing that a horse should really carry a red light on its tail, and that an old woman carrying a bundle of laundry ought to be similarly protected. Labouchere followed in the same sense. There was in consequence very little time left for the women's Bill, which was inevitably talked out.

Mrs. Pankhurst and some of her friends from the Women's Social and Political Union, were present at the House of Commons for the debate: there were also there some of the leading members of the other suffrage societies, which are most easily distinguished from the Political Union by the title 'constitutional'. Ladies of each kind of society were joined together by a common indignation. Surely they felt it was scandalous that a serious topic should be treated with this light-hearted trickery. Visitors to the Law Courts may recall, after a case has ended, a little, bedraggled knot of human beings—the unsuccessful litigant and his friends—having the intricacies of the law and the elaborate processes by which they were outwitted, explained to their puzzled minds by their legal advisers. Similar explanations—the procedure of the House, the rules of the House, the licence of debate, the importance of never curbing discussion except by the clock—were laid before the ardent ladies. They remained highly indignant and totally unconvinced. At this juncture they realized that a man had been hustled out of the Strangers' Gallery for making a disturbance. They crowded round what they imagined to be a new champion, with eager gratitude. To their chagrin they found it was Councillor Gribble of Northampton, who had protested because Parliament, instead of discussing the unemployed, had devoted its time to talking about votes for ladies. The little band moved out into the street and Mrs. Wolstenholme Elmy, with her ringlet curls looking not unlike a Cruickshank drawing of an elderly Dora Copperfield, rose to speak. She was immediately stopped by the police who pointed out that she could not address a meeting in the approaches to Parliament. The company then wandered on to the protecting shadow of Richard Cœur de Lion and close by the drawn sword, which seemed to proclaim the generosity of man's nature in the forgotten Age of Chivalry, Mrs. Elmy tried again. This time she was more peremptorily stopped, for was she not almost blocking the entrance to the House of Lords? The cluster of ladies, now joined by the sturdy figure of Keir Hardie, then moved across to the Broad Sanctuary where a short meeting was held, and names were taken by the police.

Thus mildly and obediently began the first act of militancy. The meeting was perhaps hardly as effective as one of the drawing-room meetings organized by Miss Becker. The handful of ladies felt at best that they had, under Mrs. Pankhurst's leadership, done something that was unusual and daring. The world outside was unmoved and at the very most an errand-boy broke off whistling 'Yip Ai Addie Ai A Ai A' to listen to what was being said, and perhaps a Canon, strolling back to his comfortable quarters in the Abbey Precincts, felt vaguely disturbed by an indefinable sense of impending mischief. But broadly speaking the oratory of the ladies was unnoticed—and not even *The Times* referred to the episode. Yet that May afternoon saw the first plunge by the ladies into the chilly and daunting waters of militancy, and they could comfort themselves that if the busy world had not heeded their speeches, at least their names were enshrined on those tablets of immortality—a policeman's notebook. And what was done on 12th May was to form the pattern of the future. The striking attitudes of tragedy (recalling Mrs. Siddons at her most powerful) inside the

House of Commons, the attempt to influence members by a little
surreptitious burst of oratory, the inevitable expulsion and then
the indignation meeting outside were all to follow the precedent
of 12th May 1905, till they were caught up in the flood waters of
disorder on the grand scale.

XIII

A Challenging Question to Churchill

For the moment there was a pause while the political situation unfolded as the General Election to be held at the end of the year grew nearer. The weak government of Arthur Balfour —its supporters divided into Tariff Reformers and Free Traders— was toppling to its catastrophic fall, and not even Balfour, who rode to disaster like a nonchalant juggler on a circus pony, could soften the imminent blow. The Liberals, as all the by-elections showed, were edging towards a triumph—helped by the purblind actions of their opponents whose educational policy had infuriated the nonconformists, whose policy in South Africa had disgusted humanitarians and whose policy of taxing imports had alarmed the commercial aristocrats in banking and shipping. Filled with such ample and effective ammunition Liberal candidates had little room left in their election addresses for abstruse questions like the women's vote. Although the majority of Liberals, perhaps without great enthusiasm, favoured votes for women, the most encouraging sign was the announcement by the Women's Liberal Federation that they would only support at the election those candidates who were favourable to the woman's cause. This positive threat was an advance: previously a notoriously anti-feminine Liberal candidate ran the risk of losing the local support of his branch of the W.L.F.; there had been no general pronouncement from Headquarters.

But from the women's point of view the disappointment of the election was the Labour Party. This has already been explained, but it is important to emphasize that although the Pankhursts had identified themselves closely with the Independent Labour Party in Manchester they had been unable to draw the party, as a whole, behind the women's vote. The point of difference, which was to divide the suffrage agitation from Labour after the Election, was already emerging. The Pankhursts believed that votes should be given to women as a matter of principle and of justice: they would have been satisfied if the State had agreed that merely a handful of women should vote, and here they were following the lead of all the established and constitutional societies. On the other hand the bulk of the Labour Party felt that enfranchising a few well-to-do ladies could only help the Conservatives, and that the principle of giving women the vote could only be satisfied as part of universal adult suffrage. There were of course shades of difference within the Labour Party—Keir Hardie, a loyal and devoted friend of the Pankhurst family, felt that the injustice of excluding women cut so deep that it should be remedied immediately by enfranchisement along the lines the women wished, while a few of the older trades unionists viewed the whole idea with the same masculine distaste as did Labouchere or Sir Frederick Banbury. The point of difference is well illustrated by a debate which was held two years after the election between a leading Suffragist and Miss Margaret Bondfield—destined to be the first woman in the Cabinet, and not likely to be forgotten by history for her achievement in improving the conditions of women working in shops. Her opponent had said that the quickest way to enfranchise the working-class was to give votes for women: the point being that women were more alive to social injustice than men were: in reply Miss Bondfield said: 'I entirely disagree. I say good luck to them, and may they get it. But don't let them come and tell me that they are working for my class.' There lay the real difference between the Women's Social and Political Union and the Labour movement. The Labour Party drifted further into the narrow waters of class antagonisms: the women could not follow them, and were left clinging obstinately but heroically to their rocks of principle and justice. Therefore, with the exception of Wigan, the case for woman's suffrage was fought sporadically rather than effectively throughout the General Election. None of the three Parties espoused the cause, and in the welter of party cries, the claims of the women were scarcely heard. People were too busy listening to the substantial glories of the big loaf offered to them by the Liberals in contrast with the small loaf which would be their lot under Tariff Reform, or shuddering over the horror of Chinese slavery to pay heed to the whims of a handful of clever women.

Perhaps conscious of this, as the Election drew near, some courageous ladies in Manchester determined to advertise their cause, to parade their wrongs before the flower of chivalrous manhood, entrenched in a public meeting. At that time Mr. Winston Churchill, in common with other members of the historic political families—Cecil and Cavendish—broke with the Conservative leadership on the issue of free trade: Churchill went further than most of his associates, and not only left the Conservatives, but submitted himself to the easier yoke of Liberalism. Shortly before the General Election he was adopted as Liberal candidate for northwest Manchester, and opened his campaign in the Free Trade Hall, with a large public meeting addressed by Sir Edward Grey— one of the conspicuous leaders of the moderate Liberals and certain of high office if that Party won the election. The meeting was held on 13th October 1905.

Christabel Pankhurst attended the meeting, accompanied by Miss Annie Kenney who was already almost fanatically devoted to the Pankhursts. After the speeches, questions were put principally about the Liberal attitude to the unemployed. During a pause in the questions Annie Kenney rose and asked Churchill: 'If you are elected, will you do your best to make Women's Suffrage a Government Measure?' To this no reply was given and Christabel Pankhurst then rose and held aloft a slightly tawdry banner on which was inscribed 'Votes For Women'. (Mrs. Pankhurst was also in the meeting, but she took no part in the disturbance.) The hubbub which arose was instant and deafening, and a chivalrous Liberal stalwart put his hat over Christabel Pankhurst's face. When some semblance of order was restored, the Chief Constable of Manchester who, rather strangely, was on the platform, offered to give the question to Grey if it was put in writing. The question, which was carefully drafted, asked if the Liberal Government would give votes to working women, and it was signed 'Annie Kenney' for the Women's Social and Political Union. Certainly Grey was maladroit. The candidate, Churchill, was in favour of votes for women and had so voted in the House of Commons in 1904. Lady Grey, shortly afterwards to be killed in a carriage accident, was a fervent feminist and undoubtedly influenced her husband to follow her views. Grey had therefore only to turn the question with an allusion to his own sympathies and those of Churchill. In fact he remained awkwardly silent. When it was clear that no answer was forthcoming, the ladies, locked in one another's arms, made a disturbance calling 'The Question, The Question— Answer the Question', and were hustled from the meeting. As they were being removed Christabel Pankhurst said to the stewards of the meeting and to the police: 'I shall assault you. I shall spit at you.' When order had been restored inside, Grey rose and said that he did not deal with the point 'because it is not, and I do not think it is likely to be, a party question'. Outside, the two ladies— and after they had been hustled and man-handled this showed high courage—attempted to address the crowd streaming out of the Free Trade Hall. They were immediately arrested, and Christabel Pankhurst was fined 10s. and Annie Kenney 5s. with the alternative of seven days' imprisonment for Christabel Pankhurst and three days' imprisonment for Annie Kenney. They chose the latter. The candidate for north-west Manchester, not unmindful of the mischief which these determined ladies might do to his prospects, and in youth, as in maturity, ever eager to be generous, presented himself at Strangeways Gaol to pay the fines. The Governor declined to accept his money. The outcry in the newspapers was considerable, resting on ancient precepts of Victorian governesses about 'ladylike behaviour' which were most characteristically enshrined in the pages of the *Standard*, 'Our only regret is that the discipline will be identical with that experienced by mature and sensible women, and not that which falls to the lot of children in the Nursery.' But the ladies were immensely cheered by a telegram which reached them from Keir Hardie: 'The thing is a dastardly outrage, but do not worry it will do immense good.'

This prison experience—the first endured by any women for a political cause in this country—was sufficiently long to be disagreeable, but not so long as to shatter the sense of romantic adventure nor to destroy the feeling that the path of duty was paved with hardship and suffering. As surely as Joan of Arc had

7b. Mrs. Pankhurst

7a. Jane Warton

8*a*. Sylvia Pankhurst in the East End: a post-war celebration breakfast

8*b*. On the door-step; 'the General' picketing Sir Edward Carson's house in Eaton Place

been, 500 years before, these young women were comforted by the ringing sound in their ears of mighty but compelling voices. By suffering, their personal devotion was strengthened. Annie Kenney has described how, during the prison service, they sat side by side, holding hands, and that Christabel looked 'very coy and pretty in her prison cap. She took my hand tenderly and just held it, as though I were a lost child being guided home.'

As soon as the two ladies were released from Strangeways they were welcomed back to liberty by a mass demonstration in the Free Trade Hall. The faithful Keir Hardie was the principal speaker, and the meeting was organized by the Independent Labour Party—showing the close relations still existing between that body and the Women's Social and Political Union. Crowds had to be turned away from the meeting, and the two youthful prisoners were acclaimed with bouquets and songs of liberty. Terse and straightforward as Keir Hardie's speeches always were, what he said on this occasion was eclipsed by the wit and oratory of the young Manchester girl—Christabel Pankhurst, which over and over again drew cheers from the delighted audience. On her fellow-sufferer, Annie Kenney, the effect of the speech was a combustion. 'She it was', wrote Annie Kenney twenty years later of her friend Christabel, 'who lit the fire which consumed the past.' Oldham and the mill belonged to the past: henceforth her life was given to the cause, and Mrs. Pankhurst told her that so long as they had a home she should live there.

Naturally enough these events—though they were somewhat eclipsed in the national newspapers by the long drawn but public death-bed of the Conservative Government—aroused excitement and attracted recruits to the W.S.P.U. in Manchester. Among these last was a formidable lady of Highland origins called Mrs. Flora Drummond. Her life had been soured by her height—five feet one inch. She had been destined for a career in the Post Office, and was fully trained for this, when a regulation was passed excluding any man or woman from postal employment who was under five feet two inches high. No doubt this regulation was not malignant but practical: the petite or the dwarf would alike have had a struggle to push stamps or change to the public across the broad counter of a post office. But apart from her own case Mrs. Drummond thought, not unreasonably, that the regulation fell with extra severity on women who, as a species, were shorter than men. With emphatic conviction she joined the Union. Her organizing capabilities and her slight air of swagger were, in later years, to earn her the affectionate title of 'General'. Queen Victoria once said: 'We are rather short for a Queen', and Mrs. Drummond might have paraphrased this by saying: 'We are rather short for a general.' She was a zealous and important addition of strength to the Union.

A few weeks after the welcome to Annie Kenney and Christabel Pankhurst in the Free Trade Hall, Balfour fell. The Liberals, under Campbell-Bannerman, formed a strong administration and four days before Christmas 1905 held a wildly enthusiastic meeting in the Albert Hall. The simple *joie de vivre* of the gathering was scarcely distinguishable from the spirit which was to animate countless voices in the nation four days later:

> *O come all ye faithful*
> *Joyful and triumphant.*

Mistakenly the enthusiasts from Manchester decided to interrupt the Albert Hall Meeting: their exertions made about as much impression as a church mouse, hurrying across the aisle while the congregation was singing a hymn on Christmas morning. In the flurry and hostility they held their little banner upside down.

More wisely the Union decided to concentrate through the impending election on an area where they had made progress and where they were known. Apart from the valuable sortie to Wigan, which has already been described, and apart from a visit by Annie Kenney to Keir Hardie's constituency, Merthyr Tydfil, the Pankhursts, Miss Billington, 'General' Drummond and their followers concentrated their fire on a single Manchester constituency. This was the north-west Division where the under-Secretary of State for the Colonies in the new Government, Winston Churchill, was fighting a then unknown solicitor Joynson-Hicks. The action of the ladies was not precisely logical, since Churchill had voted in favour of woman's suffrage, but they no doubt felt that he was the most prominent supporter of the Government fighting in Manchester and they were also no doubt influenced by the detestation of Liberals which marked the Independent Labour Party in its early days. They were to claim afterwards that the intervention of the Union in north-west Manchester had resulted in Churchill getting the smallest majority of the six Manchester constituencies which all returned Liberals or Labour men. This was a highly dubious claim. Churchill was fighting a difficult seat, predominantly Conservative, which had returned a Conservative for twenty years: his achievement in winning with a majority of 1,300 was resounding. The intervention of the ladies, which caused some amusement and some frayed tempers but contributed to very lively meetings, was probably of no detriment to the Liberal candidate: rather otherwise. The most lasting result of the efforts of those ladies was perhaps Churchill's superb impromptu when he said: 'I am not going to be henpecked on a subject of such grave importance.'

XIV

The Assault on London

Nineteen hundred and six—the centenary of the death of both Fox and Pitt—was politically a year of destiny. Towards the end of January the results of the General Election came rolling inexorably forward bearing on their crest a colossal Liberal triumph. Only 156 Conservatives trailed back to Westminster, leaving behind 246 of their brethren engulfed in the waters of oblivion. The Liberals almost exactly doubled their members which gave them a majority of nearly 100 over every possible combination—that is to say a majority of 100 if the Conservatives, the Irish and the Labour Party had all joined to vote against them. They were supported by fifty-two Labour members —a somewhat self-conscious portent of twentieth-century politics.[1] Four hundred and twenty members, belonging to all Parties, were avowed supporters of woman's suffrage. The excitement of the election, prolonged over several days as polling-day varied from area to area, was unrivalled, and certainly recalled the great days of 1832 when after the passing of the Reform Bill the Conservatives were swept away. For half a century after 1906 Liberals were hopefully to scan the heavens for a gleam of victory, and as they thought they saw some glint of light among the darkling scene they would murmur: 'It will be Nineteen O Six over again.' But it never was. In fact the triumph of 1906 gained strength, in restrospect, because it was the last.

The new Cabinet, which was sustained by the Liberal triumph can claim the pre-eminent place in English history. Though not named the Ministry of All the Talents, it deserved the title. In-

[1] Of the 52, 29 were, strictly speaking, Labour. The remaining 23 were 'Lib-Lab' fighting as allies of the Liberals.

tegrity and ability were represented by Grey at the Foreign Office, Asquith at the Exchequer and Bryce as Chief Secretary for Ireland; Haldane brought to the War Office a mind trained by the law to astonishing acuteness; Morley as Secretary of State for India and Birrell as President of the Board of Education made their contributions from the world of learning: Lloyd George at the Board of Trade and John Burns at the Local Government Board were the spokesmen of the new ideas inspired by progressive thinkers: all these talented men with those in junior places such as Herbert Samuel, Walter Runciman, McKenna, and Churchill were held together and inspired by the broad, tolerant but decidedly progressive mind of the Prime Minister—Campbell-Bannerman. Thus led, men and women throughout the country began to think that with the twentieth century had come the chance to remove ancient prejudices and shackles from the mind of man and clear the road for a general advance. Surely in this enlightened atmosphere, asked the advocates of female suffrage, even they could breathe more freely, could begin to assume the brave air of those marching to victory?

Although for the next eight years the Women's Social and Political Union was to fill the centre of the stage, attracting all the limelight and diverting all attention from the quieter supporters of their cause in the background, these undemonstrative supporters remained always the heart of the movement, carrying conviction by their very patience and resignation. Mrs. Fawcett—a most able chronicler of their doings and perhaps pre-eminent for intellect among all the women supporters of the agitation—once pointed out that it was from Mill that the movement had derived the reputation for practical good sense and moderation which she described as its distinguishing feature. To the shoddy arguments of the male mind that women were too volatile, too passionate for the excitements of political life, this persistent patience was a decisive retort. One other point is important. The woman's political movement had always rested on a firm basis of Conservative opinion. In Victorian times writers like Frances Cobbe had argued that the accession of women to the franchise would be a stabilizing factor, and that it was preferable that the sisters and daughters of those who had the vote should be on the voting register rather than the dregs of the working class, which would be the inevitable result of a further extension of the male franchise. There were of course Liberals and Socialists within the constitutional women's movement but its bias was decidedly to conservatism. The twin virtues of reason and moderation were shown to the best advantage by the National Union of Women's Suffrage Societies, with something in the region of 500 affiliated societies which had been formed in 1897 to close the political fissures in the movement. The headquarters of this body was in Great Smith Street, and the sad plight of its members was emphasized by the telegraphic address: 'Voiceless London'. Its President was Mrs. Fawcett and on its executive committee it could boast of famous names like Mrs. Corbett Ashby, the Liberal, Miss Margaret Ashton, the educationalist and renowned citizen of Manchester, Lady Frances Balfour, Mrs. Heitland, wife of a Fellow of St. John's, Cambridge, the eminent Scotswoman Miss Chrystal Macmillan, Miss Eleanor Rathbone, later to win laurels as a courageous member of the House of Commons, and Miss Maude Royden. Now the immediate question for 1906 to solve was the effect on this body (intellectual, professional and respectable) and its sympathizers (henceforth to be known as constitutionalists) of the Women's Social and Political Union with its daring antics and its aura of the convict's cell.

In 1906 there were three considerations which greatly weakened the effectiveness of those agitating for the vote along constitutional lines. Although individual Members of Parliament were prepared to sponsor bills for giving women the vote, no party would give them the slightest help. The history of the previous forty years seemed to underline the simple truth that without the backing of a political party, a controversial franchise measure was doomed. These ladies were like backers on a race-course, eager to follow their fancy, but denied the pleasure because there were no runners. Even the young and spirited Labour Party disappeared from the starting list in 1907 when after a stormy conference at Belfast, the Party dropped female suffrage in favour of universal adult suffrage thereby almost losing its leader Keir Hardie, who announced, after the vote was taken, that he might have to sever his connection with the Conference.

There was also the difficulty that the private Member of Parliament had far less power in the House of Commons than had been the case in Victorian times. The opportunities of a back-bencher were largely eclipsed by the better organization of parties, and by the demands of their Whips for more of the time formerly absorbed by the private member.

In the same way that they had no political party backing, they had no newspaper support whatever. Far in the background were the days when the Press gleefully fastened on the phenomenon of a woman speaking in public or a collection of ladies bearing a petition to Parliament: by 1906 the public activities of these constitutional suffrage societies aroused almost the same interest as a vestry meeting in Great Snoring.

Yet in surveying the history of the women's political movement in the twentieth century, the reader could easily overlook the work of the older societies. They formed the solid and unswaying foundation on which their more headstrong comrades could build. Miss Christabel Pankhurst once lightheartedly tossed off the generalization that the non-militant suffrage agitation was of the nineteenth century, but that the militant agitation was of the twentieth. There was no such demarcation. The non-militant agitation continued, through all the hubbub of the militants, and the still voice of reasoned argument was by no means drowned in the din. Mrs. Sydney Webb said truly when she wrote that people would never understand the awakening of women until they realized that it was not mere feminism. She linked it, with the spread of the ideals of international labour and the spirit of revolt among native peoples, as part of a general movement towards partnership among human beings. And she correctly noticed that compared with the other two the women's movement, all over the world, had been conspicuously free from militancy. Therefore in following the fortunes of the militant suffragettes the reader will not overlook the steady, powerful but orderly societies who may have been with the militants in spirit but were not of them. Their unflagging work though never conspicuous, prepared the ground for a shift of public opinion.

Nor at the beginning was there any particular antagonism between the two points of view. In London the orthodox supporters of the movement were in complete command, and they watched with amused tolerance the efforts of the wild Mancunians to transport their theories to the sophisticated civilization of the Capital. The start of the assault on London was diminutive—almost pitiful. It was marked by the arrival of Miss Annie Kenney with £2 in her pocket. Miss Sylvia Pankhurst, who was studying art in South Kensington, found a room for her in Chelsea and together the two decided to organize a meeting at Caxton Hall, with a procession, on the day of the opening of Parliament. After a few days Mrs. Pankhurst joined them from Manchester and was slightly appalled by the magnitude of what the two girls were attempting. The 'General' was at once ordered to come to London. But on February 19th, when Parliament was opened, these four had succeeded in organizing a respectable demonstration—the Caxton Hall was well filled, and they had collected about 300 working women, mostly from the East End, to march from St. James's Park Underground to the Hall. Mrs. Pankhurst and Annie Kenney spoke; when it was announced that there was no reference to woman's suffrage in the King's speech Mrs. Pankhurst urged the company to march off in procession to the House of Commons. The 'demonstration' ended in melancholy vein: the rain poured, the wind blew and the police barred the women from entering the House of Commons. They were finally admitted twenty at a time, but the busy M.P.s—most of them filled with a sense of glory at their own election—could spare nothing save a few condescending nods of polite approval to the bedraggled ladies.

Yet there were encouraging signs. Lady Frances Balfour attended the meeting and, although she was not in agreement with their methods, she saw that the Women's Social and Political Union was vibrating with life. A shade unkindly, she described her experiences to her friend Professor Saintsbury, a pre-eminent literary critic who loathed progress and Liberalism, and was shivering with terror in Edinburgh at the prospect of a Radical Government in power: 'It is a strange world!' the unfeeling lady wrote, 'I went and looked at, and sat under a huge concourse of working women, who had met to demand the suffrage "this session". They were the outcome of the women's Social and Political organization. They will have nothing to do with any of the old-established Suffrage Societies, they met under the Labour Party with their own flags and carrying their own babies. Those last, poor infants, were fed with lumps of cake. . . . Assuredly, new winds are blowing through society.' Lady Frances ended her letter by quoting a limerick, about herself, which had just won a £30 prize:

> *There's a lady whose name's in Debrett*
> *She became a great Suffragette*
> *She walked and she talked*
> *She wrote and she spoke*
> *But Adam is adamant yet.*

And now there followed close on this successful meeting an event which, in the history of the Union, was to do more than anything else to bring Adam to his senses. This was the confluence of the two Emmelines—Mrs. Emmeline Pankhurst and Mrs. Emmeline Pethick-Lawrence. The exact circumstances of this meeting are not easily unravelled, but it was clearly due to the exertions of the benign Keir Hardie. Lady Frances was perfectly correct in referring to the Caxton Hall meeting as being held 'under the auspices of the Labour Party' because Keir Hardie had personally supervised the arrangements, and had advised Sylvia Pankhurst about the hall. In his great history of England from 1870 Sir Robert Ensor calls Keir Hardie 'the ungrudging helper and mentor' of the Union: he goes on to suggest that by no means the smallest of his services lay in bringing together these two remarkable ladies. And the conjunction of the two Emmelines was arranged about the time of this first Caxton Hall Meeting. Emmeline Pethick was born in 1867—the daughter of a prosperous family, with Cornish associations, living in Weston-super-Mare. She came to London in the early 1890's—a representative of the late Victorian independent young woman—with sufficient money to exist, and to feel vaguely uneasy about the poverty surrounding her. For five years from 1890 she worked in the West London Mission as a 'Sister of the People' with special responsibilities among women. In 1895, with her friend, Mary Neal, she founded the Esperance Girls' Club and Social Settlement—and this in turn had two off-shoots—the Esperance Dressmaking Establishment, which was run on an eight-hour day, and a hostel at Littlehampton known as 'Green Lady Hostel'. By 1905 the Esperance Club, under the influence of Cecil Sharp, had degenerated into one of those embarrassing folk dance concerns, in which East-End girls, with joyful measure, were supposed to recollect the spirit and gaiety of their unknown medieval forbears. The Sitwells, in their brilliant youth, successfully pilloried these self-conscious revels. From any danger of being caught up in this 'arty' ending to a serious social experiment Emmeline Pethick was saved by marriage. In 1901 she met Frederick Lawrence—a member of a prominent and respected City family, who had been educated at Eton and was a fellow of Trinity, Cambridge. At Cambridge he had been the last in succession of a remarkable triumvirate of Presidents of the Union— Charles Masterman, the renowned Liberal thinker and politician, and P. W. Wilson—a Member of Parliament and writer who died after these lines were written. Lawrence added to his achievements by representing Cambridge at billiards—though we may rest assured that he had nothing in common with the flashy character of whom Thackeray tells us 'he had billiards written all over his countenance', because his ideals were of the highest, and he was once described as having for part of his religion 'conscious unity with the entire sentient creation'. Like his future wife Lawrence was interested in social work in London, and lived in Mansfield House University Settlement. With charming courtesy he took his wife's maiden name and hyphened it with his own on marriage—a tribute to the distinction which she had already achieved.

In 1906 Mrs. Pethick-Lawrence became Treasurer of the Union, and for the next six years she and her husband served the cause with united devotion, and if the shrewdness and business acumen of the husband were what the Union desperately needed, the eloquence and courage of the wife proved a bonus of enduring value. The historian of the future may be tempted to say that the Pethick-Lawrences made the Women's Social and Political Union respectable: that would not be correct. Rather it might be true to say that they made it a little more sensible. Mr. Pethick-Lawrence never obtruded himself, but his money, his time and his judgment were absolutely at the disposal of the movement. He was something more than just Mrs. Pethick-Lawrence's husband: he was the Prince Consort of militancy.

Mrs. Lawrence assumed the treasurership of the Union in March 1906, and shortly afterwards the organization settled into an office in Clement's Inn, conveniently close to the tempting possibilities of Fleet Street publicity. And it was about this time that the *Daily Mail* is believed to have coined the word 'suffragettes'— to distinguish them from the law-abiding suffragists and to brand them with the implications of pettiness which seem inseparable from words ending in that fashion. Their office was opposite that formidably respectable bank—Messrs. Barclays at 19 Fleet Street, which took under its protecting arm the somewhat fluctuating balances of the Union. Indeed we can almost hear the sigh of relief, uttered by the bankers in that eminent house, thirty-five years later, as they rammed the records of this embarrassing account deep into the sacks of the salvage drive.

Thus established, the Union started to open fire on the all-powerful Liberal Government—not perhaps a deadly fusillade; it was rather a steady and disconcerting peppering. In April there was a by-election in the Eye division of Suffolk, where a widely loved Liberal member had resigned after embroiling himself in the tangled finances of the mid-Suffolk Light Railway. The election was in full swing when the diminutive but alarming figure of the 'General' came striding across the peaceful Suffolk uplands. She had no money: she had no vehicle; but she got about—perhaps owing to the traps and gigs of the Tory farmers—and was not ineffective. In the same month the Union made a demonstration from the Ladies' Gallery during one of the characteristic debates, on woman's suffrage, marked by one of the usual efforts by their opponents to talk out the bill. As time drew on Mrs. Pankhurst led the shrill cries of 'Divide, Divide', and she and her following were ejected. Almost exactly a decade before, some ladies (it will be remembered) had attempted to applaud from the Gallery: their action had caused amusement and some indignation among the orthodox Suffragists. The demonstration of April 1906 was more determined than that of May 1895, and was received with icy indignation by some members of the constitutional societies who were present.

However in the following month both wings of the movement coalesced together to lay their case before the Prime Minister—Campbell-Bannerman. Miss Emily Davies—and exactly forty years had passed since she handed the celebrated petition to Mill—Mrs. McLaren and Miss Margaret Ashton represented Liberal opinion, Miss Eva Gore-Booth put forward the case for the textile workers; and the Co-operative and Temperance Movements were also represented. The members of the Union were not the kind of women to slip unostentatiously into Downing Street. They assembled by Queen Boadicea's statue on the Embankment —breathing in perhaps something of the fire and fury of that militant Queen. They were led by Mrs. Pankhurst, Mrs. Pethick-Lawrence, Keir Hardie, Annie Kenney, in clogs and shawl, and Mrs. Wolstenholme Elmy, with her grey curls, bonnet and striking face seeming to recall the graciousness of an earlier age. Indeed all five—striking and picturesque as they were—arrested the notice of the passer-by. The aged and the halt travelled in a forage lorry, adorned with a great red banner on which was inscribed in white letters: 'We demand Votes for Women this session.' To the Prime Minister, Mrs. Pankhurst spoke of the members of the Union being prepared to 'sacrifice life itself' for the ideals which they held. In his reply the Prime Minister explained that he himself favoured women having the vote, but that members of his Cabinet were opposed to the principle. It was of course notorious that the Chancellor of the Exchequer, Asquith, was among those members. The proceedings closed with a gentle hiss, and the Union leaders stepped out to address a crowd of 7,000 from the plinth of the Nelson column.

Although Campbell-Bannerman was one of the kindest of mortals, he was perhaps a little ungenerous in making specific allusion to those of his colleagues who were known to be opposed to the women. Lloyd George, under the sting of feminine interruption at a meeting at Liverpool, accidentally went much further and rapped out, in reference to the suffrage agitators, 'Why do they not go for their greatest enemy?' He doubtless meant the Conservatives, but his rhetorical question was met by cries of 'Asquith' from all over the hall. These references were coupled with Campbell-Bannerman's more general counsel to the deputa-

tion 'to go on converting the country'. Almost inevitably the
next step in the Union's campaign was to concentrate their
attack on Asquith.

On June 15th Asquith was speaking in Northampton, where a
sizeable Labour vote at the General Election had almost resulted
in handing over this stern Radical fortress, which but lately had
sheltered Bradlaugh, to the Conservatives. Mrs. Pankhurst, Miss
Billington and Miss Kenney went to hold a protest meeting against
him in the open air. This was advertised by a curious handbill
which, with comprehensive finality, branded Asquith as the
enemy of women and workers. At this time Asquith was the
target for venomous attack from the infant Labour Party—although the attacks were not characterized by the innocence of the
cradle. He was frequently greeted with cries of 'Assassin' or of
'Featherstone Murderer'. The facts behind this catcall were curious.
In 1893 there had been a long and bitter strike in the Yorkshire
and Lancashire coal pits, at a time when Asquith was Home
Secretary, and he had agreed that if necessary the magistrates
could supplement the local police by calling in the military. On
September 7th there was serious rioting at a pit called Featherstone, which belonged to Lord Masham, near Pontefract. As disorder and damage grew, the owners found that the Chief Constable, all the magistrates and all the police were enjoying what
Lord Rosebery once happily called 'the stench and villainy' of
Doncaster Races. The owners eventually found one magistrate,
called in the military who took charge, opened fire on the rioters,
and caused casualties. Although some blame could be attached to
the police and magistrates, none whatever fell to the Home
Secretary. The Committee of Enquiry found, as was obvious, that
all the faults were local—though they allowed themselves a
curious expression of regret that the soldiers had used modern
weapons. The miners would have hardly been grateful for a
random discharge of lead from a blunderbuss.

Verdicts of committees of enquiry did not weigh with the eager
ladies of the Union—they included the charge on the leaflet that
Asquith 'was answerable for the shooting down of miners at
Featherstone': and went on with a splendid piece of special
pleading that because the Government paid compensation to the

families of the dead, Asquith 'acknowledged his own culpability.' The handbill ended with the appeal in heavy type: 'Come in Crowds to oppose Asquith, the enemy of Liberty and Justice' and on the other side: 'Women! Women! Rise up and oppose Him.' But neither the women nor the workers were conspicuous by their numbers on that summer night in Northampton, which ended somewhat dismally in Mrs. Pankhurst being flung out of Asquith's meeting.

Perhaps disappointed, the women turned to a sharper form of attack. Four days later, on June 19th, a picked band called at Asquith's house—Number 20 Cavendish Square. Finding him out, they left a message that they would call again two days later. On June 21st, led by Theresa Billington, a posse of East-End women, with flags, marched into the Square—not yet an overspill for the professional gentry from Harley Street but still the home of the rich, the sedate and the aristocratic. Miss Billington went and rang the bell of Asquith's house, while the women of the East End walked round and round the Square. The police, starting to interfere, Miss Billington hurried across and slapped a policeman in the face.[1] She was arrested and led away. At that moment a further but smaller band of women, led by Annie Kenney, marched into the Square. Annie Kenney succeeded in reaching the front-door where she kept her finger pressed on the bell. She was arrested. Members of Mr. Asquith's family and some of the servants appeared at windows and began to clap. One of Annie Kenney's followers then called out with singular fatuity: 'Oh! don't do that! Oh don't do that! That is how the soldiers were sent to Featherstone.' She, with one of her companions, was arrested.

Theresa Billington appeared before the metropolitan magistrate (Mr. Paul Taylor) at Marylebone Police Court. He is believed on this occasion to have made the remark which caused lively amusement among the members of the Union—'This shall come to an end. It must come to an end. I will bring it to an end.' Faced with this example of masculine chatter and complacency Theresa Billington refused to recognize his authority to try women on the grounds that laws were made exclusively by

[1] In later life she was to say that she never regretted that slap.

men. She was fined £10 with two months' imprisonment in default of payment.

She chose imprisonment, and was in consequence the first of the noble army to endure confinement in Holloway—that dreary dungeon close to King's Cross. In a sudden and unexplained burst of bonhomie the *Daily Mirror* came forward and paid the £10 so that she was quickly released. After a slight delay, for legal reasons, Annie Kenney followed Theresa Billington into Holloway, with a two months' sentence, and her companions received six weeks. (All these sentences were accompanied with the alternative of a fine which was scornfully refused.)

Four days later Keir Hardie, supported by some members of the Labour Party, raised the matter in the House of Commons, by appealing for a reduction in the sentences, which were certainly severe. The Liberal Member for Burnley thought the sentence by no means too severe for 'those female hooligans'. Replying for the Government, the Home Secreatry (Herbert Gladstone) asserted that Miss Billington had slapped a policeman in the face three times, and after she had been arrested, kicked him twice. Keir Hardie also sought a reduction in the sentence for a woman of sixty-four—'all she did was to call out "Featherstone".' An old and respected Radical said that he had listened to Keir Hardie's allusion to Featherstone with the utmost indignation: he thought that the repeated attacks on the Chancellor of the Exchequer by the Labour Party and 'those women' were dastardly.

Keir Hardie's parliamentary action was reinforced by a sweeping article in the *Evening News* on the same day by Mrs. Pethick-Lawrence: 'The struggle has begun. It is a life and death struggle. . . . We take this cause into our own hands. We look to none but ourselves. We appeal to none but women to rise up and fight by our side, shoulder to shoulder. . . . We are not sorry for ourselves. . . . the harder the fight the better. What we are going to get is a great revolt of the women against their subjection of body and mind to men.'

From the sophisticated vantage point of the 1950's, the reader can picture the men of London going back from their work and scanning this ringing article in their evening paper. The respectable gentlemen, the professional classes, the Soames Forsytes no doubt raised their eyebrows and murmured 'Stuff': the prosperous traders—the Mr. Clutterbucks—decided that it would be best to keep the article from their wives in Surbiton or Finchley, while the young clerks and young shopkeepers—the heroes of H. G. Wells in his early days—no doubt guffawed and allowed their minds to wander over the delights of subjection. Perhaps a few thoughtful citizens saw that there might be something in it, and began to wonder what the universe might have in store for them if their little world of London was suddenly to be filled with a race of warrior women. Yet this imaginary glimpse into the future was the reality. Perhaps there is even room to regret that this power to foresee the future, to estimate the danger was denied to those who carried out the law too literally, and even to the Home Secretary himself. Though Machiavellian, the correct course would appear to have been to attempt to disperse the demonstrating ladies, to take them into custody for a few hours, but to make no charge. For the genius of these ladies—and the word is not too strong—lay in harnessing suffering to the women's cause. Prisons and 'life itself'—an emphatic phrase much favoured by Mrs. Pankhurst and Mrs. Pethick-Lawrence—were their weapons. Henceforth the case of women's suffrage was to be illumined throughout the land by the harsh glare of martyrdom. Black Marias, prison cells, prison clothes, stern wardresses endured by these eminently respectable women ceased to be the marks of shame: they became the marks of glory.

Nor will it be overlooked that for every thousand people who shrugged off these heroics with a laugh or uttered that banal but comfortable question—'they asked for it, didn't they?' there would always be one, whose deepest feelings would be touched, who would rise to answer the call. Such a one came forward during this summer and as in bearing, in character and in intellect she stands out pre-eminent among her comrades she deserves her conspicuous place in this story.

XV

The Two Emmelines and Mrs. Despard

Charlotte French was born in 1844—the second daughter of an Irish family, with distinguished connections and in comfortable circumstances. Her parents died when she was still in her teens and, with her elder sister, she helped to bring up her younger sisters and only brother—John, afterwards the Field Marshal. She was in Paris at the outbreak of the Franco-Prussian war, and shortly afterwards she met Colonel Maximilian Despard, an Irishman, whom she married. In the same year she published a novel called *The Rajah's Heir*. Colonel Despard died in 1890—there were no children—and she then threw herself, with zeal, into public work among the poor in south London. She was among the earliest of the women Poor Law Guardians; she founded some successful clubs for workmen and boys in Nine Elms; and she also founded one of the first child welfare centres in the country—in Currie Street, Nine Elms. In Battersea she associated with pioneer socialists in the Social Democratic Federation—though she was drawn away from this to the Independent Labour Party—because of that body's sympathy with the women's movement. Her popularity in south London was great, and it gained something from her splendid appearance—a long, ivory-complexioned face with snow-white hair—invariably crowned with a flowing, black lace mantilla. She generally walked in sandals. Her face was deeply lined and she seemed to move as though she bore the sorrows of mankind. Like Eva Gore-Booth she had inherited the rebellious spirit of the Irish, and she once said that her first hero was Satan in *Paradise Lost*; she was a Roman Catholic, and she used to say that she never liked to tell anyone how greatly she sympathized with him in his revolt against the heavenly autocrat. And all her political ideals were sustained by the conviction that the enfranchisement of women was the root from which all the other reforms must spring. Without this—she once wrote—'The Utopia of noble citizenship, which has been the dream of my life, will never come to pass.' The wise and great Editor of the *Daily News*—A. G. Gardiner—said that the historian searching for the significant personalities in the Suffrage Crusade, will find that no figure will arrest him more than that of this elderly woman, 'tall and slight of build, who seems in the crowd but not of it'. And he adds that there is nothing so little understood by mankind 'as a life of complete self-sacrifice and service until it is over'. Her recruitment to the Women's Social and Political Union was an addition to their ranks of a moral influence of imponderable strength. Mrs. Despard lived until the autumn of 1939, when she was ninety-five. Although her later career is beyond the range of this book, she continued a consistent support of advanced causes almost down to the day of her death. In the 1918 'coupon' election she stood for Battersea (North) as Labour candidate—polling the vote (remarkable at the time) of 5,634. Outraged by the Irish policy of the Lloyd George Coalition Government she went over to Ireland and stirred up much trouble for the authorities—an act of defiance which was especially embarrassing as her brother was Chief Secretary at the time. She went to Russia in 1930—and was besieged in Dublin afterwards by anti-Communist Roman Catholic zealots. She came to London when she was ninety-three, and attended a meeting of the comrades of the Suffrage fight in Caxton Hall. Miss Lilian Baylis knelt before her and kissed her hand.

The adherence of Mrs. Pethick-Lawrence and Mrs. Despard to the Union was made known to the world outside by a forceful demonstration at the end of October 1906. As the meeting of Parliament in that autumn grew near, Mrs. Pankhurst was pressing the Prime Minister to undertake that a measure of woman's suffrage would be granted 'this session'. He replied to these representations that no further controversial legislation could be undertaken that session—an answer which was possibly inspired by Mr. Gladstone's reply to a similar enquiry in

1884, that the Government had as much as 'it could safely carry'. Parliament reassembled on October 23rd, and on that day the Union members attended the precincts of the House of Commons to press their views on the Prime Minister. They were supported by a number of working women.[1] They sent in a message, which was taken to the Prime Minister by the Recorder of Birkenhead, the respected Liberal member for Anglesey, who quickly came back with the information that Campbell-Bannerman had nothing to add to his letter. By this time there were perhaps 200 women in the Central Hall. Round this Hall, in the majesty of marble and with resounding lapidary inscriptions, stand parliamentarians of former times. By chance rather than choice, the women were clustered round the statue of the irresolute Iddesleigh, who, in old days as Sir Stafford Northcote, had drawn the youthful fire of the Fourth Party. His experiences in life at the hands of Lord Randolph Churchill and other members of the Fourth Party were less excruciating than those in death, when these ardent ladies, climbing among his boots and clinging to his legs, attempted to address their comrades, while banners were unfurled and cries were raised. The first to scale the plinth of the statue was the diminutive Mary Gawthorpe, a school-teacher from Leeds and a pioneer for the Labour Party in that City. Miss Gawthorpe described her recreation, in a book of reference, as 'sleeping': but there was no sign of somnolence that evening, and she was always one of the most alert and lively minds among the hierarchy of the Union. She was dragged off by the police: at once the intrepid Despard advanced and took her place. She was likewise dragged down by the police but not before Mrs. Dora Montefiore cried out to a group of Members of Parliament standing idly by: 'Can you men stand by and see a venerable woman handled in the way in which we have just been handled?' The men were not moved, and the police succeeded in shepherding the women out into the street —though, in the general melée, Mrs. Pankhurst was unluckily

[1] During 1906 the presence of these working-class women from the East End was a characteristic of suffrage demonstrations. Their presence was noted by independent observers as something new. Although the fact is not stated, it is permissible to suggest that they were organized by Miss Sylvia Pankhurst, who was always in the closest sympathy with the East Enders, and was during that year the secretary of the Union. These working-class followers were less in evidence thereafter—until 1913 when they were once again skilfully organized by Miss Sylvia Pankhurst.

hurled to the ground. She was not hurt, but having the capacity of extracting the last drop of attention from any situation, she did not hurry to rise. The tempers of her companions rose and, in spite of police objections, they attempted to hold a meeting outside the entrance to the House of Commons. Ten women were arrested.

On the following morning they appeared at Rochester Row Police Court before Mr. Horace Smith, and each was fined £10 (which on principle they declined to pay) with the alternative of two months' imprisonment. The sentence was severe. It was greeted with a demonstration in court, as a result of which Miss Sylvia Pankhurst was sent to prison with the other ten. Among the prisoners were Mary Gawthorpe, Mrs. Pethick-Lawrence and Mrs. Cobden-Sanderson—the distinguished daughter of Richard Cobden. Mrs. Cobden-Sanderson was alone allowed to speak in Court, and she addressed to the magistrate a telling epigram originally used by John Burns: 'I am a law-breaker, because I desire to be a law-maker.' Shut up in the Black Maria—and the vehicle being horse drawn made a leisurely progress—on their journey to Holloway the ladies were cheered by readings from Browning's poems by Mrs. Pethick-Lawrence. The scene can be imagined: the vehicle, swaying and jolting and not free from stench: the noise and clatter of carts and carriages without: the ladies within, not timid or remorseful but naturally apprehensive, and the steady eloquent voice of Emmeline Pethick-Lawrence rising and falling as she declaimed the stirring statements of 'The Statute and the Bust'.

> *Where is the use of the lip's red charm,*
> *The heaven of hair, the pride of the brow,*
> *And the blood that blues the inside arm—*
> *Unless we turn, as the soul knows how,*
> *The earthly gift to an end divine?*

Another leading suffragette said that as soon as she entered the Black Maria she experienced that shiver of apprehension which reminded her of the journey down to the sea in one of the old-fashioned wheeled bathing machines.

On arrival at Holloway the ladies were classed as prisoners in

the Second Division though Sylvia Pankhurst—presumably because her disturbance in the Court had been especially defiant—
was placed in the Third Division. The treatment of Sylvia Pankhurst was not materially worse in the Third than in the Second
Division: the hardship lay in being segregated from her comrades.
Both Second and Third Division prisoners had to wear prison
clothes, and had virtually no privileges. On their behalf in the
House of Commons their friends vigorously contended that they
should have been in the First Division, where they would not have
had to wear prison dress and where they would have had other
privileges of seeing friends and writing.

As this point of First or Second Division treatment was to recur
throughout the remaining years of the agitation, the facts deserve
to be noted. By tradition, by a natural sense of what is appropriate
and indeed by statute the English legal system has always treated
the political prisoner in a different fashion from the common
criminal. Although the question was not precisely clear, there
could be no doubt that there were certain offences such as sedition,
seditious libel, and offences to which the Extradition Acts applied
for which the First Division is specifically laid down by the
Statutes covering those offences. The stock cases always cited in
aid of the suffragettes were those of Dr. Jameson and W. T.
Stead. The former, after his headstrong decision to invade the
Transvaal in 1896, was captured, handed over to the British
authorities, tried and sentenced to fifteen months imprisonment.

Dr. Jameson was originally sent to Wormwood Scrubbs in
prison clothes.[1] But as the result of a petition, which was largely
signed by both Conservative, Liberal and Irish members of
Parliament he was removed to Holloway as a First Division mis-
demeanant. His apologists have always suggested that his prison
experiences nearly killed him, but his biographer perhaps comes
nearer to the mark when he suggests that his breakdown may have
been due to the fact that in prison he was denied 'the blessed consolation of labour'. As an Irish Member of Parliament expressed it
he was treated with champagne suppers and 'the visits of mam-
monized members of Society'. Although Dr. Jameson's offence

---

[1] Mr. Seymour Fort in his biography of Jameson suggests that he was sent to the
Scrubbs on a technical error.

was totally different from that of the women, his transfer from one Division to the other lent force to the idea that Members of Parliament were not wasting time in urging that the suffragettes should be given the advantage of First Division treatment.

Similarly W. T. Stead, after his article 'The Maiden Tribute of Modern Babylon', exposing criminal vice in England concerning young girls, was sentenced to three months in prison for seditious libel, but he likewise enjoyed First Division treatment. The last case was, of course, prominently within the recollection of older suffragists for Mrs. Fawcett had written to Stead at the time: 'I cannot find words to tell you how I honour and reverence you for what you have done for the weakest and most helpless among women.' Admittedly the offences, which the members of the Women's Social and Political Union had committed, were not those for which any statute enacted First Division treatment. But the Prison Reform Act of 1898 more vaguely laid down that when the antecedents of a prisoner were good, First Division treatment was appropriate. For example, Lord Russell, convicted of bigamy a few years earlier, had been by his peers given First Division. But the Government, when pressed in the House of Commons, pointed out that it was never the practice to treat as political prisoners those who broke the ordinary laws for political reasons. Moreover the Government pointed out that the decision into which Division a prisoner should be placed was a matter for the magistrate or judge not for the Home Office. The most that the Home Office could do was to draw the attention of the magistrate to the provisions of the Prison Reform Act.

But the exploits of the members of the W.S.P.U. were not likely to be viewed leniently by the London police court magistrates at this period. They were, like Horace Smith at Rochester Row, for the most part elderly men—steeped in the brine of Victorian austerity. The idea of these women embroiling themselves with the police for the sake of a political ideal was something not only outside their experience but outside their comprehension. Severity was their only weapon for dealing with what they did not understand.

Although legally the stand taken by the Government was correct, it was unfortunate that at this critical moment they had not matched the new tactics of the women with imagination and ingenuity. The matter was in the hands of the Home Secretary— Herbert Gladstone—an agreeable and accomplished man. He differed from his father in supporting the female franchise, and he also differed from that illustrious man in that he lacked the force of a powerful and widely ranging mind. From the foothills of history, looking back, we can see that a fatal twist was given to the course of the Suffrage story by the events of October 1906. They were not only to rub off some of the glory of the Liberal victory earlier that year, but they were to give an immense fillip to the Union. This truth is stated with precision by Theresa Billington in her book on the Militant Suffrage Movement: she writes that with the events of October 'the first phase of the movement came suddenly to an end, and we who had struggled and foundered in shifting sand found ourselves on firm ground.'

And of Herbert Gladstone she wrote: 'He supplied to the movement the needed stimulus of passionate enthusiasm, the spirit that always rises under oppression, and he contributed to supply the second need of advertisement.'

Even more serious than the establishment of the Union was the dangerous conjunction of the militants with the constitutional suffragists. Previously these last had floated serenely, casting an amused and occasionally suspicious glance at the erratic course of their sisters. But disapproval was swallowed up in indignation at the severity of the Government and admiration for its victims. 'I hope that the more old-fashioned suffragists will stand by their comrades who in my opinion have done more to bring the movement within the region of practical politics in twelve months, than I and my followers have been able to do in the same number of years.' So wrote Mrs. Fawcett in a letter to *The Times*.

The newspapers had formerly treated the Union members as a lark: they provided, to the perceptive eye of an editor, much the same type of copy as a rag by 'varsity chaps' on rugger night in Leicester Square. This changed. And the change was quickly sensed by the members not in Holloway. Mr. Pethick-Lawrence, taking advantage of these favourable winds of publicity, announced that he would pay £10 to the Union for every day that his wife suffered the indignities of prison. This heroic subscription received some favourable notice. But it was of course equivocal, and some newspapers did not hesitate to suggest that the payment was not so much a subscription as a thank-offering. The point was carried further by the winner of a prize at a fancy-dress ball at Covent Garden who went adorned with the verse:

> *Ten pounds a day*
> *He said he'd pay*
> *To keep this face*
> *In Holloway.*

The Government perhaps saw its mistake. Within a few days of the imprisonment of the women—two were released for health reasons, one being Mrs. Pethick-Lawrence—the remainder were transferred to the First Division and when they had served half their sentence they were set free. The sentence was interrupted but the mischief was complete.

The leading members of the older suffrage societies entertained all the prisoners to a banquet at the Savoy Hotel. That well-conducted play-ground of the affluent city man has provided the background for many an important deal and for some political arrangements but possibly it has, in its long history, never afforded hospitality to a party more truly warmed by the fires of burning idealism but less fitted for the delights of trencher and beaker. Mr. and Mrs. Bernard Shaw, chumping their vegetarian nuts, were present, and sat next to one another. A few other men attended—the faithful Sir Charles McLaren, Mr. Barnard, the Liberal Member for Kidderminster, Mr. Philip Snowden and Mr. Israel Zangwill—the distinguished novelist and wit.

The women present swamped the men, and the prisoners for the most part were taken in to dinner by distinguished representatives of the suffrage societies. With simplicity, Annie Kenney writes: 'Mrs. Lawrence bought me a very pretty green silk Liberty dress for the occasion, and I wore a piece of real lace. I was so pleased with them both.' She was escorted into dinner by Miss Beatrice Harraden, who had written in the 1890's a best-selling novel *Ships that pass in the Night*. With short hair and a fringe, invariably dressed as a Liberty aesthete of the 1880's, Miss Harraden was a formidable escort for the Oldham mill girl.

There were three toasts—The King, the Royal Family and Success to the Women's Suffrage. The last was proposed by Miss Elizabeth Robins, eminent as actress and author, who had that year written a play called *Votes For Women*, and it was seconded by Miss Isabella Ford, a pioneer of many enlightened causes from Yorkshire who, with the touching simplicity of those who helped to launch the Labour Party, expressed the belief that the home of the working man should be made the centre of all that was beautiful and ennobling; in pursuit of this ideal she taught the piano to many working people. Mrs. Cobden-Sanderson and Miss Theresa Billington replied to the toast.

The enthusiasm was immense. The faithful intellectuals, who were the strength of the earlier suffrage societies, had had few enough occasions for cheering. For forty years all had been disappointments, made more bitter by the patronizing asides and contemptuous smiles of the men. Now they had a real excuse for expressing their pent-up feelings. This they did, and those who have only heard the perfunctory cheers or the mellow laughs of a conventional banquet can have no conception of the noise when applause springs from feelings, and when it is strengthened by hero-worship. Miss May Sinclair, in her novel *The Tree of Heaven*, has given an impressive word picture of how the applause struck those who were present. She described it as a strange and piercing collective sound as if 'a clear tinkling of glass and a tearing of silk and a crying as of children and of small, slender-throated animals were held together by ringing, vibrating overtopping tones as of violins playing in the treble.'

The poet has reminded us how music, when soft voices die, 'vibrates in the memory'. These soft voices raised in musical acclamation on that December evening were never again, in harmonious unison, to sing the exploits of the militants. Yet their tones were to vibrate in the memory of some of the prisoners, and to encourage them in the idea that daring exploits and prison were the rewards for bearing the sorrows of womanhood. The militants became imbued with the feeling that myriads of phantom voices were cheering them: an hallucination which was filled with mischief. And they had too a visible reminder that they were fighting for a cause. The souvenir of the banquet was a picture of

Queen Boadicea driving in her chariot: but the courageous Briton carried aloft no spear or sword, she was charging into battle, waving a banner with the weird device 'Votes For Women'.

Looking back we can see that the events of October 1906 had in reality breached the fort: the women were at that moment closer to a successful and final advance than ever before and ever afterwards until the upheaval of the war. Not only were the two sections of the movement in affectionate alliance, but the topic was given prominence in the newspapers. For years the subject of female franchise had been completely dead so far as the press was concerned. The point has been forcibly explained by Lady Frances Balfour: 'Where we could not get a line given to our meetings, the Press went after the Militants as devoted lovers.' Naturally some of the deeds of the militants, coupled with blazing paragraphs in the papers, shocked people. But on the whole there was a hardening of sympathy for the women. An example of this was seen in the opinions of that immortal novelist, almost an octogenarian and living retired under the shadow of Box Hill, who in *The Egoist* and *Diana of the Crossways* had shot a dazzling light on the dusty corners of Victorian treatment of women, and could write that he sympathized with the militants because 'their action means that women are overcoming timidity'. But although the attacking army was more united and in better shape than it was ever to be hereafter, their objective remained formidable and impregnable. Unquestionably there was wide intellectual support for the franchise claims of the women, and it came from just that quarter—writers and leaders of opinion—to which the Liberal Government was especially sensitive. But whatever their sympathies and however much they were goaded from outside, the Government was in reality faced by a problem which was insoluble. Their own divisions in the Cabinet—though they were formidable—could possibly have been overcome but the difficulty which was insurmountable was that even the most ingenious mortal living, in spite of all the sympathy for the women's cause and in spite of favourable majorities in the House of Commons, could not devise a bill for enfranchising women which would command a majority in Parliament. There was all the difference between applauding the principle, and supporting a specific Bill.

The Women's Social and Political Union was vague in defining its objective: the matter was stated thus—'To secure for women the parliamentary vote as it is or may be granted to men.' Of the 400 and more supporters of the women's vote, in the House of Commons, a considerable proportion would have abstained or voted against a Bill based on such a principle. While it is true that majorities had been obtained for such Bills in the past, they had never got further than the Second Reading. The world of difference between expressing, by a favourable vote, agreement with the principle of a Bill (which the voter knows perfectly well has no chance of getting further) and supporting a measure until it becomes an Act of Parliament cannot be too often stressed. But once the Government sponsored a Bill in these terms, and gave facilities for it, support would have fallen away from the Liberal and Labour members (who made the bulk of the 400): they would have disliked adding to the register a block of voters, based on the existing qualifications, because they would have felt that this could only strengthen the Conservatives. This point will become clearer as the manœuvres in Parliament during the following years are described. Already in 1906 it was perceptible that, except as part of universal adult suffrage, for which neither Parliament nor the country was prepared, the prospects of female enfranchisement being passed by a House of Commons, with a progressive majority was an impossibility. In consequence the Government was virtually unable to satisfy the women's demands. That being the case their only hope was to soothe not to irritate, to be guided by those spiritual qualities enshrined in the pages of St. Paul, or to recall the words of Shakespeare:

> *O! it is excellent*
> *To have a giant's strength, but it is tyrannous*
> *To use it like a giant.*

Unfortunately that was not their policy. They were however saved from the full consequences of their severities in October by the mistakes of the women. For if 1906 could be called the year of destiny in the history of the battle for female franchise, 1907 could be called the year of delusion.

XVI

Keep the Liberal Out

The threat to public order from the suffragettes, at the opening of the year 1907, disturbed the Government. In addition to the steady trickle of law-breaking from the militants, the constitutional societies organized a march from Hyde Park to Exeter Hall in the Strand on February 9th—two days before the State opening of Parliament. In spite of the heavy rain, which gave the demonstration its niche in history as 'The Mud March', between 3,000 and 4,000 people took part—an impressive total, and a far larger muster of support than the Union could command. On February 12th Mrs. Pankhurst presided over what was called A Women's Parliament at the Caxton Hall; when the ladies attending heard that once again the King's speech contained no reference to the women's vote, deploring this omission they passed a resolution which they enthusiastically decided to bear with them in procession to the House of Commons. 'Rise up, women', called Mrs. Pankhurst from the chair. Immediately the meeting marched out to cover the short distance from the Hall to Parliament Square. Alone, at the head of the women, and preceded by an inspector of police, walked Mrs. Despard. The afternoon was cold with gleaming sunshine and Mrs. Despard looked superb—picturesque but dignified. An observer once remarked that on these occasions she reminded him of the fighting Téméraire. And in the westering sunlight she certainly seemed to recall the lines of Sir Henry Newbolt:

> *Now the sunset breezes shiver*
> *And she's fading down the river,*

But in England's song for ever
She's the fighting Téméraire.

For her fighting qualities were quickly put to the test. Opposite the Abbey she and the procession were confronted by the police who told them to turn back. They continued to march. Suddenly a considerable force of mounted police rode into the procession and, with the help of the foot police, scattered the women, thumping them on the back. Mrs. Despard and other leaders were arrested. Again and again the women tried to re-form, and in the words of Mrs. Pankhurst 'the battle against the merciless hooves' lasted for some hours. Public opinion was unquestionably shocked; the *Daily Chronicle* published a cartoon the next morning called 'The London Cossack', which showed a mounted policeman riding off in triumph from the field of battle with his victorious trophies—a collection of ladies' hats.

Naturally enough the House of Commons was not unmoved by these unseemly disorders at their gates. Most members felt that a settlement, founded on reason, could not be impossible, and with this end in view W. H. Dickinson immediately took steps to introduce a woman's suffrage bill. Although Dickinson was described in a contemporary publication as 'a somewhat austere character', who had acquired social grace through his marriage to the daughter of a knight, he was both in ability and character one of the finest representatives of the revival of the Liberal Party. He was one of the victims of the unsavoury 'coupon' election of 1918, and his defeat was a symptom of the mortal blow struck at English public life by Lloyd George's coalition. He introduced his Bill, which came up for Second Reading on March 8th: it was a simple measure enacting that words importing the masculine gender, in all acts regulating the qualifications for voting, should include women, and that women should not be disqualified from voting by marriage. But immediately the Bill was debated, all the old difficulties reared their heads. The Prime Minister announced that the Government would leave the Bill to a free vote of the House without the intervention of the Whips, and he added that he himself would vote for it although he felt that it was weighted in favour of the well-to-do, and that it did not adequately affect working women. He meant that the proposals perpetuated and emphasized the property qualification for voting. The rejection of the measure was moved by two Liberal members, one of whom referred to the militants as 'a stage army'. He underlined the Prime Minister's remarks that the Bill was unduly harsh on working-class women, by arguing that a bill drafted on such lines would restore the balance of power to the upper and middle classes, which had been corrected by the Reform Bills of 1867 and 1884. Dickinson seems to have seen clearly that there was small likelihood of his bill passing, but he thought—in view of the fact that the whole question of the suffrage might have to be dealt with soon in a Reform Bill sponsored by the Government—that it was timely and wise to assert the principle that neither sex nor marriage should bar a person's right to vote. But although such expressions of principle may have had some value, the truth was that just as the women found their path to Westminster blocked by the police, so the House of Commons found it impossible to move out of their impasse. For no bill, enfranchising women, had the least chance of success unless it was a Government measure, supported by the discipline of the Whips. But so long as the Cabinet was divided, a Government measure was virtually an impossibility. However much Keir Hardie, Snowden and enlightened Liberal members might raise the matter at Question-time or by a private member's bill their well-intentioned efforts, apart from keeping the issue to the front of public attention, were of little consequence. Certainly they did nothing whatever to assuage the wrath of the militants.

Like many of its predecessors, Dickinson's Bill was talked out on March 8th. A fortnight later 'the stage army' organized a further raid on the House of Commons. Mrs. Despard being in Holloway, the procession was led by Lady Harberton. Like Mrs. Despard she was an Irish lady, and she was married to a scholarly peer who, during the First War, wrote a remarkable book called *How to lengthen our Ears*. She herself was, as Miss Sylvia Pankhurst calls her, a suffragist of the old school and, in the 1890's, had been a rather conspicuous champion of women's dress reform. She was leader of the Rational Dress movement. In 1898, wearing the emblem of the movement, which was a divided skirt, she had presented herself to the landlady of the Hautboy Hotel, Oakham—demanding refreshment. This the landlady refused— on the ground that her appearance might prove objectionable to other customers. The Cycle Touring Club sued the landlady at the Surrey Quarter Sessions, and in the course of the case, which was unsuccessful, Lady Harberton stated that she was in the habit of walking along Regent Street in her divided skirt. History does not record whether she was wearing this dress on the march from Caxton Hall to Westminster.

The reception of this deputation, which was broken and scattered, was not dissimilar from that of February 12th—except that mounted police were not used. The tussle lasted for several hours, since women, after being rebuffed by the police returned to Caxton Hall to rest before setting out to renew their efforts; to a group of these warriors, resting before another sortie, Christabel Pankhurst was heard to say: 'If possible seize the mace, and you will be the Oliver Cromwells of the twentieth century.' But they failed: although a party of working women from Yorkshire and Lancashire, disguised as sightseers, drove into Palace Yard, in a stylish waggonette, they got no further—thanks to the vigilance of the police. Both the Home Secretary and Lloyd George came out on to the street to watch the fighting. There were many arrests.

And now the scene of battle shifted. Some of the members of the constitutional societies—suffragists as they were called—began to question the wisdom of scuffling with policemen and they were supported in their doubts by even a few of the militants. London had certainly become 'Suffragette conscious', and the new task was to rouse the country. In those times there was a constant flow of by-elections, for the normal vacancies caused by death and ill-health were supplemented by each minister, on appointment to a ministry, having to submit to re-election. As soon as a by-election was well started, Mrs. Pankhurst or Christabel Pankhurst, and sometimes both, supported by as many as thirty campaigners, would descend on the constituency, hold a series of open-air meetings and generally alarm the candidates who, confronted by what are called 'uncertain factors' at election time, tend to become as nervous as a spinster in a haunted bedroom. Undoubtedly the members of the Union, partly because of their remarkable oratorical talents and partly because of the novelty of women speaking in the open, attracted crowds. They were not always respectfully treated, and at Uppingham Mary Gawthorpe had to speak through a shower of bullseyes, till finally a well-aimed china egg knocked her into the silence of a faint.

The election policy of the militants was uniform—'Keep the Government out'. This had been the policy of Parnell and the Irish in the 1880's, irrespective of whether the Government was sympathetic or not, and as has already been said that wayward character and his illogical disciples were an abiding influence on the strategy of the Pankhursts. Certainly it was a subtle point—almost too dialectical for the intelligence of the electorate—to fight that Party which was the friend. Mrs. Josephine Butler, as far back as the 1870's, had followed the same course when she was campaigning for the repeal of the Contagious Diseases Act and had had some success in Colchester where, almost single-handed, she had contributed to the decisive defeat of a Liberal Privy Councillor in a seemingly Liberal seat. But the policy was dangerous. The Liberals, whose benevolent support was essential for the passing of a woman's franchise bill, were incensed. They coined the description of Mrs. Pankhurst and her comrades as 'Toryettes'. Some Liberal supporters of the Union began to waver.

How far this by-election strategy was successful it is difficult to say. Grandiose claims were invariably made by the women. If the Liberal Government lost a seat, or if the Liberal majority was reduced, there were immediate whoops of joy, cries of victory, and martial trumpetings. An outline of these by-election results show that the losses of the Liberal Government (though heavy) were in line with the losses suffered by all governments elected with prodigious majorities. The experience of the Coalition Government after 1918 is here in point.

In fact the results suggest that the complications with Labour —rather than the efforts of the women—were the explanation for most of the Government losses. There is certainly no evidence that the suffragette tactics, though they were tiresome to Liberal candidates and alarming to the timid ones, had any real effect on the results. Still less is there any evidence that these tactics of the ladies had any effect on the Cabinet—which was the intention of using them, and their only justification.

The one year in which the intervention of Suffragettes seems at first glance to have affected the results was 1908. This was a bad year for the Government—in part explained by the pause with which it began owing to Campbell-Bannerman's prostration by illness in January, February and March—and three by-elections, in all of which the Union was exceptionally prominent, deserve a close examination.

The first was in mid-Devon, where the result was declared on 17th January 1908, and this is the only contest which lends some colour to the claims of the militants. Here there was a straight fight between Mr. C. R. Buxton, a distinguished candidate, fired with all the humanitarian zeal of his family, who was fighting to hold the seat against the same Conservative candidate who had been soundly beaten at the General Election two years earlier. The Liberals were so confident of victory that they had mourning cards printed: 'In fond and loving memory of the Tariff Reformers and Suffragettes who fell asleep in mid-Devon.' In fact Mr. Buxton was beaten, and the correspondent of the *Manchester Guardian*, commenting on the result, thought that the intervention of the women had affected the result. Some of the more ardent Devonshire Liberals evidently thought so too, for after the poll was declared, they seized Mrs. Pankhurst, who was escaping out of the back door of a shop, threw her in the mud and, but for the intervention of the police, would have placed her in a barrel and rolled her down the street of Newton Abbot.

The most remarkable of the three results was Peckham. Here a Liberal majority of over 2,000 was swept away and turned into a majority of 2,494 for the Conservative on March 24th. Carried away by enthusiasm for the cause the distinguished playright, Mr. St. John Ervine, wrote to a weekly journal: 'This Peckham election has been a revelation to me of the perfectly wonderful forces which the Women's Social and Political Union are bringing to bear on by-elections.'

The facts reveal less of these perfectly wonderful forces. The by-election at Peckham was one of the gayest but most illogical of all the pageants of Edwardian England. The scenes recalled

Mafeking, and drew the leisured classes with the alluring force of The White City or the fair on the ice in 1814 when the Thames was frozen. The explanation of this was that the brewers, stung to fury by the Liberal Licensing Bill of this year, which struck a heavy blow at the monstrous encouragement of intemperance by the liquor trade, intervened in the election on the kind of generous scale which recalled their ample vats, their strong dray horses and rotund bar-men. They poured money and beer into Peckham. Not to miss the fun the Coal Consumers' Council staged some coal vans, with sacks of coal, a large one painted with the name of the Conservative candiate and a small one with the name of the Liberal. The Conservative candidate, in a vivid phrase of the time, was floated to Westminster on beer. A curious side-line of the fight was that the election was won by a total abstainer.[1] But in spite of his personal habits his cause was carried to triumph by beer, and against the roaring of that compelling tide the pipings of the Union were not heard; their extravagant cries of 'Victory! Victory!' were not endorsed by the representatives of the newspapers reporting the Election.

Not dissimilar issues were carried north to Manchester where in the north-west division Mr. Winston Churchill, lately appointed to the Cabinet, was defending the seat against Joynson-Hicks and a bearded Labour candidate from Burnley. Hicks, later to become a prominent politician, was a strange mixture for a Manchester seat—a London solicitor who was an ardent motorist and a stubborn temperance reformer. But, as in Peckham, the victuallers, the coal men and the women hurled themselves into the fight behind their dour and slightly embarrassed champion—the Conservative candidate. The election also provided a picturesque amalgam in a weird society formed out of Women's Suffrage and liquor. This was called the Manchester Barmaids' Association, and was formed by Eva Gore-Booth and Esther Roper because certain aspects of the Liberal Licensing Act were thought to bear unfairly on the employment of women in public houses. The Barmaids' Association took premises in Corporation Street, and held a special meeting for their robust and cheerful protegées. A few days before the Election ended, the people of Manchester were

[1] Mr. (now Sir Henry) Gooch.

astounded to see a coach 'of the olden time' drawn by four white horses and covered with placards about the barmaids. On the box was the Countess Markievicz, who drove through the streets with the incomparable skill of one trained in the Irish school of equitation. At a packed meeting in the Coal Exchange the Countess said: 'I have come over from Ireland to ask men to vote for Joynson-Hicks because he is the only candidate who takes a straight and decent view on the barmaids' question.' At the huge rally of all parties, and their strange satellites, which was held in Stevenson Square on the eve of the poll, the arrival of the great coach stirred the maximum interest even at the expense of the Social and Political Union whose members were speaking from a lorry. While it remains to add that the citizens of Manchester preferred the egregious Hicks to Churchill—an act of disloyalty which he met with graceful courtesy—it cannot be said that the women contributed to the unfortunate result. In truth the game was up—when the members of the Union had to contend with brewers, coal merchants and Countess Markievicz—they were outshone. Perhaps the historian could argue that they were the pioneers of spectacular intervention at by-elections, but even the most resolute statistician would find it difficult to argue that— except in the case of mid-Devon—they had any substantial effect on the result.

XVII

A Split—The League is Formed

This by-election strategy though it was often expounded and defended by the leaders of the militants—Mr. Pethick-Lawrence wrote a short pamphlet on the subject in 1909— carried with it a more serious danger than the alienation of the Liberals. It defined and widened one of the gaps between the militants and the older societies. The strategy of these constitutionalists—as far back as the time of Miss Becker—had been to question each candidate, and then advise their sympathizers to vote for the one who gave the most favourable answer. This was generally the Liberal. In many cases the electorate in 1907 was offered the risible spectacle of the militants fighting a raging, tearing campaign against the Liberal on whose behalf a second group of ladies was working more quietly but no less wholeheartedly. In this year Mr. Bertrand Russell, encouraged by the constitutional societies, stood at a by-election in Wimbledon as a Women's Suffragist. He polled nearly 4,000 votes but, because he bravely asserted his belief in Liberalism, his cause was not espoused by the militants. All these developments help to explain the criticism of the leadership of the Union which became strident throughout this summer of 1907. In September personal difficulties, fired by criticism of the anti-Government policy of the Union, led to a combustion. The critics of the Union leadership concentrated attack on the constitution of the Union which Mrs. Pankhurst described as being 'not worth the paper it is written on'.[1] When the leaders of the Union had first come to London in 1906 some attempt had been made to draft a constitution. This

---

[1] Letter in possession of London Museum.

draft had been agreed at the Conference of members held in October 1906: by the constitution it was decided that the annual conference of members should be held each October, that there should be an Executive Council consisting of the officers and delegates from each branch (some forty branches of the Union had been formed outside London), and that there should be an emergency committee consisting of officers and organizers and two members appointed by the Conference. The Executive Council was to meet quarterly.

The critics complained that the Executive never met, and that in reality the Union was controlled by the Emergency Committee on which Mrs. Pankhurst and the paid organizers (two of whom were her daughters) were in the majority. Mrs. Pankhurst and her family were to some extent subsidized by the Union and, considering the circumstances in which they were left at Dr. Pankhurst's death and their services to the cause, such an arrangement was not unreasonable. But the critics argued that as the union was appealing to the public for £20,000, control of the Union should be more widely based. To these critics Mrs. Pankhurst answered swiftly and pugnaciously. At an Emergency Committee meeting on September 10th she announced that:

1. The committee would at once proceed to the election of a new committee.
2. The Conference would be abandoned.
3. The Constitution would be annulled.

In reply to the Secretary of the Union, Mrs. Despard, she announced that in future she would not have anyone on the Committee who was not in complete accord with herself. These sweeping changes were supported by Mrs. Pankhurst, Mrs. Pethick-Lawrence and the five paid organizers; Mrs. Despard and one other withdrew. Some valued members of the Union supported Mrs. Despard—notably Mrs. Billington-Greig[1] and Mrs. How-Martyn. These ladies decided to hold the October conference, and their revolt was in fact supported by a small majority of the branches. They adopted the name of the Union while Mrs. Pankhurst and her associates called themselves the National Women's

---

[1] Theresa Billington married in this year Frederick Louis Greig. On marriage husband and wife took the joint name of Billington-Greig.

Social and Political Union. The Conference was duly held and no doubt correctly asserted its right to 'the name, funds, property and literature now held by the National Union in Clement's Inn.' To enquirers Mrs. Pankhurst sent out a letter from Clement's Inn which contained some winged shafts against her old comrades, and a claim to omniscience, much beloved by later dictators of the twentieth century. 'At last we faced the whole thing. We foresaw every contingency and every possibility and, we decided to show fight . . . the seceding camp is made up of every dissatisfied and disappointed person and is held together by no bonds of union such as the bonds which unite the real workers.'[1] Like all who enjoy hurling the thunderbolts of political dictatorship, Mrs. Pankhurst could not resist blackguarding her opponents, depicting the difference between what she thought right and wrong with the harsh outline of a child's drawing. Although no precise account of the events after the Conference in October 1907 has been published, it seems reasonable to suppose that temperate councillors (probably Mr. and Mrs. Lawrence) came forward to keep the peace. Mrs. Despard and her associates renamed their organization the Women's Freedom League, while Mrs. Pankhurst and her followers reverted to the original title of the Union, dropping the prefix 'National'. Although women's organizations are sometimes regarded as addicted to squabbles and faction, both Union and League, after the first sharp engagement, distinguished themselves by their magnanimity. In particular the Women's Freedom League stressed the point that litigation would only waste time and money, and they stated their agreement with the Union by demanding enfranchisement 'this session' which was, of course, Mrs. Pankhurst's favourite slogan.

The League opened offices at 18 Buckingham Street off the Strand, subsequently moving to Robert Street between the Strand and the river. The Union remained in possession of the premises in Clement's Inn. That inn lies to the west of the Law Courts and, though greatly changed and modernized, it still possessed some of the tradition and atmosphere of its ancient dignity and attracted, both for residence and work, the type of independent citizen who likes to live near the heart of London

[1] Manuscript in the London Museum.

and within ear-shot of the roar of the Fleet Street presses. Mr. and Mrs. Pethick-Lawrence had a flat in Clement's Inn, and it was here that the Union had its office, later moving to the ground floor to offices formerly occupied by the Land Registry—Number 4—'the real home of the Militant Movement' as it was described by Annie Kenney.

The Union had no president or chairman—merely a committee with treasurer and secretary. After the split, the Committee consisted of four members and four officers. The Committee members were Mrs. Wolstenholme-Elmy, Miss Annie Kenney, Miss Mary Neal and Miss Elizabeth Robins. The officers were Founder and Honorary Secretary—Mrs. Pankhurst, Joint Honorary Secretary Mrs. Tuke, Organizing Secretary Miss Christabel Pankhurst and Honorary Treasurer Mrs. Pethick-Lawrence. The auditors were Messrs. Sayers and Wesson of 19 Hanover Square: the Bankers were still Messrs. Barclays of 19 Fleet Street. From Clement's Inn was edited *Votes for Women*: though occasionally rabid, this journal was conducted with force and judgment by Mr. Pethick-Lawrence, and it could be argued that its propaganda value to the movement was worth all the 'marches' and 'battles' which sprang from the lively mind of Mrs. Pankhurst. Although Mr. Lawrence never obtruded himself, the organization of the Union rested on his aptitude and foresight. Few political societies have ever been better organized. The telephone number was Holborn 2724 with three lines: the telegraphic address was Wospola London—a name, and possibly a number, which no doubt have their niche in the archives of Scotland Yard. Henceforth the Union was in reality a dictatorship, and on the horizon could be observed the dark clouds of sex war. The vote was becoming, as Sir Robert Ensor says, less desirable on its own account than as a symbol of sex equality. Nothing perhaps illustrates this better than a remark of Mrs. Pankhurst at one of the Caxton Hall meetings. A questioner had asked whether a march to Westminster was the wisest strategy at that juncture: with asperity Mrs. Pankhurst answered from the Chair: 'Be true to your own sex.'

The most obvious result of the split was that there were now two militant suffrage societies. But the League gradually drifted away from disorder to what might be called orderly militancy.

Mrs. Despard and her followers adopted a policy of what was described as 'constitutional militancy', the clearest example of this being tax resistance. Although Edmund Burke is often credited with being the first to evolve the maxim that those who are not represented should not be taxed, it was in fact an accomplished Lord Chancellor (Camden) who put into words this constitutional truth. At the time of the American War of Independence he said: 'Taxation and Representation are inseparably united. God hath joined them: no British Parliament can put them asunder.' The claim therefore that women who paid taxes should be represented in Parliament was not weak. As far back as 1870 two courageous Quakers in Bristol—the Misses Anne and Mary Priestman—had refused to pay their taxes till at last the authorities seized their dining-room chairs and put them up for auction. In 1904 Mrs. Dora Montefiore had carried this action a stage further by barricading her house, which was in Hammersmith, against the bailiffs. A considerable crowd collected to see these excitements, and she flung open a window upstairs and proceeded to lecture its members on the importance of women having the vote. Another lady was besieged in her home in Bromley for six months, and a refinement on the conventional resistance of income tax was made by Miss Octavia Lewen, the distinguished doctor, who resisted the charge for armorial bearings. Mrs. Despard's furniture constantly appeared in the auction rooms, and was generally bought in by a sympathizer. This kind of protest (though it was not ineffective) lacked the vividness of 'a march' or 'a battle' and almost inevitably the more dazzling tactics of the Union threw the League into the shadow.

The League also took an active part in by-elections against the Government, and here their policy was indistinguishable from that of the Union. After the Peckham by-election Churchill used a characteristically robust—and not unjust—phrase about the women allying themselves 'to the tail of a public-house made agitation'. It was not wise, and he was thereafter pursued by a prominent member of the League—Miss Maloney armed with a resounding muffin bell. She attempted to drown all his speeches in the open-air, and was given the soubriquet of La Belle Maloney.

In the excitements of the Bermondsey by-election in the autumn

of 1909, two members of the League adopted violent tactics
probably unpremeditated by their headquarters. Mrs. Chapin—
she was an American lady—and Miss Neilans dashed into two
booths on polling-day and poured some acid—pyrogallic acid
which was much used in photography—into the ballot boxes.
Mrs. Chapin was described in a contemporary women's journal as
'having seen much of our streets'; what she saw filled her with a
sense of uncontrollable indignation, and she performed her act of
militancy with the thoroughness of an angry American. A somewhat anaemic returning officer—no doubt long immured in the
temperate atmosphere of Government departments—was ill-
prepared for the rude blasts of Mrs. Chapin's onslaught. He
attempted to frustrate her attack, and in the tussle some of the
acid splashed his face. He immediately called out: 'Oh my eye—
Constable arrest this woman.' The ladies were tried at the Old
Bailey before Mr. Justice Grantham, whose antique opinions and
flamboyant personality made him (as may be well supposed) a not
very sympathetic judge in such a cause: he caused great offence by
saying that one of the accused was obviously enjoying herself in
court. Miss Neilans was sentenced to three months' imprisonment,
and Mrs. Chapin to four. The case caused some stir, but it seems to
have been a spontaneous attack, and not planned from headquarters.

But if the two Societies met as allies on the by-election field,
they were distinguished, as has been explained, by the more overt
militancy of the Union. And one further point of difference may
be remarked. Although the origins of the Union lay in Manchester,
its strength was London. Essentially it belonged to the metropolis.
At its peak, just before the 1914 war, it had thirty-four branches or
local unions in London alone; whereas the total number of its
branches outside London was only fifty-four. The League had
sixty-four provincial branches, and the non-militant societies
some hundreds. Israel Zangwill, the distinguished novelist,
speaking at Exeter Hall at the beginning of 1908, asserted that if
the women's suffrage movement had been 'only a metropolitan
exotic, a society luxury, it would soon pine away.' The Union—it
could be argued—was something of a London particular which
might have been dispersed by some sudden change in the climate

of popular feeling. The older societies—and even to some extent the League—gained strength from representing opinion outside London—opinion which was not swayed by the excitements of London.

And perhaps to demarcate the difference between itself and the League the Union became more martial. The new Secretary of the Union was Mrs. Mabel Tuke, who had spent much of her earlier life cantering across the Veldt, and on coming to England was a pioneer of the artful graces of Morris dancing. She generally started her letters to members of the Union 'Dear Soldier, in the Women's Army' or more briefly 'Dear Fellow-Soldier'. And with the assumption of these distinctly warlike airs the Union finally cut itself off from the Labour Party, whose fundamental belief in peace and brotherhood, accorded ill with the spectacle of these ladies calling down as their champion the great god Mars. And those who stayed within the bristling fortress of the Union tried to attach the stigma of socialism to their former comrades with the suggestion that the spirit of socialism had taken wing out of the Union into the League. Although Mrs. Despard was a member of the Independent Labour Party the allegation that the League was 'Laboury' (a strange adjective of the time) was not correct. But the effort of Mrs. Pankhurst to use Labour sympathies as a brand of opprobrium for their opponents is an interesting indication of the distance they had travelled from the days of Dr. Pankhurst and the Independent Labour Party.

The developments of September and October 1907 were a mortal blow to the strength of the Union—not perhaps obvious on the surface because it was to wax in ardour and fighting zeal—but henceforward its exertions (though they were to be intensified) were confined to a narrower field. Under the virtual dictatorship of the Pankhursts and of the Pethick-Lawrences, the Union became enormously more efficient, but it missed the driving power of the more diverse supporters of the early days. As was clearly illustrated in the case of Parnell there are tactical advantages in a political movement attaching itself to an individual, but the danger of narrowing the effectiveness of the movement stands out no less clearly. The members of the Union were not unlike Napoleon's Old Guard at Waterloo: those veterans were to fight with fortifying devotion but they lacked the feeling that the people of France were behind them—a feeling which had impelled them to victory in earlier days. In the women's movement adoration for the leader and complete subordination to her 'word of command' were not enough: they might lead to triumph but they could not lead to victory.

Nothing is easier (and few things more pointless) than to make a great man foolish by looking at some chance observation he has made and then, as it were, directing on it the wisdom of the years and smiling with superior scorn at its appearance after half a century. Yet some words of Keir Hardie so precisely sum up the feelings of a true democrat on this question that they deserve to be recalled. Writing in 1907 he said: 'We witness on every hand unchallenged male dominance, arrogant armaments, harsh and unfeeling administration of the law.' And then he added: 'with the incoming of the mother element into politics this would be gradually changed.' While it certainly would not be true that all early Labour men shared this point of view, the matters which Keir Hardie mentioned—militarism and legal harshness—pressed heavily on their supporters and some reflection of these discontents had been a source of strength to the women's cause. These new stirrings in politics and something of the fervour of Labour idealists had flowed into the women's movement through the Union: by drifting away from their labour moorings, as they did in 1907, the leaders of the Union not only lost some of their force but they were at the mercy of the wild gales of the ensuing years which were to drive some of them into the weirdest courses. With vehemence they contended for mastery in politics but they were guided by different principles and different prizes from those with whom they were battling. They were like a strange yachtsman who entered his boat not to win the cup but to foul his fellow competitors.

Of softening the masculine austerities of politics, of introducing the mother element they showed no sign: rather as 1908 advanced they seemed to introduce the tactics of the jungle—and to remind observers not so much of the mother as of the lioness. The same point is expressed more genially by Mr. Howard Spring, in his novel, *Fame Is The Spur*, when he writes of a militant suffragette: 'She turned into a fierce flame of a woman.'

XVIII

Clinging to their Chains

For the next two years the history of the women's suffrage movement is a tale of disorders and skirmishes, never perhaps on quite such a bloodthirsty scale as the language of the leaders suggested, but fought with courage, ingenuity and mounting tempers. With that formidable character in *Paradise Lost* Mrs. Pankhurst and her daughter seemed to cry: 'My sentence is for open war.'

The first shot was fired by Mr. Haldane—the Secretary of State for War—who was a great master of the vivid phrase, and his subsequent career was to remind politicians that striking expressions sometimes linger in the memory of critics and enemies to the doom of the speaker's career.[1] On 8th January 1908, at a meeting of the Scottish Liberal Council in Glasgow, he stated that, although ultimately the suffrage could not be withheld from women, the vexatious methods of the militants had injured the women's cause in Parliament. As the ensuing years were to emphasize, this statement was correct but he weakened his position as an Olympian and sympathetic commentator by adding 'men do not like being fought with pin-pricks: women might wage war but they should not do it with bodkins'. Friendly advice, coupled with such shafts, was not likely to mollify the little group in Clement's Inn.

Three weeks later King Edward VII, on a day of sparkling January sunshine, opened Parliament and it was noticed that he was received with more fervour along the route than at any time

---

[1] His statement that Germany was his spiritual home was used against him with deadly effect by his political enemies when war started in 1914.

since his accession. On the way, four members of the Women's Freedom League broke through the soldiers and police and very nearly reached the coach with a petition which they wished to present to the King. The League also marked the occasion by chartering Captain Spencer to fly his dirigible across London. The feminist balloonist, Miss Matters, armed with a hundredweight of leaflets, accompanied him. They travelled across the Capital from the Welsh Harp to Coulsdon Valley at a hieght of 2,500 feet, and Miss Matters made a not ineffective distribution of her literature over the Mall.

At Westminster the King narrowly escaped a worse experience. At the State opening of Parliament, a gallery on the way to the House of Lords is arranged for members of the public, who may view the procession, having been admitted by tickets distributed by peers or members of the House of Commons. The King and Queen, wearing their crowns and robes, move slowly hand-in-hand through this gallery, accompanied by little other protection than members of the Court, whose varied accomplishments do not always include the nimbleness necessary to protect their master from some importunate petitioner. The sovereign is lightly protected on these occasions, since all is governed by deference and good manners.

Those who only picture Philip Snowden as the rather tight-lipped exponent of orthodox Socialist finance may find difficulty in recalling that in his prime he was an audacious rebel, who delighted in shocking the conventional. As is shown by the following letter he took the somewhat rash step of giving his privileged ticket to the Secretary of the League.

10 Baron's Court Road,
West Kensington W.
Saturday, 25th January '08.

Dear Mrs. Martyn,

I am sending you a ticket of admission to the Royal Gallery of the House of Lords. It will admit one person, who will have no difficulty in handing her petition to the King. All I ask is that you will say to the Press, if they ask you how you got the ticket, that it was given by a friendly M.P. Mention no name.

I would suggest that you choose to do this thing some woman of gentle and refined appearance as well as intrepidity of spirit as such would receive more favour in the eyes of His Majesty. Why not your sweet self?

> With kindest greetings,
> P.S.

In fact the opportunity was missed perhaps because a diversion was caused, just before the King came, by the removal from the House of Lords of a somewhat bizarre gentleman who claimed to be a peer.

These attempts to petition the King were the work of the League, but the Union was naturally not idle, though its quarry may have been somewhat less exalted. A few days earlier, members of the Union attended in Downing Street, where it was known that Ministers were meeting to discuss the programme for the ensuing session. One of the women, Edith New, began to address the knot of women and sightseers: the police moved across to stop her: she had chained herself, with a nurse, to the area railings. Confronted with this first example of a baffling device, the police must have sent across to Scotland Yard for files and hack-saws. Miss New bravely continued to cry: 'Votes For Women'. In the confusion, a taxi-cab drove up and out of it dashed 'the General': eluding the police, entangled in Miss New, the nurse and the chains, she stormed into No. 10, and was ejected by some scandalized private secretaries and cabinet ministers. This was dismissed at the time as one of those eccentric demonstrations which marked the beginning of 1908; they grew more familiar as the year went on. Both Mrs. Drummond and Miss New, who each refused to enter into recognizances, were sent to prison for three weeks.

A few days after this—on January 24th—a successful meeting for women only was held in the Queen's Hall at the instigation of the Women's Liberal Federation.[1] This was followed by a deputation from the National Union of Women's Suffrage Societies to the Chancellor of the Exchequer—Mr. Asquith—on the day after the opening of Parliament. In his reply he made some points which were obvious though they could not be popular. He said

[1] Possibly the first occasion on which a political party has organized an exclusively women's meeting.

that even if the Cabinet had been unanimous, they could not initiate legislation on a matter of such constitutional importance unless it were first laid before the country at a general election: nor did he feel able to hold out hopes that the Government would grant facilities for the passing of a private member's bill on the subject. Probably he was right in thinking that a change of this magnitude needed to be discussed at a General Election: though in the future he was to be attacked for introducing Home Rule without any such mandate. The manœuvres in Parliament were largely conducted with an eye to publicity for the women's cause, and here the private member could play a part.

This last point entered the realm of practical politics when it became known that Henry Stanger had been lucky in the ballot and that his Bill would come up for Second Reading at the end of February. Stanger's Bill, which was identical with that introduced in the previous year by Dickinson, stirred the militants to great exertions—tempered by their experiences in 1907. As before, the beginnings of the parliamentary session were matched by the opening of a women's parliament which met in Caxton Hall on February 11th for three days. A deputation 'marched' from the Hall to carry a resolution to the Prime Minister at the House of Commons: on this occasion it was led by two Chelsea portrait painters—Miss Marie Naylor and Miss Florence Haig. At the same time an amusing ruse was attempted in Parliament Square. Two furniture pantechnicons, drawn by horses, were being slowly driven past the Houses of Parliament. When the second of these vehicles was opposite the door of the Stranger's Entrance, the back was opened and out leapt twenty-one determined ladies. They had unluckily forgotten that, after being closely confined in the dark van, they would be blinded on coming out into the light. Half of them rushed off in the wrong direction, and made a brave sortie against Westminster Abbey. A few penetrated the House, and many were arrested. This exploit should be known in history as the Battle of the Nieces since the captains of the van were three nieces of eminent men—Maud Joachim (niece of the violinist) and the Misses G. and M. Brackenbury, nieces of General Sir Henry Brackenbury, who had made a great name for himself, in a position where names are too often covered in obloquy, as

Director-General of Ordnance at the War Office during the Boer War.

Their forces somewhat depleted by fifty arrests, the members of the Convention were greatly cheered by the arrival on the last day—February 13th—of Mrs. Pankhurst fresh from a by-election campaign in South Leeds. (The figures showed a catastrophic fall in the Liberal majority compared with the General Election two years previously, though the Liberals held the seat: but the result seemed to be accounted for by the Conservative having taken a large slice of the Labour vote, an event for which the ladies could hardly claim the credit.) But whatever the effect on the voters of Mrs. Pankhurst's visit to the impressionable city of Leeds, she could look back on a triumphant open-air meeting on Hunslett Moor, said to be attended by 100,000 people,[1] whose shouts were still ringing in her ears as she slipped into her chairman's seat at Caxton Hall. Though she was still limping as a result of her rough handling by the Devonshire Liberals she insisted, amid a good deal of excitement and emotion, on herself leading yet another deputation to the Prime Minister at the House of Commons. 'The General' succeeded in inducing the driver of a passing dog-cart to give her crippled leader a ride, but the driver was stopped, and Mrs. Pankhurst ordered out by the police. She struggled forward on foot, supported by four other women—their arms linked. She was arrested. On the following day she was sentenced to find sureties in £20 for twelve months' good behaviour or six weeks in prison. She chose the latter. In her own memoirs she described her feelings after she had changed into prison clothes, and the cell door was closed: 'My first sensations when the door was locked upon me were not wholly disagreeable. I was desperately weary, for I had been working hard, perhaps a little too hard, for several strenuous months. . . . I was glad to throw myself on my hard prison bed and close my eyes.'

Though solitary confinement may be a harsh punishment for children, it is not always unwelcome to adults. Miss May Sinclair makes the point clearly in her novel to which reference has already

---

[1] Although the concourse on Hunslett Moor might seem at variance with the suggestion earlier, that the suffragettes did not substantially affect by-election results, it will be appreciated that they invariably roused the maximum curiosity.

THE CAT AND MOUSE ACT

PASSED BY THE LIBERAL GOVERNMENT

9. 'Cat and Mouse'—a W.S.P.U. impression of Mc-Kenna's Act

10. 'The Modern Inquisition'—a W.S.P.U. impression of forcible feedin

been made. Her heroine had marched on one of these attacks on the House of Commons; and after she had been arrested and imprisoned, she says: 'After the crowds of women, after the meetings and speeches, the endless talking and the boredom, the cell was like Heaven. Thank God it's always solitary confinement. The Government doesn't know that if they want to make prison a deterrent they'll shut us up together.' Mrs. Pethick-Lawrence has also confessed that she experienced times of 'great mental peace and happiness in the solitude of the prison-cell'.

When the time came for Mrs. Pankhurst's release, the Governor asked her if she had any complaints. She answered politely that she had no complaints of him or of the wardresses and then fiercely added: 'Only of this prison, and all of men's prisons. We shall raze them to the ground.' Undoubtedly the treatment of women in prisons was lagging behind the humanitarian feelings of the twentieth century, and the arrival of well-to-do prisoners had the effect of drawing attention to abuses and hardships. Though it is only a side-line of the suffrage story, the improved treatment of women prisoners, which resulted from the indignation of these 'political' prisoners was an important chapter in prison history. H. G. Wells, in a characteristically truculent remark, thought that the sole achievement of militancy was that it led to improved conditions in prison for the female malefactor. But perhaps the feeling of these ladies cut deeper than he thought. It was not only the indignities of prison life which struck them: it was rather the system's indifference to the individual, the bitter knowledge that men made the laws and laid down the prison rules—feelings that struck Mrs. Pankhurst forcefully when she heard the cries of a woman giving birth to a child in the prison hospital. And Miss Evelyn Sharp, with the sensibility and imagination of a perceptive writer, puts the pathos of these matters with force and subtlety; she is describing how she went to see a militant friend in Holloway; a wardress walked across the yard with her, and turned and said: 'It's pretty here in summer.'

The second reading of the Stanger Bill was held on February 28th while Mrs. Pankhurst was still in Holloway. The course of the debate need not detain the reader, since it was marked by the same arguments and, from the opposition, a repetition of ancient follies which had characterized all the previous debates. Mr. Snowden remarked that it was the twenty-third debate that had taken place on this issue since Mill first raised it in 1867. Sir John Rees—the Liberal Member for Montgomeryshire—was in the process of trying to talk out the Bill with such elegant observations as this: 'Petticoat is a good thing, and government is a good thing, but it does not follow that petticoat government is a good thing.' He was interrupted by Lord Robert Cecil—a distinguished member of a family which invariably showed great sympathy for the women's cause—who moved that the question be put. This motion the Speaker accepted: and the figures were 271 for Mr. Stanger's Bill and only 92 against.[1]

[1] In the majority for the Bill were 218 Liberals (with some Labour included), 32 Unionists and 21 Irish Nationalists: 53 Liberals (with some Labour) voted against, and were supported by 27 Unionists and 12 Irish Nationalists. The small number of Unionists voting is noticeable.

XIX

Pageantry on the Streets of London

But amid the ancient arguments and froth of a woman's suffrage debate there was a curious contribution from Herbert Gladstone. He was, as has been said, a supporter of the female franchise, and he was possibly trying to wean the women away from militancy to more peaceful demonstrations. But his speech reads almost like a tocsin to Clement's Inn, and sounds strangely from the Home Secretary who was pursuing the militants with vigour. 'Comes the time'—he said—'when political dynamics are far more important than political argument. . . . Men have learned this lesson and know the necessity for demonstrating the greatness of their movement and for establishing that *force majeure* which actuates and arms a Government for effective work.'

Gladstone spoke in February 1908, and by mid-summer the women, both militant and constitutional, had taken him at his word and given a demonstration in the centre of London which was calculated to touch the fancy of even the most worldly Edwardian. For one of the contradictions of that comfortable epoch was that in the midst of affluence, in the steady pursuit of success, the Edwardians, in spite of all kinds of over indulgence, had a weird hunger for the picturesque. This showed itself in a remarkable spate of pageants organized by Mr. Louis N. Parker. He passed from St. Albans to Coventry, from Bury St. Edmunds to the Isle of Wight, from Chelsea to Cheltenham and from Winchester to Pevensey: at a wave of the Parker wand county ladies strolled among ruins as medieval princesses, mayors thundered across wet meadows disguised as crusaders, the rotund figures of Edwardian gentry did not look amiss as dignitaries of monastic life while burgesses tried to feel comfortable masquerading as Hengist and Horsa. These pageants of 1907 and 1908 were gay and harmless—a little battered by rain in the first year and occasionally giving rise to local feuds—best revealed perhaps by an icy little sentence in the 'Annual Register' about the Coventry pageant: 'Disputes as to the costume of Lady Godiva were eventually settled.'

Taking advantage of this fleeting gala spirit, the Suffragists staged an impressive spectacle on June 13th. From a starting-point on the Embankment 13,000 women proceeded along Pall Mall, up St. James's Street and down Piccadilly and Knightsbridge to the Albert Hall. The predominant feature of the spectacle was a display of innumerable banners—worked and embroidered with all the art and emphasis of the early twentieth-century needle-woman. Some were blazoned with Boadicea, Joan of Arc and Queen Elizabeth: and it is gratifying to record that one banner carried the effigy of the immortal Becker. Close to this banner walked those who had been her comrades—the aged Emily Davies, Dr. Garrett Anderson and Mrs. Fawcett. At the head of the professional women and graduates walked Mrs. Ayrton—wife of the eminent electrical engineer and herself an illustrious student of Girton, who had made a particular study of sand ripples. There was a special section for writers, who walked beneath a splendid piece of embroidery named with a title (which would have delighted Parker)—'The Scrivener's Banner'. The cockney onlooker was not slow to call out: 'Here come them Scavengers.' Beatrice Harraden, Elizabeth Robins and Evelyn Sharp marched in this section. After them came artists, actresses, nurses, gardeners, typists, shop assistants, factory workers and—rather emphatically last—home makers. Although members of the Union took part in this procession, since many of the rank and file belonged to more than one suffrage society, the Union itself did not. On the other hand the League did, its officials and members walking immediately behind the home makers, and Mrs. Despard was one of the speakers at the Albert Hall.

The principal procession formed behind a beautifully worked banner which culminated in the blazing word 'Rectitude'; at its head walked Mrs. Pankhurst, dressed as always in impeccable taste, side by side with Mrs. Wolstenholme Elmy, looking maybe a shade theatrical with her silver ringlets, a long flowered dress stretching to the pavement, and carrying a handsome bouquet.

The demonstration was successful and striking, but it was totally eclipsed by the display of *force majeure* organized by the Union ten days later. For their demonstration they chose Hyde Park and Sunday, June 21st, for like the Labour Party, from which they sprang, they saw the propaganda value of the Day of Rest. The preparations were carried forward with spirit: on the Thursday before the 21st 'the General' hired a motor boat and, equipped with a megaphone, moored herself for some time opposite the Terrace of the House of Commons where the members were enjoying tea. 'Come to the Park on Sunday' she cried, salting her invitation with such inducements as; 'There will be no arrests.' 'You shall have plenty of police protection.' Inspector Scantlebury, who was responsible for maintaining order in the precincts of the House of Commons, launched a police boat to attack this marauder, but 'the General' sailed away in triumph.

The 21st was blessed by fine weather. Special trains were run into London, and following the example of the parliamentary reformers in the 60's, the organizers arranged for seven processions to converge on the Park from different parts of London. The Chelsea contingent was dressed entirely in white—not perhaps the quarter of London in which the onlooker would most readily look for innocence or the emblem of a blameless life. There was less needlework than in the procession of the Constitutionalists but perhaps more colour—for this was the first occasion that the suffragette colours—purple, white and green were used—principally as scarves and sashes. (White and green were the constant colours of all the suffrage societies: purple was the distinguishing addition of the Union.)

On arrival the crowd was addressed by leaders of the Union from a number of impromptu platforms. At the end—about 5 o'clock in the evening—a bugle sounded, and then the Resolution was put which called upon the Government to give votes to women without delay. This was followed by another bugle and the shrill cry, thrice repeated—'Votes For Women'. Miss Sylvia

Pankhurst has described how she was almost startled, on getting to her lorry, by the crowd spread out around her: 'Over the whole of the area there was to be seen not a single blade of grass.' On the following morning *The Times* published a long descriptive account of the gathering, and calculated the number of people attending as more than half a million. The writer added: 'Like the distances and numbers of the stars, the facts were beyond the threshold of perception.'

Scanning the heavens, like our fathers of old, for signs and wonders we may well ask ourselves 'What did this gigantic gathering portend?' When it is remembered that about 70,000 people attended the great Reform meeting in the Park in 1867, which was thought to have exercised an irresistible pressure on the House of Commons, it could surely be argued that the reluctant Members of Parliament would have yielded before an orderly crowd seven times as large as that of 1867. But the Government, considering the reports of the meeting, which came in from the police, can have had little difficulty in deciding that much of the crowd was drawn to the Park with the hope of seeing some fun on a summery afternoon. Mrs. Pethick-Lawrence had spent £1,000 in advertising the meeting, with a plan of the exact site in Hyde Park, on all the principal hoardings in London and the provincial capitals. The crowd flocked to Hyde Park animated not so much by a burning sense of women's wrongs as by a listless desire to be amused by the fun of the fair. Mrs. Pankhurst and 'Chrissie'—as the London crowd called her daughter—were in the eyes of that crowd not so much the eloquent exponents of an ideal, as the rivals of a purveyor of cheap pills or of a witty salesman of a remnant of bombazine. The matter is put beyond speculation by this letter from Helen Fraser[1] one of the speakers at the meeting.

'The crowd was about half a million—the day was lovely . . . at the platforms there was much rowdyism—Christabel's, Mrs. Pankhurst's and Mrs. Martel's.[2] At mine we had a splendid hearing and had the shout also. [She must mean by this the cry of Votes For Women which followed the bugle at the end.] It seemed to

[1] She had been organizer of the Union in Glasgow.

[2] An Australian from New South Wales who had stood as a parliamentary candidate after the women were given the Commonwealth franchise in 1902. She was very active in the Union at this time.

me however that the vast mass of people were simply curious—
not sympathetic—not opposed—simply indifferent.'[1] And H. W.
Nevinson put the same point with characteristic forcefulness
when he wrote: 'If the Liberal Government had burnt one of the
leaders alive the audience "would have shrieked with indignant
delight and gone home to tea." ' Of course the day was a triumph,
but was it a triumph for the female franchise? Was it not even
possible that the orderly but picturesque 13,000 were a greater
force majeure than the half million sparring alongside the rostrums
in Hyde Park?

And great as these demonstrations were they coincided with a
weakening of the women's support within the Government. After
some weeks of increasing physical weakness the Prime Minister,
Campbell-Bannerman, resigned. Shrewd and benign, but surprisingly Radical in his views, he had been acceptable to the
Labour and extremist supporters of the Liberal Government, and
there was no warmer advocate of the women's cause in the
Liberal Cabinet. On March 27th he sent for Asquith and told him
that he was a dying man and added: 'You have been a wonderful
colleague, so loyal, so disinterested, so able. You are the greatest
gentleman I have ever met.' A week later Campbell-Bannerman
resigned, and Asquith formed a new Government. The change
could not be welcome to the women's suffrage agitators, and
henceforth their attacks on the Liberal Government were accentu-
ated by much abuse of the new Prime Minister personally.

Although a study of Asquith's character is beyond the scope of
this book, it is important to emphasize that his move to 10 Downing Street sharpened the temper of the struggle. It was not only
that a sympathizer in the person of Campbell-Bannerman had
made room for an enemy, but Mr. Asquith's particular gifts—his
critics called them 'the lawyer's mind'—made him especially anti-
pathetic to women pursuing their goal with fervour but without
logic. With the courtesy of the true intellectual he tended to con-
vey his meaning obliquely—often helped along with a shaft of
wit—rather than by bawling a blunt negative. This gave rise to
some misconceptions and accusations against him. Once when he
was still Chancellor of the Exchequer he received a deputation

---

[1] Manuscript in London Museum.

from members of the older suffrage societies. Miss Isabella Ford expatiated on the views of working women, finally offering to take Mr. Asquith on a tour of meetings of working women in Leeds. After a pause Asquith was heard to say: 'The prospect does not greatly attract me.'

He brought to public life gifts of intellectual fastidiousness which are as rare as they are valuable. The idea of converting a human being's reason by parades, marches and fighting the police was incomprehensible to him. The more the women marched, the less his reason marched with them. Therefore the work of the militants strengthened his opposition to the vote. The women pursued him with much shrill invective—some of which was not without its effect in damaging his standing in the country—but he remained like a rock, which by reason of its natural formation, repels the froth and fury swirling round it.

XX

Inside Bow Street Police Court

This sharper war with Asquith and the Liberal Government was signalized by a brisk engagement on June 30th. After a meeting in Caxton Hall, the leaders of the Union marched to Westminster and endured a prolonged evening scuffle with the police. Not unnaturally the women who faced this unpleasant ordeal were prone to exaggerate the ferocity of the police and to translate events into words which are more fittingly kept for the carnage of a real battlefield. An unpleasant development on June 30th was the intervention of louts—robust Edwardian youths sturdier, more virile and less unpleasant than their imitators fifty years later—who rushed into the fray with the zest of a Rugby football scrum. These mercenaries were sometimes mistakenly regarded by the women as plain clothes policemen. The clearest— and one of the least passionate—accounts of what those fights were like has been written by Miss Kitty Marion. She has described it in these words—

'The police, including plain-clothes men, posing as the hostile crowd, broke our ranks by shouldering in and pushing us away in every direction, and as each of us tried to proceed singly towards the House, petition in hand, two and three policemen, one on each side taking us by the arm and shoulder, quite unnecessarily pinching and bruising the soft under-arm, with the third often pushing at the back, would run us along a little distance and fling us, causing most women to be thrown to the ground unless they were big and strong enough, like me, to lean well back while being run.'[1]

[1] Miss Marion's manuscript diary in the London Museum.

Among the spectators who watched the struggle from Palace Yard were Gladstone himself, Rosebery and Lloyd George. They were no doubt anxious to see for themselves how the police discharged their difficult task. Meanwhile, taking advantage of the general concentration of attention on Westminster the intrepid Edith New, accompanied by Mrs. Leigh, went to Downing Street and broke some of the Prime Minister's windows with stones. 'It will be bombs next time' one of them genially observed.

As the blazing summer of 1908 faded in the margin of winter the temper of the public rose. Unemployment grew formidably: parades of unemployed were held: there were hunger marches: a Prince of the Blood was hooted in Glasgow. Taking advantage of these disturbed feelings, the Union held a meeting in Trafalgar Square on the Sunday before the opening of Parliament and appealed for support from the public 'to help the suffragettes to rush the House of Commons.' Handbills were distributed announcing the time for this scrimmage as 7.30 on Tuesday evening, October 13th. The police, armed with ominous notebooks, attended in force at the meeting. A warrant for the arrest of Mrs. Pankhurst, Christabel Pankhurst and 'the General' was issued from Bow Street by the magistrate, Mr. Curtis Bennett, on the grounds that they had been guilty of conduct likely to provoke a breach of the peace.

Mr. H. G. Wells writes in *The New Machiavelli* that there had been 'a pretty deliberate' appeal from the Union leaders to the unemployed to join forces with them. No doubt this was why the authorities took a serious view of these developments in the autumn of 1908. The ladies did not at once surrender to the summons, and attended a Caxton Hall meeting where they were received, as Mrs. Pankhurst intended, with ringing cries of personal devotion. Surrendering later in the day, fixed by Clement's Inn for rushing the House of Commons, they spent the night in the somewhat dingy cells attached to Bow Street. In answer to Mrs. Pankhurst's complaints to friends in the House of Commons, a burly colonel, who sat for one of the Aberdeen divisions and had all the joviality which even to this day seems to characterize members of Parliament from those parts, came at once to see her in her cell: Colonel Murray immediately ordered three splendid dinners to be sent across from the Savoy which the ladies enjoyed together, by the light of wax candles, in the matron's room.

Meantime considerable crowds had gathered at Westminster controlled by a massive force of police. Mrs. Pethick-Lawrence, who was in charge of the meeting at Caxton Hall, sent forth a squad of eleven women to march to the House of Commons with the words: 'Oppose with spiritual force the material force arrayed against you.' The resulting 'battle' was similar to those earlier in the year, and it was watched by several members of the Government including Mr. Lloyd George and his youngest child.[1] Later in the evening Keir Hardie's secretary, Mrs. Travers Symons, who was allowed inside the Houses of Parliament in the course of her duties, acting on impulse rushed into the Chamber and advanced on the Speaker calling on members to deal with the women's question first. She was removed by an attendant.

On the next day, October 14th, the magistrate agreed to an adjournment of the case of the three leaders for a week, and the trial opened on October 21st. On that day the proceedings began with a remarkable personal triumph for Christabel Pankhurst, since the prisoners had successfully subpoenaed Lloyd George and Herbert Gladstone to give evidence. Christabel Pankhurst had, it will be remembered, read law and she examined her distinguished witnesses with ability. It transpired that Lloyd George had been seen at the Trafalgar Square meeting—again accompanied. by his youngest child. They had stood and listened for a short time to Mrs. Pankhurst speaking. Christabel Pankhurst examined him closely on his understanding of the word 'rush' in the leaflet, which had been pressed into his hands at the meeting. Reinforced by *Chambers's Dictionary* she suggested that it really only meant to demand eagerly or do something in a hurry, and when Lloyd George seemed reluctant she asked the magistrate, quoting Taylor on Evidence, whether she might not treat him as a hostile witness. Coming on to the evening of the opening of the session she said that she understood that Lloyd George had walked, with his youngest child, from Downing Street to the House of Commons. (Lloyd George as Chancellor of the Exchequer was then living at 11 Downing Street.) She asked him whether he had thought it

[1] Now Lady Megan Lloyd George.

safe to bring her out. 'Certainly', he replied. 'She was very amused.' She then closed her examination by taunting him with allusions to the Welsh graveyard case. (In his ardent, early days Lloyd George had advised a Nonconformist family to break open the locked gate of a church cemetery and bury their dead there in defiance of the clergyman.) Lloyd George stubbornly (and correctly) maintained that he had not incited the crowd to violence.

Mrs. Pankhurst followed her daughter, and fastened on what was perhaps the weak point in the Chancellor of the Exchequer's case—namely taking his daughter to watch events, which the Government thought might develop into a dangerous breach of the peace. Mrs. Pankhurst: 'You took her out to be amused by the sight of the crowd?' Lloyd George: 'She wanted to see the crowd and I took her out.'

Miss Pankhurst then called Marie Brackenbury—the landscape painter—and asked her whether Mr. Horace Smith, the elderly police-court magistrate at Westminster, when sentencing her for her part in the disturbances earlier in the year, had said: 'I am doing what I was told to do.' The magistrate snapped out to Christabel Pankhurst: 'You must not put that question.' But Marie Brackenbury's emphatic statement that Horace Smith had used these words, was clearly audible. Christabel Pankhurst then called the Home Secretary. The opening part of his examination was occupied with an attempt by her to put the Horace Smith point to Gladstone, with its obvious implication that the magistrates were only acting on the instructions of the Home Office. Curtis Bennett successfully thwarted this. She then turned to Gladstone, observed that he had watched the demonstration from Palace Yard, and asked if he felt afraid. She finally took him through his speech in the House of Commons about *force majeure* sentence by sentence, closing her examination with the ringing challenge: 'Why don't you give us the vote then?'

The defendants then called other witnesses who treated the matter with the right degree of banter. Miss Evelyn Sharp, who was on the deputation to the House of Commons on October 13th, said that she had eluded the largest policeman she had ever seen in her life, and that the whole proceedings had reminded her of a rush at hockey. But if these events were to be reduced to the terminology of the hockey field, the police might have retorted that the tactics of the ladies had something in common with the bully. The irrepressible Colonel Murray gave evidence that the crowd in Trafalgar Square was composed of exactly the type of men and women who go to church on Sunday in Scotland.

Then Christabel Pankhurst made her speech. She started by a long tirade against Horace Smith; Curtis Bennett, with that amused tolerance which is often a characteristic of members of the Bar when their professional friends are under attack, allowed her to say that Horace Smith had settled in conjunction with the Government that Miss Brackenbury was guilty 'before the evidence was heard. . . . The Liberal Government has outdone the monarchs of old time in their attempt to corrupt the fountain of British justice'. Horace Smith who had 'forgotten his duty to us, to the public and to his profession deserves to be hounded out of civilized society'. And lest Curtis Bennett should tend to feel complacent, she referred to his court, Bow Street, as 'the Star Chamber of the twentieth century'. Later she pointed her finger at Mrs. Travers Symons, who was a spectator in Court, and said: 'She is the only woman who succeeded in rushing the House of Commons, and she has got away scot-free.' She pointed out that the crowd on October 13th was not so violent as the press of people, which had assembled outside St. Margaret's, Westminster, to watch the wedding of Mr. Winston Churchill in the previous month.

Mrs. Pankhurst then followed with a remarkably eloquent and effective speech. She began by saying that she had married a man 'whose wife I was and also his comrade in all his public work'. Saying that she had lived longer than her daughter and could therefore look at the question more broadly, she left the debating points which Christabel had made, and ended with a moving appeal to the magistrate—'We want you to use your power to decide this case—but we want you, sir, if you will, to send us to trial in some place more suitable for the trial of political offenders than an ordinary police-court. I do not know what you will do: I do not know what your powers are: but I do think, speaking as a woman to a man, I do say deliberately to you—I think your experience has been a large one—I come here not as an ordinary law-breaker.

We are here not because we are law-breakers: we are here in our effort to become law makers.'

In giving judgment Curtis Bennett referred to the speeches of the defendants as 'able'. He referred to the famous case of *Wise* v. *Dunning*[1] as absolutely deciding the question of the jurisdiction of his court to try political cases. He bound the defendants over, and in default he sentenced Mrs. Pankhurst and 'the General' to three months and Miss Pankhurst to ten weeks. They naturally all refused to be bound over. They were not given First Division Treatment. 'The General' was released because of ill-health after nine days, and Mrs. Pankhurst and her daughter were both released a few days before Christmas.

The case inevitably was greatly publicized. Illicit photographs were taken of the magistrate and of the cabinet ministers in the witness box; from one of them the faithful Mr. Pethick-Lawrence can be seen sitting immediately behind the prisoners in the dock.

Max Beerbohm visited Bow Street during the case and wrote a memorable description of the clash between Christabel Pankhurst and Lloyd George. He emphasized that she was a most accomplished comedian: '. . . do not suspect me of a cheap sneer. The description is but a part of the truth about her. But it is the part with which I, as a dramatic critic, am mainly concerned. She has all the qualities which an actress needs, and of which so few actresses have any. . . . Her whole body is alive with her every meaning. . . . As she stood there with a rustling sheaf of notes in one hand, the other hand did the work of 20 average hands. But "work" is a dull word for those lively arabesques with which she adorned the air of the police court. . . . As she stood there, with her head inclined merrily to one side, trilling her questions to the Chancellor of the Exchequer, she was like nothing so much as a little singing bird born in captivity.' Max Beerbohm also thought that Herbert Gladstone came better off from the ordeal than did Lloyd George 'whose Celtic fire burned very low: and the contrast between the buoyancy of the girl and the depression of the statesman was almost painful. Youth, and an ideal on the one hand; and, on the other, middle age and no illusions left over.'

[1] The result of disorderly scenes in a Roman Catholic area of Liverpool where a 'No Popery' agitator had attempted to hold meetings.

And as she captivated the mind of the wise and witty writer, so her punishment commanded the respect and sympathy of the newspapers. The Liberal *Daily Chronicle*—at that time especially sensitive to any whispers from Lloyd George—regretted that the magistrate had imposed such a severe sentence. A more resounding protest came from the defendant's old comrades—now the Women's Freedom League. On October 28th, a week after the conclusion of the case at Bow Street, while Members of Parliament were discussing the Licensing Bill the proceedings were suddenly interrupted by cries of 'Votes for Women' close behind the brass grille of the Ladies' Gallery. Attendants dashed forward, and found that three ladies Miss Helen Fox, Miss Muriel Matters,[1] and Miss Tillard had securely chained themselves to the grille, and padlocked the chains with yale locks of formidable proportions. The officials of the House of Commons could do nothing except put their hands over the ladies' mouths, who were none the less occasionally able to emit little squeaks of 'Votes For Women'. Reinforcements were summoned, and it was decided that the only thing to do was to remove the grille with the ladies attached, in a manner somewhat recalling Samson, who when involved in a difficult situation with a lady, removed the doors of the city. Simultaneously there were disturbances in the Lobby and round the Cœur de Lion statue.

There was also a steady stream of protest about the treatment of the three ladies—especially the point about First or Second Division treatment—in the House of Commons. Perhaps the most effective came from Swift MacNeill, an Irish Protestant member of long standing, with all the fiery irresponsibility of his party, who had once assaulted the cartoonist Harry Furniss in the Lobby for what he deemed an insulting picture. He told the Home Secretary that he had delayed his holiday in Ireland because he could not have enjoyed it without raising the treatment of Mrs. Pankhurst first. He had to be satisfied with the information that the ladies were treated to a rather more comfortable chair than was customary for prisoners in the Second Division.

But to us looking backwards there is a certain melancholy—a

---

[1] She was later to float over the House of Commons in a dirigible painted 'Votes For Women'.

golden glint of autumn—about these Bow Street triumphs. Although the publicity was immense, and although even the most stubborn foes applauded the ingenuity and eloquence of mother and daughter, and although everywhere people contrasted the sincerity and courage of the three women with the narrow cell and broad arrow of their treatment by the authorities they were committed to a course which was fatal. For each of their escapades —disturbances at meetings, intervention at by-elections, marches to Westminster in defiance of the police and now the use of courts of justice for propaganda—achieved publicity but exhausted it. They could only advance by means of fresh and ever more venturesome clashes with law and order. And what would be the consequence of these on public opinion?

The answer to that question is not readily given. The militant tactics, in welding together the zealots of the movement, in illustrating the truth—as did the spectacle of an early Christian being thrown to a hungry lion—that there is strength through suffering, were of the greatest service to the Social and Political Union. But the fact that their exploits attracted enormous crowds did not mean that public opinion was with them any more than the curious Romans, watching the lion enjoying its Christian dinner, were in sympathy with the victim.

11. Funeral of Emily Wilding Davison; the cortege crossing Piccadilly Circus

12. Funeral of Emily Wilding Davison; the coffin at Victoria Station

XXI

'The Women of England are Clamouring Outside'

When the case at Bow Street came to an end, fifteen months lay ahead before the first General Election of 1910. Before considering the fiercer strategy of the militants in this important period for the Government, the reader should not skim over certain developments in the larger battle of politics, which explain why woman's franchise was increasingly elbowed to the back. After a bad year in 1908—partly explained by the change of Premier and partly by the unpopularity of the Government's attack on the Drink Trade—the position of the Liberals strengthened in 1909. Asquith—and as Chancellor he had been regarded as a somewhat austere and aloof personality—won not only the admiration of his following in the House of Commons but their affection. Now that he was in the first place he showed a warmth of feeling, with which he had not been credited. The parliamentary correspondent of the *Daily Express* put the matter succinctly—'As he led his big army, he won them more and more as men'. 1909 saw the introduction of Lloyd George's 'people's budget'. From the peaks of taxation among which mankind moves in the 1950's the proposals of Lloyd George look as comfortable and uneventful as the smoke rising from the cooking of Sunday dinners in a village in the valley. But they were assailed with a ferocity not known in English politics since the Reform Bill. The reason for this was that they included a super-tax for the first time, and also a 20 per cent tax on the unearned increment of land value—a blow at the lucky higgler who happened to own a few

fields on the fringe of a town, as well as the large landowner. Mr.
Balfour set the tone for Conservative attack, by remarking in the
House of Commons that the Budget was known as a democratic
budget; he then added: 'Let them not associate democracy with
robbery.' In the autumn the House of Lords, in defiance of the
Constitution under which they were excluded from tampering
with money bills, rejected the Budget as they had rejected the
Government's Licensing Bill. Throughout 1909 political tempers
grew hot—fired by a series of coruscating attacks on peers and
Conservatives by Lloyd George and Churchill, and by a more
venomous and less scrupulous attack on the Liberals from the
newspapers owned by Lord Northcliffe. The flames were fanned
by the obvious extinction of a part of the huge Liberal majority
when the election came, and the resulting confidence of the Conservatives. Amid this rousing hullaballoo the cries of the women
were scarcely heard.

They valiantly continued to concentrate attack on Asquith,
though Churchill and Lloyd George also came under fire. On 17th
September 1909 Asquith was speaking in Birmingham, where the
streets were barricaded against the women. The Prime Minister
showed courage in going to Birmingham which, even in the
Liberal triumphs of 1906, was solidly Conservative, and the anti-
Liberal bias of that city—coupled perhaps with memories of nine
years earlier when the patriotic bloods of Birmingham had driven
Lloyd George to escape their fury in the guise of a police constable
—led to extraordinary precautions—including the erection of a
large tarpaulin over the glass roof of the Bingley Hall where the
Prime Minister was to speak. From time to time the audience of
10,000 was startled by a sound of crashing: outside it was found
that two courageous women, Mrs. Leigh and Miss Charlotte
Marsh, had climbed on to the roof of an adjoining building and
were removing the slates and throwing them at the Bingley Hall.
A vain attempt to dislodge the ladies with fire hoses was made,
and the police had eventually to capture them, like any burglar,
after a spirited chase over the roof tops. Lloyd George, in his
celebrated speech in the great hall of the 'Edinburgh Castle' in
Limehouse on July 30th—the speech which contained the immortal apostrophe 'Ah! the Dukes! They all knew the Dukes,

especially in the East End!'—had to contend with much suffra-gette disturbance at the beginning. He had caused great offence on a previous occasion, when his meeting was interrupted, by calling to the stewards: 'Throw them out ruthlessly.' Later this was to have a sequel. Speaking at the Albert Hall, Mr. Lloyd George was much interrupted. H. W. Nevinson, an excitable man, leapt up in his seat and cried out: 'Is it to be ruthlessly again, Mr. Lloyd George?' The Welshman, though a past master at dealing with Conservative heckling, never relished hostile questions if they were directed from his left flank. Recognizing Nevinson Lloyd George contented himself with the almost plaintive retort: 'Oh Mr. Nevinson I am surprised at a man of your education asking that question.' At a meeting at Louth a few months later he said, when some women began to interrupt him: 'I see some rats have got in: let them squeal, it does not matter.' Such exchanges from the leading supporter of the women's franchise in the Cabinet show something of the dangers of the policy which the Union was following, and the way in which it succeeded in forcing friends into the opposition.

Churchill managed to treat the attacks on him with more geni-ality, although they were severe. At Bristol Railway Station he was attacked by Miss Theresa Garnett, flourishing a dog-whip and crying: 'Take that in the name of the insulted women of England.' Luckily the blows miscarried, Churchill coolly pocketed the whip, but he might have been a little more flustered if he had known that his assailant had lately been charged with biting a wardress.

And as England advanced towards a General Election hardly any prominent Liberal escaped the attention of these ladies. Under the platform, inside the organ of the Albert Hall, disguised as a telegraph boy, or springing among the chimneys in gymnastic dress they dogged the Liberal Cabinet ministers like some aveng-ing ghost in a Dickens novel. They jumped on Mr. Asquith when he was playing a game of golf with Herbert Gladstone at Lympne, and the unhappy Lloyd George was the victim of a brilliant manœuvre. He was speaking in the Queen's Hall, addressing him-self in particular to the Nonconformist vote with allusions to 'the Carpenter of Galilee' and a statement that in rural England the little, unsightly red-brick chapel was often the only place that would stand up to the baronial castle. Coming out, and glowing with the memory of these charitable sentiments, he went straight to his car and a suffragette followed him and by a masterly manœuvre managed to slip into the car behind him and lock the door. She then gave him a severe lecture followed by a good shaking, while the chauffeur struggled to undo the car door. As she stepped triumphantly out, she narrowly escaped some mischief from the crowd who showed their disapproval in no uncertain manner.

Though occasionally these varied devices may have been local and spontaneous, they were for the most part planned by the master-minds in Clement's Inn. The following letter illustrates the care with which the leaders directed their missionaries.

17th July 1909

Dear Mrs. Cullen,[1]

Mr. Winston Churchill is to address a meeting at Norwich on Monday, July 26th. I wonder if you would go there a few days beforehand to rouse the people and get a great crowd at his meeting. . . . No doubt you can get hospitality while in Norwich, and the Union would gladly pay out of pocket expenses. I am writing to the I.L.P. to say that we shall send someone about the middle of next week, and whoever goes will be prepared to address their Sunday meeting.

Yours sincerely,

CHRISTABEL PANKHURST

Six days later Miss Pankhurst wrote again to Mrs. Cullen saying: 'We send you another helper in the person of Miss Jarvis. She is ready for arrest.'

The Pankhursts and Pethick-Lawrences, reviewing their strategy, must have realized that acts of militancy, if they were accompanied by pageantry on the streets, gained greatly in effect. The two processions of the summer of 1908 had illustrated the truth of this: while they reminded the women of the sufferings of

---

[1] This letter is in the London Museum, and it is interesting because it shows that although the Union and Independent Labour Party had drifted far apart, they still had some contacts—especially in their fancy for Sunday meetings which at that time were viewed with horror by orthodox politicians.

those imprisoned, they emphasized the strength of the following behind the policy of Clement's Inn. For this reason a number of demonstrations, which were spectacular but orderly, were held throughout 1909.

On April 16th a procession was held, and marched from the Marble Arch to the Aldwych Theatre to celebrate the release of Mrs. Pethick-Lawrence. The procession was led, on a day of bright spring sunshine, by Miss Elsie Howey, the daughter of the Rector of Finningley, in Nottinghamshire: wearing armour and carrying a banner of the Union colours, she rode astride a heavy but splendid white horse. Although the connection of the Maid with the ladies who attempted to march to the English House of Commons—and it was doing this on February 24th that Mrs. Lawrence had been arrested—was not obvious, the explanation of the prominence of the French patriot on this occasion was that two days later Joan of Arc was to be beatified at St. Peter's, Rome. The procession was a long one with an immense display of Union colours: included in it was a carriage, draped in the Stars and Stripes, which carried the American delegates to the International Suffrage Society which was meeting in London at this time. At the end of the procession came a motor-car, adorned at each of the four corners with the flag of purple, white and green. The driver, with the slightly embarrassed but humorous expression of a Londoner in such circumstances, was the only sombre figure in the cavalcade. Alone, standing in the back, holding a bouquet in her left hand and waving a scarf of the Union colours in her right hand travelled Mrs. Lawrence—the heroine of the day. The procession was effective.

After her release Mrs. Lawrence was presented with a motor-car by the Union. A conspicuous vehicle painted in purple, white and green it likewise gained distinction from being driven by the first liveried chauffeuse to be seen in London. Not to be altogether eclipsed by London, Cambridge (the town of bicycles) could boast of a lady's bicycle painted in the same colours. The proud owner wrote to *Votes For Women*—'it is really the most beautiful bicycle I have ever seen. It is not at all aggressively suffragist, as it is very sober.' History does not record how the light-hearted undergraduates of Cambridge viewed this sober machine.

A few days later a large and successful bazaar was held in Prince's skating rink; there the decorations, principally of ladies with the wings of angels in the pre-Raphaelite style, were the work of Miss Sylvia Pankhurst illustrating the text—'They that sow in tears shall reap in joy.' At one end of the hall was a prison cell, accurately reproduced, and inhabited by an erstwhile prisoner who could describe to the curious exactly what happened in reality. Again this bazaar was a success, over £5,000 being taken for the Union.

Meanwhile familiar tactics were by no means dropped. On June 29th a deputation set out for the House of Commons from the Women's 'Parliament' at Caxton Hall. A squad of eight ladies, cheered by the band of the Union which played them out of the Hall, marched to Parliament Square: they were led by Mrs. Pankhurst, Mrs. Saul Solomon, widow of a former Prime Minister of the Cape of Good Hope, and Miss Annie Neligan, a retired headmistress. Mrs. Pankhurst, with her distinguished though venerable companions, was admitted to the House of Commons. On hearing that the Prime Minister would not receive her she struck a police inspector on either cheek. She and her companions were arrested. When they came before the Magistrate, Lord Robert Cecil, who was a practising member of the Bar, defended them and applied for the case to go to the High Court. This was granted, but the authorities did not proceed further with the case—no doubt because of the distinction of Mrs. Pankhurst's companions. As soon as news of their arrest got back to Caxton Hall their followers made repeated sorties against the House of Commons throughout the evening. A crowd of many thousands watched the struggle and over 100 women were arrested. Many windows in Government Departments were broken by stones. At the height of the battle, in the central lobby of the House of Commons, where were several Members of Parliament and their friends, a distinguished man suddenly called out: 'The Women of England are clamouring outside.' He was unceremoniously hustled out to join them. This was Mr. Laurence Housman.

Often repeated as these demonstrations were, they seemed with every repetition to play afresh on the emotions like some unvarying and familiar pageant of royalty. The milling crowds in Parliament Square, the police on foot and on horseback and then the white-faced, but determined little squad of ladies, sallying forth at intervals as the summer evening turned to dusk and darkness, brushing aside the jeers of the lout and the hooligan till at last they found their refuge in arrest and the friendly protection of the police. In two masterly paragraphs in *The New Machiavelli* H. G. Wells has described how this particular demonstration struck 'Lord Barham and me'—two typical Edwardians strolling down from St. James's after a comfortable dinner. They noticed the look of 'heroic tension' on the faces of the women, and then after describing the sea of people and array of police Wells added —and surely this is correct?—'the scuffle that ended in the arrests was the poorest explosion to follow such stupendous preparations.'

For there indeed lay the principal weakness of these fighting tactics. They drew enormous crowds but did not convert them. Though it is guesswork, an analysis would probably be broadly accurate which showed that 80 per cent of the crowd was curious, 10 per cent hostile and 10 per cent sympathetic. Moreover the statement can be made with confidence that if there had been any considerable body of sympathizers in the crowd the task of the police would have been made much more difficult, and the effectiveness of the protest magnified. Something of this seems to have been appreciated by the Women's Freedom League. At the beginning of 1909 they attempted to petition the Prime Minister. The intrepid Miss Matters rose in her balloon, and showered leaflets over the centre of London arguing that a petition to the Prime Minister was in nowise illegal but was perfectly constitutional. On February 18th members of the League attempted to bear the petition to Mr. Asquith at the House of Commons, but Mrs. Despard and some others were arrested. After this experience the League devised a scheme of peaceful picketing: from July 5th to October 28th a little group of patient women could be seen outside the House of Commons waiting to waylay the Premier and hand him the petition. (Owing to the long-drawn discussions on the Budget, Parliament sat through the autumn, being adjourned on October 8th for ten days.) Throughout the long nights of the Budget sittings they remained at their action stations—the gates of New Palace Yard or St. Stephen's Porch. Wells has described them: 'There were grey-headed old ladies standing there, sturdily charming in the rain; battered looking, ambiguous women . . . north-country factory girls, cheaply dressed suburban women; trim, comfortable mothers of families; valiant-eyed girl graduates and undergraduates; lank, hungry-looking creatures, who stirred one's imagination.' And then he adds: 'I found that continual siege of the legislature extraordinarily impressive—infinitely more impressive than the feeble-forcible "ragging" of the more militant section.'

The Government obviously distinguished between the two militant bodies—the League and the Union—treating the former with consistent restraint. In August they had found it necessary to arrest some members of the League (including Mrs. Despard and Mrs. Cobden-Sanderson) for picketing Downing Street. They were defended at Bow Street by Tim Healy, then an Irish member, always a warm-hearted supporter of the women's vote and afterwards the first Governor-General of the Irish Free State. With the rounded eloquence of the Irish he said: 'They have not pulled down any railings, but they have armed themselves with a piece of cardboard and a piece of paper, and they knock at the Official Door, and they stand in rain, and hail and shine in front of the Official Residence, and they say "Great Men of England receive our prayer". And the Great Men of England say "I refer you to the police".' They were subsequently tried at the Old Bailey, where they were fined and their fines were paid for them anonymously.

XXII

The Hunger Strike

Mrs. Pankhurst and other leaders of the Union had shown the world how courage and disregard for authority could carry forward a great cause. And now from this time to the end, the cause was to be sustained by the ideals of suffering and sacrifice. These gave it the impetus to survive not only the ingenuity of successive Home Secretaries but internal divisions and some loss of popular support. Although suffering and sacrifice were to be displayed to the world in highly dramatic forms by the Union over the next few years, their forceful expression by the League outside the House of Commons and how they were applauded by a shrewd observer like Wells will not be overlooked. A popular woman writer of those times (Miss Olive Schreiner) gave expression (in possibly rather too fine language but well understood in the tense days when she was writing) to the idea that women could only reach their goal through suffering: 'Down the banks of labour, through the waters of suffering: there is no other way to the Land of Freedom.'[1]

And at this juncture there arrived in the ranks of the Union a distinguished recruit who seemed in her bearing and mind to enshrine all the frustrations and sorrows of her sex. Lady Constance Lytton was the second daughter of the Viceroy of India, the granddaughter of Bulwer Lytton the novelist, and the great granddaughter of the remarkable Mrs. Wheeler who had made her curious contribution to the cause in its earliest days. Lady Constance was at this time in her late thirties, living with her mother and reputed to have been disappointed in a love affair with an army

---

[1] *Dreams* by Olive Schreiner.

officer of some note. She had helped her mother's sister Mrs. C. W. Earle with a book which had much success and which is still deservedly enjoyed *Pot-pourri from a Surrey Garden*. She and her aunt shared the profits on this book. Her godmother and relative Lady Bloomfield, who was a writer of some success at the time, died in 1905 leaving some money to Lady Constance. Not being in particular need of this money, she decided to use it on something that was useful. She has described how by chance she heard of a piece of social work that 'contained an element of spontaneous joy', which she contrasted with 'the oppressive jackets' of ordinary philanthropists. The sophisticated mortal of the mid-twentieth century is almost ashamed to have to confess that the source of all this uninhibited joy was the revival of folk songs and folk dancing. There was something undeniably incongruous about Lady Constance's life with the militants, which was to move to the stately cadences of tragedy, beginning with the light-hearted leaping of the rustic dance and the inspired cheerfulness of 'Hey Nonny No'.

She made the acquaintance of Mary Neal and attended the Esperance Club. Here it should be emphasized that the Esperance Club was a club for working women with the idea of social regeneration through the spontaneous joy of song and dance. The name, with its associations of progress to a better state of affairs, was doubtless suggested to Mary Neal or to Mrs. Pethick-Lawrence by the battle-cry in *Henry IV*: 'Now, *Esperance*! Percy! and set on.' Cecil Sharp, who was prominent in the Club in its early days and who did more than any other individual to revive these songs and dances, broke with Mary Neal because there was, to his way of thinking, too much emphasis on social uplift and too little on artistic elegances. Sir Osbert Sitwell, with the help of his distinguished brother and sister, has done much to correct public taste on these matters, and to damp down some of the extravagances which followed from Sharp's enthusiasm. He has, with characteristic wit, pointed out how highly successful Sharp was in collecting English folk-songs from the Apalachian Mountains in Florida. But to be fair it should be added that in those Dark Ages, when the Edwardian upper and middle classes never looked beyond their own sleek well-being, there was courage, sympathy and understanding shown by those who attempted to colour the lives of working women with something other than the scrubbing brush or a glass of white port.

At the holiday headquarters of the Esperance Club in Little-hampton Lady Constance met Mrs. Pethick-Lawrence and Annie Kenney. In her book, the latter after emphasizing the streak of sadness in Lady Constance's character, has drawn attention to her instinctive sympathy with the working-class militants and has emphasized the importance to the movement of someone of her standing and character. Walking arm-in-arm round the rain-drenched garden at Littlehampton the mill hand and the Viceroy's daughter discussed the problems of working women. Lady Con-stance thought social reform was of greater moment than any barriers of sex: Annie Kenney replied: 'I can only tell you that I, who am a working-class woman, have never known class distinc-tion and class prejudice stand in the way of my advancement, whereas the sex barrier meets me at every turn.' This visit to Littlehampton was in 1906, and Lady Constance's conversion began then, but proceeded gradually.

She first comes to the front after the disturbances over 'Rush the House of Commons' in the autumn of 1908, when she lobbied Members of Parliament to try to obtain First Division treatment for Mrs. Pankhurst, Christabel and 'The General'. She was of course personally well-known to many of the leading men in both the Conservative and Liberal parties, and her arrival at the House of Commons was remarked. After the first day of the trial—it will be remembered that it opened on October 13th and was then ad-journed for a week—Lady Constance evidently tried to enlist the support of Mr. Arthur Ponsonby. He had been private secretary to Campbell-Bannerman and he had succeeded him as Liberal Member for Stirling, earlier that year. To the Liberal Party and later to the Labour Party he brought remarkable gifts, unimpaired by timidity or convention and strengthened by the humanitarian feelings of a deeply sensitive nature. His reply to Lady Constance is interesting because it shows how even those whose minds were most naturally attuned to suffering and injustice were antagonized by militancy. 'I think'—he wrote on October 14th—'that militant tactics were effective up to a point. They have got beyond that point . . . they have got the House of Commons for the time being dead against them and are rapidly alienating opinion in the country.'[1]

She was allowed to visit the three ladies in their cells at Bow Street: on entering these melancholy surroundings, she at once recalled the word *puanteur*, which means smell of deadness, and it reminded her how that odour had seemed to haunt Dostoievsky's accounts of his imprisonments. A few days later she heard Mrs. Pankhurst recalling in the dock how she had heard, when she was in prison before, the cries of a woman giving birth to a child. Mrs. Pankhurst had added: 'We believe that if we get the vote we will find some more humane way of dealing with women than that.' Such aspirations vibrated the chords in Lady Constance's sensitive personality. She was ready for a demonstration. At the beginning of 1909 she was prominent in the attack on the House of Commons when Mrs. Pethick-Lawrence was arrested. She was far from strong, having a weakness of the heart, and she has herself described how on this occasion she was doubled up for want of breath and was 'physically incapable of speech'. She was arrested. Always delightful and humorous she has recalled how, waiting for her case to come on at Bow Street, she stood opposite the constable who had arrested her like 'partners waiting for a country dance to strike up'. In prison she suffered from the deference due to rank. When she told the chaplain, who was in charge of the prison library, that *Esther Waters* by George Moore ought to be included in the Library he answered: 'Your ladyship is such a good judge of books that I should wish to leave the choice entirely to you.' Owing to her heart she was put in hospital but she chafed at not being able to join her comrades in the cells.

And now as Lady Constance's part in the story moves slowly towards its tragic ending, a new development of the year 1909 introduced a more challenging note. In that summer Miss Wallace-Dunlop,[2] equipped with a block and printer's ink, succeeded in stamping on the stone wall of St. Stephen's Hall, in the Houses of

[1] MS. letter in London Museum.

[2] Marion Wallace-Dunlop: born in Scotland; daughter of Robert Wallace-Dunlop, C.B.; author of *The Magic Fruit Garden*; *Fairies, Elves and Flower Babies*; exhibitor at Academy.

Parliament, a quotation from the Bill of Rights about the right of the subject to petition the King. The transcription was smudged, and to put the matter beyond doubt she repeated the offence a few days later. She was sentenced to a fine for damaging the stone-work or one month's imprisonment. She arrived in Holloway on July 1st, and at once warned the Governor that unless she were placed in the First Division she would refuse to eat anything. This warning she put into force on July 5th. The prison authorities tried every means to coax her to feed, even leaving a tray of delicious food—quite unobtainable in any Division—by her bed all night. Mr. Howard Spring, in his excellent reconstruction of those events in *Fame Is The Spur*, hardly exaggerates when he des-cribes a wardress coming in to a suffragette with a beautiful tray of tea daintily arranged, pouring out the tea and slicing the cake. But Miss Wallace-Dunlop did not carry the name of the Scottish hero for nothing, and she resolutely refused all inducements to make her eat. 'What would you like to eat to-day?' asked doctors and wardresses anxiously. 'My determination' was the reply. The delicacies followed the coarse bread and skilly out of her cell window. On the Thursday she was released faint and starving but triumphant.

Apparently Miss Wallace-Dunlop conceived the idea of starving herself, without direction from the Union leaders, and she had hit on something which was to prove an intractable problem to the authorities. The idea of a hunger-strike seems to have been copied from the tactics of political prisoners in Tsarist Russia, and it may cause surprise that such a device should have caused any embarrassment to the stony-hearted gaolers in Muscovy. But Miss Wallace-Dunlop bravely took this step into the unknown, bravely plunged into 'the waters of suffering', and her courage deserves to be acclaimed. Mr. Pethick-Lawrence wrote to her on the day after her release—'the power of the human spirit is to me the most sublime thing in life—that compared with which all ordinary things sink into insignificance.

'If I needed anything more than this great and splendid move-ment, which I am privileged to assist, to make life worth living, it would be found in what you have done. I value the knowledge of it as I value the great facts of life: and I pray that if ever in my own life some great hour of trial comes, the memory of it will be with me to give me courage and faith and endurance.'[1]

Throughout the summer of 1909 disturbances in Holloway were fairly general: the suffragettes gaining their premature release after hunger striking. But in September the Government struck back. After Mrs. Leigh had been sent to prison for her part in disturbing Mr. Asquith's meeting in Birmingham in September, she at once went on hunger strike. The Government decided that she should be fed. They no doubt chose Mrs. Leigh partly because she was very contumacious (she had bombarded the roof of Haldane's meeting with slates only the month before she attacked Mr. Asquith in Birmingham) and partly because she had shown good physique and gymnastic prowess in climbing over the roofs. The process of forcible feeding is disagreeable. Nourishing liquid[2] is passed into the mouth through a tube or, where the person is very refractory, by tubes through the nostrils. Doctors, wardresses and nurses attended this form of treatment. Although forcible feeding is a disgusting topic—and the gruesome details lost nothing in the telling when recounted as propaganda by the victims—it was not dangerous. Some doctors—including Sir Victor Horsley, perhaps the finest and most enlightened surgeon of that time—argued that it was dangerous but it would appear to the layman that such arguments were based on natural repugnance rather than scientific facts. Forcible feeding is of course a familiar form of treatment in lunatic asylums.

The hunger strike was accompanied by much disorder of a more general kind—cells were damaged, and whenever they could, the women broke the cell windows. Miss Emily Wilding-Davison, who was serving a prison sentence in Manchester for interrupting a meeting addresses by Mr. Runciman, contrived by some extraordinary legerdemain to barricade the door of her cell and when the doctors came to feed her, access was effectively barred. Expostulation and force were alike tried in vain. By chance the Prison visiting committee—largely composed of the civic worthies of Manchester were at the prison at the time, and they said, in their unimaginative way, 'Turn the water hose on her.'

[1] Manuscript letter in London Museum.
[2] The mixture fed through tubes was Valentine's meat juice and lime juice cordial. This was varied with Benger's Food or beef-tea.

This the warders proceeded to do. The poor woman, drenched and battered, with the water rising in her cell had to yield. She was taken to hospital and released. The Government could not possibly justify such behaviour, and Gladstone in the House of Commons confessed that the Visiting Committee had made a serious mistake. In December Mrs. Leigh brought an action in the High Court against the Home Secretary claiming that forcible feeding was illegal, and asking for damages.

The case came before the Lord Chief Justice—Alverstone—not perhaps a great ornament of the Bench, but an inveterate songster in Victorian drawing-rooms. He is believed to be the only Lord Chief Justice who was also a chorister—he sang in the choir at St. Mary Abbot's in Kensington for forty years. But this agreeable warbler of plain song, this chanter of innocent ditties round the piano, was not at home among the rough realities of suffragette warfare, and his handling of the case was unsympathetic. Mrs. Leigh brought her action against the Home Secretary, the Governor of Birmingham prison (Captain Percy Green) and the prison medical officer, Dr. Ernest Helby. Mary Leigh was not only a lady of spirit, but she was endowed with a command of neat English, and she recalled in court how she had said to the doctor at the time: 'If you force it into my mouth, I term that an operation: if by the nose I term it an outrage.' Dr. Helby showed great patience and kindness. The prison matron seems to have been a sterner character. In Court she said that she well remembered the arrival of Mrs. Leigh who entered the prison arm-in-arm with other suffrage prisoners and singing the 'Marseillaise'. Twenty panes of glass were broken, and she expressed her full feelings of outraged bumbledom when she added of Mary Leigh: 'I would have given her a good box on the ears.' A number of doctors gave evidence to the effect that forcible feeding was an ancient practice, common in lunatic asylums, and that it could be applied with beneficial consequences to the health of patients in hospital. In the course of his summing-up, Alverstone—influenced no doubt by the simple Christian doctrines he had imbibed at St. Mary Abbot's—said: 'It was wicked folly to attempt to starve themselves to death.' After only two minutes' consideration the jury returned a verdict for the defendants.

The Hunger Strike

Miss Davison was more successful in her action against the Visiting Committee at Strangeways: she won her case although the County Court Judge (E. A. Parry) rather strangely limited the damages to £2 on the grounds that the incident had provided copy for 'a vivacious and entertaining account in the Press'.

XXIII

Lady Constance in Disguise

These severe and unpleasant developments in the second half of 1909 had the effect of welding the militants into an ever-tighter and more devoted band. Each felt that the sufferings of the other were a call to share in these tribulations: they crowded the banks eager to immerse themselves in the cruel waters of suffering. No one perhaps felt this more acutely than Lady Constance. She was determined that neither health, nor a natural timidity nor her aristocratic connections should deter her from sharing the horrors which her sisters were facing. Accompanied by Mrs. Nevinson, Miss Dorothy Pethick[1] and some other women she journeyed to Newcastle where Lloyd George was to address a great Liberal demonstration on the Budget on October 9th. (It was at this meeting, which was confined to men, that he referred to the House of Lords as composed of '500 men chosen by accident from among the unemployed.') In the evening of October 9th, surrounded by a large miscellaneous crowd of urchins and sightseers, and escorted by two stalwart but complacent gentlemen, Lady Constance advanced along the streets of Newcastle. She picked her way along the tramlines. As she approached the place of the meeting, she saw Sir Walter Runciman's magnificent motor-car. Knowing that Lloyd George was Runciman's guest, she threw her stone at the bonnet of this car. The scene recalls the grim determination of the idealist, striding forward, with her motley escort. Her target was hardly worthy of the occasion, for it was merely the insignia of Edwardian wealth, the burnished, expensive car, with translucent glass and gleaming

---

[1] Sister of Mrs. Pethick-Lawrence.

brass. The stone must have been of moderate dimensions since it carried the inscription: 'To Lloyd George. Rebellion against tyranny is obedience to God. Deeds not words.' Perhaps it would be a little difficult to support the statement about tyranny with strictly biblical authority, and it was unlucky that Sir Walter Runciman, like the Whig candidate for Cambridge who was struck in the face by a dead cat intended for his fellow candidate, Macaulay, was the innocent recipient of this important stone. Lady Constance was fined £4. She refused to pay and was sent to prison for a month. She immediately refused to eat. After two days she was released as was Mrs. Nevinson, who had been sentenced for striking with an axe, concealed in a bouquet of hideous chrysanthemums, the barriers which the police had put up to contain the crowds for the Lloyd George meeting.

No doubt Mrs. Nevinson was treated with leniency as a member of the League and as the wife of an eminent writer. Lady Constance was a member of the Union, and it was inevitably whispered that her speedy release was only explained by her rank —a tale which was formally denied in the House of Commons but which had a sequel with disastrous consequences for Lady Constance. No doubt she was in reality freed because of the weakness of her heart. Yet the authorities in picking and choosing which of the women should be forcibly fed were perhaps open to criticism: in selecting the young, the robust and the plump they seemed to be reducing a serious business to the level of the poulterer's shop.

Readers may reasonably wonder why there was no greater volume of public indignation over forcible feeding. The Liberal press accepted it mutely. It is true that both Brailsford, one of the pioneers of Labour journalism and Nevinson, who was of course both interested and afflicted by the turn of events, resigned their positions as leader-writers on the *Daily News*. They wrote a joint letter to *The Times* which ended: 'We cannot denounce torture in Russia and support it in England, nor can we advocate democratic principles in the name of a party which confined them to a single sex.' But these views were not general, and there can be little doubt that the increasing disorders of 1909 had antagonized opinion, and on that account stifled the inevitable criticism of this outrage. Churchill was certainly not far from the mark when he said to a deputation from the League: 'I am bound to say I think your cause has marched backwards.'

Indeed the volume of support behind the protests against forcible feeding was small: it was certainly insufficient to decide the Government to alter their inexorable measures. To just a handful of sensitive men and women at the time and possibly to most human beings to-day—for although many virtues may have grown dim with the advance of the twentieth century, sympathy with suffering has developed apace—the bare recital of the facts in prosaic questions and answers in the House of Commons is more striking than pages of indignant adjectives. Mr. Percy Alden—a humanitarian of courageous and independent personality of a type which, with the eclipse of the Liberal Party, has taken flight from Westminster—put this question on October 20th: 'I beg to ask whether all the Suffragist prisoners in Newcastle Gaol are being fed by force; whether any representation has been made by the registered medical adviser of Miss Rona Robinson, M.A., a suffragist sent to one month's imprisonment in the Second Division for breaking a window in Liverpool Gaol to the effect that owing to the weakness of her heart and throat forcible feeding in her case would be highly dangerous: and if so what steps he proposes to take.' Gladstone replied: 'Only three of the seven suffragist prisoners in Newcastle prison are being fed by tube. The others are now taking their food from the officers without active resistance. Rona Robinson was released yesterday morning on medical certificate.' Although the phrase 'forcible feeding', with its emphatic alliteration, may have erred on the side of exaggeration, the Government usage of 'feeding by tube' was prosaically inept.

Charles Masterman—the dazzling though at times unpredictable apostle of the new Liberalism—had the disagreeable task, as under-secretary to the Home Office, of announcing the inauguration of forcible feeding. He dismissed it lightly as 'hospital treatment' and asserted that it was often used in the case of prisoners who were 'weak-minded' or 'contumacious'. After the Bermondsey ballot-box case the Home Secretary blandly announced: 'Mrs. Chapin takes her food quietly. Miss Neilans has refused her food . . . the medical officer has had to feed her by tube. Her health is not suffering.' More generally Mr. Gladstone, said in an answer to a statement by Mr. Hugh Law that the practice of forcible feeding was 'filthy and disgusting', 'I do not agree. . . . Honourable members have made no protest against this practice, which has prevailed for very many years past in asylums, in prisons, and hospitals, and the effect of which has been grossly exaggerated.'

Although in the House of Commons stalwarts like Snowden and Keir Hardie were unceasing in their efforts to brand the Government's handling of this issue as illiberal and inhumane their protests were received with respect but without concurrence. Indeed there were signs that Members of Parliament saw traces of comedy rather than tragedy in the development of militancy. Mr. Arnold Lupton, perhaps the only successful candidate in the 1906 election to have fought on a push-bike, whose principal concern was with the abolition of compulsory vaccination, and whose intervention in any debate was the signal for uproarious laughter, asked the Home Secretary whether he had been advised that 'the best way of securing law and order in the streets outside this house is firmly and sternly to refuse to all ladies the honour of imprisonment.' Mr. Hugh Law, a product of Rugby and Oxford who through a passion for Gaelic had drifted into Irish Nationalist politics, pointed out that the Home Secretary had refused to let a prisoner in Holloway, Miss Maud Fitzherbert, enter the precincts of the House of Commons to see her cousin, the Member for West Donegal (himself). He then asked with an air of innocence: 'Will the Right Honourable Gentleman afford me the same protection against my creditors as he affords me against my relatives?'

And in the meantime, while some Members of Parliament were jesting, the thought of hunger strikes and tube feeding reverberated in the mind of Lady Constance with the inexorable urgency of a tocsin. Her friends and comrades in arms were being tortured. She must be at their side. She must share their sufferings. How could she if she was to be met at every turn with the cry that she was delicate and a lady of rank? In this dilemma she showed that it was not for nothing that she was the grand-daughter of the great romantic novelist. Drawing on a favourite theme of Victorian fiction, she decided to disguise her rank. Like Lady Isabel in

East Lynne or Lady Dedlock in *Bleak House* she would, by a change of dress, escape from the traditions and conventions of her class. Like most members of the aristocracy, brilliant at an impromptu charade, she played her part to perfection.

On 14th January 1910, accompanied by a Mrs. Baines, she went, disguised as a seamstress—the very word seems to carry with it a picture of a respectable woman of the working-classes in Victorian times—and addressed a meeting of people outside Walton Gaol in Liverpool—where hunger striking and forcible feeding were at their height. She urged the crowd to advance into the prison and demonstrate: she stopped speaking and led the way. Though the speech might have been deemed by an attentive listener a shade too polished for the appearance of the agitator, the disguise was good: she was in the clothes of a working-woman and had cut her hair and was wearing spectacles. She had studied her clothes with care. The sleeves of her dress were too short: she was wearing grey, woollen gloves and (a subtle touch) on the collar of her coat she pinned three tawdry brooches. They were of the kind which a village child pins proudly to its bosom on an occasion of royal rejoicing. But those brooches carried no emblems of kings or queens but portraits of Mrs. Pankhurst, Christabel and Mrs. Pethick-Lawrence. She was at once arrested, on approaching the entrance to the prison, and gave her name as Jane Warton. On the next day she was sentenced to fourteen days' hard labour. She at once started the hunger-strike and she has described how through the fitful sleep of her first night in prison she dreamed of fruit. Delicious peaches and nectarines and vast melons established themselves in her mind. The next day came the less agreeable reality of nourishing broths and feeding tubes. The doctor, who examined her heart, with some disregard for the facts and for the dignity of the English language, pronounced it 'perfectly ripping'. With pathos but without restraint she has described in her book *Prisons and Prisoners*[1] the precise sensations of one who endured what Master-

[1] Messrs. Heinemann who published this book, introduced it with this note: 'The Publisher hopes that fault will not be found if he disclaims agreement with some of Lady Constance Lytton's views, expressed in this volume, notwithstanding the fact that he is glad to offer it to the public. He feels that personal disagreement over details should not hinder him from publishing this splendid story of heroism and unselfishness.'

man blandly called 'hospital treatment'. After some days the suspicions of the prison authorities seem to have been aroused. The tone of the doctor changed: 'I do beg of you, I appeal to you, not as a prison doctor but as a man to give over. You are a delicate woman.' To the Home Office the prison doctor wrote, developing his suspicions: he added: 'she has a nose of a somewhat Wellingtonian bend.' In fact Lady Constance's nose, though pronounced, was particularly straight, and the doctor presumably referred to the Duke as a symbol of the aristocratic nose. A day or two afterwards she was released.

The episode was dramatic and in its way damaging to the Government which could hardly escape the implication that the peer's sister was cherished in prison while the seamstress was not. Soon afterwards Lady Constance was stricken by paralysis and, although this was not brought on solely by Walton Gaol, for the excitements of those times roused feelings which were too passionate for a frail constitution, the circumstances stood by themselves as a condemnation, on the heroic scale, of the methods by which the Government was attempting to break the resistance of the Union. Not everyone would endorse the somewhat florid prophecy of Mrs. Pethick-Lawrence that 'children yet unborn will be taught the story as though it were that of Philip Sidney and they will say in their hearts "I too will be fearless and chivalrous and brave. I too will belong to the Knighthood of the Holy Ghost".' But for all that, Constance Lytton illumines the rather wild years of militancy with the radiant colours of courage and devotion, made the more conspicuous because they emerge from a background of meekness and simplicity.

XXIV

Conciliation and King Edward's Death

And now as the General Election of 1910 grew near some estimate of the achievements of the militants may be attempted. No one looking back would wish to minimize —or indeed could succeed in minimizing—what they had done. In the six and a half years which had passed since the little band of ladies met in Manchester, they had stormed their way to the front of public attention. In Fleet Street, in the Law Courts and in Parliament they had become personalities of the first rank. Mr. A. G. Gardiner wrote at the time with characteristic vividness, but without exaggeration, when he said: 'Out of the little group of half a dozen women who used to meet in a room in Manchester has emerged the movement which has shaken the whole fabric of politics.'

Yet it is fair to add that in the English political system there is no point in shaking the whole fabric of politics unless the earthquake is accompanied by a shift in public opinion. Of this there was no sign. Certainly some young women—high-spirited, independent and ardent—were drawn to the battle as a result of militancy, and it created a *corps d'élite* of which possibly the whole movement stood in need. But at the same time it created a strong opposition. In 1909 a petition, with a quarter of a million signatures, against giving women the vote was presented to Parliament. For the first time an anti-suffrage League, with Lord Cromer and Lord Curzon prominent, each an illustrious pro-consul of imperial Britain, was formed. Among the leading women in the opposition movement were Lady Jersey, prominent for charm and intellect in late Victorian society, Mrs. Humphrey Ward, the distinguished novelist, and Miss Violet Markham happily still living. No doubt some of the supporters of these ladies were drawn from believers in the species of trash, about women, which is to be found in the pages of Marie Corelli or of Elinor Glyn. An example from the former illustrates the point: Marie Corelli is playing the well-worn chord that women have all the political influence they need without the vote—'A clever woman sits at home and, like a meadow-spider, spreads a pretty web of rose and gold, spangled with diamond dew. Flies or men, tumble in by scores, and she holds them all prisoners at her pleasure, with a golden strand as fine as a hair. Nature gave her at her birth the right to do this, and if she does it well she will always have her web full.' But some of the support of 'The Anti's' (as they were known) was more formidable. Mrs. Humphrey Ward and Miss Markham were the spokesmen of sensible people who felt, not without excuse, that a predominance of women in the electoral system accorded ill with a country which was bravely shouldering great imperial responsibilities. Miss Markham originated a telling phrase when she spoke of the absence of a vote as 'the symbol of disinterested service'. The militants enjoyed laughing at the Anti's—'the priceless Anti's' they were called in the lady's slang of the time. But such mirth was somewhat hollow. It was hollow because the 'Anti's' strengthened the hand of the parliamentary opposition—including the opposition inside the Cabinet—to the whole idea of votes for women.

And there in Parliament the issue lay interlocked with all the ingenuity and subtlety of a Chinese puzzle. Shaking the whole fabric of politics, like some Samson who thinks that force rather than manipulation is the way to unlock the device, was not the answer. And it is of course against the parliamentary background and not against the swaying crowds in Parliament Square or even against the flaring headlines of Fleet Street that the achievements of militancy must be judged. Edwin Montagu, then at the dawn of his astonishing and blazing career in public life, said in the House of Commons in 1907 that the militants 'are, if I may say so, entirely ignorant of the exigencies of parliamentary life'. To under-

stand exactly what Montagu meant the reader should look back
once more to the parliamentary scene after the Liberal triumph in
1906. For the first time for several decades that House of Commons saw no woman's suffrage group formed from members of
all parties. Such a group—it will be remembered—was one of the
creations of Miss Becker and in fact it was responsible for bringing
forward the annual woman's suffrage bill. There seems no clear
explanation why in 1906 it ceased to exist, unless the diminished
Conservative Party found difficulty in raising adequate representation for such a group. Although the group no longer existed both
Dickinson's Bill in 1907 and Stanger's Bill in 1908 were of the old
type, designed to appeal to all parties—and in fact winning the
support of all parties. In 1906 the Liberals, in all the glory of a
membership of nearly 400, felt that they were strong enough to
form a woman's suffrage committee, which was exclusively
Liberal. In 1909 this body introduced an adult suffrage bill which
was to give the vote to all persons of full age both male and
female. These Liberal suffragists knew that a bill, so framed,
would shed all right wing Liberal support and naturally all Liberal
opponents of the women's vote, but they could count on fairly
solid Labour and Irish support.

The Bill was introduced in March 1909 by Mr. Geoffrey Howard
—favourite son of the alarmingly temperate Rosalind Lady Carlisle and, on his own account, a Liberal of force and enlightenment. In the opening of his speech he cut himself off from the past
—from the patient manœuvres of Miss Becker to secure an all-
party majority by saying: 'I personally do not believe any great
reform of this kind can be passed on non-party lines.' The debate
followed the usual course except that Snowden, from the Labour
benches, pointed out that the Bill was repudiated by all the suffrage
societies. This was correct, and it is explained by those societies
regarding the vote as a matter of justice, and not something to be
tagged on as part of a further extension of the male franchise. The
Prime Minister intervened in the debate and carried Mr. Geoffrey
Howard's point further by saying that a measure of this kind, if it
was to become law, should not only be a party measure but should
be sponsored by the Government 'and be carefully moulded under
the stress of prolonged and deliberate parliamentary discussion'.

He himself, with some of the Cabinet colleagues, voted against the Bill which was carried by the narrow majority of thiry-four, but as the Government was not prepared to devote time for its further discussion the Liberal Bill, like its all-party predecessors, was doomed.

Here the reader will notice that as Asquith was perfectly correct in saying that, on a highly controversial issue, the only Bill which had any chance of succeeding was one sponsored by the Government so the folly of the militants in devoting all their fire at the Liberals becomes more glaring. Although such a policy may have seemed brave and gay, it did not greatly differ from the convulsion of the drowning man who puts all his strength into an attempt to drag down with him the friend who has come to his aid.

Nothing illustrates this more clearly than the sweeping political events which followed Howard's Bill. Lloyd George's Budget was introduced on 29th April 1909: after tumultous debates inside and outside Parliament it was rejected by the House of Lords on November 30th—the voting was 350 to 75. This vote made an election inevitable and—what was more to the point—made inevitable that it would be fought with intense vindictiveness on the narrow front of the Budget and the right of the Peers to curb the House of Commons. All minor issues were swept on one side, and the agitations of the militants had about as much effect on the main struggle as did the officers in Wellington's army on the outcome of the Peninsular War, when they went tally-hoing after the fox. The women were also handicapped by the obvious fact that a band of thirty or forty women, concentrated at a by-election, could make themselves felt: spread over some 600 constituencies at a General Election they became ineffective. They probably had no influence on the result.

A small point illustrates this. Hilaire Belloc, in spite of being the son of one of the pioneers of suffrage from mid-Victorian times, was a vigorous opponent of women being given the vote: he was standing for Salford (South) which he had captured from the Conservatives by a small margin for the Liberals in 1906. He received a circular from the supporters of woman's suffrage which he answered with courageous terseness:

King's Land, Shipley, Horsham
December 6th.

Dear Madam,

I am in receipt of your letter of the 3rd instant. In my opinion the agitation to which you refer is grossly immoral, and I will have nothing to do with it.

I am your obedient servant,

H. BELLOC

The ladies decided that all the polling booths in South Salford should be picketed with women, telling all electors that it was their duty to keep Belloc out. The result was a triumph for Belloc who held a difficult seat—which was in fact lost to the Liberals in the second election of 1910 when he was no longer the candidate.

The result of the election, and it is a burning lesson to all politicians of the strength and resilience of Conservative opinion in England, was a formidable reverse to the Liberal Party which lost 100 seats. The Liberals now depended for their majority on the somewhat docile Labour group—sobered by having lost a substantial slice of their numbers—and the more volatile Irish. Mrs. Pankhurst exulted over the result, mistakenly claimed much of the credit for it, and, in her book, she has described how she and her friends plastered the hoardings during the Election with posters about forcible feeding—'it was splendid ammunition and it told'.

But here again Mrs. Pankhurst revealed her lack of political sense, for she was really firing her howitzers at her own side. In this she was not alone. In a manifesto, issued on the last day of 1909 and signed by Mrs. Pankhurst and Christabel, and Emmeline Pethick-Lawrence and Mabel Tuke they urged 'every Liberal, whether man or woman, to help us in stamping out the false and spurious Liberalism affected by Mr. Asquith and the Government.' Even Mr. Pethick-Lawrence, a shrewd political observer, could deceive himself into believing that the women had swayed the result, and write after the election 'the suffragettes were responsible for losing the Government thirty or forty seats, thus making their majority dependent on Irish support.' And as the coterie of ladies returned after the election to Clement's Inn, decking themselves out in all the glory of their self-imposed laurels, they might well have been asked in words somewhat similar to those used by the Roman tribune:

'Wherefore rejoice? What conquest bring ye home?'

For judged from any angle the result of the election was unlucky. The virtual equality of the two chief parties led, as in history it always has, to a period of the bitterest political acrimony. More particularly for the cause of woman's suffrage it was a disaster. They had lost a majority which was broadly favourable: and there had been a great access of strength to the Conservative party which, though individuals were sympathetic to the women's cause, was in essence antagonistic. The only glint in a dark sky to which the women could point was that militancy had won political notice for the cause. This is clearly brought out by some facts about members' election addresses. During the debate on Geoffrey Howard's Bill Mr. K. W. Forster—a Kentish member with a deserved reputation on the cricket field—said that only thirteen members had mentioned woman's suffrage in their election addresses in 1906. He was subsequently corrected in the debate and it was established that thirteen was the number who had referred to adult suffrage, whereas forty-eight had mentioned woman's suffrage. Out of a total of 670 members both figures were meagre. On the other hand in 1910, it was noticed by the *Manchester Guardian*, that at least 250 candidates mentioned woman's suffrage in their addresses. The credit for the enhanced attention given to the question must be accorded to the militants.

On the eve of the General Election at a rally of 10,000 men, held in the Albert Hall, and described in the pages of *The Times* as 'boiling over with enthusiasm', the Prime Minister outlined the Liberal programme and included in it this important definition of Liberal intentions on the woman's franchise.

'Nearly two years ago I declared on behalf of the present Government that in the event, which we then contemplated, of our bringing in a Reform Bill we should make the insertion of a suffragist amendment an open question for the House of Commons to decide. Through no intention and no fault of ours, that opportunity for raising the matter has been taken away.' He meant of course by those words that the life of the Government had been cut short by the action of the Lords, and he added that the Declaration would hold good in the New House of Commons, 'and that the women's cause should be no worse off in the new Parliament than it would have been in the old.'

When all the results of the election were declared and before the two chief antagonists—Liberalism and Conservatism—settled down to the bitterest fight of our history, there was a moment's pause, like the prolongation of that fleeting handshake which introduces the round of boxing. For 1910—that year of portents and achievement, the year which saw the death of King Edward, the appearance of Halley's comet and the spectacular flight of Mr. C. S. Rolls across the Channel and back in ninety minutes, seemed for one instant of time to check the political passions of the Englishman. We can almost imagine that in the sunlit but impassive days which followed the death of the King, statesmen caught some distant gleam of those mortal battles which lay ahead of them after 1914. Public men seemed during that summer of 1910 determined to make one last effort to assuage the wrath of parties which was absorbing the energies and bellicose spirit of the British people. At mid-summer the leaders of the Liberal and Conservative parties met behind locked doors at 10 Downing Street, for many weeks, in an attempt to unravel the tangle over the House of Lords. There was even talk of a coalition—recalling the wise but graphic forecast of an almost forgotten mid-Victorian (Bernal Osborne) that if the deluge does occur 'from it will spring a rainbow, in which the various tints of party will be combined'. From this general relaxation of temper the suffrage issue was not excluded. In fact a shade more forbearance on all sides might, in this year of grace, have broken the inflexible difficulties by which it was encumbered.

Taking advantage of Asquith's undertaking and of the altered situation following the General Election a strong parliamentary committee was formed to further woman's suffrage, with 25 Liberals, 17 Conservatives, 6 Irish Nationalists and 6 Labour men. Lady Constance's brother, Lord Lytton was chairman of the Committee and Mr. Brailsford the secretary: this body was known as the Conciliation Committee, and throughout the spring and early summer the members of it were busy concocting a bill which might prove acceptable to the new House of Commons. The

Women's Social and Political Union decided to suspend militancy before the election, as the Women's Freedom League had also decided to do.[1] The precise circumstances in which this truce came about are now difficult to unravel. The official history of the Woman's Suffrage Movement, as Miss Metcalfe's book might fittingly be called, states that the leaders were informed that the Government wanted to give way, but did not wish to seem to give in to militancy. It appears most improbable that any official intimation of that kind was given to the suffrage leaders. Mrs. Pankhurst says that the proposed abolition of the Lords veto made the political situation 'strained and abnormal', and for that reason the Union leaders decided on a truce. Miss Sylvia Pankhurst is no doubt nearest the mark when she says that rumours were abroad that the Government was disposed to relent. Taking advantage of these rumours, Lady Constance, her brother Lord Lytton and Brailsford probably persuaded the leaders of the Union that a truce would be statesmanlike. Certainly the formation of this strong committee of parliamentarians (undaunted by all the provocations of former militancy) is much to the credit of the patience of political men. Some of the leading militants, thanks to the generosity of the Pethick-Lawrences and the respite of the truce, travelled to Bavaria to see Anton Lang in the Passion Play. In this benign atmosphere the Committee bent to its task.

The Bill eventually propounded was simple. The first clause enacted: 'Every woman possessed of a household qualification, or of a ten pound occupation qualification . . . shall be entitled to be registered as a voter, and when registered to vote. . . .'

The household qualification meant that every woman owning a house, a part of a house or even a room, provided she had full control over it, could vote. The occupier of premises valued at £10 *per annum* brought in the small shopkeeper.

The second clause of the Bill enacted that marriage should not disqualify—but that husband and wife could not both qualify for a vote in respect of the same property.

The obvious criticism of this measure was that in order to win

---

[1] Militant action, i.e., action involving breaches of the law, was suspended. Intervention against Liberal candidates in the country was, of course, not illegal, and was carried on with vigour by the Union, with speeches and canvassing.

Conservative support, the Committee had gone too far down the road to meet them. The property qualification was dominant, and there was no vote for the mill-hand, or the housewife tied to a drinker in the Mile End Road—whose claim to a vote had always been strongly urged in suffrage propaganda. But such political subtleties did not assail the innocent minds of the leaders of the Union. The principle was conceded: that was sufficient, and therefore let the Bill be welcomed. And during those crucial but peaceful weeks the Union did what was possible to keep the cause vividly in the public eye.

In March the Albert Hall was filled, and Mrs. Pankhurst gave medals to those, including Lady Constance, who had suffered for the cause. At this meeting a telegram from a supporter in Birmingham, promising £5 to the funds, was read out: it ended: 'glimpses I have seen of women's lives in Morocco make me, if possible, more earnest than before.' But although these sentiments were loudly applauded their relevance was not obvious since not even the most fervid opponent of the women's vote, and not even Mrs. Humphrey Ward herself, was suggesting that the customs of Morocco—that happy land of sheikhs—should be transported across the ocean to England. This particular meeting was advertised by a parade of parasols—those emblems of leisured womanhood—manufactured in the purple, white and green of the Union with Votes For Women embroidered on them in silk. Shortly afterwards supporters of the suffrage even attempted a sortie into the very fortress of the male sex—the racing track at Brooklands. Here, it has to be confessed that mankind did not appear to advantage. The Edwardian racing motorist looked particularly unkempt in the shaggy horror of Norfolk jacket and knicker-bocker, and his appearance was not softened by tweed caps and monstrous goggles. A courageous worthy, rejoicing in the name of Mr. Bischoff, christened his Triumph motor bicycle 'The Suffragette'. Those versed in these matters will appreciate that the Triumph was conspicuous among all the early motor bicycles as an especially sober and reliable machine—not given to the temper and spirits of militancy. Wearing the tricolour sash of purple, white and green, with streamers of the same strident combination flying from his handle-bars, the audacious Bischoff rode round the track, opening his throttle with eagerness to establish the victory of The Suffragette. He came in last but one.

Although King Edward had died, the spirit of pageantry, which had given life and colour to his reign, lived on. Four days after the Conciliation Bill was introduced in the House of Commons, the Union staged a vast and successful procession through the streets. At the head of all marched Mrs. Leigh—the first to endure forcible feeding. Behind rode 'the General' on a splendid charger: she was full of jests and animation, her personality ensuring for the marchers a popular reception from the crowd of sightseers. The Honourable Mrs. Haverfield,[1] with Miss Vera Howey acted as mounted marshals. All three ladies rode astride. Behind the General came the women's band. After this came the contingent of prisoners which attracted much notice. There were 617 women, and they were dressed in white, carrying aloft tall staves surmounted by a broad arrow. Although they looked a shade too cheerful— even Lady Constance was photographed smiling—they were highly effective—somewhat reminiscent of a procession of Christian witness on Good Friday. Mrs. Pankhurst was especially striking in a white cloak. Prominent in the procession were the learned ladies, some 800 strong, who named themselves the 'Regiment of Portias'. Mrs. Garrett Anderson was in the van of this group, and it was noticed that, rather unexpectedly, they marched with fine military precision. Immediately behind the Portias, looking a shade abashed, came a male squad from the University of Cambridge.

The Women's Freedom League was represented by a detachment headed by Mrs. Despard, carrying a bunch of arum lilies. She had a great ovation, though some of the spectators—perhaps veterans from the Boer War—called out as she passed 'Good old French'. The cry was hardly appropriate since at that time brother and sister were on the worst of terms. Yet it was understandable for in the early days of the twentieth century the leading soldiers— Roberts, Kitchener and French—had a great following among the London populace.

---

[1] She formed a remount camp for horses left to die on the veldt during the South African War. She generally wore a hunting stock and small bowler hat. She lived at Marsh Court, near Sherbourne.

The women athletes had a special section, at the head of which was a banner with Diana and her hound, carried by conspicuously vigorous ladies who were dressed for the gymnasium. Immediately behind them came the sweated workers. The writers had a special section, each member carrying a large goose quill. The actresses section included Miss Lena Ashwell, then at the height of her renown, her arms full of pink and white peonies. The musicians followed beneath a banner inscribed with the rather meaningless words: 'The rest may reason and welcome: 'tis we musicians know'—a curious line from the poet Browning. The rather grim little representatives of the Fabian women were closely followed by the Garden City contingent—all bearing large green boughs.

There were some cheering portents. At Hyde Park Corner, Countess Russell was present in her victoria, which was gorgeously decked in the colours of the Women's Freedom League. This lady was an American whose marriage to Lord Russell, a decade previously, had been the occasion of a celebrated trial for bigamy in the House of Lords. Also at Hyde Park Corner was the conspicuous figure of Bernard Shaw: he waved to his wife who was marching with the writers. As the ladies came bravely swinging along Pall Mall they were closely observed by the Archbishop of Canterbury who was standing on the balcony of the Athenaeum.

There was a small contingent of men and this included A. J. Webbe,[1] who left the Surrey and Middlesex cricket match, to march behind Laurence Housman.

While it is an obvious truism that pageants are not politics, the display—notwithstanding this—was a vivid reminder that the contribution of women to English national life was now so vigorous and varied that any exclusion became at once glaring and difficult to justify. Perhaps that may have impressed any Members of Parliament who happened to be watching, for they rather than the public or the newspapers were the target at this juncture. Even the remarkable sum of £5,000 which was collected in the Albert

---

[1] Webbe was a fine cricketer of the old school who had played for Harrow in the 1870's. Although suffrage propagandists contrived to suggest that he walked off the field to join Laurence Housman, he would seem merely to have left a match which he was watching.

Hall after the march was of small consequence compared with the feelings of members of the Commons. There lay the battlefield, and the augurs were not favourable.

The first reading of the Conciliation Bill, which was introduced by Shackleton the respected Labour member for Clitheroe, was carried without a division on June 14th. But there was a short debate in the course of which a strident voice was heard to say: 'I offer it implacable resistance.' The speaker was the redoubtable member for Walton—F. E. Smith. He was as good as his word, and when the Second Reading was held on July 11th and 12th he intervened with a speech which for argument and force was one of the best ever made against the principle of woman's suffrage. He began by emphasizing what was the undoubted weakness of the Bill when he said: 'I honestly believe it is a Conservative Bill in its policy', but he went on to say that in the long run it could only lead to the enfranchisement of all women. He then went on to argue that the doctrine of the right to vote was, as he expressed it, 'as dead as Rousseau'. He pointed out that the oriental population of the Empire, which was two-thirds of the whole, detested government by females and that far from 'No Taxation Without Representation' being accepted in the modern world, our Indian fellow subjects paid taxes, but did not vote. He argued in conclusion that women might be able to impose duties on men (e.g. conscription) which they were prevented from carrying out themselves because of their sex. Shortly after Smith had finished, Hilaire Belloc made a characteristic point. He referred to a remark of Shackleton that the House of Commons should recognize the intelligence of women from the fact that they wrote books: 'I confess'—he went on—'it turned me cold. There is perhaps nothing which an educated man or woman can do which requires less intelligence than the writing of books.' Such sentiments must have fallen harshly on the ears of the aged Madame Belloc, who was listening to the debate from the Strangers' Gallery.

Then followed Lord Hugh Cecil in a speech which was never forgotten by those who heard it and must by reason of its subtle wit be assured of immortality. Dealing with F. E. Smith's argument that men, owing to their superior physique must always enforce the laws which they were therefore entitled to make, Lord

Hugh alluding to his own frail constitution said: 'I presume that I shall be disfranchised, and that Eugene Sandow [the famous strong man of those times] will become a plural voter on a great scale.' The main point of his speech was an analysis of his sensations as a voter: 'I have a vote myself'—he said—'I exercise that vote in the City of Oxford in support of my noble friend [Lord Valentia, who as an Irish peer, was not prevented from sitting in the Commons and represented Oxford]. But when I go to Oxford to exercise my vote I am not at all conscious of performing a function either difficult or sensational or particularly masculine. When I go through the streets, where my education as a voter begins, I see many posters, none of which seem to me very convincing—some of which tell me that Tariff Reform will greatly lessen unemployment, and others that it will reduce the working classes to black bread and horseflesh, with neither of which anticipations I am able to agree. I then go, in a mood not very joyful, to the polling-booth.' He then describes the process of voting, and how the moment he had put his voting paper in the box 'I was seized with a strong nervous apprehension that I had inadvertently voted for the candidate whom I did not intend to support. . . . It is a serenely tranquil, an austerely refined, and from beginning to end a thoroughly ladylike operation.'

But to the consternation of the Conciliation Committee both Lloyd George and Churchill attacked the Bill and voted against it. Churchill, who had offered his blessing to the work of the Committee, in fact killed the Bill. Loud and long were the cries of traitor by which he was assailed, and the accomplished Lord Lytton attacked him in the Albert Hall with vehemence. Churchill's speech was effective because he showed that the Committee, in trying to rope in Conservative support, had produced a bill which was not democratic. He explained how it would lead to faggot-voting, i.e., a wealthy man could give property to his wife and daughter and enfranchise them. He also drew a cheerful picture of the prostitute, enjoying a vote under the Bill on her premises, and then losing the vote when she made a respectable marriage. Asquith closed the proceedings with a speech which was not designed to mollify the militants—'the cause'—he said—'which cannot win its way to public acceptance by persuasion, argument, organization and by the peaceful methods of agitation is a cause which has already in advance pronounced upon itself its own sentence of death.'

The voting was 299 in favour and 189 against. But the Bill was doomed by the size of the minority. The Government, with such a clear division of feeling, was justified in refusing to give further facilities for the Bill. In any event by a majority of 150 the House agreed that the Bill should go to a Committee of the whole House which was tantamount to no further progress.

In reality the Conciliation Bill had shared the fate of the previous bills on the woman's vote. It was saluted in the House with a polite majority and then like the corpse, after the Last Post, passed to dumb forgetfulness with dignity and decorum. But the Conciliation Bill showed this important difference from the succession of bills of earlier days. The debate had lasted two days, and had been marked by outstanding speeches from all the leading men in the House. Woman's Suffrage had for the first time accorded opportunity for a full-dress debate: it had provoked serious thought and splendid oratory from Asquith and Balfour, from Churchill and Austen Chamberlain, from Lloyd George and Alfred Lyttelton, from Snowden and Keir Hardie. As often in its history the House of Commons reflected, by rising to the occasion, the depth of feeling in the country over an issue which, in Snowden's happy phrase, 'divided parties like a flash of crooked lightning.' The seriousness with which Parliament treated the issue of woman's suffrage in 1910 must in justice be counted as one of the achievements of militancy. For would peaceful parades, lobbying Members of Parliament and gatherings in Belgravian drawing-rooms have achieved the same end? The debate (though disappointing to the ardent spirits of Clement's Inn) was in reality a measure of their success.

Yet some ominous points had made their appearance. There was always the danger that the Cabinet, feeling the irritation of the public with some of the acts of militancy, would lose their patience. And there were clear signs throughout that tranquil summer of 1910 that the Government was preparing sterner and more ruthless measures if militancy should start again. Herbert Gladstone—kindly, honourable but not a successful Home Secretary had gone to South Africa as Governor-General, and had been succeeded at the Home Office by Churchill. Almost the first act of the new Home Secretary was to introduce a scheme of prison reform. These changes included altered treatment for people sent to prison with no element of moral turpitude, who were no longer to wear prison clothing, or to be searched or to take the regulation bath. They were to be allowed food from outside, to take regular exercise and to talk during exercise. The new Home Secretary gave orders that women suffragists were to have the benefit of those new regulations provided, of course, that they behaved and kept the ordinary rules. But it was known that accompanying these concessions—which were obviously wise because by taking the horror out of prison life he had removed some of the romance from it—(and had they been introduced earlier they might have removed much of the mischief from the agitation) he had issued far stricter instructions to the police, and had been carefully examining the problem of forcible feeding. It is believed that, with characteristic desire to savour all aspects of life, he had himself forcibly fed in private. But his whole speech in June was in his best fighting vein with scant sympathy for the women's case and read, in conjunction with the scathing close of Asquith's speech, suggests that the Cabinet had their plans laid and were awaiting the next move of the militants with confidence. Only the benign, good intentions of the Conciliation Committee kept the peace through the summer of 1910.

On their side too the women were not unprepared. As early as May of that year Mrs. Pethick-Lawrence had written in a private letter,[1] in words which were characteristic of her emotional but effective style: 'If the scheme miscarries then we shall know that the great Artificer has need of the furnace again and the smelting-trough and the anvil, and we shall be ready with glad hearts.' At this point it is fair to observe that the needs of the great Artificer were less urgent than those of the Vulcans of militancy in Clement's Inn. For, as has been already emphasized in these pages, the directors of the policy of the Union, having once embarked on militant action, were inexorably obliged to go on. For both their membership and their funds were, to some degree, kept together

[1] MS. in London Museum.

by the excitements of militant action. Their opportunity to resume the fight came with the autumn of 1910. When Parliament met in that November, Mr. Asquith announced on November 18th that the negotiations between the Liberal and Conservative leaders had collapsed, that there would be an immediate General Election on the House of Lords and that the Government would take all the time of the remaining session for its own business. This of course meant that the Conciliation Bill or any amended version of it would have to be abandoned.

The tactics of the women followed their well-worn course. Apprised of what was likely to be said in Parliament, they arranged a meeting, while Asquith was speaking, in the Caxton Hall and as soon as he finished they sent off waves of women to the House of Commons, with a deputation to the Prime Minister, to withdraw the veto on the Conciliation Bill. The leaders who, according to the established routine, were admitted to the House of Commons by the police, were Mrs. Pankhurst and Mrs. Garrett Anderson. This venerable but picturesque figure—she was seventy-four and wore a fur bonnet tied under the chin with white ribbons —was the epitome of Victorian feminism—sensible, dignified and attractive. Her presence commanded the immediate respect and attention of the police who escorted the two ladies to the House of Commons. But their comrades who followed, and attempted to reach Parliament Square throughout the afternoon, were given a less cordial reception.

In the annals of the suffrage movement this cheerless November afternoon was ever afterwards referred to as 'Black Friday'. The recollection of those taking part in the demonstration provides a lurid picture. The wife of a Dublin professor had a punch on the nose and was hurled by a constable, in front of a mounted police-man, with the encouraging order 'Ride over her'. The gallant Mrs. Leigh, ever at the heart of trouble, was knocked flat in the road by an inspector who said to a constable: 'Take the cow away.' A lady, unmarried and verging on middle age, was grasped with firm affection by a young policeman and like Mrs. Proudie, on a different occasion, she screamed: 'Unhand it, sir' only to be told: 'My old dear, I can grip you where I like to-day.' As was observed by another victim: 'The police have such strong, large hands, that when they take hold of one by the throat or grasp one's side or ribs they cannot possibly know how tightly they are holding.' Yet another lady observed: 'What I complain of is the continuous beating and pinching. If any of us develop cancer in the body in after years we shall have no cause for surprise.' A married lady went up to a policeman and announced with some importance that it was her intention to reach Downing Street or die. 'Die then' he replied seizing her by the hair. Throughout the proceedings women, including the aged and eminent Mrs. Saul Solomon, were seized by the breasts, and a cripple on a tricycle was pushed into a side-street where the valves of the tyres of her machine were taken away.

The whole scene was a strange manifestation of feeling in a civilized people. But the women were mistaken in trying to throw the odium for what happened on to the police. Certainly the methods of the police had changed. When Gladstone was Home Secretary, the ladies advanced: threw themselves against the cordon of police with the abandon of those taking part in a Highland Schottische and sank, with relief, into the protective custody of the first friendly policeman. On 'Black Friday' the police deliberately delayed their arrests, treating those political ladies as though they were a party of bibulous charladies, trying to force their way into a public-house after closing time, who would soon realize that after all home was the best place. The ladies were, in popular language 'pushed around', instead of being arrested. Among the crowd were the inevitable roughs and cackling youths who, as the police flung the women out of the road, received them with coarse epithets and coarser endearments. And if a young policeman, perhaps fresh from a study of the latest novel of Ethel M. Dell, seized a middle-aged spinster and, provoked beyond endurance, whispered: 'You have been waiting for this for a long time' we can scarcely blame him. Churchill had of course to defend the police in the House of Commons and he was loudly cheered when he refused any enquiry into vague charges brought by irresponsible persons. Later Churchill denied that any fresh instructions had been issued to the police, but he asserted that in the future 'with a view to the avoidance of disagreeable scenes, for which no one is responsible but the disorderly women police officers are to make arrests as soon as there is occasion'. He won the delighted approval of the police and Commons alike when he referred to the Women's Social and Political Union as 'that copious fountain of mendacity'.

It seems most likely that the Home Office did not issue any orders to the police, but that the warning of the Superintendent, which was given in an address to all police going on duty, rather over-emphasized the importance of only arresting the women as a last resort. The release of all the women on the following morning (an astute move) was evidently prompted by Churchill and the Home Office.

Four days later the members of the Union, with support from the Women's Freedom League, made a surprise attack on Downing Street when there was a thin police defence. In the scrimmage the Prime Minister had to be hustled into a taxi and Augustine Birrell, who adorned the government with his wit and learning, received damage to his knee-cap. Several windows were smashed. There was a curious little sequel to this day which, probably because the police were taken at a disadvantage, was fought by them with vigour. Churchill came into the street and seeing the hapless Mrs. Cobden-Sanderson pinned against some railings by a squad of police called out: 'Take that woman away, she is obviously one of the ringleaders.' The words 'that woman' were possibly infelicitous when applied to the daughter of immortal Cobden—and to a lady who mixed freely in the social circle of the Government. They were overheard by a young member of a distinguished Jewish family—Hugh Franklin, a relative of Churchill's colleague Herbert Samuel. Franklin was a strong male sympathizer with the militants and had in fact been arrested on 'Black Friday', though with the others he had been released on the following day.

A few days later, in the last week in November Churchill was firing the opening shot in the second General Election of that year with a characterstcally robust condemnation of the Conservatives to the electors of Bradford. Coming back by train he had waht *The Times* described as an 'unpleasant experience'. Walking down to the restaurant car from his first-class compartment he was suddenly confronted by Franklin in the corridor who, raising a dog-whip, called out 'Winston Churchill, take that you cur'. The blow was fortunately intercepted by Detective Sergeant Sandercock, who was travelling with the Home Secretary. Franklin was sentenced to six weeks imprisonment and had to be, forcibly fed.

Shortly after this episode—at the end of December—Herbert Samuel, who was an opponent of giving way to the women, was himself the victim of a curious attack. A suffragette took off one of her boots and hurled it at the front door of his house—31 Porchester Terrace. The boot broke the door—possibly not a great tribute to the quality of the timber used in the construction of that agreeable terrace.

Some of the excuse for further militancy was removed by Asquith who gave an undertaking that the Liberal Government if returned, would give facilities for a suffrage bill provided it permitted of free amendment. This satisfied the Freedom League and the Constitutionalists who set about persuading parliamentary candidates to give pledges of their support for female franchise. Their task was not easy, for the attention of candidate and voter alike was absorbed by the House of Lords, which to the Conservative seemed a gallant St. George about to slay the dragon of Radicalism, while to the Liberal that House seemed to embody the malign spirit of influence and riches—a spirit which existed to ensure that whatever the colour of the government of the day the principles of the Conservative party should always control the destinies of the nation. Into this unpromising arena stepped two candidates, committed to the women's cause as suffrage supporters and fighting beneath the banner inscribed 'Votes For Women'. The one, who fought St. Pancras (East) polled twenty-two votes, the other who fought the Camlachie Division of Glasgow polled thirty-five votes. There was also a species of primitive Gallup poll on the women's question during this election. At Hornsey reply-paid postcards were sent out to 22,350 registered voters asking for their opinion on whether women should have the vote. Only 7,500 bothered to answer, and of these only 2,200 were favourable. The miserable polls of the suffrage candidates and this meagre response to the informal poll at Hornsey were decisive proof of the difficulty of trying to fight the women's cause outside the protection of party.

The Union carried on some desultory acts of militancy through-out the election. There were the usual attempts on Cabinet Ministers, and Mrs. Mackworth—now an honoured figure in weekly journalism—succeeded in jumping on the running-board of Mr. Asquith's motor-car, when he was on his way to an election meeting at St. Andrew's. She has described the scene: 'We gazed at each other. I a little dazed at having succeeded so easily: he leaning back in his car, looking white and frightened rather like a fascinated rabbit.' Those who knew Mr. Asquith will hardly recognize him in this description: his principal anxiety under attack was lest the women should try to tear off his clothes. But as in the January election, the suffrage issue was submerged by the wild waves of party; through the storms ooer the House of Lords, the cry of 'Votes For Women' was scarcely audible.

XXV

From Prison to Citizenship

The result of the election in December 1910 was substantially the same as that in the previous January. The Liberals and Conservatives were exactly equal with 272, and the Government depended on a majority of 126 provided by the Irish and Labour parties. The position of the Government was not weak, but it demanded care, and a consideration for the susceptibilities of those allies who provided the majority. Plainly the bill to hobble the House of Lords, for which, irrespective of the Irish, the country had shown a clear majority, was the first preoccupation of the new House of Commons. This Bill, after debates of dramatic force unmatched in British parliamentary history, was passed by both Houses on 10th August 1911. But the reform of the House of Lords left in its wake great bitterness between the Conservatives and Liberals—feelings which were intensified when the ambitious and pragmatical Bonar Law seized the Conservative leadership. Although Conservative leaders felt deeply and sincerely outraged by Liberal measures after the second election of 1910, they called up depths of passion which were dangerous and unprecedented. Inevitably the bias of Liberals—stung by the violence and malevolence of Conservative spokesmen—swung sharply to the left. From the suffrage aspect this was important because Liberal opinion was hardening against increasing the anomalies of the existing electoral system by grafting on to it a female franchise, and was increasingly turning to adult suffrage (in which women could be included) as the essential objective.

This seems to explain the failure of the next Conciliation Bill. When the new Parliament was elected, the Conciliation Committee was formed again, and the Bill was altered to meet the objections which Churchill had raised. The new Bill was introduced by Sir George Kemp, chairman of a thriving flannel manufactory at Rochdale, who although a gentleman of fashion and a member of White's Club, was none the less a valued Liberal and had succeeded in beating Joynson-Hicks in Churchill's old Manchester constituency in the first election of 1910. Passing from triumph to triumph he succeeded in unhorsing Bonar Law for this same constituency, which had been hardly fought four times in as many years, at the December election.

But he was less successful in transposing the zest and vitality of Manchester electioneering to the Conciliation Bill. The debate, which was held on May 5th, was somewhat listless, no front-bench men spoke, the majority in favour was large (167) but the Bill was once again doomed by being committed to the House. The Cabinet, in a number of statements by Ministers, said that no further time could be spared by the Government that session (their energies were fully absorbed by the House of Lords) but that the Prime Minister's pledge that time would be found during the life of the Parliament held good. They undertook to devote a week to a bill on the lines of the Conciliation Bill and, amid the sombre gloom of a banquet at the National Liberal Club, Sir Edward Grey agreed that the word 'week' should be given an elastic interpretation.

The militants, conscious that the House of Lords filled the attention of the public and mindful of the approaching Coronation, were glad to lay down arms; all sides were comforted by an assurance from the Prime Minister, in a letter to Lord Lytton, that the Government were 'unanimous in their determination to give effect, not only in the letter but in the spirit,' to his promise before the election. Mrs. Pankhurst left in the summer for an extensive tour of America.

On the Saturday before King George V was crowned on June 22nd—the women, militants and constitutionalists alike, joined in a vast procession through the London streets: gilded by June sunshine, which was absent from the crowning of King George, this pageant of womanhood was a consummate spectacle, reminding all who saw it not only of the achievements of women but of their gradual emergence from their tribulations in Victorian times. Yet in spite of the sun, the smiling faces and the prodigious success of the whole, a certain melancholy pervades the scene—its mournful countenance plainly visible to us looking back. For on looking to what was to follow the reader can see that much of the pent-up enthusiasm and idealism, which were the inner springs driving these women to their demonstration, were destined to be shattered in the convulsions of 1914. The trumpets of rejoicing, the confident, high-pitched voices of the women sounded bravely, but the destiny of the world was not to be guided by the hopes of these enthusiasts; the sounds of jubilee were not to be thrown back by the future, they rather obeyed the injunction of the poet 'answer, echoes, dying, dying, dying'.

While it was massing, the procession filled the Embankment along its whole length from Blackfriars to Westminster, and through the side-streets to Whitehall. Once again 'the General', mounted, rode at the head. The prisoners, a much larger force than in 1910 for they were almost 1,000 strong, marched beneath the banner 'From Prison to Citizenship'. They were dressed in white. Behind them came a pageant of women, which included one of the great parliamentary abbesses of medieval times, and the homely countenance of Lydia Becker. It was on this occasion that Lady Strachey, tall and conspicuous, a widow and the mother of ten distinguished children, was asked by an urchin scampering along the fringe of the procession: 'Don't yer wish yer 'ad a 'usband?' Her reply: 'Not wishing to commit bigamy, I don't' was characteristic but must alas! be regarded as apocryphal. And perhaps the feelings of the great majority of those taking part were admirably expressed by the headmistress of a famous girls' school: 'I shall hate and loathe the very thought of it, but of course I will be there.' An observer at the time remarked that the contribution from the constitutional societies was 'unexpectedly large'.

The two truces, the large majorities for each Conciliation Bill in the House of Commons and the very considerable undertaking given by the Liberal Cabinet in the summer of 1911 naturally filled the whole of the women's movement with hope. Hardly would the historian be exaggerating who argued that it was the first really substantial advance since the days of Mill. Not unnaturally the militants claimed at the time, and have claimed since, that their zeal gave the impetus which forced the movement forward, and that the events of 1911 were a triumph for Clement's Inn, for the Trinitarian Dictatorship as they were dubbed by a former comrade.

There can be no doubt whatever—and even the most censorious critic of militancy would not demur to the truth of this judgment —that the militants had attracted in the newspapers a prominence for the suffrage question which was new and fortifying to the whole movement. Miss Becker and her disciples had—before the dawn of militancy—been virtually ignored in the newspapers, once the novelty of what they were doing had worn off. The suffragists were at the time—and have always been—generous in giving the militants full credit for what they did to rouse public attention to women's suffrage. Lord Baldwin well caught the sense of urgency which the militants brought to the movement when unveiling the statue of Mrs. Pankhurst outside the Houses of Parliament; he said on 6th March 1930 'If Mrs. Pankhurst did not make the movement, it was she who set the heather on fire.'

At the same time many suffragists lamented that clamour and hysterics were news, whereas reasoned argument was not. *The Times*, at this period always very spiteful against the women, adopted this lamentation and carried it further by arguing that the militants had only harmed the cause with public opinion. An attempt to rebut this argument by a leading constitutionalist gave rise to a strange little episode this year.

In the summer Lady Selborne, wife of a former Governor of the Transvaal, sister of Lord Salisbury and President of the Conservative and Unionist Women's Franchise Association, wrote a letter to *The Times* enclosing a letter from Lady Constance, which was published, with appropriate prominence. The point of Lady Constance's letter was to show that a drawing-room meeting held by Lady Selborne in her London house received no publicity worth mentioning 'while if I threw a stone at the Prime Minister's carriage I should get a column on the front page.' Immediately Holford Knight, who two decades later was to close a disappointing career in Labour politics as a kind of professional mute at the memorial services of illustrious men, rushed into the controversy with a letter saying that the late Dr. Crippen attracted quite a respectable amount of publicity to 'his cause but I never understood that was a measure of the public's sympathy'. But Knight's amusing intervention was speedily eclipsed by Lady Selborne who wrote again and said: 'I must first confess that Lady Constance did not write the letter I enclosed to you—I borrowed her name for the moment.' Lady Constance's sister called this 'a mild and harmless deception', but the *Daily Express* was nearer the mark with a paragraph headed "La Belle Stratagem" which shed crocodile tears for the dignity of *The Times* thus the victim of 'an ennobled hoax'. Lord Hugh Cecil leapt to the defence of his sister: 'It seems to be strangely imagined'—he wrote—'that Lady Selborne has introduced a novelty and an indecent novelty—a sort of literary harem skirt—to a scandalized world.'[1] He pointed out that his sister's letter had been designed to criticize the paper's mistaken sense of news value, and he drew a parallel between his sister's letter and the parable with which Nathan the prophet had rebuked King David though he thought that the latter had been attended with more satisfactory fruits of penitence than his sister's attempt to rebuke *The Times*.

In a familiar witticism Wilde once wrote: 'There is only one thing in the world worse than being talked about, and that is not being talked about.' No doubt the leaders of the Union would have cordially endorsed the truth of this epigram, but the whole question of the distinction between notoriety and publicity was subtle and not easily decided. The newspapers, just getting into their full stride of snappy sensationalism for the first time in English history, unquestionably did much to encourage Clement's Inn but many of the newspaper headlines, though they may have flattered the Trinitarian triumvirate, were damaging to the women's cause. (The *Daily Mail*, which was the leader of the popular papers at the time, always gave the minimum attention to the escapades of the militants, as a matter of policy. But it was alone in this—even the *Standard*, the organ of Conservatism and at that time on its death-bed, attempted to revive itself by giving exceptional space to the suffrage question.)

[1] The harem skirt—a narrow skirt which was the fore-runner of the hobble skirt—had lately reached England from Paris.

Nor will it be overlooked that the press in holding up shocked hands at militancy, was not leading opinion it was merely falling into line beside it. To thousands of God-fearing citizens the behaviour of the Pankhursts and their friends seemed not dissimilar from the activities of Peter the Painter against whom the forces of the Crown, with the police, had been employed in the siege of Sidney Street, off Mile End Road in January 1911. The feelings of these worthy citizens were well caught in some verses by Rudyard Kipling—not possibly in his happiest vein but certainly not ineffective. They contained the verse:

When Nag the basking cobra hears the careless foot of man,
He will sometimes wriggle sideways and avoid it if he can.
But his mate makes no such motion where she camps beside the trail.
For the female of the species is more deadly than the male.

To an extent the Women's Freedom League struck the happiest note by a series of escapades which were successful and amusing but not riotous. These attracted notice in the newspapers but avoided the condemnation which accompanied the press accounts of the fiercer militants. The League organized a boycott of the ten-yearly census of the population which was held on 2nd April 1911: the women spent the night with friends, in empty houses with 'No Vote No Census' chalked on the walls, or in the delights of 'rinking' at the Aldwych skating rink. Somewhat to the disappointment of those organizing this protest, the Government did not enforce the £5 fine or month's imprisonment which was laid down as the penalty. No doubt the elimination of a few hundreds of women did not invalidate the figures, and John Burns, who as President of the Local Government Board, was the Minister responsible replied, when asked why the Government had not prosecuted the absentees, 'In the hour of success, mercy and magnanimity must be shown.' *Punch* enlivened the episode by observing that the ladies must have taken leave of their census.

The League also paid great attention at this time to the possibility of harnessing spiritual force to the suffrage cause. The Spiritual Militant League was formed in March and it was laid down that members of this League should attend church services with the idea of evoking spiritual force to advance social justice

13. Mrs. Despard in Downing Street: a group of sympathizers

14. Mounted Police clearing Trafalgar Square after a Suffragette meeting—May 1913

for women. This League issued a long manifesto, protesting against the indignities to women in the marriage service of the Church, inevitably animadverting on the words of the clergyman: 'I pronounce that they be man and wife together', and suggesting that the use of man instead of husband implied all kinds of indulgences for the male. The *Daily Herald*, which had just embarked on its precarious start in life, followed this up by suggesting that a Guild of Honour should be formed by women who should undertake to bear no children until the vote was won.

The League took its part in the celebrations which were held in 1911 to celebrate the tercentenary of the Authorized Version of the Bible. A packed meeting was held in the Albert Hall addressed by the Archbishop of Canterbury, the American Ambassador and the Prime Minister. In the course of Asquith's speech a large banner was unfurled with this text from the prophet Isaiah 'to loose the bonds of wickedness, to undo the heavy burdens and to let the oppressed go free' with the expected advice that the way to obtain these desirable ends was 'Votes For Women'.

There were further signs in this year of the linking of the suffrage movement with religion. The Catholic Women's Suffrage Society (with Blessed Joan of Arc as patron) was formed in 1911, the Free Church League had been formed a few months earlier and the Jewish League was formed a few months later, as was the Scottish Churches League.

Moreover there had been over the past few years a general accretion of strength to the suffrage cause among the professional classes. The actresses and artists had their own society: there was a Civil Service society, a Welsh society formed at the time of the Coronation procession in 1911, a London Graduates Union for men and women, an arts and crafts society called The Suffrage Atelier, a society for Scottish University Women and perhaps most remarkable of all a society for Gymnastic Teachers, with a membership of ninety-seven. This weight of opinion gave the impression that only a few months separated the women from their goal. The vote was round the corner. In Kentucky Mrs. Pankhurst was asked: 'When will English women vote?' She answered: 'Next year.'

XXVI

'War is Declared on Women'

This prospect, which seemed at once alluring but conclusive in the festive summer of Coronation Year, was unhappily lost in the fogs and frosts of Guy Fawkes. On November 7th the People's Suffrage Federation sent a deputation to Asquith. This body had only had an existence of eighteen months but it was influential and respectable. On its executive were some of the paramount names in both Liberal and Labour parties, which included Mrs. Francis Acland, wife of a Junior Minister, Mr. W. C. Anderson a Labour candidate and afterwards a Labour Member of Parliament, Miss Bondfield, the first women member of a Cabinet, Miss Llewellyn Davies, an enlightened social worker, Miss Mary Macarthur, Mr. J. S. Middleton, for long secretary of the Labour party, Mr. Walter Rea, a sound Liberal member who, with Mr. Arthur Henderson of the Labour party, was Treasurer of the Federation, Mr. George Roberts, the Labour member for Norwich and Mr. and Mrs. G. M. Trevelyan. Now no Prime Minister could afford to ignore the representations of an organization such as this which was broadly based on enlightened opinion. The Federation believed that woman's suffrage could only be carried through in alliance with the progressive forces in politics, and would also have to be accompanied by a reform of the franchise system. The deputation of November 7th pointed out that from a total population in Great Britain of 45,000,000 people, only 7,500,000 had votes.

Thoughtful Liberals always felt that this exclusive franchise had greatly helped the Conservatives, and really explained their considerable success at the 1910 Elections. The inevitable consequence of the bitterness of Conservative polemics, as has already been emphasized, was to make the Liberals increasingly turn to ideas of broadening the franchise. This was immediately shown in the Prime Minister's reply to the Deputation, which went a great deal further than public opinion expected. After prefacing his remarks by the statement that the Government was bound by its pledges on the Conciliation Bill, he came down strongly on the side of adult suffrage, announced that the Government would introduce a bill to give effect to this in the next session and that it would be capable of amendment to include women. Long-drawn and immediate were the yelpings from Conservative leaders but they were drowned by the piercing cries from Clement's Inn. 'Treachery' screamed Mrs. Pankhurst from across the Atlantic: 'War is declared on women' answered Christabel from London. She went on: 'The Government's latest attempts to cheat women of the vote is of course inspired by Mr. Lloyd George. The whole crooked and discreditable scheme is characteristic of the man.'

The reason for the indignation of these ladies was that they wanted the principle of the justice of the women's claim admitted by some such measure as the Conciliation Bill, which was solely concerned with women: they bitterly resented the idea that the Government should have adulterated the principle by mixing it with the enfranchisement of more men. The difference was perhaps narrow and seems, from the vantage point of to-day, trifling. And just as the Irish Home Rule question in the 1880's had divided the older societies, so party politics introduced fresh discords into the franchise agitation at the dawn of King George's reign. By a weird conjunction, the Conservative members of the older societies and the Union were together in their support of the Conciliation Bill. In fact Mrs. Pankhurst and her daughter Christabel were far more at home in Conservative circles than they were in progressive surroundings. Miss Sylvia Pankhurst has stated that from 1910 onwards her sister 'had entered aristocratic Conservative circles'. Some members of the Labour party—Keir Hardie and Snowden—were also in sympathy with this strange alliance. But the great bulk of Liberal-minded supporters of the women's franchise saw nothing outrageous or treacherous in the policy propounded by Asquith.

He followed this announcement by agreeing to see a deputation from all the suffrage societies—an occasion when he was at his best—listening attentively to all the speeches and in his reply singling out that of Mrs. Despard for special compliment and praise. He chaffed Christabel saying that she had come, offering terms of peace, with a pistol in one hand and a dagger in the other. But he left the ladies in no doubt that he remained opposed to giving the vote to women, but that he was perfectly ready to leave the matter to the Commons, provided the whole ramshackle electoral system was overhauled and modernized.

And now Lloyd George added his spoon to the pot. On the day after Asquith had received the deputation of the suffrage societies there was an announcement in the *Daily News* over the initials P.W.W.[1] stating that Lloyd George had placed his services at the disposal of 'the great and growing suffrage party' and was prepared to move an amendment, giving women the vote, to the Reform Bill. Some days later he spoke at Bath—not perhaps the ideal choice—for the city was built on leisure and riches and rheumatism—but explained by the presence of the Liberal Federation which was holding its annual meeting there. He detailed the political moves which had at last opened the road for a democratic measure 'which will enfranchise not a limited class of women, chosen just to suit the Tory canvasser', but would include the wife of the working-man. 'That explains' he went on 'the fury of these anti-Liberal women.' He thought that as duels were vanishing all over Europe so wars might end if women were armed with the vote. His speech included a characteristic passage, which was to usher in a fiercer outbreak of militancy and forms the prelude to the next chapter.

[1] Philip Whitwell Wilson, a Liberal member from 1906 to 1910 and thereafter one of the most esteemed contributors to Liberal journalism. See also p. 138.

XXVII

Smashing the Windows

'I do not say there have not been cruel women in history, but on the whole it has been the salvation of the race that with the welter of cruelty which through the ages filled the earth with the moaning of the tortured, the sex stood with unpolluted hands at the altar of mercy.' Gratifying and eloquent as this tribute may have sounded, when spoken by Lloyd George hard by the genteel splashings of the Pump Room, it was no substitute for the vote and it was no consolation to those who were voteless. Nor did this tribute to women accord well with the coterie in Clement's Inn, who were even then as Lloyd George spoke, preparing to transform the battle for the vote into the battle of the sexes. For there were no altars of mercy in Clement's Inn. A few days before Lloyd George spoke Mrs. Pethick-Lawrence, in the absence of Mrs. Pankhurst who was in America, hurled her cohorts into battle with the police in Parliament Square. She urged them to sacrifice themselves 'for the great sin whose root is in sex domination'. Over 200 women were arrested including Mrs. Pethick-Lawrence herself, who fought with the police for twenty minutes, Lady Sybil Smith and five members of the Duval family—mother, three daughters and a son.[1] Shortly afterwards Mr. Asquith was refused a hearing at the City Temple, where he was to speak to mark the coming-of-age of the Mansfield House Settlement in Canning Town. Mr. Ramsay Macdonald, who was present, des-

---

[1] Victor Duval born 1885, a Liberal, who resigned active party work on founding the Men's Political Union for Women's Enfranchisement. Shortly after his release in 1911, he married Miss Una Dugdale, of the distinguished Warwickshire family. This marriage caused public comment because of the deletion of the word 'obey' and was one of the earliest weddings at which the omission was made.

cribed the scene as 'disgusting and degrading', and added a characteristically confused observation that if 'he thought the cause had come to this' (and it was alas! only too obvious that it had) 'I would go into the Lobby every time against it.'

At the end of the year Mrs. Swanwick, sister of the artist Sickert, and a leading suffragist of integrity and influence, wrote a letter to the *Nation* which bitterly attacked the Women's Social and Political Union and which contained the sentence 'I would rather be loyal to my own conception of reason and right than to any theory of sex loyalty laid down by a self-chosen architect.' For as 1911 ended, events began to show that sex loyalty was the dominant theme of the leaders in Clement's Inn, and the attentive listener could even hear the alarming sounds of drum beat and bugle summoning the faithful to arms, to take their action stations in the battle of the sexes.

Mrs. Pankhurst returned from America, and on February 16th 1912, she addressed a meeting of liberated prisoners—'We don't want to use'—she said—'any weapons that are unnecessarily strong. If the argument of the stone, the time-honoured, official, political argument, is sufficient, then we will never use any stronger argument. And that is the weapon and the argument that we are going to use next time. . . . I am taking charge of the demonstration, and that is the argument I am going to use.' Mrs. Pankhurst, frail and essentially feminine, was not an accomplished stone-thrower. In her hands stones and even flints, not unlike the arrow in Longfellow's song 'which fell to earth I knew not where' were apt to leave a plate-glass window unscathed. After her speech, and in preparation for the threat thus openly made, she was known to have been busily practising in the dusk against a hay-stack.

Most people would feel that Mrs. Pankhurst was overstating her case in calling stone-throwing 'a time-honoured, official, political argument'. It was of course frequently used in the eighteenth century against those refusing to illuminate their houses in honour of some mob hero: it was used against the Clubs during the dock strike of the 1880's, and it was used against Apsley House at the time of the Reform Bill. In none of these cases did the argument convince or convert, and if stone-throwing could be honoured with the description of an argument, it was an argument which, Mrs. Pankhurst was quickly to find, carried with it its own refutation. Such an 'argument' finds its own murky level with the angry cracks and splinters in the pitiful shop-windows of German tradesmen in London in August 1914.

A week after this speech, the militants marked their final breach with the suffragists by attending a great meeting, organized by the constitutional supporters of woman's suffrage, at the Albert Hall, and by doing their best to disrupt the speeches. Mrs. Fawcett was in the chair, and Lloyd George, generously and not without courage, had agreed to speak. The Albert Hall boxes were filled with society leaders of the female suffrage, including the Duchess of St. Albans and the Duchess of Marlborough. As Lloyd George rose to speak he was assailed, in the words of a newspaper, 'by a single, whizzing cry of *Traitor*'. The interruptions were intolerable. At last an elderly lady rose immediately in front of Lloyd George. She was wearing a black satin dress and a white mob cap. For a moment Lloyd George flinched. This apparition from Victorian days—for such she seemed to the majority of the meeting—turned to the body of the Hall and called in stentorian tones: 'Couldn't you behave like ladies for once?' She seemed to embody the patient dignity of nineteenth-century womanhood calling across the decades to the tomboys of the twentieth. The burden of the Chancellor of the Exchequer's speech was that woman's suffrage was essential in face of the labour unrest and the social problems, which must be the primary concern of any Government in the future. Mrs. Snowden, who followed him, spoke of the wear and tear on any speaker of constant interruptions and said 'I would rather a thousand times have had my nerves flayed than that our distinguished guest should have suffered from this discourtesy to-night.' In this speech Lloyd George threw a douche of cold water on the suggestion that the question of woman's suffrage should be submitted to a referendum of the nation. This had been advocated at the beginning of 1912, and it had found strong support in the columns of the *Westminster Gazette*—the mouthpiece of official Liberalism.

The extent of opposition, roused by the tactics of Clement's Inn among the general public, was shown six days later when the Anti-Suffragists filled the same Hall. The orthodox politicians' speeches were made by Lord Cromer, Lord Curzon, F. E. Smith and 'Lulu' Harcourt (the Colonial Secretary) but the meeting was captured by Miss Violet Markham who used figures, with great effect, to show how meagre had been the contribution of women in the political field which was open to them—namely in local politics. She gave figures to show that there were at that time only twenty-one women on town councils and three on county councils. Miss Markham included in her speech the ringing sentence 'Renunciation is eternally better than possession'.

On the following day, March 1st, the militant opponents of the 'Anti's' expressed a contrary view with force. As four o'clock struck that afternoon almost every shop-window round Piccadilly Circus, up Regent Street and along much of the length of Oxford Street was broken by women striking them with hammers, which had been concealed in their muffs or in their clothes. At the same time Mrs. Pankhurst drove in a taxi-cab to Downing Street, accompanied by Mrs. Tuke and Mrs. Marshall. Getting out, the ladies threw stones at the Prime Minister's windows: Mrs. Marshall—whether by design or accident history does not relate—hit the Colonial Office, rather a wild shot as it meant that she had missed the whole of the conspicuous and tempting façade of the classical target at which she was aiming.

This wholesale stone-throwing—repeated a few days later in Kensington, was organized, concerted and serious. Mrs. Pankhurst had announced to all the world, a fortnight before, what was planned. And in its trivial way the following advertisement which appeared in *The Vote* immediately after Mrs. Pankhurst's speech showed that many people were expecting wild times ahead —'Suffragists, who are preparing for strenuous times and who may be compelled to wear glasses are advised to go to Mr. John Piggott, 117 Cheapside, London, for a pair of his rimless eye-glasses, with patent clip, warranted to fit any nose and to keep place in all circumstances.'

But if the window-breaking was clearly premeditated, the victims were in no sense mollified by that, nor even by learning that it was in the time-honoured excuse 'a political act'. Occasionally of course the humour of the Londoner broke through, and a jeweller put a large placard in his window which read 'Ladies, if we had the power to grant it, you should have the vote right away. Please do not smash these windows they are not insured.'

SIDNEY MARKS

But generally indignation was unbounded, and there were serious suggestions that the ducking stool should be used for the triumvirate of Clement's Inn, and that the public should pay to watch the fun—the money, thus obtained, being used to repair the windows.

Including the little party of three in Downing Street more than 200 women were arrested and went to prison. The majority of them were students, nurses and artists though one was a lady of seventy-nine. Dr. Ethel Smyth—a composer of distinction with a character of force—was among them. The behaviour of these ladies in prison was not good, and was of course marked by much hunger striking. A number of them, taking exercise, caught sight of Dr. Ethel Smyth inside her cell and at once broke into the suffrage song, the music for which she had specially written—

> *Shout, shout—up with your song,*
> *Cry with the wind for the dawn is breaking;*
> *March, march, swing you along,*
> *Wide blows our banner and hope is waking.*
> *Song with its story, dreams with their glory,*
> *Lo! they call and glad is their word;*
> *Hark, hark how it swells,*
> *Thunder of freedom, the voice of the Lord.*

Dr. Smyth was observed at the window of her cell, beating time with her tooth-brush.

But not all the ladies who smashed the windows and suffered imprisonment, had the spirit of Dr. Smyth, nor were they by any means Maenads as they were dubbed by *The Times* with cruel erudition. (The Maenads were the frenzied and tipsy followers of Bacchus.) The correspondence of one has survived and, although they have no high lights, the letters reveal the almost touching simplicity of the writer, and the complete absence of either hysteria or drama.[1] The sentiments deserve the attention of the reader, because they are by no means uncharacteristic of the followers of Mrs. Pankhurst.

[1] Among the manuscripts in the London Museum.

The writer is Mrs. Terreno, an Essex lady married to a gentleman of Argentine origin. She was fifty-four at the time, and had been a suffragist since the 1870'2, but had joined the Social and Political Union in 1908, and the events of 'Black Friday' determined her to get arrested. She was a musician, living at Rockstone House, Pinner; her pleasure in life was a game of croquet. The charge against her was breaking the windows of an engineering firm called Stedall's in Oxford Street. She was able to scribble a note in Court to her husband, dated March 2nd, 'Dearest Husband. Do not worry. I am quite all right, and we are to refuse bail, so I suppose I shall be sent to prison to-day.' And then later: 'My trial comes off on Wednesday, March 20th at Sessions. Bail £200. I did not think I was worth so much.'

On March 5th she wrote to say that the Prison Authorities made an attempt to prevent the prisoners from conferring with Mrs. Pankhurst 'so we fought for her and won . . . we were put into our cells by force and then broke our cell windows and everything that we could . . . we only took our meal on Sunday evening after receiving her instructions that we were to eat. . . . We obey her absolutely.' Before she went on hunger-strike, she told her husband that her forbears had fought in the Crusades, 'and I feel their old war-like spirit coming out'. She complained that when forcibly fed she was stuffed like an Xmas Turkey. And when Mrs. Pankhurst with Mrs. Pethick-Lawrence rejoined them in Holloway on a subsequent charge she wrote 'I cannot tell you the joy it is to have our leaders with us . . . the sight of their dear faces has cheered everyone. . . . They join in all games just like the rest, and make themselves perfectly adorable.'

The window-smashing, coupled with the species of adoring but self-sacrificial loyalty to the Clement's Inn leaders (of which this letter affords a characteristic example) determined the Government to strike at the leadership. They could be assured of public support, and it was possible that militancy, thus wounded, might expire. The Piccadilly window-breaking had taken place on Friday, March 1st, and on Tuesday, March 5th, the police arrived in Clement's Inn with warrants for the arrest of Mr. and Mrs. Pethick-Lawrence, Mrs. Tuke, and Christabel, on a charge of conspiracy. Mrs. Pankhurst was in custody for her Downing Street stone, Christabel Pankhurst happened to be out, heard what had happened and fled to France. The police ransacked the office and searched Christabel's flat. As sometimes happens on these occasions, the police contrived to give an extra twist to public prejudice by letting it be known that they had found a bookshelf in the flat 'with a rather mixed selection of works, many of them French'.

After preliminary hearings at the Magistrates' Court at Bow Street the defendants, with the exception of Mrs. Tuke who was acquitted, were committed for trial at the Old Bailey.

In the interval before the trial began Mr. Pethick-Lawrence wrote to his wife: 'We are to stand where the great and noble have stood before us all down the ages. We are to be linked with those who have won the everlasting homage of the whole human race. If next week you and I were to be crowned King and Queen in the presence of an adulating people, how paltry would be the honour in comparison.'[1]

The case came up in May before a distinguished judge (Coleridge—son of J. D. Coleridge who long years before appeared with Dr. Pankhurst in the case of *Chorlton* v. *Lings*). The conduct of Coleridge was much blackguarded by the sympathizers with the prisoners who no doubt felt that his vicarious contact with Victorian feminists should have made him partial to their cause in the twentieth century. But Coleridge would seem to have conducted the case impeccably—he was outstandingly fair-minded—but he was criticized by the women because he would not accept the contention of the defence that a political motive mitigated the offence.

The conduct of the case was seemly—in marked contrast to the suffrage cases tried in the High Court by Mr. Justice Darling, where all was ribaldry and jest. The only divergence from gravity was when Mrs. Pankhurst called her only witness—Dr. Ethel Smyth. Mrs. Pankhurst asked her if she had taken part in the demonstration of the previous November. (That, it will be remembered, was the resurgence of militancy after the truce when Mrs. Pethick-Lawrence led the attack on the House of Commons.) Dr. Ethel replied that she would have done so 'but as a matter of fact

[1] Manuscript letter in London Museum.

I was very badly bitten in a dog fight a week before.' Mrs. Pankhurst then asked about Mr. Hobhouse's speech. (Charles Hobhouse, an influential but somewhat peppery Liberal member of
Parliament, had said at Bristol that he did not see, in the woman's
suffrage cause, 'the kind of popular feeling which led to the burning of Nottingham Castle in 1832 by man agitating for an extension of the franchise in the Reform Bill.'[1] The observation, seems
to have been offensive and provocative.) On reading it Dr.
Ethel wrote to Clement's Inn 'I am coming, I don't see how
any self-respecting woman after that can stay at home.' All
this she explained, with gusto, in answer to Mrs. Pankhurst's
question.

She was then asked by Mrs. Pankhurst about her window-
breaking on March 1st. 'I would be very happy to say whose
window it was', she briskly replied. 'It was the window of a gentleman, who made, I thought, quite the most objectionable remark
about women's suffrage that has ever been made, and that was
when he said, in answer to a deputation of women, that he would
be very happy to give the vote to women if all women were as
intelligent and well-balanced as his own wife. Well, I thought that
was the most impertinent thing I had ever heard, and also the most
fatuous, because it was as if he thought that he had got the pick of
the basket. So I said to myself: That is the window I am going to
break.'[2]

The Prosecution had no difficulty in showing that Mrs. Pankhurst and Mrs. Pethick-Lawrence had, in their speeches, openly
encouraged their following to attack property. Mrs. Pethick-
Lawrence had said in the Town Hall at Kensington on 30th
November 1911: 'The only way to bring them to their senses is to
touch their property.' Mrs. Pankhurst's speech on February 16th
has been already quoted. An examination of the archives at
Clement's Inn has revealed such letters as the following:

[1] The burning of Nottingham Castle actually took place in October 1831 not in
1832. It might have been more stimulating to the militants if Hobhouse had referred
to the attack the same evening on Mr. Chaworth-Musters' house outside Nottingham. Mrs. Musters (Byron's friend) had to spend the evening hiding in the shrubbery,
and was believed to have died from the experience.

[2] She is referring to 'Lulu' Harcourt who had married an American wife. She had
broken the windows of his home in Berkeley Square.

29th February 1912

Dear Colleague,

Will you come to the Gardenia Restaurant, Catherine Street, W.C. on Monday at 6 p.m. .... On no account reveal the contents of this letter to anyone or speak of it to anyone, even although you know that they may have the same information as yourself.

Yours sincerely,

CHRISTABEL PANKHURST.[1]

A code telegram was read; it ran: 'Silk, thistle, pansy, duck, wool, E.Q.' which, being interpreted, meant: 'Will you protest Asquith's public meeting to-morrow evening, but don't get arrested unless success depends on it. Wire back to Christabel Pankhurst, Clement's Inn.'

From the dock Mrs. Pankhurst made a masterly speech, running over the history of the Union, dwelling on the events of 'Black Friday' when the police had showed 'a kind of ferocity in dealing with us' which had 'compelled us to take this other step'. She also stated: 'We are not the kind of people who like to brag a lot: we are not the kind of people who would like to bring ourselves into this position unless we were convinced that it were the only way.' Her daughter Sylvia has noticed that on this occasion her mother was 'in the flood-tide of the last great energies of her personality before the disintegrating ravages of old age' began to steal upon her. Mr. Pethick-Lawrence, trained to the Bar, conducted his own defence and won the admiration of all for the skill and composure with which he spoke. The jury found all defendants guilty but recommended them for leniency 'on account of the undoubtedly pure motives behind the agitation'. The Judge sentenced them all to nine months' imprisonment.

But the unhappy consequences of this case did not end with the imprisonment of the defendants, for in addition, they were ordered to pay the costs of the prosecution. Although the Manager of Barclays Bank at 19 Fleet Street had appeared in the witness-box and stated, with sleek, professional pride, rather like a haberdasher showing off a choice roll of shirting, that the Union's was a beautifully conducted account, with upwards of £100,000 passing

---

[1] Manuscript in London Museum.

through it, the Pankhursts personally had no money. In reality a personal debt, such as this order to pay the costs, could only effect the Pethick-Lawrences. Mr. Pethick-Lawrence naturally declined to pay, and the contents of his home near Dorking were sold by order of the authorities to meet the costs of this case. In the following year Robinson and Cleaver, Swan and Edgar, Swears and Wells, the White House Linen Specialists and T.J. Harries sued the officials of the Union for the damage to their windows. This case they won, and were awarded £364. Again this expense fell on the rich member of the triumvirate and because he declined to pay he was made nominally bankrupt. Taking advantage of his unfortunate plight, the Committee of the Reform Club expelled him from membership of that ostensibly enlightened institution.

XXVIII

The Emmelines Part Company

The events of the early days of March were as fatal to the suffrage cause as were the ides of March to Caesar. Although the exact effect of these attacks on property in delaying votes for women is a matter for debate, the balance of historical opinion would undoubtedly support the contention that they postponed the vote. Sir Robert Ensor says with truth that had militancy 'not been persisted in, some kind of Women's Suffrage Bill would probably have passed the Commons between 1906 and 1914'. In the dock Mrs. Pankhurst exclaimed 'I am convinced that public opinion is with us.' She doubtless believed it: but the indiscriminate window-smashing of March 1st proved that public opinion, like a badger which is baited, can turn on those it normally tolerates. She, her daughter and the Pethick-Lawrences led their little army with brilliance, but they led it to disaster. The first fruits of this disaster was a split in the Triumverate.

Throughout the summer the strain on the leadership was severe. After the stress of the dock at the Old Bailey, followed by imprisonment, and a stretch of forcible feeding (which Mrs. Pankhurst succeeded in escaping by brandishing a ewer in the face of the apprehensive doctor when he came to her cell) both Mrs. Pankhurst and the Pethick-Lawrences were in need of peace and quiet. Christabel Pankhurst was settled in Paris, and in order to fill the void in the leadership she appointed Annie Kenney to the first place. The letter which she wrote on this occasion deserves to be quoted, because it emphasizes the curiously conspiratorial atmosphere in which these ladies existed. 'Beloved Annie—The bearer of this note is a good friend of the Cause. She, with another friend, helped me to escape. She will tell you where I am, and give you an address that will find me. Keep this a secret. . . . I want you to take supreme charge of the whole Movement during my absence, and while Mother and Mrs. Lawrence are in prison. . . . Come quickly, and bring with you a member who understands the language of the country that I am sheltering in. Disguise yourself, and watch closely for Scotland Yard men. . . . What a day when women win the vote! Press on and give all our loyal ones my love and my faith that each one will obey orders that will be sent through you by me, and by unity we shall win through. Come to me at the first possible moment. Christabel.'

Donning the weeds of a widow, Annie Kenney set off to join her exiled chief in Paris.

Each week, throughout the spring and summer of 1912, Annie Kenney went to Paris for consultations; together the two young women conducted 'Votes for Women' with an emphasis on wilder militant tactics. When the Pethick-Lawrences got back to work they questioned the wisdom of further instalments of extreme militancy, and urged that the movement should pause before embarking on an extension of the attacks on property. Such attacks, of course, implied organized arson—the next inevitable step. Christabel came over from Paris, during August, for discussions with her mother and the Lawrences. Their differences could not be resolved, and at a great meeting in the Albert Hall in October Mrs. Pankhurst announced that henceforth she and her daughter, Christabel, would be the sole guides of the Union, whose headquarters would be transferred to Lincoln's Inn House in Kingsway, and that Christabel would edit a new periodical on behalf of the Union—to be known as *The Suffragette*. Mr. and Mrs. Lawrence would still work for the women's cause outside the Union, and would continue to edit *Votes for Women*. And passing quickly from these personal discords as if she were anxious to chase away any dark forebodings in her audience, Mrs. Pankhurst roused her meeting to enthusiasm with the blithe words of command: 'I invite this meeting to rebellion.'

But the writing was on the wall. At the two previous Albert Hall meetings, with the Lawrences, who excelled in the art of raising money, present, £16,000 had been collected—a striking

15. Attempt to enter Buckingham Palace: Mrs. Pankhurst being removed
by a police inspector

16. Attempt on Buckingham Palace: an arrest

total from the two audiences. At the single meeting in October the collection fell to £3,600. In commenting on the dispute, Annie Kenney was surely right when she said: 'Christabel won, the fight continued, but the Movement, as a Movement, lost.' That it did not founder was entirely due to the Lawrences. Although they felt their virtual expulsion and its circumstances acutely, they never attempted to form a rival group or to draw with them—and this they could have easily done—a section of the Union members. Such magnanimity is rare in the history of British political organizations, and prejudice—apt to think that women's societies are more a prey to warring factions than those of men—will search in vain for supporting evidence for this misconception among the ruins of the proud triumvirate. In their breach with Mrs. Despard in 1907 and with the Lawrences five years later the Pankhursts were steering a headlong course: they were only saved by the beacon lights of sense, friendship and loyalty to the cause, shown by those whom they hurled overboard. The most that the Lawrences or Mrs. Despard allowed themselves to say was to emphasize the danger to the cause if the leadership persisted in the wildest tactics. Mrs. Despard wrote in *The Vote* in March 1912: 'We have not the least respect for plate-glass windows or for the usual British idea of "respectability" and "womanliness" but we care too deeply for our Cause to endanger its chance of success, however slender that chance may be.'

How slender that chance had become will be seen at once on considering events in the House of Commons after March 1st.

The Conciliation Bill, broadly similar to the Bill of 1911, was given its first reading in February and came up for debate on its second reading on March 28th. It was moved by Mr. Agg-Gardner, Conservative member for Cheltenham, and seconded by Sir Alfred Mond, the Liberal industrialist who sat for Swansea. The supporters of the Bill naturally made the greatest efforts to disentangle the principle behind it from the doings of the militants. Mr. Charles Roberts, son-in-law of the formidable suffragist Lady Carlisle, who sat for Lincoln, neatly suggested that if they were going to condemn the women because of the behaviour of the extremists they should do away with the University vote because of the disorderly conduct of the member for Oxford University (Lord Hugh Cecil) who had shouted down Mr. Asquith. But such appeals were in vain. The result of the division showed how alarmingly the support had thinned. Instead of the usual comfortable majority of 100 and more, the Bill was defeated by fourteen votes. It is true that some thirty of the Irish members had voted against the Bill, for technical reasons concerned with the procedure of the House of Commons. But on top of that there were many abstentions and defections.

Mr. Asquith spoke, and the effect of his speech was remarked by those reporting the scene. He started with the kind of allusion at which he excelled, bringing in the hoary argument of Victorian feminists about the pathos of George Eliot being barred from the ballot-box, while her gardener was honoured with the dignity of a vote. He agreed that the argument was unanswerable, but he thought it no more relevant than saying that it was a shame that Shakespeare (or Bacon) should have had the same number of votes as his tradesman. More seriously he went on to argue that the case for saying that Parliament was careless of the interests of women or children could not be sustained and, while he regretted having to be unsympathetic to many public-spirited women, he thought there was no case historically or constitutionally for enfranchising a large class without clear proof that both the class and the country wished it. *The Times* observed that the House followed Mr. Asquith in his arguments which that paper described as 'admirable'. *The Nation*, not always a friendly critic of the Liberal Government, observed at this time how Mr. Asquith 'had grown out of all knowledge as a personage. It is no longer mere appreciation of his parliamentary gifts but an attitude of devotion.' The paper went on to argue that the warm, personal feelings of the Liberal members for Asquith personally made any appreciable shift of opinion on the suffrage issue 'unlikely'. At about this time Sir Max Beerbohm drew his celebrated cartoon of Mr. Asquith: he sits reflectively smoking a cigar, while round his head whirl a hunting-crop (the peers) a pick-axe (the trades unions) a hatchet (the suffragettes) a sabre (German soldiers) and a blackthorn stick (Carson). Below are written the lines from 'The Lady of The Lake'

Come one, come all, this rock shall fly
From its firm base as soon as I.

The personal vendetta of the militants against Asquith had undoubtedly contributed to these feelings. And so it was that in addition to the weighty and persisting political difficulties by which the question of women's franchise was dogged, the debate on March 26th showed that militancy had not only antagonized much parliamentary support, it had fortified the outstanding opponent of the women's cause.

XXIX

An Obscene Letter to 'The Times'

And then, just as it seemed as if militancy might be given the *coup de grâce*, it was revived by one of those unexpected blunders from the other side, which lend fascination to all political struggles. In this case the blunder took shape as a letter from a voluble doctor. This curious epistle, which was about the length of that from St. Paul to Philemon, occupied three columns of *The Times*, and trenched rather than touched on topics best confined to the consulting room of a gynaecologist. To some extent *The Times* had provoked the letter by publishing ten days previously, at the time of the window-breaking, a leading article headed 'Insurgent Hysteria'. This article included these words 'the hysterical, the neurotic, the idle, the habitual imbibers of excitement are always at the service of those who offer them an opportunity of gratifying the ruling passion. Some of them are out with their hammers and their bags full of stones because of dreary, empty lives and high-strung, over-excitable natures: they are regrettable by-products of our civilization'.

On this canvas the doctor slashed his paint. He was Sir Almroth Wright, physician to St. Mary's Hospital, son of a divine and brother to the Librarian of the London Library. He pronounced militancy as a mental illness set up by sex: he suggested that nearly 50 per cent of all women went crazy in middle-life, and that their minds were always liable to gusts of periodic excitement. 'Woman looks upon her mind' he wrote 'not as an instrument for the pursuit of truth, but as an instrument for providing her with creature comforts in the form of agreeable mental images.' Another pronouncement was that 'the mind of woman is always

threatened with danger from the reverberations of her physio-
logical emergencies . . . it is with such thoughts that the doctor
lets his eyes rest on the militant suffragist.' He also stated that in
matters of public morality 'one would not be very far from the
truth if one alleged that there are no good women, but only
women who have lived under the influence of good men.' He
analysed the militants within two different types. The first he
called the sexually embittered 'whose legislative programme is
licence for themselves or else restriction for men'. The second he
gracefully alluded to as 'the incomplete'. 'Their programme' he
wrote 'is to convert the world into an epicene institution in
which men and women shall everywhere work side by side at the
self-same tasks and for the self-same pay.' The eminent doctor
then added this comment 'Even in animals—I say, *even*, because in
these at least one of the sexes has periods of complete quiescence
—male and female cannot be safely worked side by side, except
when they are incomplete.' Perhaps the most curious aspect of this
letter is that *The Times* should have published it. The Editor gave
it to the world on the morning of the debate on the Conciliation
Bill.

What effect this remarkable effusion had on the debate, it is
difficult to say, but it rallied opinion outside the House of Commons to the victims. *The Nation* drily observed 'Sir Almroth paints
with a coarse brush'. Mrs. Humphrey Ward, the leading anti-
suffragist, wrote to *The Times* 'repudiating for myself and, I have
no doubt whatever, for thousands of men and women who feel
with me on the suffrage controversy, all connection with the
bitter and unseemly violence which that letter displays. *Non tali
auxilio.*'

One other softer breeze fanned the embers of militancy. From
the early summer onwards events in the House of Commons had
begun to attach some humanitarian sympathies to the scattered
forces of the Union. A new Secretary of State for Home Affairs
was reigning in Whitehall, Mr. Reginald McKenna having ex-
changed offices with Mr. Churchill ('with punctilio' as the latter
expressed it) in the autumn of 1911. McKenna was a representative of the new men in politics. To family or tradition he was indebted for no advancement: he was certainly not blessed with the

flaming gifts of a Lloyd George nor had he the kind of supreme intellectual equipment which made an Asquith, or a Morley or even a Carson acceptable throughout the social political fabric of London. But with Runciman, Samuel, and Illingworth on his own side, and with others on the Conservative and Labour benches, not yet emerged from the unknown, he represented the new forces—the experienced and competent professional men—prepared to take a hand at running a Department as they might run their family business or office. McKenna—one of the chief victims of the destruction of Liberalism in British politics—has been persistently underrated partly because his gifts, illumined by no great powers of imagination nor by high flights of eloquence, infuriated the 'brilliant' men and the old-fashioned 'traditionalists' in English politics. To the suffragette problem he brought none of the easy-going sympathies of Herbert Gladstone nor the masterly ingenuity of Churchill: he decided his policy, defended it with clarity but without sentiment in the House of Commons, and did not try to assuage the wrath of the tender-hearted. A good instance of this occurred at the end of March. A Lancashire Liberal member asked whether there were cockroaches and 'other abominations' in Mrs. Pankhurst's cell at Holloway. Joseph King—a diverting Member of the House pilloried in *Punch* as the Mad Hatter to whom he bore some slight resemblance—interjected with some of the inconsequence of the personality he was thought to resemble: 'I suppose he means mice.' Undeterred by laughter McKenna gave a coldly factual answer, which did not diminish merriment: 'Such things'—he said—'exist only in the imagination of the questioner. The cell is bright with a sunny aspect.'

Lady Frances Balfour once said of McKenna that he was ignorant of women and ignorant of society in all its graded shades. No doubt in the eyes of one who was the daughter of a duke such disabilities were formidable. Certainly they drew on McKenna the fury of those aristocratic supporters of the female franchise—Lord Hugh and Lord Robert Cecil. Their attack was concentrated on the ancient topic of First Division, which came prominently before the House of Commons after the Conspiracy Trial at the Old Bailey. McKenna decided that the prisoners should be given First Division treatment: but this the prisoners declined to accept unless it were also given to the other women—serving their sentence for the stone-throwing of March 1st, many of whom were on hunger-strike.

Lord Robert Cecil raised this matter on June 28th: arguing that all should be treated alike and saying—not without justice—that the leaders of militancy commanded more sympathy and support in the House than did their unknown followers. He ended with a ferocious attack on McKenna saying that every office he had held had been stained, during his tenure, by miscarriages of justice. He alluded to the Swansea School Scandal, where the Local Education Authority had withheld salaries of teachers in a church school and the Board of Education, with McKenna at its head, had refused to carry out the recommendations of their own public enquiry, and to the Archer-Shee case, where a young naval cadet had been expelled from Osborne, a case which had developed when McKenna was First Lord of the Admiralty, and now to the militant suffragette scandal. Keir Hardie—though he was only speaking for a section of the Labour party on this—voiced with matchless simplicity the feelings of humanitarians about forcible feeding, striking perhaps a more responsive chord on the Liberal benches than among his own comrades, 'When you see them weak, thin and emaciated . . . when you feel, as they put it, that this outrage is equal to the worst form of outrage that can be perpetrated upon a woman—every feeling is violated.' On the other hand there were plenty of harsh voices crying from the Conservative benches. 'If they will not eat, then let them die.' Such expressions were encouraged by another remarkable medical man, Doctor Percy Wilde of Bath, who wrote to his newspaper to say that there was no such thing as a hunger strike, for hunger was not felt after two days, and starvation was the best cure for chronic disorders which did not yield to ordinary treatment.

Apart from a reference to Lord Robert having poisoned the wells of truth by his personal attack, McKenna took his stand with effective precision on the facts. He said that a political motive neither aggravated nor extenuated an offence. The women were committed to prison for having broken the law. He pointed out that over the past thirty years a Home Secretary had only inter-vened on three occasions to move a prisoner from one Division to another—in the cases of W. T. Stead in 1885, Jameson in 1896 and the Pethick-Lawrences and Mrs. Pankhurst that year. He read to the House a letter which he had received from the Judge—Lord Coleridge, drawing attention to the jury's appeal for clemency. Coleridge also added this observation: 'I should be the first to advocate their being treated as First Class Misdemeanants or to approve of any judicious revision of sentence. But I could not do so in face of the attitude of defiance which they thought fit to adopt.' McKenna went on to explain that the prisoners had subsequently undertaken, through their solicitor, that, while they were in prison, they would not direct or control the commission of any acts whatever, whether legal or illegal. They confessed that the responsibility of controlling the movement from prison was too great. Referring to the other women prisoners, serving their sentences for the events of March 1st, McKenna added that it was fully within his province to advise the Sovereign to remit part of the sentences, but that could only be a revision of the time they served, not a revision of class which was a matter for the Law. 'What pedantry!' ejaculated Lord Hugh Cecil. Mr. John Ward—the Liberal-Labour member for Stoke, who was known in the House of Commons as 'the handsome navvy', rose to express his regret that so much time had been devoted to the rights and wrongs of 'wealthy and influential people well able to look after themselves'. Only sixty-nine members had supported Lord Robert, but it was clear that as soon as the difficult problems of prison, hunger-striking and forcible feeding were discussed the feeling of sympathy with the women (whatever their offences) emerged to soften the condemnation of their tactics.

XXX

The Constitutionalists Progress

Other matters, not connected with militancy, strengthened the women's cause at this time. The League still steadily fostered the refusal to pay taxes—an Ipswich lady was sent to prison for declining to pay the licence on her pet dog and Laurence Housman's sister Miss Clemence Housman was also imprisoned for ignoring a debt of 4s. 6d. to the Inland Revenue authorities. The Duchess of Bedford announced that she would not pay the property tax on Prince's Skating Rink. (Prince's was a popular rendezvous with leisured Edwardians. Gracefully and without exertion, amply skirted ladies mingling with experts from Canada or Scandinavia skimmed the length of the great building. Observers watched from a protected gallery, and all were soothed by a Hungarian band playing waltzes and mazurkas.) A newspaper, reporting this decision, commented that it looked like being a cold summer for the tax collector. But perhaps the most effective of these tax resistance cases was the Wilks case in September 1912.

Dr. Wilks was a lady doctor with a considerable private income. Following the example of Mrs. Despard and other leaders of the League she had steadily refused to pay any income-tax. Her husband was an L.C.C. teacher with a salary of £160 a year. His father Mr. Mark Wilks had been one of the founders of the London School Board, and the roots of the family were deeply embedded in Liberalism and Nonconformity. The Government—in one of those moments of routine madness which afflict even the most adroit members of the Civil Service—prosecuted Mr. Wilks for the refusal of his wife to pay tax, and he was sent to prison. The outcry in Liberal quarters was loud—the *Manchester Guardian*

265

carrying a headline 'Wilks and Liberty'. At a crowded protest meeting at the Caxton Hall, Bernard Shaw (and with him income-tax and wealthy wives were always rather sensitive points) brought the meeting to its feet with this comment on the struggle for the vote.

'As a man, I have been able to bear with a certain amount of equanimity the delay of the reform, so long as I saw before me the inspiring spectacle of a number of women heroically sacrificing themselves: but now that the women have taken to sacrificing the men things are rather altered.'

Lloyd George—the Minister responsible—was severely attacked at this meeting, and shortly afterwards the heroic Wilks was set free.

In October a spectacular march of women from Edinburgh to London was organized by The Qui Vive Corps—the words seeming to conjure up memories of one of Mr. Arthur Marshall's delightful impersonations. The Corps was formed by two fashion-able ladies—Mrs. Frederick Cavendish-Bentinck and Mrs. Robert de Fonblanque, a hunting lady who lived at Petworth in Sussex. The marchers set off bravely, some 300 strong, with Mrs. Despard at the head during the six miles from Edinburgh to Musselburgh. As they started Mrs. de Fonblanque sent a telegram to her sister: 'Just off. Pray heaven we save the sweated women and children.'[1] The meaning of this telegram may be somewhat obscured unless it is remembered that many of the idealists behind the woman's vote saw it, as not only desirable in itself, but as opening the door to glories unperceived by the languid eye of man. They felt that, with the vote, would come the promised time of which their church-going sisters, with differing implication, sang—

> *That war shall be no more,*
> *And lust, oppression, crime,*
> *Shall flee Thy face before.*

Six women completed the whole 400 miles, but the force re-

---

[1] 'Sweated Industries' were much to the front in the political imagination of the time. The investigation into poverty at York by Seebohm Rowntree and many later enquiries in all parts of the country maintained public attention on this question, as did the successful Sweated Industries Exhibition organized by the *Daily News* in 1906. Women too often afforded the very worst examples of sweating by the em-ployers.

mained constant, shedding numbers and recruiting afresh as it marched. The leaders were received at Downing Street, and the whole episode, which was an effective piece of organization was not perhaps without its lesson for the unemployed marches of the 1930's.

Another fine achievement, unsullied by militancy, (though in this particular instance it would have been scarcely out of place) was afforded by Mrs. St. Clair Stobart. After experiences in the Veldt in South Africa, she had returned to England, and formed a Women's Convoy Corps. This held an annual camp in the summer, and the idea behind the Corps was to get the wounded in war from the fighting line to the base hospital. Her corps was fully trained by the time of the Balkan War in 1912, and she took out a detachment for service with the Bulgarian Army. She did this in the teeth of opposition from the British Red Cross, who announced that it would send men only to the war zone. 'Men'—wrote Mrs. Stobart, with understandable indignation—'who knew more about the rules of football than of hospital work.' The women endured great hardships, described with modesty by Mrs. Stobart in her book *War and Women* which was published in 1913, and they achieved a resounding success. Few would disagree with Mrs. Stobart's conclusion that 'the purblind policy of shielding women against their will from a knowledge of truths, however unpleasant these may be, is disastrous not only for women, but for the community at large'. Certainly Mrs. Stobart and the Women's Convoy had gone some way in refuting the hoary argument that women should not vote because they cannot fight.

There was unquestionably throughout 1912 an access of strength and an increase of activity in the ranks of the constitutionalists. Miss Sylvia Pankhurst suggests that some of this was due to their desire to show sympathy with militancy. Undoubtedly that is correct, but perhaps more of it was really due to the feeling that there was a perceptible change in the opposition. For whatever feelings may have been stirred by militancy it remained true that women were now being acclaimed for taking an active part in spheres—such as the march from Edinburgh to London or the Balkan War—which would have been inconceivable in the days of Miss Becker. Points like this were far more likely to diminish the intellectual opposition of men like Asquith, coupled as they were with the knowledge of the part played by women in many branches of the Government service, than the strident interruptions of militancy. The gradual absorption of women into the working life of the nation was an astonishing development of the first decade and a half of the twentieth century: it has received scant notice because it has been eclipsed in the popular imagination by what was to emerge after 1914.

XXXI

Strange Colours at Balmoral

Yet any hopes of a gradual compromise along the lines of reason were reduced by the outbreak of militancy in its most frenzied form developing with the summer and autumn of 1912, as a consequence of the split in the Triumvirate. Instead of marches on Westminster, property was attacked with stones and fire; instead of disrupting meetings of ministers, leading suffragettes subjected members of the Cabinet to personal violence.

At a reception given by Asquith's brother-in-law at his house in Queen Anne's Gate a lady guest went up to the Prime Minister, seized him by the lapels of his dress coat, gave him a tremendous shaking, calling out loudly: 'How dare you come here, when women are being forcibly fed in prison?' There had been a similar occurrence at a Government reception at the India Office in honour of the King's birthday in June. A lady, wearing a pink evening dress, gripped the Prime Minister by the shoulder while her husband poured out, in voluble expostulation, the views of this devoted pair on Votes for Women. According to a newspaper version Mrs. Asquith was believed to have boxed the ears of the cheerful lady in her pink dress.

A more unfortunate incident occurred at Aberdeen at the end of November. Lloyd Geoge was speaking there and made a lively attack on landlords and Conservatives, and added in passing that women would have had the vote that year but for militancy. Mr. Joseph Farquharson, whose paintings of sheep and shepherds in the Highlands are well-known, was bowling along to the meeting in his car when the windows of his car were smashed—he having been mistaken for the Chancellor of the Exchequer. On the following day, the Reverend Forbes Jackson, a Baptist minister from Aberdeen, was leaving the station when he suddenly received lashes across the head and shoulders from a dog-whip. He was not exactly soothed on finding out that his assailant, Miss Emily Wilding Davison, had thought he was Lloyd George escaping in disguise. Well might the Reverend Mr. Jackson have adapted the words of the Duke of Wellington, when a stranger tried to get into conversation with him by addressing him as Mr. Smith: 'If you believe that, you will believe anything.'

Some months later, Lord Weardale, who as Philip Stanhope had been a prominent Radical Member of Parliament, stepped out of a taxi at Euston, where he was catching a train for Northampton to attend the wedding of Lord Spencer's daughter, when he received a severe whipping. A suffragette had mistaken him for Asquith. When the magistrate remonstrated with her for striking an elderly gentleman of nearly seventy, she merely commented that men who torture women ought to be thrashed. Lord Weardale was possibly more fortunate than the doctor at Holloway who was set on by two or three women, as he was going to his work in Holloway, and thrashed with a sjambok. The doctor was hauled to safety by some male prisoners.

Miss Wilding Davison, who attacked the Baptist Minister at Aberdeen was something of a solitary moving in the van of militancy and seeking no encouragement from the leaders of the Union for the startling acts of defiance which she committed in the name of that Society. Certainly she had enjoyed a busy twelve months because in December 1911, without telling the Union leaders, she had set fire to a number of pillar-boxes in Westminster by dropping inside them a lighted rag steeped in paraffin. She was sentenced to six months' imprisonment, and while she was in Holloway there occurred a curious incident which attracted some parliamentary notice. The incident was described with drama in some of the suffrage journals as an attempt to commit suicide—but it seems to have been more of a demonstration of despondency. One afternoon in June, having visited the lavatory, she refused to go back to her cell. While the prison officials were arguing with her she threw herself off the landing, falling on the wire-cage about eight feet below, which was fixed to prevent prisoners from attempting suicide. She lay for a time on the wire, and then threw herself on to the stone staircase—a distance of about five feet. She told the medical officer that she had made these attempts because she had 'a feeling that a tragedy was wanted'. Exactly a year later she was to provide one.

This year also the militants paid increased attention to the Royal Family. On 9th September, at night, they went to Balmoral and King George was scandalized to find that all the flags on his private golf course had been removed in favour of ones in purple, white and green. Advancing closer to the Castle they had painted an impudent slogan on the fountain which Queen Victoria had set up to the memory of the Keeper of her Privy Purse—'Good Sir Thomas Biddulph'. Biddulph was described by the Queen as 'a wonderfully disinterested and unselfish man', and it is difficult to picture the words which, had the Queen survived, she would have used to describe the outrage.

And uglier shadows began to darken the scene. In July Mr. Asquith went to Dublin, and perhaps encouraged by the general acclamation with which he was received he delivered a speech in the Theatre Royal of an eloquence and vision, recalling the oratory of the giants of English politics, and making—it has to be confessed—the full-throated rantings of Carson and Bonar Law sound more noisy than sensible. On his arrival in Dublin he had driven with the Irish Nationalist leader, Redmond, to the Chief Secretary's Lodge, where he was staying, and the indomitable Mary Leigh succeeded in tossing a hatchet into the open carriage. Mr. Redmond was slightly wounded in the ear. Undeterred by being nearly lynched by the crowd she went in the evening to the Theatre Royal, when it was empty, and attempted to set fire to it. At the same time a friend of hers went to the cinema, filled her handbag with gunpowder and attempted to drop a match on this swiftly manufactured bomb. Both ladies were sentenced by the Irish Courts to five years' penal servitude.

A few days earlier an attempt had been made to burn Mr. Harcourt's historic house at Nunesham. A policeman had discovered two ladies equipped with inflammable material at two in the morning, sheltering under the wall of the house. One, Miss Helen Craggs was arrested: the other, who escaped, was believed by the constable to be called Smith. Here the police made an almost inevitable mistake. They hurried off to Hook and arrested Dr. Ethel Smyth, for what could be more natural than that the lady who stoned Harcourt's London home should be involved on this occasion? She was completely innocent, and greatly enjoyed the pleasure of proving the police wrong.

The police were certainly sorely tried. On one occasion a policeman saw the actress, Miss Kitty Marion, tugging violently at a fire alarm. 'What's the matter?' he asked. 'I want to get the Government out,' was the inconsequential reply.

Such, clearly displayed in 1912, were the uncomfortable trials which the Government might expect if the struggle went on. Was there a chance that even at the eleventh hour the horrors of arson by amateurs might give way to a parliamentary settlement of the dispute? There was a pause while once again the forces of commonsense were deployed in the House of Commons.

Asquith, it will be remembered, had agreed to introduce an electoral reform bill, which was to be capable of amendment to include women. This measure, known as the Franchise and Registration Bill, was introduced in June 1912 and it destroyed all plural voting including the University and City franchises, and it abolished all property qualification for the vote. The proposals were certainly advanced, but even when full allowance is made for the shock to Conservative feelings, to their natural alarm at seeing property (which they regarded as one of the buttresses of the English political system) being ruthlessly cut out, the debate which followed showed how severely they had suffered in changing their leader from Balfour to Bonar Law. The latter intervened with a series of harsh gibes about the Liberals having to jerrymander the constitution because they did not dare to face the existing electorate. Balfour, on the other hand, speaking in the calm of a Friday morning indulged in some reflective warnings which have lose little of their freshness after forty years. In a modern democracy he thought it was difficult to maintain an Assembly worthy of the people's respect and confidence. 'Democracy'—he said—'was the only parent with no inclination to be proud of its own children.' As the House of Commons became ironed into uniformity with 'men of enduring vitality and brazen lungs, all apparently moulded in the same form' so the respect of the public for Parliament would begin to wither.

Although such sombre musings may seem far removed from the brisk doings of the militants, the uncertainties of public men about the future of the franchise as a whole, were not the smallest of the difficulties against which the problem of votes for women must be set. The Committee stage of the Franchise and Registration Bill was postponed until 1913. Militancy continued sporadically throughout the autumn and winter of 1912, but the real importance of the controversy at that time was centred on the women's suffrage amendments to the Franchise Bill, which were being planned, and to certain developments between the Labour party and the women's movement.

The parliamentary Labour party—although it produced outstandingly devoted supporters for the women's cause—was by no means unanimously behind the idea of enfranchising women. Out of a total of 42 members of the parliamentary Labour party some 20 to 25 generally went into the lobby in favour of votes for women. For what the claim was worth the parliamentary Labour party could probably show a bigger percentage of support for the women than in the other parties. However, more significant than the votes of the small parliamentary Labour party was the resolution carried at the annual conference of the party in Birmingham in 1912, to the effect that no franchise bill would be acceptable to the Labour and Socialist movement which did not include women. The miners—not always the most liberal-minded section of the working-class electorate—voted solidly against the proposal, but it was carried by 919 to 686.

The consequences of this vote on the women's societies was curious. Mrs. Despard, on behalf of the League, acclaimed the decision as fulfilling a cherished dream of hers, and the leading non-militant body, the National Union, agreed to support all Labour candidates except where a Labour candidate happened to be standing against 'a tried, Liberal friend'. The leaders of the Women's Social and Political Union, perversely, did not welcome these new allies. At the end of 1912 Miss Christabel Pankhurst was writing of there being 'war between women and the official Labour party', and there is no doubt that the Pankhurst family was drifting far from their Labour origins. The *Daily Express*, which has always had a fancy for social distinctions and a keen nose for the more expensive furs, drew attention to the smart appearance of Union members. The militants, according to this paper, were 'gowned in the height of fashion, wearing the purple, white and green under their wraps of sable and ermine'. The charge was not without foundation, for the success and notoriety of the Union had attracted support from the leisured classes. This, together with Mrs. Pankhurst's and Christabel's partiality for Conservative drawing-rooms, may have deflected the Union from its original loyalty to the Labour movement, and no doubt helped to widen the breach with the Lawrences, who were Labour party sympathizers from the earliest days.

But some part of the indignation of the Pankhursts with Labour sprang from a startling episode in the autumn of 1912 which originated with that popular Labour member who has been described as too often allowing his 'bleeding heart to govern his bloody head'. Mr. George Lansbury had been elected for Bow and Bromley, defeating Mr. Amery, in the second election of 1910. He had been a vociferous advocate of the women's vote, and in the summer of 1912, in the House of Commons, he strode towards the Prime Minister shouting: 'You will go down to history as the man who tortured innocent women. You ought to be driven from public life.' In November he resigned his seat, and stood for re-election in order to test opinion on woman's suffrage. He was defeated by 700 votes. The Labour party formally condemned his action, which had naturally been received with paeans of joy by the leaders of the Women's Social and Political Union, and this helped to keep antagonisms alive between official Labour and the Union.

At this juncture Miss Sylvia Pankhurst came more vigorously to public notice. She had for long been on terms of close personal and political friendship with Keir Hardie, was in accord with the Labour movement and understood the point of view of the working-class voter. In the autumn the Union, marching in step with many philanthropic bodies at that time, began to take interest in the East End—each prosperous branch of the Union—Kensington, Chelsea and Paddington—renting a shop in the East End, staffing it and equipping it with literature. 'Slumming' was a word which had had a vogue for exactly twenty years, in the sense that the East End of London existed as a vast field for charitable exercises. But long before that, Ruskin had pointed out that the best men in every generation invariably made the mistake of thinking that almsgiving, comfortable words from the pulpit or exhortations to patience, all administered to the unfortunate, were substitutes 'for the one thing God orders for them—justice'. When the excitements of the Bow and Bromley by-election were over, the ladies from the Union prepared to dismantle the shops, to put up the shutters—their task done, and to take away their gay clothes and confident talk which had shown to advantage in the grey unhappiness of the human dwellings which lined the district from Old Ford to Bromley. But while the others left, Miss Sylvia Pankhurst remained—determined that the East End should be roused to cry for justice for one-half of the human race.

These developments outside Parliament, with their subtle fissures and alignments of feeling, led to a certain lack of cohesion in the supporters of Votes for Women, inside the House of Commons—which was reflected in a strangely confusing assortment of amendments to the Franchise Bill. There were four. The first, in the name of the Secretary of State for Foreign Affairs, Sir Edward Grey, proposed to delete the word 'male' from the Bill. This of course revived a hoary constitutional problem, dating back to the days of Brougham and would not have given any woman a vote, without subsequent litigation, and was in fact designed by Grey merely to open the way for the later amendments. The next amendment embodied Labour party policy, and stood in the name of Mr. Arthur Henderson. This envisaged the enfranchisement of women on the same terms as men. This might have added as many as ten or eleven million new voters to the Register. The third amendment, in the name of Mr. Dickinson, aimed to enfranchise all women householders and the wives of householders over 25. This was called the Norwegian amendment.[1] The fourth amendment, standing in Mr. Alfred Lyttelton's name, followed the terms of the Conciliation Bill.

---

[1] Later in 1913 Norway conceded the franchise to all women at twenty-one. At the time of these discussions in the House of Commons the Norwegians were considering limiting it to women of twenty-five and over.

The debate opened on January 24th, and it was marked by a high level both of oratory and seriousness—which characterized the later phases of the struggle in the House of Commons. The Government itself set an example by showing their concern that the matter should be fairly settled, and allowing members of the Cabinet to speak on differing sides.[1]

Sir Edward Grey, owing to a sudden disturbance in Turkey, had not felt able to leave the Foreign Office, and his amendment was moved in a graceful speech by Mr. Alfred Lyttelton. He was followed by 'Lulu' Harcourt, who in spite of certain elegances of appearance and perfection of dress, was in his advanced opinions and clarity of mind a worthy representative of the great Lancashire constituency of Rossendale. His speech, although a stern critic might say that it was rather too humorous and that he had taken full advantage of the chance to aim a few shafts at his friends in the Cabinet, was a striking success, the extent of which both surprised and delighted the House of Commons. He began by quoting Lloyd George that a mandate from the country was needed, before the House of Commons could give votes for women. Harcourt commented: 'Only one member (Lansbury) has tried it and his example and experience afford no encouragement to others.' He then quoted Sir Edward Grey saying: 'Adult suffrage at one stroke is more than the country would at present accept.' Harcourt drily added: 'And so we shall find him clinging to the business end of the wedge, which is so dear to the heart of every timid reformer.' Harcourt again turned to Lloyd George, who wished for adult suffrage for men, but limited suffrage for women. He reminded the House that domestic servants came under Lloyd George's exclusion, but that he had lately received a deputation from them, in connection with National Insurance, and had described their views as 'relevant, emphatic and sound'. He asked why should Lloyd George wish to deprive them of the vote. 'He has not hesitated to take their threepences. Does he fear to take their opinion? It reminds me of the old epigram, slightly altered, that if there is one thing worse than the cant of equality,

---

[1] This formed the precedent for the well-known 'Agreement to Differ' in 1932, when the Liberal and Labour members of the National Government trounced the Ottawa agreements, imposing tariffs, in the House of Commons while remaining members of the Government which had imposed them.

it is the recant of equality.' He ended by saying that his views had
not been affected by the 'attempt to burn my house—or rather the
children's wing of my house.'

The Conservatives chortled with glee. Lord Hugh Cecil rose to
say that the frenzied zeal of Harcourt reminded him of Peter the
Hermit, who organized the First Crusade. He thought Harcourt
very like Peter the Hermit 'except in costume and cleanliness of
person'. He considered the speech most damaging to the Government, and he added: 'it was delicious to listen to.' But the game
was played out and the referee, in the person of the Speaker,
brought everything to an end with a long authoritative blast of the
whistle. On the following day in answer to a question from the
Prime Minister the Speaker said that if an amendment approving
woman's suffrage were carried, it would cause such a fundamental alteration in the Bill that—in accordance with the rules of
the House—the Bill would have to be withdrawn.

The verdict was completely unexpected by the Government.
Asquith was placed in a decidedly unenviable position, because
he and the Government would be accused of having deliberately
tricked the women. The facts, though explained by the niceties of
parliamentary procedure, were, to those outside, a glaring damna-
tion of Liberal treachery and of Asquithian perfidy. The *Observer*,
with justice, blamed the Law Officers of the Crown for having
advised the Cabinet badly and especially the Solicitor-General,
'that solemn model of a pundit on a monument, Sir John Simon'.
But Asquith shouldered all the consequences of this fiasco, thank-
ed the Speaker for having prevented a waste of parliamentary
time. 'It was our honest intention to carry out the pledge we had
given'—he said—'I am bound to say so much lest it should be
suggested either that in this matter we have treated an important
point of procedure with inadvertence and neglect and, still more,
that it should be suggested that there has been anything in the
way of sharp practice.' 'Resign! Resign!' called out the cheerful
Winterton supported by the less respectable 'Paddy' Goulding.[1]
Looking across to this strange pair, chanting in uneasy union,
Asquith raised his eyebrows and asked in mild surprise: 'On
Women's Suffrage?' He ended by promising that, although noth-

[1] A Conservative member with a partiality for intrigue, afterwards Lord Wargrave.

ing further could be done that session, the Government would give facilities for a private member's bill on woman's suffrage.

This was introduced in May, and although the speeches were good, there was a certain lack of reality about them. The Prime Minister and the Foreign Secretary were the only spokesmen from each side of the divided Cabinet. Asquith explained that the House of Commons was perfectly competent to take the step of giving votes to women if they thought fit, nor would there be any question of his resigning if they passed the measure. He thought that the arguments against the Bill would lose much of their force if it could be shown that there was a real demand for it in the country, or if it could be shown that the interests of women suffered through their being excluded. Grey, concentrating on this last point, said: 'Wages, labour, housing, land, temperance, taxation, education and every question that deals with the efficiency and standard of human life and home life—as long as no women have votes, your democracy on all these points will be hopelessly incomplete.'

In the course of his speech Asquith had observed: 'I am sometimes tempted to think, as one listens to the arguments of the supporters of women's suffrage, that there is nothing to be said for it. I sometimes am tempted to think when I listen to the arguments of the opponents of women's suffrage that there is nothing to be said against it.' Perhaps he was in particular prompted to this reflection by Ramsay Macdonald who ended a remarkable oration in favour of woman's suffrage by urging the House to make them 'co-partners with men as citizens, so that the State may have the rich, the domestic, the wonderful experience of the woman who has lived, thought and felt and who desires to throw all that at the feet of the State so that the young and the aged, the rich and the poor may be blessed by the partnership'.

And Asquith may well have felt that the speech of Mr. J. A. Grant—the member for West Cumberland—on the other side well justified his feeling that there was nothing to be said against it: 'In controlling a vast Empire like our own, an Empire built by the mental and physical capacity of men, and maintained, as it always must be maintained, by the physical and mental capacities of masterly natures—I ask myself: Is there a place for women?'

In rebutting Mr. Grant's spendidly masculine argument, Lord

Robert Cecil pointed out that from the days of Deborah to Queen Louise of Prussia there had been a succession of women who showed a high, imperial spirit. F. E. Smith then made a delightful intervention: 'My noble friend in his speech alluded with enthusiasm to the performance of Deborah who, I suppose, may not unreasonably or with any undue levity be treated as being the pioneer of the militant movement.' Lord Hugh Cecil, rushing to the succour of his brother, rose immediately F. E. Smith sat down and rapped out: 'One of the peculiarities of this controversy is that it disorders the faculties of even the ablest men.'

At times the attendance was thin, but the standard of debate was high, marked by deep feeling. It was almost the fiftieth time the House of Commons had discussed a bill to give full citizenship to women—and it was also the last. This debate in May 1913 ended that long series of bills and amendments running back over Edwardian times, past the Jubilee of Queen Victoria to the half-century before when Mill rose to speak 'his eyebrows working fearfully'. To us looking back there is a certain melancholy about these ultimate discussions—but a melancholy redeemed by the conviction that the House of Commons had very faithfully reflected the anxieties and uncertainties which afflicted public opinion on this issue. Inevitably, as Asquith had pointed out, the arguments were threadbare which in the days of Lydia Becker, of Mrs. Bodichon and of Madame Belloc had seemed bright and convincing. But the speakers themselves were undaunted. They stepped out their measure, like a party dancing a quadrille in a modern ballroom, conscious that they were somewhat remote from the flood-tide of passion, but full of grace and spirit. But the Bill was lost by forty-eight.

XXXII

'Burning to Vote'

Outside the House of Commons it seemed that the fate of these suffrage bills was monotonously frustrating, for the principles at the heart of every woman's suffrage bill had been constantly lost in the labyrinth of procedure or of party manœuvre. Impatiently waiting, the women could only believe that they had been tricked. They were like the companions of a child, which is trying its luck in a maze: irritated by the non-appearance of their charge they begin to convince themselves that what was inevitable was deliberate.

In a speech in the House of Commons some ninety years earlier, Brougham quoted a remark of Burke's which he said should be painted in gold above the hall of every deliberative assembly— 'Where there is abuse there ought to be clamour, because it is better to have our slumbers broken by the fire bell, than to perish amidst the flames in our bed.' The militant suffragettes, when they realized that they had lost the battle in the House of Commons, showed that they were determined to have the best of both worlds: the alarm should sound and the public should burn. Whipped up by Christabel Pankhurst from the boulevards of Paris, and egged on by the plaintive but deeply moving eloquence of her mother in London, the women of the Union adopted a general policy of secret arson—directed at property but not at human life. It was called 'secret' because the perpetrators did their best to avoid discovery: there was no question of courting arrest which had been their declared policy during the demonstrations on the streets and during the window-breaking. They were, as was observed at the time, 'burning to vote'.

During the days immediately following the withdrawal of the Franchise Reform Bill in January, and the defeat of the Woman's Suffrage Bill in May, the attacks of the militants showed ingenuity and variety. Miss Jackiedawra Melford—the daughter of a leading actor—perched herself on the top deck of a motor-bus which in those sturdy times was open to the heavens: from this vantage point she drove along Victoria Street, firing stones from a powerful catapult into the windows of the buildings passed by the bus. The professionals at many of the golf courses round Birmingham were startled to find that some of their putting greens had, during the night of January 30th, been burned by acid with the slogan 'Votes for Women'. A few days later the orchid-house at Kew was wrecked, rather in the style of the handiwork of a party of boisterous undergraduates after a stimulating dinner: the windows of the house were smashed, plants knocked out of their pots and all the labels removed. The reader can almost hear the muttered imprecations of the gardeners as they arrived to restore order. On the next day the windows of the Reform Club were broken as were those a little farther along the same street, of that innocent old son-in-law of Queen Victoria—Prince Christian—whose fancy, in his old age, was merely for peace and quiet and for an occasional dish of sucking-pig.

But a few days later the attacks grew sharper. The militants made the mistake of returning to Kew, where they set fire to the Tea Pavilion. A girl, Olive Wharry, was arrested and brought before the local magistrates' court. She threw a directory at the head of the Chairman—Councillor Bisgood. Although she aimed from a distance of six feet, she fortunately missed her target. A little later in the year the citizens of Dudley were alarmed by an explosion at midnight. A gun captured from the Russians in the Crimean War had 'spoken'—primed and fired, not without courage, by a suffragette. In March two railway stations were burned down—Saunderton on the Great Western near Princes Risborough, and Croxley Green near Watford.

There was a more serious manifestation. Sir George Riddell, a generous and sincere friend of Lloyd George, who was Chairman of the *News of the World*, lived on the edge of Walton Heath Golf Course and was providing congenial neighbours for himself by

building a house for Lloyd George and also for Charles Masterman close to his own. This little nest of ardent Liberals, in the
midst of the conventional decorum of Surrey suburbanism, had
caused some comment. The *Morning Post* referred to it as the first
fruits of the Liberal rural housing programme. Lloyd George's
house was not finished when the militants, on February 19th,
succeeded in placing two bombs in it. The one placed in the bedroom exploded and did damage: the other failed to go off. 'The
General', with military terseness, commented to the press: 'It is
grand.' The *Daily Express*, just coming under the stimulating
guidance of Lord Beaverbrook, nicknamed the militants 'the
Bombazines'. But the matter was of course serious and when Mrs.
Pankhurst openly declared: 'I accept all responsibility for the
bomb outrage', the authorities had to act. She appeared before the
Epsom Bench, carrying a bouquet of lilies of the valley. She was
committed for trial and subsequently sentenced to three years'
imprisonment.

Faced with this situation the Government had to increase their
resources for curbing the militants. It will be appreciated that
imprisonment, accompanied by the hunger strike, even after a
spell of forcible feeding, frequently led to the prisoner being released long before the sentence was served. This outwitting of
authority could perhaps be excused for street affrays or window-
breaking but it was altogether inappropriate for the more serious
actions by which the authorities were now confronted. Greatly
irritated, some people were once again urging that the hunger
strikers should be left to starve to death—even Members of
Parliament were heard to express such sentiments, though perhaps few of them would have agreed with Lady Bathurst, who
issued the following pronouncement to the press from her important home in Belgrave Square, showing that not for nothing
was she the daughter of the proprietor of the *Morning Post*.

'When a suffragette has been convicted, first have her well
birched (by women) then shave off her hair, and finally deport
her to New Zealand or Australia.' The instinct of some human
beings, alarmed at what was happening, was to resort to methods
of barbarism. In the House of Commons, in the middle of March,
1913, Mr. Harold Smith, a more savage member of the family than

his brother F. E. and with primitive qualities unredeemed by the sparkling intellect of his elder brother, fiercely attacked McKenna for being too lenient to the women. In his reply McKenna denied that the militants committed offences knowing that the Government was powerless to punish them: he gave figures to show that since 1st January 1913, 66 suffragists had been received in prison— 35 had served their sentences, 23 were still in prison, and 8 had been released because they refused to take their food. He paid sensible and balanced tribute to the women's courage and to all the difficulties for the prison authorities to which this gave rise. He told the House of Commons how they refused to be examined by a doctor, how they surreptitiously starved themselves, how 'one of the prisoners, quite recently, before going to bed at night, sponged herself all over with warm water and then lay on her bed, without any bed-clothes, the whole of the cold night'. He added, 'we know by bitter experience that we cannot deal with them except by taking each individual case as it arises, and exercising patience, forbearance and humanity.' Turning to the suggestion that if he had courage he would let the women die, he said: 'I wonder if it requires more courage to let some helpless woman die because she has mistaken political opinions, and has broken a window, or to face the obloquy showered upon my head by the honourable member for Warrington (Harold Smith)'. The stately embodiment of Conservatism, Sir Frederick Banbury, interrupted the Home Secretary to say that if he did leave these women to carry out their threats to starve themselves to death: 'Nothing would happen. Only one or two would die.' McKenna went quickly on: 'I think you would find thirty or forty would come forward to die. They are fanatical and hysterical women, who no more fear death in fighting what they believe to be the cause of women than the natives of the Soudan feared death when fighting the battle of the Mahdi.'

The question of deportation was strongly urged. Lord Robert Cecil, rather surprisingly, suggested St. Helena: another member urged the claims of the diminutive islands of Rum, Eigg and Muck, and the Isle of Man inevitably met with much approval.

A fortnight after this debate, on April 3rd, McKenna asked the House of Commons to give a second reading to the Prisoners

(Temporary Discharge) Bill. This gave the Home Secretary powers to release a prisoner, whose health was suffering: the prisoner would remain free while complying with certain conditions but if they were violated could be re-arrested. The House agreed to this, without any great show of enthusiasm: it was named by Lord Robert Cecil 'the Cat and Mouse Bill'.

'They no more fear death in fighting what they believe to be the cause of women than the natives of the Soudan feared death when fighting the cause of the Mahdi.' Those words were spoken by McKenna in March: their truth was proved with an emphasis, which was pitiful but final, in June. On June 4th the Derby was run, and after the leading horses had passed Tattenham Corner, Emily Wilding Davison, eluding the police on the rails, ran on to the course and threw herself in front of the last group of horses, which were somewhat bunched. By chance—because it was quite impossible to pick out the purple, the gold braid, the scarlet sleeves, of the Royal Colours, and aim at an individual horse owing to the speed at which they were coming and the way in which they were grouped—Miss Davison fell in front of the King's horse Anmer, bringing it down and injuring the jockey. (The race was won by the favourite but this horse was immediately disqualified by the Stewards for 'bumping and boring'. This was of course entirely irrespective of Miss Davison, as her action had not, in the opinion of those responsible, affected the result of the race). Miss Davison was picked up, and the colours of the Union were found sewn inside her coat. She was taken to Epsom Cottage Hospital, and her injuries were thought to be serious but not mortal. With judicious impartiality King George sent to enquire for the jockey, and Queen Mary enquired for Miss Davison. The jockey speedily recovered; Miss Davison, after an operation on the head, which was performed by a prominent male supporter of militancy, died on the Sunday following the Derby.

On Saturday, June 14th, her body was born in triumph from Victoria to King's Cross with a pageantry which recalled the obsequies of princes. Thousands of women took part in the cavalcade—marching in groups dressed in black, purple or white —those wearing black carried purple irises, those in purple—red peonies and those in white—laurels. At the head of the procession were the usual mounted outriders immediately followed by a standard-bearer, with a banner, on which was embroidered: 'Thoughts have gone forth whose power can sleep no more. Victory. Victory.' Then followed hunger-strikers, the clergy, standard-bearer with a banner: 'Greater love hath no man than this that a man lay down his life for his friends', personal friends, the body, relations, a standard-bearer and banner: *'Dulce et decorum est pro patria mori'*, hunger-strikers, Mrs. Pankhurst's carriage,[1] standard-bearer and banner: 'He that loseth his life shall find it.' Members of the Union, women doctors and women graduates and a double band closed the great procession. A halt was made at St. George's Church, Bloomsbury, where the Reverend C. Baumgarten conducted a short service. The Great Northern Railway then bore the coffin northwards for burial in the grave of the Davison family at Morpeth.

As is usual on occasions of national rejoicing or sorrow, leaflets were printed and hawked among the crowd of sightseers. The dead woman was depicted in her mortar-board, and readers were reminded that she had won first-class honours in English at Oxford. The letter-press of the pamphlet was curious, for it was strongly political and 'left-wing'. There were references to the struggle for widows to live 'on the pittance paid for Government clothing', the sweating system with women working for less than 1s. a day, the 110 babies out of every 1,000 who died within the first year of birth, the women bought and sold into a life of shame, and the little children 'outraged and defiled'. 'These wrongs will continue undiminished so long as the womanhood of the country' is held in subjection and dishonour. It ended with the strange assertion: 'And so she offered up her life as a petition to the King.'

The great procession was respectfully received by Londoners, except at one or two points where racing men voiced their protest. Clever but headstrong, Emily Davison had always tended to walk alone—she was the first to use fire, and she had been the first to talk openly of life being sacrificed for the cause. There is

---

[1] Mrs. Pankhurst, dressed in deepest mourning, was arrested under the 'Cat and Mouse Act' just as she was stepping into her carriage. Her empty carriage followed the hearse—rather in the Victorian fashion when eminent persons sent their carriage, with blinds drawn and with no occupants, to join a funeral as a mark of respect to the deceased.

evidence that the Union leaders did what they could to damp down these promptings, but theirs was no doubt the responsibility because she only typified, to the ultimate point, the consequence for a sensitive human nature of the brave deeds and loud words which poured forth from the militants. The foolishness of what she did is too obvious to need stressing: and her action was made neither worse not better by the orgy of sentiment with which it was acclaimed. Minds prone to believe that everything works out for the best and that no sacrifice is pointless were doubtless comforted by the leading article in the *Daily Herald* which ended with this remarkable sentence: 'But we are all battling in the faith that nothing in the struggle and sacrifice is in vain, and that the end will be harmony and joyance.' Most thinking mortals will sense the tragedy in the fate of a human being impelled to destruction by the mystic call of sacrifice: the kind of futile political optimism, which merely saw it as a prelude to 'Merry' England, to a world of dancing swains and tripping maids, to wonderful scenes of sylvan joyance, reveals humanity at its most disheartening—the moralist at the graveside.

And in addition to the moralist, the joker was unluckily not far away, for a few days afterwards Miss Davison's feat was given a slightly ludicrous twist by a maniac. When the race for the Gold Cup at Ascot was being run; a middle-aged gentleman rushed in front of the favourite, brandishing a revolver in one hand and a small flag of the suffragette colours in the other. He stopped the favourite, who was leading, and brought down horse and jockey. He himself was seriously injured, but the indignation of the betting gentry was strong—especially when it was learned that he had carried a Bible in the fly-leaf of which was written: 'Oh the weariness of these races and the crowds they attract.' This demonstrator was found to be Mr. Harold Hewitt, an old Harrovian and a Cambridge man. The police reported—and possibly this was the most alarming thing about him?—that he lived in Bloomsbury.

XXXIII

'I Don't Know What We Are Coming To'

The leaflet distributed at Emily Davison's funeral draws attention to what was, as this struggle drew to its close, an unfortunate but developing emphasis in the policy of the Union. Such an occasion as the funeral of this very brave, if very mistaken, woman was not appropriate for a discussion of prostitution or the ravishings of children. If Sir Almroth started 'the sex war' the Union's leaders carried it on—and seemingly not without relish. As Miss Sylvia Pankhurst expresses it (and she did not approve the development) they began to argue that 'women were purer, nobler and more courageous; men were an inferior body greatly in need of purification'. She is also no doubt correct in saying that Mr. Pethick-Lawrence threw in his lot with the militants partly to prevent the struggle for votes turning into a battle of the sexes. The unfortunate direction in which events were running was made clear when Mrs. Pankhurst was tried at the Old Bailey, in April, 1913, for inciting the commission of the bomb outrages in Lloyd George's home. She appeared before Mr. Justice Lush; though a conscientious lawyer and popular at the Bar he displayed some weakness on the Bench, and allowed Mrs. Pankhurst to introduce many irrelevancies. In her speech at the close of the case Mrs. Pankhurst managed to introduce a swiping, random blow at the English judiciary. She said: 'A painful thing occurred many years ago. An assize was opened, the prisoners were waiting for trial, but one of the judges did not take his place in court. There were cases to be tried at that assize—there was a case of a wretched man charged with a horrible offence. . . .' At this point Lush interrupted her and said that she must not go on with what she was saying. With scarcely a pause she got round his prohibition as follows: 'I have been told that I cannot refer to the provocation which women have received in the administration of the law: that I cannot tell you of a Judge of Assize found dead in a brothel. . . .' Lush boiled over with indignation, and told her that she was guilty of a most shameful want of decorum, but she had made her point.

These advertised shortcomings of mankind were given additional piquancy for the taste of the public (though it could of course be argued that these matters need no titillation) by what was known as the Piccadilly Flat Case in August 1913. A Piccadilly Flat—it has to be confessed—strikes a note of warning in the mind of even the most easy-going moralist, and the particulars of the case seemed to rouse one of those periodic surges of public curiosity which are not easy to explain. The details were rather unusual—though somewhat paltry and hardly worth the excitement. 'Queenie' Gerald (the occupant of the flat) was charged with keeping a brothel. On the premises were found whips, birches and correspondence. A gentleman, named in the case and called Morris, fled the country. No doubt—and it has happened before—Queenie Gerald's little establishment became an object of attraction to gentlemen in well-to-do circumstances. There was, among the correspondence, a letter from a cadet at Sandhurst enquiring, with the innocence of one educated at a good public-school, whether Queenie could oblige him with a virgin. Queenie was sentenced to three months in the Second Division.

At once there were complaints in Parliament, contrasting the light sentence for a 'procuress' with that imposed on a high-principled suffragette. McKenna was as ever perfectly resolute, and he pointed out that Queenie Gerald only procured prostitutes, and that though paid as a procuress she, in fact, defrauded her clients. Then the Government was accused of hushing up the correspondence and it was said that gentlemen's names were discovered which the prosecution declined to reveal. From this it was an inevitable step to assert, with the blindness of party rancour, that members of the Cabinet were among Queenie's patrons. *The*

Globe newspaper, at that time tottering to its fall, was in the hands of a Jewish Conservative. Day after day its readers were indulged with delectable bits about Queenie Gerald and her illustrious clients from the Liberal front bench. The Labour party (not always too particular about its comrades-in-arms) joined this rather putrid quest. The case coincided with a series of articles which Christabel Pankhurst was writing in *The Suffragette*. These articles were subsequently published in the form of a book called *The Great Scourge and How to End it*. The publisher was David Nutt. The scourge was of course venereal disease, and the theme of the book is sufficiently revealed by Miss Pankhurst's cure—'Votes for Women and Chastity for Men.' The arguments and facts fortunately need not detain the reader, but Miss Pankhurst did not hesitate to weave into her narrative the much-published facts of Queenie Gerald, and she wrote: 'In the Piccadilly flat case, with its foul revelations and its still fouler concealments, is summed up the whole case against votes for women.' Perhaps the last word on this unwise development in militancy is best left with a woman. Miss Rebecca West, then at the very dawn of her distinguished career, described in an article in *The Clarion*, at that time an advanced journal on the Labour side, how she spent a penny in buying *The Suffragette*. With forceful wit she pointed to the harm which these scoldings of men by Miss Pankhurst were likely to do.[1] She ended: 'There was a long and desperate struggle before it became possible for women to write candidly on subjects such as these. That this power should be used to express views that would be old fashioned and uncharitable in the pastor of a Little Bethel is a matter for scalding tears.'

And now in the spring of 1913 the struggle entered its final phase. The death-throes of militancy or the birth pangs of the enfranchisement of women, as the reader cares to regard it, gave rise to the wildest scenes. Many houses were destroyed, but condemnation of the militants will be tempered by the reflection that they always chose unoccupied houses and sometimes the more out-

---

[1] Perhaps illustrative of what she had in mind was an article in *The Winning Post* by a gentleman calling himself 'Robert le Diable'. 'Is the pure-minded Christabel aware that a brothel is a temptation to youth provided by her own sex? Yet the inmates may be preferable to the ice-bound, callous creature called a suffragette. There is at least a touch of nature even if abused, in the one while the other is stone.'

rageous follies of the Victorian manufacturing classes. A hideous and bogus baronial castle, built by a manufacturer of 'turkey-red' —a colour which can hardly be acclaimed as an aesthetic triumph —was burned in the Vale of Leven, and was reputed to have cost the owner or his insurance company £70,000. In the summer of 1913 the women could point to a not dissimilar success—the destruction of a bungalow outside Bolton valued, with its contents, at £20,000. This expensive cabin belonged to Sir William Lever, afterwards Lord Leverhulme, who at the time of this singeing of his fortune was staying at Knowsley where King George and Queen Mary were also guests. The Lancashire police were provoked at not being able to make an arrest. A few weeks later Mrs. Rigby,[1] the wife of a prominent doctor at Preston, was arrested for placing a bomb in the Liverpool Exchange Buildings. At the end of the initial proceedings before the magistrates, when she was remanded, she asked to be allowed to make a statement in Court. This was granted, and she began with an eloquent discourse about the fire at the Lever bungalow, which she described as 'a beacon lighted for the King and country to see that there were some insupportable grievances for women.' Here the magistrate interrupted her, saying that he could not see what bearing the question of the bungalow had on her remand. Mrs. Rigby went on: 'It has this bearing. I lighted the fire alone that night. I walked there and did it alone.'

In addition to these, and numerous other empty private houses, the railway station at Oxted, the croquet pavilion at Roehampton and the University Football Pavilion at Cambridge were all burned. In 1914 the outstanding episodes were the burning of the pier pavilion at Yarmouth, of the Bath Hotel at Felixstowe and (the most scandalous of all the outrages) the burning of Wargrave Church. A fine south London church—St. Catherine's, Hatcham—had been destroyed in the previous year. Bombs of a somewhat feminine manufacture, were placed in offices and warehouses, in Lime Street Station at Liverpool, in St. George's, Hanover Square and a contraption was hung over the back of the Coronation Chair in Westminster Abbey. This consisted of one of the large-scale

---

[1] A very early member of I.L.P. She illustrates the connexion between advanced politics and the Suffrage workers—especially in the North.

bicycle bells, in fashion at that time, which on being struck revolved with a prolonged melody. Each half of the bell contained a chlorate explosive mixed with iron nuts. All these activities—and there were many others throughout the country—showed variety, ingenuity and courage. To the public they were somewhat dangerous (but not very) and extremely vexatious. A detailed account of all these bangs and burnings—including the firing of toy pistols from the gallery of the House of Commons—can be found in the Annual Register or in the books of Miss Metcalfe or Miss Sylvia Pankhurst. Like the misdoings of the Kings of Israel they are chronicled elsewhere—and no doubt, like the actions of those temperamental sovereigns, these escapades assumed larger proportions to those who watched them than they do to posterity. The perpetrators of these deeds were naturally determined that they should lose nothing in the telling. When for example the orchid-house at Kew was damaged, and a lady snicked a telegraph wire between London and the north, *The Suffragette* came out with blazing headlines—'The War Continues. Valuable Orchids destroyed at Kew. Glasgow isolated from London.' The nervous and those who reasonably objected to the idea of a young woman directing all these disorders from the comforts of a Parisian flat were constantly urging McKenna to fiercer retribution. He remained resolute, resisting all attempts to push him into a more ruthless policy. He never denied the gravity of the issue by which the Government was faced, but he was able to show that the number of fires attributed to the militants were only a fraction of the average yearly total, and that some, for which the Union claimed the credit, were the work of ordinary criminals —such as the worthy who burned down his house to secure the insurance money and left many suffragette pamphlets lying about at the scene of the 'disaster'.

The 'Cat and Mouse' Act had some success, but in its application to the leaders of militancy, it focused too much attention on them of which they were quick to take advantage. Both Mrs. Pankhurst and her daughter Sylvia, who was conducting a well-found political campaign in the East End of London, constantly outwitted the authorities, and appeared in public as semi-invalids —the victims of Liberal brutality. There is no need to discount their sufferings which, from the moment of imprisonment, included a refusal of all solid food and all liquid. When the ladies were sufficiently reduced they were set free, but as they never gave the undertaking for good behaviour, they were liable to arrest at any moment. Mrs. Pankhurst was generally seen in public with a nurse—a gorgon of a woman who looked like a matron of a lesser public school—and invariably planted her formidable person between the police and her patient. At a meeting at the London Pavilion, where Miss Kenney was re-arrested under the Act, sympathizers attempted a rescue. After a scuffle with the police, some helmets and other trophies were captured: these were put up to auction and fetched over £300 in the meeting. Miss Sylvia Pankhurst, whose courage captured the imagination of her East End sympathizers (themselves not unfamiliar with evasive action where the police were concerned) was frequently saved from arrest by clever disguise or by the weight of the faithful—as it were the swarm around the queen. She generally appeared in public on a stretcher to emphasize her debilitated state, and looked not unlike a medieval princess, travelling in a litter, to make her last devotions at some shrine. The weakness of the Cat and Mouse treatment was that the leaders were able to use it as a means of enhancing their sufferings and thereby playing on the powerful emotions of their followers. Mrs. Pankhurst's hold over the faithful was never more complete than during these closing months of the struggle.

The Government no doubt hoped by striking at the leadership to decapitate the movement, and McKenna was also able to point out, with truth, that virtually all the women who committed the outrages were paid by the Union. In fact he believed that militancy only existed on the subscriptions of rich women: they paid their tools, as he expressed it, 30s. or £2 to go about the country and commit outrages. McKenna might here have quoted some lines, in vogue a few years earlier, which seem to catch the spirit of these vengeances—

> *O I've seen a girl or two in my time*
> *Yet I never saw such a vixen;*
> *She's light blue eyes and bonny brown 'air,*
> *And they call her the Slasher of Brixton.*

The Government had raided the headquarters of the Union on 23rd May 1914—no doubt with the intention of unravelling the names of the large subscribers, so that the victim of militancy could bring a legal action against those who financed the operations. McKenna said later that if the means of Revenue of the Union could be destroyed, the power of Mrs. Pankhurst and her friends would finish.

The Union funds for the year ending in February 1914 were £37,000, which was a formidable sum—the largest ever achieved by the Society.[1] The possibility of striking at militancy through the subscribers to the Union was given no adequate chance because of the outbreak of war.

The policy of the Union was accompanied by a complete lack of respect for any institution, except human life. They seem, in retrospect, a curious blend of Cromwell's Ironsides, the Irish Fenians and some shady little body of leftists scheming in an upper room off Tottenham Court Road. In earlier days they had used the courts of justice for propaganda: from 1913 they treated the courts with contempt. During a trial at the Old Bailey, following the burning of a house at Hampton, a hammer was thrown at the judge and a tomato at prosecuting counsel—Mr. Archibald Bodkin afterwards Director of Public Prosecutions. Miss Nina Boyle, on being sentenced at Bow Street, called cheerfully to the magistrate: 'Good morning, Mr. Pecksniff, we shall meet again.' The magistrate might excusably have pointed out that Charity and Mercy 'those not unholy names' did not seem conspicuous in the leaders of the Union. 'The General', also at Bow Street, called across the Court to the counsel prosecuting her: 'You sit down, you Jack-in-the-Box. You have been earning your living easily enough by hounding down women. You have come from Bluebeard at the Home Office.' McKenna, most domestic and respectable of mankind, scarcely deserved this thrust. That morning 'the General' was at her best. She broke out of the dock and advanced

---

[1] £4,500 was due to contributions raised by Mrs. Pankhurst on her visit to America at the end of 1913. Miss Sylvia Pankhurst, in her book gives the income of the Union as follows: 1906/7, £3,000; 1907/8, £7,000; 1908/9, £20,000; 1909/10, £32,000; 1910/11, £29,000; 1911/12, £25,000; 1912/13, £28,000. The figures show how militancy stimulated revenue: the decline in 1910/11 and 1911/12 could be explained through militancy being discontinued during the truce of those years.

with threatening aspect on the rather anaemic solicitors and their clerks who moved instinctively towards the Bench. The policemen in court closed with her but she managed to seize a policeman's whistle and hurl it at the magistrate. Sir Henry Curtis-Bennett, who was the magistrate at Bow Street and consequently tried many of the leading suffragists, was set on by two young women when he was enjoying the breezes on the North Down Cliffs. Although he was a large man he was borne some way towards the edge by his assailants.

Church services were frequent targets for attack. One Sunday in St. Paul's Cathedral in August 1913 the officiating clergyman had intoned the sentence which ends 'and to shew thy pity upon all prisoners and captives' when forty women began to chant:

> *Save Emmeline Pankhurst*
> *Spare her! Spare her!*
> *Give her light and set her free*
> *Save her! Save her!*
> *Hear us while we pray to thee.*

Art galleries were much favoured. In June 1913 a Romney was slashed by a lady carrying a butcher's cleaver. How she contrived to hide this—unless she was admitted to the Gallery carrying a carpet-bag—seems mysterious. Sargent's portrait of Henry James, given to that eminent man by artistic and literary friends to mark his seventieth birthday, was slashed at Burlington House; again a chopper was used. And a few days later Herkomer's portrait of the 4th Duke of Wellington was also damaged in Burlington House. But—from the aspect of aesthetics—the most serious mischief was that caused to the Rokeby Venus on 10th March 1914 in the National Gallery. The effects of the attack can be seen to this day. The damage was done by Miss Mary Richardson,[1] and her statement was not calculated to mollify public opinion: 'I have tried to destroy'—she said—'the picture of the most beautiful woman in mythological history because the Government are destroying Mrs. Pankhurst—the most beautiful character in

---

[1] Miss Richardson seems to have started a long and troublous career by rising in the middle of luncheon in the Holborn Restaurant and clamouring for the vote. Affluent gentlemen in the middle of their business luncheons pelted her with bread. She was arrested no less than nine times between July 1913 and June 1914.

modern history.' At Bow Street she described the Home Secretary as having made 'the criminal code into a comic Valentine'. 'I am not afraid of dying', she went on. 'He cannot coerce me. He cannot make me serve my sentences. He can only repeat the farce of releasing me. Either way mine is the Victory.' As she left the dock, on her way out to the prisoner's door, she was seized by a girl and kissed.

And it was perhaps inevitable at this stage of the combat that the militants should have attempted to drag on to their side those powerful forces which rest above the warring factions of British politics. The Church of England has always been especially vulnerable to this kind of approach. Although their services had been ridiculed by the militants, the clerics, sympathetic to the women's cause, no doubt felt that in turning the other cheek they were obeying those calls of meekness and long-suffering patience which had been recommended by St. Paul. The Bishop of Lincoln,[1] who as a former canon of Manchester had imbibed the stimulating opinions of that city, was conspicuous in showing sympathy for the militants—as were a few other prominent men in the Church— including the Headmaster of Repton, William Temple. A meeting was held on 6th December 1913 in the Queen's Hall organized by these and other Church leaders as a protest against forcible feeding, but it was noticed that the audience was more obviously in sympathy with militancy than were the speakers. A few months earlier a little squad of clergymen, wearing the low-crowned clerical hats of those times, marched in brave array, escorted by the police, to Downing Street to protest against the Cat and Mouse Act. The diminutive but engaging F. L. Donaldson[2]—familiar to worshippers at Westminster Abbey in more recent times—was at the head of the posse. At Downing Street the deputation was politely received. But the Church won no politeness from the militants in return. In 1914 they adopted the practice of picketing Lambeth Palace. The Archbishop, Randall Davidson, who was

[1] Edward Lee Hicks (1843–1919) a strong temperance reformer, pacifist and sympathizer with female suffrage. His opinions delayed his advancement: Mr. Asquith appointed him to Lincoln in 1910.

[2] Frederick Lewis Donaldson, b. 1860. Educated Oxford, Vicar of St. Mark's, Leicester, 1896–1918. Canon of Westminster and Archdeacon from 1937. One of the founders of the Church Socialist League. Died 1952.

nothing if not humane sent for one of these patient watchers and
assured her that he would consider the matter of forcible feeding.
The lady in question, Mrs. Dacre Fox, then described her inter-
view at an enthusiastic meeting of the Union in these terms: 'I can
only say that as I sat looking at that old man, the feeling which
was uppermost in my mind was that of contempt. . . . I wondered
if Calvary had almost been in vain.'

And the final authority outside party politics, which remained
as a target for militant abuse, was the sovereign. Abuse was forthcoming in 1914. In the summer the members of the Union made a
sustained and determined attack on Buckingham Palace in an
attempt to petition the King. It was stated in the House of Commons—and not denied—that the King was confined to the Palace
for four hours. On this occasion Mrs. Pankhurst was arrested,
borne off from the Palace gates in the arms of a burly inspector—a
scene which has provided one of the most familiar photographs
of the whole of the suffrage struggle. More vexatious to King
George were the occasional personal insults to which he was
liable. There was an interruption and some screaming from women
when, with Queen Mary and the King and Queen of Denmark,
who were paying a state visit, he went to the Opera at Covent
Garden. On the afternoon of May 23rd the King and Queen went
to a special matinee of *The Silver King* at His Majesty's. During the
performance a lady, chained to her seat in the stalls, called loudly
and repeatedly to the King: 'You Russian Czar up there.' A
reference to the King was received with prolonged hissing at a
subsequent meeting of the Union.

On June 4th an extraordinary and successful ruse was achieved
during the presentation of debutantes at Court. Lady Blomfield—
the widow of an architect of some note, who was the son of a
renowned Bishop of London—had arranged to present her two
daughters. She became suspicious that the fever of militancy was
burning within them, and decided on the evening of the Court not
to take them. (She had to go herself as she was presenting another
young lady.) Her daughters, after she had gone, went to the
Palace and explaining to the somewhat innocent court official that
their mother was ahead with their tickets, had no difficulty in
making their entry. One of them—at the moment of prostration

in an exquisite curtsey before the King—called out: 'Your Majesty, stop forcible feeding.' Courtiers rushed from all directions and Sir Douglas Dawson (Comptroller of the Lord Chamberlain's Department) led Miss Blomfield away leaving a small piece of finery, in a crumpled heap, at the feet of the King. Lady Blomfield, who was in another room added to the confusion, when she heard what had happened, by falling into a faint. On the next morning Lady Blomfield said to the newspapers that the episode 'was deeply deplored by the whole family'. A great worker for imperial and patriotic causes Lady (Massie) Blomfield also issued a statement to the newspapers that she was able to reassure her many friends that she was only distantly related to the perpetrators of this insult to the King. That evening the King described the episode in his diary adding the observation—'I don't know what we are coming to.'

XXXIV

The Vote at Last

Well might the observer, looking back to those agitating months in 1914 which were the prelude to the First War, wonder with King George what they might portend. The rumblings of Civil War in Ireland, the struggles of Capital and Labour which pointed to all the bitter feuds of class war, and the sex war in London (for though some of its manifestations were outside, its roots lay in the metropolis) seem symptoms of such a malignant temper that the chronicler of those times feels positive relief in the knowledge that they are all to be swept into oblivion by the sacrifice of a million British dead in battle. Such an ironical state of affairs seems almost to justify the extraordinary remark of that Austrian despot who decided that war, like some gigantic cupping operation, is necessary from time to time to carry away the accumulated ill-humours of mankind. And the danger for those attempting to see these matters in true perspective is that the impending catastrophe is so immense that it dwarfs what went before. Like the pages of an exciting tale, which are leading up to the great crisis of the story, they seem to encourage only perfunctory notice. Consequently the mistaken idea is fostered that war creates social change and social revolution: it does nothing of the kind, for at most it accelerates tendencies already conspicuous. 'The war gave women the vote' or 'Women won the vote by their work in the war' is a comfortable sentiment often expressed, but like many such easy sayings it bears no approximation to truth. The spirit which animated women to serve in the hospitals near the front line, to drive motor transport on the fringe of battle, or to take the place of men in many public services at home may have been spread by war: it was certainly not created by war. While it is obvious that the experiences of a 'bombazine' were not without their advantages when it came to driving a general within sound of the shells in Flanders, the contribution made by women was more firmly based than in the experiences of a small section of women. A glance at a far wider canvas than militancy emphasizes the change which was stealing over the nature of women in the years before the war began. They had become independent in outlook and circumstances to an extent which would have pleased but slightly startled a pioneer of the 1860's. They crowded the schools and colleges: they banged their forceful selves across the hockey field: they invaded the golf courses, and assumed the airs of champions on the lawn-tennis court: they took up careers, went to work in the City and most suggestive of all they made their own friends.[1] The contrast between the young lady of those pre-war years and little Miss Prunes and Prisms—the finished product of Victorian womanhood—is too obvious to need emphasis. Mrs. Humphrey Ward gives an admirable portrait of the typical young lady of those times in her novel *Delia Blanchflower*. Delia has all the crispness and assurance of her contemporaries, and it is no shock to meet her, staying in a hotel in Switzerland alone and holding forth to a slightly frumpish collection of survivors from Victorian habits with the confident assertion: 'There is a new age coming, and it will be the age of the free woman.'

Much of the force behind this change found its way into the non-militant suffrage movement—whose numbers and funds increased prodigiously in the years immediately before the war. Some have argued that the constitutional societies absorbed many new members who were roused by the militant drum but could not march to it. There is certainly some truth in that, but more in the fact that a reform which had seemed freakish now appeared acceptable and inevitable. In the summer of 1914 the National

---

[1] The Victorians always supposed that the circle of acquaintance of any individual in fairly affluent circumstances was bounded by relations and the established friends of the family. To form private friendships outside that circle was very rare in Victorian times, and still unusual in Edwardian times. It explains the remark, which strikes so strangely on modern ears, made by Sir George Sitwell to his eldest son, 'Such a mistake to have friends, dear boy.'

Union of Suffrage Societies organized a highly successful demonstration in London—a great concentration of women, who had marched from the north, south, east and west to foregather in Hyde Park. They were marshalled by Sir Francis Fletcher-Vane, of Hutton-in-the-Forest, prominent in the Boy Scout movement and (rather unexpectedly) a Liberal; it was admitted on all hands that the arrangements for such a vast concourse were perfect. These non-militant marchers were everywhere received with respect. This display of constitutional strength, backed up as it was by the knowledge that it rested on the support of many of the most balanced leaders of both sexes—unquestionably began to pave the way for the conversion of even the bitterest opponent of the 'Vote'.

Militancy remained the obstacle. The contrast between the patient strategy of the constitutionalists and the frenzy of the militants is so sharply defined that it is difficult to believe that they were each founded on the same cause. In fact the militant suffrage movement seems so remote from any logical historical causes that the reader may be tempted to class it with those sudden romantic flowerings of the human mind like the Rebellion of 1745 or the Great Exhibition of 1851 as being of little real importance.[1] Yet this would be wrong. For it was at once a triumph, and a dangerous portent, to detach an agitation of this kind from politics and bind it to persons. As long as the Pethick-Lawrences were prominent in the Union, militancy was used as a political weapon. The marches on St. Stephen's or the smashings of windows were made to coincide with debates at Westminster: it was forceful but not illogical political intimidation. With the departure of the Lawrences from the Union, militancy became the servant of the Leader. Every time that Mrs. Pankhurst was sentenced or re-arrested under the Cat and Mouse Act the fires blazed and the bombs exploded. Within twenty-four hours of Mrs. Pankhurst being sentenced to three years' imprisonment at the Old Bailey in April 1913—a country house was burned down at Chorley Wood, an attempt was made to blow up Oxted Station and to wreck a train at Stockport and some paintings by Victorian artists were

---

[1] Mr. Christopher Hobhouse in his entrancing book on The Great Exhibition of 1851 says, 'As for the importance of the Great Exhibition it had none.'

damaged at the Art Gallery in Manchester. Although Continental 'Leaders' of a later decade in the century would not have relished the comparison with a woman, the precedent was there. Parnell possibly—but Mrs. Pankhurst certainly—mark the flight of reason and of respect for authority from the battle of politics. While it may be true, as Lord Winterton observed, that militancy was only 'the blood relation' of Lloyd George's violent speeches, and that it was an almost natural product of the frenzied politics of the pre-war years it was the only storm—and many threatened—which actually burst.

And even after the deluge had started there is evidence that it could have been more effective if it had been used as a political and not a personal weapon. This was shown by the exertions of Miss Sylvia Pankhurst who was working on a very narrow front and with a mere handful of support compared with the resources of her mother and sister; her campaign in the East End of London, after the Bow and Bromley by-election, linked militancy with the traditional forces of revolt. Although there were here the same feelings of personal loyalty to Miss Pankhurst's leadership, they were subordinated to the task of rousing the spirit of the East Ender. Although she showed the greatest courage—she was constantly arrested, adopted the hunger and thirst strike and was repeatedly forcibly fed—she used her sufferings to attract followers to the cause among the women of the East End. A letter from her was, for example, published in the *Daily Chronicle* on 19th March 1914 to her mother: 'I am fighting, fighting, fighting. I have four, five and six wardresses every day, as well as the two doctors. I am fed by stomach tube twice a day. I resist all the time.' And when McKenna met her long after the battle was over, he went up to her and said: 'You are a very brave woman.' If the war had not intervened her exertions and her influence with the working-class movement must have had a decisive bearing on the history of the struggle. As it was, deputations of East End women began to make themselves felt in the environs of Whitehall, and Miss Pankhurst's greatest success was leading a deputation to Mr. Asquith in June 1914. The working women were received with politeness by the Prime Minister, and it was obvious that he had moved a long way towards recognizing the women's vote as having entered the

realm of practical politics. In his reply, after complimenting the
ladies on the way in which they had stated their case, he gave the
impression that the pressure of industrial and social questions on
the time of Parliament made it inevitable that the interests of
women would have to be represented there. The significance of
this deputation and its friendly reception by Mr. Asquith were
widely noticed at the time, but its consequences were lost amid
the dire events of high summer. If the object of militancy was to
exert pressure on the Government, then it could certainly be
argued that Miss Sylvia Pankhurst's efforts were of no less importance than the crimes of arson committed in the names of her
mother and sister.

Yet before the militant burnings and bombings are dismissed as
of little consequence, the reader will recognize that in addition to
all the obvious qualities of loyalty, tenacity and high courage,
militancy showed something (admittedly in an exaggerated form)
of the spirit of uncertainty, of unrest, of dissatisfaction which
characterized not only the women of that time but the whole of
the more intelligent of the younger generation of both sexes. The
old, assured world, built on the wise conventions of the Victorians, was slowly dissolving long before the German soldiers
thundered into Belgium in August 1914. Militancy was a product
of that old world in dissolution, and although it antagonized
thousands of people from the cause of women's suffrage it revealed those unexpected depths in the character of women which
were to make the vote inevitable. Perhaps this aspect of the struggle
has never been expressed with more grace and force than by a
speech of Lady Constance Lytton's brother, Lord Lytton, in the
House of Lords. Addressing the conventional critics of militancy
he said: 'You see in it only the folly and the wickedness: but I also
see in it the pity and the tragedy . . . I have seen the exhibition of
human qualities which I consider to be as rare and as precious as
anything which a nation can possess. I have seen these qualities
given to a cause which is in itself as great and as noble a cause as
you could well find, but given in such a way as to defeat the very
objects that they sought to obtain. . . . And that to my mind is a
tragedy.'

However foolish and extravagant the actions of individuals

may appear to us to-day, the hopes and ideals which lay behind the struggle for the franchise were, as Lord Lytton said, noble.

Mrs. Pankhurst or Mrs. Fawcett may—if their inmost feelings could be laid bare—have wanted the vote as a triumph for their sex, but they desired it no less eagerly because they felt that women could contribute something to the public life of the nation. This aspect of the cause was finely expressed by the present Poet Laureate in a speech to women at the Queen's Hall in 1910. His theme was that the whole national life could be raised only through the joint endeavour of man and woman. And he ended: 'You have proclaimed for the first time that the old rule of sex is dead: and that the new rule of human beings, of comrades, may begin to make this world liker a star, and life something liker what God breathed into the clay.'

That sense of missionary fervour gave the suffrage movement its strength: it gave the members their sense of solidarity. 'No companionship can ever surpass the companionship of the militants', wrote Annie Kenney with simplicity. 'The suffrage campaign was our Eton and Oxford, our regiment, our ship', wrote Rachel Ferguson in *The Victorian Bouquet*.

Yet the future which seemed to all progressive minds—to Liberals, to Radicals, to Labour enthusiasts, to Socialists, to Pacifists and to Feminists—full of promise for the amelioration of the human race was, as these good people peered forward from the golden optimism of the summer of 1914, about to be given by Fate a twist of ferocious cruelty. Keir Hardie wrote more truly than he supposed when he observed at the beginning of 1914: 'The womb of time is again pregnant, and no one can say with any certainty with what issue.' Every intelligent observer can see— and there are hundreds of books in print to emphasize the point— that August 1914 ended a civilization. But it also—and this was the deeper tragedy—destroyed the world which was forming. To that world, wise, good, patient, far-sighted men and women had looked forward: to its realization they had devoted their lives. No doubt the moralist would cry, with Edward Fitzgerald, that such disappointments cease to be tragic for they are commonplace:

The Vote at Last

Alike for those who for TO-DAY prepare,
And those that after some TO-MORROW stare,
A Muezzin from the Tower of Darkness cries,
Fools your reward is neither Here nor There.

But whatever the opinions of the moralist, it is indisputable that the culmination of the struggle for the women's vote was unworthy both of the courage and idealism which had inspired the fight. The epilogue was meagre.

Within one month of the declaration of war on 4th August 1914 all militancy was suspended, all suffragette prisoners were set free, and Mrs. Pankhurst and Christabel were addressing recruiting meetings. Two and a half years later on 28th March 1917 Mr. Asquith declared himself in favour of women's suffrage.[1] The Electoral Reform Bill which gave the vote to all women when they were thirty passed the Commons in December 1917, after having been discussed intermittently throughout that year, and became law in January 1918. An attempt to delete the clauses of the Bill giving votes to women had been attempted in June 1917. Though many of the old performers—Sir Frederick Banbury, Sir Charles Hobhouse, Lord Hugh Cecil and Lord Robert Cecil— stepped out with all their old grace and distinction, the glory had departed from the occasion. Mr. George Thorne, the greatly respected Liberal member for Wolverhampton, said: 'the fight is out of the whole struggle. It is absolutely clear that the fight is won.' The figures confirmed this; 364 members voted in favour of woman's suffrage, only 23 against. There was no demonstration, but when the clerk read out the figure '23' there was heard, clearly audible from the Ladies' Gallery, the sound of a woman's derisive laugh.

[1] Although *Punch* signalized the conversion with an amusing cartoon of a conductress welcoming Mr. Asquith on to a bus with the words 'Better late than never', and although many thought that Asquith coupled his change of opinion with the patronizing benediction that women had won the vote through their work in the war, neither of these do justice to the facts. Asquith had always been opposed to a partial enfranchisement of women. The Speaker's Conference, appointed by Asquith when he was still Prime Minister in 1916, had reported in favour of adult suffrage for men and women. To Asquith this was reasonable and acceptable, because, in his own words, 'it removed the illogical restrictions by which the grant of the franchise had been clogged'. It was the perpetuation of these illogical restrictions by the proposals for the female franchise before 1914 which was the principal reason for his hostility.

In November 1918—and it was almost the last act of the famous House of Commons elected in 1910—a Bill to enable women to stand for the House of Commons was hurried through both Houses of Parliament. Polling-day was on December 14th, only four weeks after the defeat of Germany, and it was observed that all the zest and colour and excitement of electioneering was gone. The women—especially in London—voted in strength but undemonstratively. Several prominent women came forward as candidates but only one—the Countess Markievicz—was successful. She was elected as a Sinn Feiner for South Dublin. In common with the other seventy-two Sinn Feiners elected to the House of Commons she never took her seat. The following stood unsuccessfully:

Miss Christabel Pankhurst (Coalition) Smethwick	8,614
Miss Mary Macarthur (Mrs. Anderson) (Labour) Stonebridge	7,587
Mrs. Despard (Labour) N. Battersea	5,634
Miss Alison Garland (Liberal) S. Portsmouth	4,283
Miss Violet Markham (Liberal) Mansfield	4,000
Mrs. Dacre Fox (Independent) Richmond	3,615
Mrs. Lucas (Unionist) Kennington	3,573
Mrs. Pethick-Lawrence (Labour) Rusholme	2,985
Mrs. E. Phipps (Independent) Chelsea	2,419
Mrs. How Martyn (Independent) Hendon	2,067
Mrs. J. McEwan (Liberal) Enfield	1,987
Mrs. Corbett Ashby (Liberal) Ladywood (Birmingham)	1,552
Mrs. Oliver Strachey (Independent) Chiswick	1,263
Mrs. Eunice Murray (Independent) Bridgeton	991
Miss W. Carney (Sinn F.) Belfast	395
Hon. Mrs. MacKenzie (Labour) Welsh University	176

Ten years after this General Election, in 1928, the age limit of thirty was removed, and women voted on an equality with men, at the age of twenty-one. This new body of the electorate, in the easy-going slang of the 1920's, was christened 'the flapper vote'. When the proposals were debated, a few of the old stalwarts tried to stir the long-dead embers and F. E. Smith (then Lord Birkenhead) in a debate in the House of Lords, obliged to vote for the measure, because it was introduced by a Government of which he was a member, but making no secret of his detestation of it, advised his fellow peers to vote for the Bill 'with resolute resignation'.

Mr. Pethick-Lawrence, by this time a respected addition to the Labour benches in the House of Commons, spoke in the debate in that house and said that the speeches of the opponents of the Bill: 'seem to be the echo of a far-distant bell that I have heard ringing over and over again.' The Bill passed the House of Lords in May 1928, and at the General Election a year later women voters comfortably outnumbered men.

As the outlawed half of the human race, a century after the publication of William Thompson's book, walked in work-a-day fashion into the polling booths to vote, few of them were conscious of the storm and stress which lay behind what Lord Hugh Cecil had once called, 'a very simple operation'. If Lord Lytton was correct in perceiving tragedy for the individual in sacrifice for a noble cause through tactics which were ill-conceived there was certainly sadness—if not tragedy—in the culmination of a struggle, long endured and bravely fought, which was to end as it had begun, to shuffle off the stage much as it had drifted on the stage, with scant attention and few applauses. For when at last women won their victory ('What a day that will be' Christabel Pankhurst had written at a bleak moment of the fight) the event was scarcely heeded, so engrossed was mankind with other matters, preoccupations of the world war. For like some obliterating tempest the war seemed to impose oblivion on the years which preceded it. The curious observer picking his way back to those times before 1914 feels not unlike someone wandering over a fair-ground from which humanity has been driven to shelter by a sudden deluge. There lie the scraps of paper, the scattered debris of gaiety—all the fun of the fair silent and sheeted. He can scarcely conceive it as it was, crowded with humanity, gay and brilliant; the stalls, garishly lighted, and tempting humanity with anything from flashing jewellery to pigs' trotters: the men bawling their wares: the crash of the ball on the coconut: the boat-swings, rising and falling, filled with passengers laughing and screaming: and the grand stud of galloping horses, magically revolving, among the gleaming brass, with whistle shrieking and music playing. Yet none of these things quite explain the colour and animation of the spectacle before the storm broke. For it was the ardour and high spirits of human beings which lent force and life to the scene, and it was those qualities which illumine the struggle for the women's vote, and lift it above the dust and turmoil of party strife.

Appendix I

Biographical Index

Every woman mentioned in the text of the book has been included in this biographical index, even when the information available is meagre. The notes are not designed to be concise biographies: their purpose is rather to give readers (without the labour of searching through out-of-date books of reference) sufficient information to identify each name. I have here and there, included the addresses, where some of the prominent suffragettes lived during the height of the agitation. The initials W.F.L. and W.S.P.U. stand respectively for Women's Freedom League and for Women's Social and Political Union—the two leading militant suffrage organizations.

ACLAND, ELEANOR; born *c.* 1877; eldest daughter of James Cropper; married Francis Acland 1905; an influential personality in many progressive causes; died 1933.

AMBERLEY, VISCOUNTESS; Katherine Louisa Stanley, born 1842; daughter of 2nd Lord Stanley of Alderley; married Viscount Amberley, son of 1st Earl Russell, 1864; died 1874.

ANDERSON, MARY REID; daughter of J. D. Macarthur, of Glasgow; born 1880; married W. C. Anderson, chairman of executive of I.L.P. Organizer of women workers in industry, and a distinguished personality in the Labour movement; died 1921.

ASHBY, MRS. CORBETT; born 1882; daughter of C. H. Corbett; married A. B. Ashby, Barrister-at-Law; educated Newnham College; distinguished member of the Liberal party; address: 22 Langside Avenue, Putney.

ASHTON, MARGARET; born 1856; distinguished through life by

her devotion to Manchester; formed with Miss Olga Herz the Manchester branch of the Women's Guardian Association; a Liberal; chairman of Manchester Suffrage Society 1906; helped to found Women's International League 1915; member of Manchester City Council; Henry Lamb's painting of her refused by Manchester Art Gallery because of her pacifist opinions; died 1937; address: 8 Kinnaird Road, Withington, Manchester.

ASHWELL, LENA; daughter of Commander Pocock, R.N.; married Sir Henry Simpson, K.C.V.O., 1908; won distinction on the stage; manager, Kingsway Theatre; author of several books on dramatic subjects and an autobiography—*Myself a Player* 1936.

ASHWORTH, LILIAS; *see* Hallett.

AYRTON, MATILDA CHAPLIN; born 1846; refused admission to examinations for medical degree; married 1872 William Edward Ayrton; mother of Mrs. Israel Zangwill; died 1883.

BABB, MISS; no information available.

BAGOT, LADY; Theodosia, daughter of Sir John Leslie, Bt., born 1865; married Joscelyne Bagot, M.P., 1885, afterwards a baronet; secondly in 1920 the Reverend Bellingham Swann; died 1940.

BAINES, JENNIE; spent her youth in Birmingham; captain in Salvation Army; married to bootmaker; sent to prison 1908, for addressing a crowd outside a meeting in Leeds Coliseum and saying: 'If these tyrants won't come to us, we must go to them.'

BALFOUR, LADY FRANCES; daughter of 8th Duke of Argyll; married Eustace Balfour 1879; died 1931.

BATHURST, COUNTESS OF; Lilias Margaret Frances Borthwick, only surviving child of first and last Lord Glenesk; married 7th Earl Bathurst, 1893.

BAYLIS, LILIAN; born in London, 1874; daughter of E. W. Baylis; Manager, 'The Old Vic'; C.H. 1929; died 1937.

BECKER, LYDIA ERNESTINE; born in Lancashire 1827; secretary of Manchester Women's Suffrage Society, 1867; editor, *Women's Suffrage Journal* 1870–90; member of Manchester School Board; died 1890.

BEDFORD, DUCHESS OF; born 1865; daughter of a Hampshire

country clergyman, Archdeacon Tribe; educated Cheltenham Ladies' College; married 1888 11th Duke of Bedford; popularly known as 'The Flying Duchess': her pioneer work in nursing and surgery was remarkable, as was her achievement in learning to fly when she was sixty: she was lost over the North Sea in 1937.

BEEDY, MISS. No information available.

BELLOC, ELIZABETH RAYNER; born 1830; daughter of Joseph Parkes; married 1867 Louis Belloc; died 1923.

BELLOC-LOWNDES; *see* Lowndes.

BESANT, ANNIE; born in London 1847; daughter of W. P. Wood; married Frank Besant, vicar of Sibsey; they were legally separated 1873; joined Fabian Society 1885; converted to theosophy; died 1933.

BICESTER, LADY; *see* Smith, Lady Sybil.

BIGGS, CAROLINE ASHURST; daughter of Joseph Biggs of Leicester; born 1840; lived in Notting Hill Square; edited *Englishwomen's Review*, 1870 to her death; died 1889.

BILLINGTON, THERESA; born Preston 1877; daughter of William Billington, shipping clerk; married 1907 Frederick Louis Greig: Publications: *Towards Women's Liberty*, *Militant Suffrage Movement* 1911; *Consumer in Revolt* 1912; *Woman And The Machine* 1913; address: The Myth, High Possil, Glasgow; now lives at Wimbledon.

BLACKBURN, HELEN; born 25th May 1842 at Valentia Island; 1874 Secretary to London Central Committee for Woman's Suffrage; 1880 Secretary to Bristol and West of England Society; 1887 Secretary of London Central Association till 1895; author of *A Record of the Women's Suffrage Movement in the British Isles*; died 11th January 1903 in Westminster.

BLOMFIELD, ROSAMUND SELINA; daughter of Right Reverend Charles Graves, Bishop of Limerick; married Rear Admiral Sir Richard Massie Blomfield 1877.

BLOMFIELD, LADY; Sara Louisa eldest daughter of Matthew Ryan; married 1887 as his second wife Sir Arthur Blomfield, A.R.A.

BODICHON, BARBARA LEIGH; born 1827; daughter of Benjamin Smith, M.P. for Norwich; married Dr. Eugene Bodichon, 1857; endowed Girton College, Cambridge; died 1891.

BONDFIELD, MARGARET GRACE; born Somerset, 1873; Assistant Secretary, Shop Assistants Union, 1898–1908; Minister of Labour 1929–31; M.P. Northampton, and Wallsend; Privy Councillor 1929; died 1953.

BOUCHERETTE, EMILIA JESSIE; born in 1825; the head and last survivor of an old established Lincolnshire family; a strong Conservative; founded and edited (1866–71) the *Englishwomen's Review*; died at Willingham, near Market Rasen, 1905.

BOYLE, NINA; born 1866; member W.F.L.; published a number of novels; associated for many years with the Save the Children Fund; died 1943.

BRACKENBURY, GEORGINA AGNES; born 1865; daughter of General Charles Brackenbury, R.A.; portrait painter; speaker for W.S.P.U.; lived with her mother and sister at 2 Campden Hill Square, London; died 1950.

BRACKENBURY, MARIE VENETIA CAROLINE; born 1866; landscape painter; speaker for the W.S.P.U.; sister of above; died 1946.

BRADDON, MARY ELIZABETH; born 1837; daughter of Henry Braddon, solicitor; successful novelist; published *Lady Audley's Secret* 1862; married John Maxwell 1872; died 1915.

BRAILSFORD, EVAMARIA; married Henry Noel Brailsford; her maiden name was Jarvis.

BUCHAN, DOWAGER COUNTESS OF; Maria daughter of William James; married first Jervois Collar and secondly 13th Earl of Buchan; died 1899.

BUTLER, JOSEPHINE; born 1828; daughter of John Grey of Dilston; secretary to Ladies National Association for Repeal of Contagious Diseases Act; married George Butler, Canon of Winchester; died 1906.

CANNING, HON. EMMELINE ROSABELLE, only daughter of the 1st Lord Garvagh; unmarried; died 1898.

CARLISLE, COUNTESS OF; Rosalind Frances daughter of 2nd Lord Stanley of Alderley; married 9th Earl of Carlisle, 1864; noted temperance reformer and strongly Liberal; died 1921.

CARNEY, W. No information available.

CAVENDISH-BENTINCK, MRS. FREDERICK; Ruth Mary St. Maur; married Frederick Cavendish-Bentinck 1887.

CHAPIN, ALICE; born New Hampshire; married H. M. Ferris 1885; publications: *Letters from Famous Musicians*; *At the Gates*; address: Haslemere, The Drive, Golders Green.

COBBE, FRANCES POWER; born 1822; only daughter of Charles Cobbe of County Dublin; philanthropist and voluminous writer; published her autobiography in 1904; died 1904.

COBDEN, JANE; *see* Unwin.

COBDEN-SANDERSON, ANNIE; fourth daughter of Richard Cobden; married 1882 T. J. Cobden-Sanderson, bookbinder and printer; member W.S.P.U.; seceded with Mrs. Despard to W.F.L. 1907; died 1926.

COMBERMERE, VISCOUNTESS; Susan Alice, eldest daughter of Sir George Sitwell, Bt., married Viscount Combermere 1844; died 1869.

CORELLI, MARIE; *see* Mackay, Marie.

CRAGGS, HELEN MILLAR; born 1888 in Victoria Street, London; daughter of Sir John Craggs, for many years secretary of King Edward's Hospital Fund; several times arrested; member W.S.P.U.

CRAIG, ISA; *see* Knox.

CULLEN, LOUISE; born 1876; went to Australia 1912; worked for the women's movement there; a magistrate in Sydney; widow of Joshua William Cullen.

DAVENPORT-HILL, FLORENCE; born 1836; youngest daughter of Matthew Davenport-Hill, reformer of criminal law; active worker for reform of poor law; died unmarried.

DAVENPORT-HILL, ROSAMUND; born 1825; eldest daughter of Matthew Davenport-Hill; elected to London School Board for City of London, 1879–97; enlightened pioneer in education; died 1902.

DAVIES, EMILY; born 1830; daughter of the Reverend John Davies, Rector of Gateshead; prominent in the founding of Girton; publications: *The Higher Education of Women* 1866; *Thoughts on Some Questions relating to Women* 1910; address: 17 Glenmore Road, N.W.3; died 1921.

DAVISON, EMILY WILDING; member of a north-country family; educated Oxford, 1st class Honours in English; long record of imprisonment; died 1913, after throwing herself in front of a horse during the Derby; recreations: swimming, cycling and study; address: Longhorsley, Northumberland.

DELL, ETHEL M.; *see* Savage, Ethel M.

DESPARD, CHARLOTTE; born 1844; daughter of Captain French; married 1870 to Maximilian Carden Despard; publication: *The Rajah's Heir* 1870; President, Women's Freedom League from its formation; address: 2 Currie Street, Nine Elms; died 1939.

DICKSON-POYNDER, LADY; Anne Beauclerk, daughter of R. H. D. Dundas; married 1896 Sir John Dickson-Poynder, afterwards 1st Lord Islington.

DORSET, COUNTESS OF; Anne born 1590; daughter and heiress of 3rd Earl of Cumberland; married first 1609, Richard, Earl of Dorset, secondly 1630 Philip, Earl of Pembroke and Montgomery; author of an autobiography; died 1676.

DREW, MARY; daughter of W. E. Gladstone; married Rev. Harry Drew, 1886; died 1927.

DRUMMOND, FLORA; 'The General'; born Manchester; daughter of Mr. Gibson; brought up in Isle of Arran; married first Joseph Drummond, and secondly Alan Simpson who was killed by a V.1 in 1944; stopped by police for riding astride in Rotten Row; leading member of W.S.P.U.; presided at unveiling of statue of Mrs. Pankhurst by Mr. Baldwin 1930; died 1949.

DUVAL, UNA HARRIET ELLA STRATFORD; eldest daughter of Commander Dugdale, R.N.; married 1912 Victor Duval; imprisoned 1909; published: *Love and Honour but not Obey*.

EDWARDS, AMELIA ANN BLANFORD; born in London of East Anglian farming stock 1831; on staff of *Saturday Review* and *Morning Post*; noted Egyptologist; died unmarried 1892.

EDWARDS, MATILDA BARBARA BETHAM; born Westerfield, Suffolk, 1836; friend of Madame Bodichon; wrote novels for sixty years of which *Lord of The Harvest* and *Kitty* are remembered; died at Hastings 1919.

ELIOT, GEORGE; born 1819; the famous novelist; died 1880.

ELLIS, SARAH; born Sarah Stickney, a member of the Society of Friends; married William Ellis, a missionary, as his second wife in 1837; author of many books including *The Poetry of Life, The Women of England*; died 1872.

FAWCETT, MILLICENT; born 1847; daughter of Newson Garrett;

married 1867 Henry Fawcett, M.P.; author of *Political Economy for Beginners*, a life of Queen Victoria and other biographies, and a history of the Suffrage Movement; address: 2 Gower Street, W.C.; died 1929.

FERGUSON, RACHEL; born Hampton Wick, 1893; co-founder of juvenile branch of W.S.P.U. 1910; writer of many successful books including *The Brontes went to Woolworth's* and *Victorian Bouquet*.

FITZHERBERT, MAUDE; probably the unmarried daughter of John Knight Fitzherbert, a member of the Tissington family.

DE FONBLANQUE, FLORENCE; daughter of G. Sparagnapare; married 1891 Robert Fonblanque; originator of Women's March from Edinburgh to London; recreation: hunting; address: Duncton, Petworth, Sussex.

FORD, ISABELLA ORMSTON; born of Quaker stock, Leeds; pioneer in trades union work for women in Leeds and Bradford; member I.L.P.; with her sister gave concerts primarily for working people in Leeds Hall, Leeds; author of *Miss Blake of Monkshalton* and two other novels; died 1924.

FOX, DACRE. No information available.

FOX, HELEN. No information available.

FRASER, HELEN; organizer for W.S.P.U. in Scotland in early days; Liberal candidate for Hamilton, Lanark, in elections of 1922 and 1923.

FRY, SOPHIA; daughter of John Pease, of East Mount, Darlington; married Theodore Fry, later created baronet, 1862; died 1897; founded Women's Liberal Federation.

GARLAND, ALISON; President of Women's Liberal Federation, 1934–36; died 1939; familiarly known as the Lloyd George in petticoats.

GARNETT, THERESA; very active in W.S.P.U. from about 1909; concerned in the attempt to attack the Home Secretary (then Winston Churchill) at Bristol; now on Executive Committee of Suffragette Fellowship.

GARRETT, ELIZABETH; born 1836; daughter of Newson Garrett of Aldeburgh; qualified to practice medicine through Society of Apothecaries, 1865; married 1871 J. G. S. Anderson; generally known as Mrs. Garrett Anderson; died 1917.

Biographical Index

GAWTHORPE, MARY; born Leeds 1881; daughter of John Gawthorpe; school-teacher; member of Leeds Committee for feeding school children; organizer Women's Social and Political Union 1906–11; many times imprisoned; recreations: sleeping not talking.

GLASIER, KATHERINE BRUCE; born 1868; daughter of Rev. S. Conway of Walthamstow; educated Newnham; joined Fabian Society 1890; married J. Bruce Glasier, 1893; editor of *Labour Leader* 1916–21; socialist speaker of great force and charm; author of two novels; died 1950.

GLYN, ELINOR; daughter of Douglas Sutherland; married Clayton Glyn 1892; author of many successful novels; died 1943.

GLOYNE, MRS. No information available.

GODWIN, MARY; born 1759; daughter of Edward John Wollstonecraft; lived with Gilbert Imlay; married William Godwin 1797; died the same year in giving birth to her daughter who afterwards married Shelley; published *Thoughts on The Education of Daughters, Vindication of the Rights of Women.*

GOLDSMID, LOUISA SOPHIA; daughter of Moses Asher; married 1839 Sir Francis Goldsmid, Bt.; died 1908.

GORE-BOOTH, EVA SELINA; born *c.* 1875, second daughter of Sir Henry Gore-Booth, of Lissadell, County Sligo; writer; collected poems first published, 1898; died unmarried 1926.

GORE-LANGTON, LADY ANNA; daughter of 2nd Duke of Buckingham and Chandos; married 1846 William Gore-Langton, M.P.; died 1879.

GREY, DOROTHY; daughter of Shalcross Widdrington; married Sir Edward Grey, Bt., afterwards Lord Grey of Fallodon 1885; killed in a carriage accident 1906.

GREY, MARIA GEORGINA; born 1816, daughter of Admiral Shirreff; married William Grey 1841; pioneer of training for women teachers; died 1906.

GROTE, HARRIET; born 1792; married George Grote 1820; published biography of her husband 1873; died 1878.

HAIG, FLORENCE E., R.B.A.; born about 1860; sculptress.

HALL, ANNA MARIA; born 1800; her father's name was Fielding; married Samuel Carter Hall, 1824; published several novels; died 1881.

HALLETT, LILIAS; daughter of Cobden's associate, Henry Ashworth (1794–1880); lived at Claverton Lodge, Bath; married 1877, Professor Hallett.

HARBERTON, VISCOUNTESS; Florence Wallace, daughter of William Legge, Malone House, Antrim; married Lord Harberton, 1861; died 1911.

HARRADEN, BEATRICE; born 1864; daughter of Samuel Harraden; publications: *Ships that pass in the Night*, *In Varying Moods*, *Katherine Frensham* and other novels; address: 10 Netherall Gardens, Hampstead.

HAVERFIELD, EVELINE; born 1867; daughter of 3rd Lord Abinger; married 1887 Major Henry Wykeham Brooke Tunstall Haverfield; married secondly Major Balguy 1899; resumed the name of Haverfield the same year; formed a remount camp for horses left to die on the veldt during South African War; generally wore a hunting stock and small bowler hat; address: Marsh Court, near Sherborne; died 1920.

HEITLAND, MARGARET BATESON; daughter of Rev. W. H. Bateson, D.D., Master of St. John's College, Cambridge; born 1860; worked on 'The Queen'; married 1901 W. E. Heitland, Fellow of St. John's. Active worker for woman's suffrage in Cambridge; died 1938.

HIGGINBOTHAM, MRS. No information available.

HILL, ROSAMUND. No information available.

HILL, OCTAVIA; born 1838; housing reformer; co-founder of National Trust; died 1912.

HOGGAN, MISS. No information available.

HOUSMAN, CLEMENCE; born *c.* 1864; daughter of Edward Housman, solicitor, of Bromsgrove; imprisoned 1911; died 1956; address: Greycott, Swanage.

HOW MARTYN, EDITH; born Cheltenham, 4th August 1875; father's name was How; educated, boarding school at Bath; North London Collegiate School for Girls, Scholar: University College, Aberystwyth; B.Sc. London; married 1899 Herbert Martyn; Independent candidate for Hendon 1918; Member, Middlesex County Council; Lecturer, Westfield College; went to Australia 1939; died after 1945.

HOWEY, ROSE ELSIE NEVILLE; born Finningley Rectory, Notts.;

long series of imprisonments; hid herself in organ at Colston Hall, Bristol, to interrupt a Liberal speaker; member of W.S.P.U.; announced her intention of giving up her life for the suffrage cause; recreations; riding, driving and hockey; address: Holly Lodge, Cradley, Malvern.

IRBY, ADELAIDE PAULINA; daughter of Leonard Irby; died unmarried 1911.

JAMESON, ANNA BROWNELL; born 1794; daughter of D. B. Murphy miniature painter; married Robert Jameson, 1825; separated soon after marriage; author of many books on artistic subjects; died 1860.

JARVIS, KATHLEEN; believed to have died shortly before the Second War.

JEX-BLAKE, SOPHIA; born 1840; daughter of Thomas Jex-Blake, Proctor of Doctors' Commons; founded London School of Medicine for Women 1874; gained legal right to practise 1877; died 1912.

JOACHIM, MAUD; born London at end of 1860's; daughter of Henry Joachim, a London wool merchant and grand-daughter of Sir George Smart the distinguished organist; of independent means.

JOICEY, probably ROSANDRA; daughter of Reverend John Ewen; married John Joicey 1867; died 1912.

KEARY, ANNIE; author of *Caſtle Daly*, *A York and Lancaſter Rose*, *A Doubting Heart*; died at Eastbourne 1879.

KENNEY, ANNIE; born Springfield, Lancs., 1879; went to work in a cotton mill, half-time, when she was ten years. Corresponding student of Ruskin College; one of the leaders of W.S.P.U.; many times imprisoned; married James Taylor; her son an officer in the Royal Air Force; died 1953.

KNIGHT, ANN; Quakeress; lived at Quiet Home, Chelmsford; advocate of universal suffrage in 1840's, and 1850's; friend of Brougham and Cobden.

KNOX, ISA; born 1831; daughter of John Craig, hosier of Edinburgh; married John Knox, iron merchant; published verse and fiction; died 1903.

LAWS, HARRIET. No information available.

LEIGH, MRS.; leader of W.S.P.U.; many times imprisoned.

LEWIN, OCTAVIA MARGARET SOPHIA; born at Ware, daughter of Spencer Lewin; educated, Girton; distinguished doctor; member of Convocation, London University; died 1955.

LINTON, ELIZA LYNN; born 1822; daughter of Reverend James Lynn; married 1858 William James Linton; separated; published successful novels and autobiography; died 1898.

LLEWELLYN-DAVIES, MARGARET; daughter of Reverend J. Llewellyn-Davies, a prominent Christian Socialist; educated Queen's College and Girton; 1889 became general secretary of the Women's Co-operative Guild; 1922 elected president of Co-operative Congress; died 1944.

LOCKWOOD, JULIA; daughter of Salis Schwabe; married 1874 Sir Frank Lockwood, M.P.

LOWNDES, MARIE ADELAIDE (Mrs. Belloc Lowndes); daughter of Louis Belloc and Bessie Parkes; married F. S. Lowndes; author of many notable books including *The Lodger* 1913; died 1947.

LUCAS, MARGARET BRIGHT; born 1818; sister of John Bright; married Samuel Lucas, journalist and politician; temperance reformer; died 1890.

LYTTON, LADY CONSTANCE; born 1869; daughter, 2nd Earl of Lytton; imprisoned; author *Prisons and Prisoners* 1914; address: Homewood, Knebworth, Herts.; died 1923.

MACARTHUR MARY; *see* Anderson.

McEWAN, MRS.; wife of John McEwan, a City merchant; active in local government work at Enfield.

MACKAY, MARIE; born 1855; daughter of Charles Mackay, songwriter and journalist; wrote many highly successful novels; wrote as Marie Corelli; died 1924.

MACKENZIE, MRS. H. M.; stood as Labour candidate for Welsh Universities at General Election, 1918.

MACLAREN, PRISCILLA; daughter of Jacob Bright, of Green Bank, Rochdale; married as his third wife Duncan MacLaren, Lord Provost of Edinburgh and M.P. for that City; died 1906.

MACMILLAN, CHRYSTAL; born Edinburgh; daughter of John Macmillan; educated Edinburgh and St. Leonard's School, St.

Andrews; matriculated Edinburgh University 1892 (the year in which women could matriculate); B.Sc. 1896; Berlin University, 1900.

MALONEY, DOROTHY; known as La Belle Maloney; died in 1920.

MANNING, ANNE; born 1807; daughter of William Oke Manning; author of many historical tales; died unmarried 1879.

MARION, KITTY; born in Westphalia about 1870; came to England for a career on the music halls in the 1880's; appeared under the name of Kitty Marion; active member of W.S.P.U.; many times imprisoned; went to America in 1914, and assumed American nationality; died 1944.

MARKHAM, VIOLET; youngest daughter of Charles Markham and grand-daughter of Sir Joseph Paxton; married 1915 Lieut.-Colonel Carruthers; a leader in many branches of woman's work and a successful author.

MARKIEVICZ, CONSTANCE GEORGINE; born *circa* 1870; eldest daughter of Sir H. Gore-Booth; married 1900 Casimir de Markievicz; Irish patriot; elected for St. Patrick's Dublin to House of Commons in 1918 election; she polled 7,800 against 3,700 for her Nationalist opponent, a gentleman in the meat trade, who had sat for St. Patrick's since 1892; elected to Dail for Dublin; died 1927.

MARLBOROUGH, DUCHESS OF; Consuelo, daughter of William Vanderbilt; married 9th Duke of Marlborough 1895; published *The Glitter and The Gold* 1954; married secondly Lieut.-Colonel Balsan.

MARSH, CHARLOTTE; born 1887 in Northumberland; organizer for W.S.P.U. in Nottingham; recreations: golf and swimming.

MARSHALL, EMILY KATHERINE; born, Westhoughton Vicarage, Lancs.; daughter of Rev. Canon Jacques; married 1904 Arthur Marshall; many times arrested; recreations: golf and gardening; address: Turpin House, York Street, Buckingham Gate and Theydon Bois.

MARTEL, MRS.; born New South Wales; stood as parliamentary candidate, 1902, after women given Commonwealth franchise; active member of W.S.P.U. in its early days.

MARTIN, VIOLET (1862–1915); born at Ross House, Co. Galway,

whence she took her pseudonym. Collaborated with her cousin Edith Somerville in a series of novels about Irish life.

MARTINEAU, HARRIET; born 1802; daughter of Thomas Martineau of Norwich; successful writer and journalist; died 1876.

MATTERS, MURIEL; born near Adelaide, 1880; a Montessorian; married and now known as Mrs. Matters Porter; lives at Hastings.

MAXWELL, LILY; of her no trace seems to have survived.

MELFORD, JACKIEDAWRA; daughter of Mark Melford; she and her father sympathized with woman's suffrage; married W. Colegate.

MERRINGTON, MARTHA; A Poor-Law Guardian in 1870's.

METCALFE, A. E.; author of *Woman's Effort*, 1865–1914 published by Basil Blackwell in 1917; one H.M.'s Inspectors of Schools.

MILL, HARRIET; born 1807; daughter of Thomas Hardy; married 1826 John Taylor; married J. S. Mill secondly 1851; died 1858.

MONTEFIORE, DORA; born Hove 1850; daughter of Barrow Fuller; married George Montefiore; went to Australia; returned to England and joined Social Democratic Federation; Member W.S.P.U.; died 1934.

MORGAN, SYDNEY; born *c.* 1783; daughter of Robert Owenson, actor; married Sir T. C. Morgan, surgeon; published novels and books of travel; lived in Dublin and latterly in London; died 1859.

MURRAY, EUNICE; born 1879; daughter of David Murray, Ll.D.; leading member of Women's Freedom League; address: Moorepark, Cardross, Dumbartonshire.

NAYLOR, MARIE; an artist living in Chelsea: she was killed in the Blitz.

NEAL, MARY, C.B.E.; born 1860; one of the pioneers of country holidays for wage earners; founded seaside holiday hotel for wage earners; encouraged spread of folk-dancing; awarded C.B.E. for this work in 1937; magistrate at Littlehampton; died 1944.

NEILANS, ALISON ROBERTA NOBLE; born London 1884; Member of Women's Freedom League; sentenced to three months' imprisonment by Grantham J.—November 1909; forcibly fed; subsequently and until her death in 1942 General Secretary of the Association for Moral and Social Hygiene.

NELIGAN, ANNIE; born 1833 at Cork; served with British Red Cross in Franco-Prussian war; headmistress Croydon High School 1874–1901; address: Oakwood House, Croydon.

NEW, EDITH; born at Swindon; joined W.S.P.U. 1906; devoted rank and file member; many times imprisoned; address: 1 Diamond Terrace, Greenwich.

NICHOL, ELIZABETH; generally known as Mrs. Pease Nichol; born 1807; daughter of Joseph Pease of Darlington; married 1853 John Pringle Nichol, the astronomer; died 1897.

NIGHTINGALE, FLORENCE; born 1820; reformer of hospital nursing; died 1910.

ORR, ALEXANDRA SUTHERLAND; born 1828; sister of Lord Leighton; married Sutherland George Gordon Orr, 1857; friend of Browning, and a strong supporter of Browning Society; published *Browning's Life and Letters* 1891; died 1903.

PARKES, ELIZABETH; eldest daughter of Joseph Priestley; married Joseph Parkes, 1828; mother of Madame Belloc; died 1877.

PANKHURST, ADELA; born 1885; now Mrs. Walsh; went to Australia shortly before the First War; prominent in Australian Women's Guild of Empire.

PANKHURST, CHRISTABEL; born Manchester *c.* 1880; W.S.P.U. leader 1903–14; editor *Suffragette*; Coalition candidate for Smethwick 1918; now active in heralding the personal, visible and powerful second Coming of the Lord Jesus Christ; created D.B.E. 1936.

PANKHURST, EMMELINE; born Manchester 1858; married Richard Pankhurst 1879; founder of Women's Social and Political Union 1903; in Canada after the First War until 1926; joined Conservative party in 1926 and adopted as candidate for Whitechapel; died 1928.

PANKHURST, ESTELLE SYLVIA; born Manchester *c.* 1882; daughter of Richard and Emmeline Pankhurst; mother of Richard Pankhurst; educated High School for Girls, Manchester, Royal College of Art, South Kensington; active in Women's Social and Political Union 1903–14; opposed First War; editor *New Times* and *Ethiopian News*; author of history of Suffragette Movement 1912 and 1931, and many works in support of Ethiopia.

PATERSON, EMMA ANNE; born 1848; daughter of Henry Smith, schoolmaster; married Thomas Paterson 1873; organizer of trade unions among women; first woman admitted to the Trades Union Congress; died 1886.

PETHICK-LAWRENCE, EMMELINE; born *c.* 1864; daughter of Henry Pethick, Weston-super-Mare; founded 1895 Esperance Girls' Club; Treasurer, W.S.P.U. 1906–12; joint editor *Votes For Women* 1907–14; author *Does a Man Support His Wife?*, *My Part In A Changing World* 1938; address: Mascot, Holmwood, Surrey; died 1943.

PETHICK, DOROTHY; born *c.* 1870; youngest daughter of Henry Pethick, Weston-super-Mare. In 1914 joined Women's Auxiliary Service (Women Police).

PHIPPS, EMILY; teacher; born Devonport; B.A., London; Headmistress, girls' school at Swansea; President National Federation of Women Teachers.

PRIESTMAN, ANNE. No information available.

PRIESTMAN, MARY. No information available.

PROCTOR, ADELAIDE ANN; born 1825; eldest child of Bryan Waller Procter; hymn-writer and poetess; died unmarried 1864.

RATHBONE, ELEANOR; born Liverpool *c.* 1865; daughter of William Rathbone, M.P.; educated Kensington High School and Somerville, Oxford; Member of Parliament for combined English Universities 1929–45; secretary Liverpool Women's Suffrage Society from 1898; died 1946.

RHONDDA, LADY; Margaret Haigh; born Prince's Square, London, 1883; daughter of D. A. Thomas, afterwards 1st Lord Rhondda; married 1908 Humphrey Mackworth; obtained divorce 1923; member W.S.P.U.

RICHARDSON, MARY; brought up in Canada; grand-daughter of a bank manager; describes herself as having battled with her fists against boys on behalf of her own sex; poet and novelist; *Laugh A Defiance*, an account of her suffrage experiences, published recently.

RIGBY, EDITH; married; joined I.L.P.; member Executive Council of Women's Labour League; secretary Preston W.S.P.U. from 1907; imprisoned several times; recreations: walking, cycling and music; address: 28 Winckley Square, Preston.

Biographical Index

ROBINS, ELIZABETH; born Louisville, Kentucky, 1863; married
George Parkes; came to England as a widow in 1889; made her
name as an Ibsen acress; author of *The Magnetic North*—a
successful novel and many other books; died at Brighton, 1952.

ROBINSON, RONA. No information available.

ROPER, ESTHER; born about 1870; student and graduate of
Victoria University, Manchester; died 1938.

ROSS, VIOLET; *see* Martin, Violet.

ROYDEN, MAUDE; youngest child of Sir Thomas Royden, Bt.;
educated Cheltenham Ladies' College, Lady Margaret Hall,
Oxford; Assistant Preacher, City Temple 1917–20; Minister of
the Guildhouse, Eccleston Square; married 1944 Reverend
G. W. H. Shaw; died 1956.

RUSSELL, LADY JOHN; Frances Anna Maria; daughter of 2nd Earl
of Minto; married Lord John, afterwards Earl, Russell, 1841;
died 1898.

RUSSELL, COUNTESS; Marion, daughter of George Cook of
Cumbernauld; married 2nd Earl Russell, 1901; obtained a
divorce, 1915.

SACKVILLE-WEST, VICTORIA; born 1892, daughter of 3rd Lord
Sackville; married 1913 Harold (now Sir Harold) Nicolson;
author of many successful books.

ST. ALBANS, DUCHESS OF; Grace, daughter of Bernal Osborne,
M.P.; married 10th Duke of St. Albans 1874; died 1926.

SAVAGE, ETHEL M.; born Streatham 1881; a highly successful
novelist, perhaps *The Way of An Eagle* being her outstanding
book; married Lieut.-Colonel C. Savage 1922; died 1939.

SANDHURST, LADY; Margaret, daughter of Robert Fellowes;
married 1854 Sir William Mansfield, afterwards Lord Sandhurst; died 1892.

SCATHCHERD, MRS. CLIFF. No information available.

SCHREINER, OLIVE EMILIE ALBERTINA; born 1855 in Cape
Colony; married S. C. Cronwright 1894; wrote *The Story of
An African Farm*, published 1883; died 1920.

SELBORNE, COUNTESS OF; born 1858; daugher of 3rd Marquess of
Salisbury; married 1883 Earl of Selborne; President, Conservative and Unionist Women's Franchise Association; died
1950.

SHAEN, EMILY; born *c.* 1825; daughter of Henry Winkworth, silk merchant; married 1851 William Shaen; died 1887.

SHARP, EVELYN; born London, 1869; married as his second wife H. W. Nevinson in 1933; a notable author; on staff of *Daily Herald* 1915–23; twice imprisoned for suffrage activities.

SHAW, CHARLOTTE FRANCES; born in Ireland; maiden name, Payne-Townshend; married George Bernard Shaw 1898; died 1943.

SHIPTON, MOTHER; reputed prophetess; *Life and Death of Mother Shipton* published in seventeenth century.

SHIRREFF, EMILY ANNE ELIZA; born 1814; daughter of Admiral Shirreff; educationalist; Mistress of Girton 1870; died unmarried 1897.

SINCLAIR, MAY; born in Cheshire; daughter of William Sinclair; educated, Ladies' College, Cheltenham; has published novels since 1904.

SMITH, MARY. No information available.

SMITH, LADY SYBIL; daughter of 6th Earl of Antrim; married Vivian Hugh Smith, afterwards first Lord Bicester, 1897.

SMYTH, ETHEL; born Sidcup 1858; daughter of Major General J. H. Smyth; composer and author; D.Mus., Oxford; D.B.E. 1922; died unmarried 1944.

SNOWDEN, ETHEL; born 1881; daughter of Alderman Annakin; married Philip Snowden, 1905; member, Executive, Fabian Society; member National Union of Women's Suffrage Societies; author *The Feminist Movement, Through Bolshevik Russia*, etc.; died 1946.

SOLOMON, MRS.; born in Scotland 1844; Principal, Good Hope Seminary 1873; married Saul Solomon 1874; life-long abstainer and woman suffragist; first President of the Social Purity Alliance, Cape Town; twice arrested; imprisoned March 1912; address: Les Lunes, Sumatra Road, N.W.

SOMERVILLE, EDITH OENONE; born Corfu *c.* 1860; daughter of Lieut.-Colonel Somerville, of Drishane, Co. Cork; President Munster Women's Franchise League; Master of West Carberry Foxhounds; author with Miss Violet Ross, q.v., of *Some Experiences of an Irish R.M.* and many other novels; address: Drishane House, Skibbereen, Co. Cork; died 1949.

SOMERVILLE, MARY; born 1780; daughter of Sir William Fairfax; married 1812, as her second husband, William Somerville; scientific writer of distinction; died 1872.

STERLING, ANTOINETTE; born New York State; married 1875 John Mackinlay; a popular contralto in England and America; died 1904.

STEWART, LADY HELEN; daughter of 9th Earl of Galloway; married 1896 W. C. Mellor, M.P.; died 1903.

STOBART, Mrs.; daughter of Sir Samuel Bolton, Bt.; married first St. Clair Stobart, secondly John Stobart Greenhalgh; member of Council of World Congress of Faiths; taken prisoner by Germans in 1914, narrowly escaped being shot; author of several successful books.

STRACHEY, JANE MARIA; born 1840; daughter of Sir John Grant of Rothiemurchus; married 1859 Lieut.-General Sir Richard Strachey; signed petition for women's suffrage presented to House of Commons by J. S. Mill 1867; member National Union of Women's Suffrage Societies; died 1928; address: 67 Belsize Park Gardens, Hampstead.

STRACHEY, RACHEL; daughter of B. F. C. Costelloe; married as his second wife Oliver Strachey; died 1940.

SWANWICK, ANNA; born 1813 in Liverpool; member of Council in both Queen's and Bedford Colleges, London; assisted in foundation of Girton; published translations from Greek and German; died 1899.

SWANWICK, HELENA; born 1864 in Bavaria; daughter of O. A. Sickert; lecturer Westfield College, Hampstead; contributor to *Manchester Guardian*; address: 26 Lawn Crescent, Kew Gardens.

SYMONS, MRS. TRAVERS; private secretary to Keir Hardie; born, 1873; daughter of Robert Williams, architect; member, W.F.L.

TAYLOR, CLEMENTIA; daughter of John Doughty, of Brockdish, Norfolk; married Peter Alfred Taylor, M.P. for Leicester 1842; died 1908.

TAYLOR, HELEN; born 1831; daughter of John Taylor, druggist, and his wife afterwards Mrs. J. S. Mill; edited H. T. Buckle's miscellaneous works; elected after a fierce election to London School Board in 1876; stood as parliamentary candidate for

North Camberwell at election of 1885; after turbulent meetings she was refused permission to stand by the returning
officer; presented J. S. Mill's library to Somerville College;
died unmarried 1907.

TERRENO, JANIE; born Finchingfield, 1858; daughter of Thomas
Beddall; married 1885 Manuel Terreno; joined W.S.P.U. in
1908; writer of music 'Sur la Glace' (waltz), 'On the Neva'
(mazurka); recreation: croquet; address: Rockstone House,
Pinner.

TILLARD, MISS. No information available.

TOD, MISS. No information available.

TREVELYAN, JANET PENROSE; daughter of Mr. and Mrs. Humphrey Ward; married 1904 Professor G. M. Trevelyan.

TUKE, MABEL; born *c.* 1870; married and lived much in South
Africa; worked with Mrs. Pethick-Lawrence in Esperance
Girls' Club; secretary of W.S.P.U.

UNWIN, EMMA JANE CATHERINE; born 1851; daughter of Richard
Cobden; married T. Fisher Unwin, 1913; elected to first
London County Council 1889; she continued to sit on the
Council until disqualified by the High Court; died 1947.

WALLACE-DUNLOP, MARION; born in Scotland; daughter of Robert
Wallace-Dunlop, C.B.; author *The Magic Fruit Garden*,
Fairies, *Elves and Flower Babies*, etc.; exhibitor at Royal
Academy; address: Ellerslie Tower, Ealing.

WARD, MARY AUGUSTA; born 1851; daughter of Thomas Arnold;
married 1872 T. Humphrey Ward, fellow and tutor of Brase-
nose College; successful novelist, her most famous book,
Robert Elsmere, published in 1888; died 1920.

WEBB, BEATRICE; daughter of Richard Potter, M.P.; married 1892
Sidney Webb, afterwards Lord Passfield; a writer, and pioneer
of political thought; died 1943.

WEBSTER, AUGUSTA; born 1837, daughter of Vice-Admiral
George Davies, chief constable of Huntingdonshire; married
Thomas Webster, law lecturer at Trinity College, Cambridge;
member of London School Board; writer and poetess; died
1894.

WEDGWOOD, FRANCES; daughter of Sir James Mackintosh;
married Hensleigh Wedgwood, the philologist, 1832.

WEST, REBECCA; born 1892; Cicily Isabel, daughter of Charles Fairfield, Co. Kerry; married 1930 H. M. Andrews; author of many successful books.

WHARRY, OLIVE; believed to have died some years ago.

WHEELER, MRS.; daughter of an Archdeacon in Ireland; married Francis Massy Wheeler; her only child to reach maturity—Rosena, afterwards the wife of Bulwer Lytton, was born in 1802.

WILKS, ELIZABETH; born about 1866; practised as a doctor in Hackney; helped to found Women's Tax Resistance League.

WINKWORTH, EMILY; *see* Shaen, Emily.

WINKWORTH, SUSANNAH; born 1820; daughter of Henry Winkworth, a silk merchant; philanthropist and translator from the German; died unmarried 1884.

WOOD, ELLEN; born 1814; daughter of Thomas Price, glove manufacturer at Worcester; married Henry Wood 1836; successful novelist; her most famous book was *East Lynne* 1861; died 1887.

WOLSTENHOLME-ELMY, ELIZABETH C.; born 1834; teacher; first secretary of Manchester National Society for Women's Suffrage; fighter for fifteen years for married women's property act; lived before marriage at Moody Hall, Congleton; after her married was known as Mrs. Wolstenholme-Elmy; militant, suffragette; died 1918.

WOOLF, VIRGINIA; born 1882; daughter of Sir Leslie Stephen; married 1912 Leonard Woolf; a notable novelist and critic; died 1941.

YONGE, CHARLOTTE MARY; born 1823; daughter of W. C. Yonge; author of many successful novels in the middle of the nineteenth century; died 1901.

Appendix II

Date of Enfranchisement of Women Abroad

Countries printed in italics were given the woman's vote before Great Britain.

Albania: 1946
Argentina: 1947
Australia: 1902
Austria: 1919
Belgium: 1920–48
Bolivia: 1945
Brazil: 1946
Bulgaria: 1947
Burma: 1922
Canada: 1918
Ceylon: 1931
Chile: 1949
China: 1947
Costa Rica: 1936
Cuba: 1940
Czechoslovakia: 1919–20
Denmark: 1915
Dominican Republic: 1942
Ecuador: 1946 (Voting is compulsory for men, voluntary for women)
Egypt: 1956 (Voting is compulsory for men, voluntary for women)

El Salvador: 1946
Finland: 1906
France: 1946
Germany: 1919
Greece: 1949
Guatemala: 1945 (with qualifications)
Honduras: 1955
Hungary: 1945
Iceland: 1915
India: 1921–35
Indonesia: 1949
Israel: 1948
Italy: 1945
Japan: 1945
Jordan: 1955 (educated women only)
Korea: 1948
Lebanon: 1952 (with qualifications)
Liberia: 1945
Luxembourg: 1919
Mongolian People's Republic: 1944

Date of Enfranchisement of Women Abroad

Netherlands: 1919
New Zealand: 1893
Norway: 1913
Pakistan: 1921–35
Panama: 1946
Philippines: 1937
Poland: 1919
Portugal: 1945 (with qualifications)
Rumania: 1946
Sweden: 1921
Syria: 1949 (with qualifications)

Thailand: 1932
Turkey: 1934
Union of South Africa: 1930
Union of Soviet Socialist Republics:
  1917
United States of America: 1920
  (though a few individual
  states had had it earlier)
Uruguay: 1942
Venezuela: 1947
Yugoslavia: 1945

Index

Abbesses, attendance in Parliament, 20
Acland, Mrs. Francis, 242
Acland, Sir, T. D., 60
Acton, first Lord, 91
Adullamites, 44–5
Agg-Gardner, J., 257
Albert Hall, 130, 180, 195, 225, 227, 241, 247, 256
Albert, Prince Consort, 43, 75
Alden, Percy, 211
Aldwych, 240
Aldwych Theatre, 197
Alexandra, Queen, 173
Alford, H. (Dean of Canterbury), 56–7
Allan, William, 90
Alverstone, Lord Chief Justice, 207
Amberley, Lady, 53, 60, 74; speech in Stroud, 1870, 74–5, 78
Amberley, Lord, 60, 70
Amery, Leopold, 274
Anderson, Elizabeth Garrett, 19, 49, 180, 224, 230
Anderson, W. C., 242
Anmer, 284
'Annual Register', 180, 291
Anti-Suffrage League, 215–16, 247
Anstey, T. C., 65, 67, 73
Apothecaries, Society of, 49
Apsley House, 246
Archer-Shee case, 263
Ashton, Margaret, 134, 140
Ashwell, Lena, 225
Ashworth, Henry, 52
Ashworth, Lilian, 52
Asquith, H. H. (afterwards Lord Oxford and Asquith), 15, 74, 93, 107, 133, 140; attacks on by Labour and W.S.P.U., 141–3; reply to suffrage deputation, 174–5; succeeds to Premiership, 183–4, 185, 186, 193; attacks on by militants, 194–5, 198, 217–19; statement on woman's suffrage before election of January 1910, 220–1; 227–8, 230, 232, 234, 236, 241; favours adult suffrage, 242–3; 245–6; speech against Conciliation Bill, 1912, 258–9; 262, 268, 269, 271, 272, 274, 277, 278, 279; receives deputation of working women, 301–2; 304
Asquith, Mrs., 269
Athenaeum, The, 225
Australia and Woman's Suffrage, 121
Authorized Bible, Tercentenary Celebration, 241
Ayrton, Mrs., 180

Babb, Miss, 88
Bagot, Mrs., 99
Baines, Jennie, 213
Baldwin, Stanley (afterwards Lord Baldwin), 238
Balfour, A. J. (afterwards Lord Balfour), 99, 107, 125, 130, 194, 228, 272–3
Balfour, Lady Frances, 120, 134, 136, 137, 154, 262
Balmoral, 271
Banbury, Sir F., 122, 126, 283, 304
Bantry (first Lord), 25, 30
Barclays Bank, 139, 167, 253–4
Barnard, E. B., 152
Bastiat, 38
Bath Hotel, Felixstowe, 290
Bathurst, Lady (wife of 7th Lord), 282
Battersea, 145–6
Baume, Pierre, 30
Baumgarten, Reverend C., 285
Baylis, Lilian, 146
Beach, Walter, 84
Beales, Edmund, 46
Beaverbrook, Lord, 282

Index

Becker, Hannibal, 55

Becker, Lydia, 54; attends Mme. Bodichon's lecture, 1866, 55; forms Manchester Women's Suffrage Committee, 55; founds literary and scientific society in Manchester, 55; appointed secretary, Manchester Suffrage Committee, 56; forms permanent committee in Manchester, 61, 63, 64, 67; canvasses candidates at General Election, 1868, 68, 72; moves resolution at public meeting, 73-4; death, 78-81; 82, 86, 88, 95, 164, 180, 217, 237, 238, 268, 279

Bedford, Duchess of (wife of 11th Duke), 265

Beedy, Miss, 88

Beerbohm, Sir M., 190, 258

'Before the Bombardment', 116

Begg, F. F., 84

Belloc, Hilaire, 41, 218-19, 226

Belloc, Madame, see Parkes, Bessie

Bentham, Jeremy, 25

Beresford-Hope, P., 86

Berkeley, F. H. F., 59

Bermondsey, 168-9

Besant, Mrs., 78

Biddulph, Sir T., 271

Biggs, Miss, 88

Bill of Rights, 205

Billington, Theresa, 17; joins W.S.P.U., 119-20; 130, 141; imprisoned, 142-3, 151; leaves W.S.P.U., 165

Bingley Hall, Birmingham, 194

Birrell, A., 133, 232

Birth Control, 70

Bischoff, Mr., 223-4

Bisgood, Councillor, 281

'Black Book', The, 33

'Black' Friday, 229-32, 250

Blackburn, Helen, 16, 120

Bleak House, 47-8

Bly, Sarah, 21

Blomfield, Lady, 296-7

Blomfield, Lady (Massie), 297

Blomfield, Miss, 296-7

Bloomfield, Lady, 202

Boadicea, 141, 154, 180

Bodichon, Mrs., 41, 48; organizes 1866 Petition to Parliament, 49; reads paper at Manchester meeting of Association for Advancement of Social Science, 54-5; 279

Bodkin, Archibald, 293

Bonar-Law, Andrew, 235, 236, 271, 272

Bondfield, Margaret, 126, 242

Borchardt, Louis, 55

Bottomley, H., 108

Boucherette, Jessie, 41; organizes petition to Parliament, 1866, 49

Bovill, Sir W., 68

Bow and Bromley, 274-5

Bow Street Police Court, 187-92, 203-4, 251, 294, 295

Bowyer, Sir G., 64

Boyle, Nina, 293

Brackenbury, Georgina, 175

Brackenbury, Marie, 175, 188-9

Brackenbury, Sir H., 175

Braddon, Miss, 50

Brailsford, H. N., 210, 221

Bradlaugh, Charles, 66, 96

Bright, Jacob, joins Manchester suffrage committee, 55-6; Liberal candidate Manchester, 63-4, 73; leads suffrage supporters in House of Commons, 83-6, 90

Bright, John, 38, 44, 60, 83; fears of clerical influence, 88

Bristol, Suffrage Society in, 61, 94

Brixton, 86

Broadhurst, H., 101

Bromley, 168

Brooks's Club, 94

Brougham, Lord, 54, 275

Browning, Robert, 51

Bryce, James (afterwards first Lord), 133

Buchan, Countess of, 89

Buckingham Palace, 296-7

Buckingham Street, 166

Budget of 1909, 193-4, 218

Burke, E., 168

Burlington House, 294

Burns, John, 133, 240

Butler, Josephine, 52, 99-100, 160

Buxton, C. R., 161

Buxton, T. F., 60

By-Elections, and suffragette strategy, 159-63, 164, 274

Byles, Sir J., 68

Caernarvonshire, 79

Cairnes, Professor, 56

Cambridge University Football Pavilion, 290

Camden, first Lord, 168

Camlachie (Glasgow), 233

Campbell-Bannerman, Sir H., 130, 133;

Index

receives deputation from suffrage
societies, 1906, 140; 146–7, 157–8, 161,
183, 203
Canning, Miss, 89
Carlisle, 7th Lord, 39–40
Carlisle, Rosalind, Countess of, 217
Carney, Miss, 305
Carson, Sir E., 258, 271
'Cat and Mouse' Bill, 284, 291–2, 295
Catholic Women's Suffrage Society, 241
Cavendish-Bentinck, Mrs. F., 266
Cavendish Square, 142
Caxton Hall, 136, 137, 156, 159, 175,
176, 185, 186–7, 198, 230, 266
Cecil, Lord David, 13
Cecil, Lord E., 60
Cecil, Lord Hugh, 64, 226–7, 239, 257–8,
262, 264, 277, 279, 304, 306
Cecil, Lord R., 178, 198, 262–4, 279,
283, 284, 304
Census, 240
Chadwick, Sir E., 84
Chamberlain, Austen, 228
Chamberlain, Joseph, 66, 107
Chapel-en-le-Frith, 115
Chapin, Mrs., 169, 211
Charles II, 20
Chartism, 38, 66, 108
Chesterfield, fourth Lord, 22, 23
Chinese slavery, 127
Chorley Wood, 300
Chorlton v. *Lings*, 67–8
Christian, Prince, of Schleswig-Holstein,
281
Church of England, 51; clergy of, 51, 57
Churchill, Lord Randolph, 147
Churchill, Winston, 121; joins Liberal
Party, 127; contests N.W. Manchester,
127–31; and Free Trade Hall meeting,
127–9, 133, and Manchester by-elec-
tion, 1908, 162–3, 189; attacks by
militants, 194–6, 211; attacks Concilia-
tion Bill, 227–9; and 'Black' Friday,
231–2; 236, 261, 262
City Franchise, 272
City Temple, 245–6
Clarion, The, 289
Clarion Cycling Club, 110
Clay, James, 44
Clement's Inn, 139, 166–7
Clitheroe, 104, 226
Coal Consumers' Council, 162–3
Cobbe, Frances Power, 50, 100, 133
Cobden, Jane, 17, 86

Cobden, Richard, 34, 38
Cobden-Sanderson, Mrs., 148, 153, 200,
232
Colchester, 160
Cole, G. D. H., 98, 107, 111
Coleridge, Sir J. (afterwards first Lord),
68, 86
Coleridge, second Lord, 251
Colonial Office, 248
Combermere, Viscountess, 89
Conciliation Bill, 221–34; clauses of,
222; second Bill, 235–6, 243, 257–8,
275
Conciliation Committee, 221–34, 235–6
Conservative Party, 45; changing charac-
ter of at end of nineteenth century, 98;
132, 217, 219, 220–1, 235; opposition
to adult suffrage, 243; 272
Conservative and Unionist Women's
Franchise Association, 238
Constitutional Women's Suffrage Socie-
ties, 133–4, 135, 137, 159; and London
demonstration, 1908, 180–1; 243–4,
299
Contagious Diseases Act, 76, 100, 160
Cook, J. D., 71
Cooke, Radcliffe, 89
Co-operative Movement, 140
Corbett-Ashby, Mrs., 134, 305
Corelli, Marie, 216
Corn Law League, 38
Corrupt Practices Bill, 96
Courtney, Leonard, 80–1, 84
Covent Garden Opera, 296
Craggs, Helen, 271–2
Craig, Isa, 48
Crippen, Dr., 239
Cromer, first Lord, 215, 247
Cromwell, Oliver, 21
Cross Street Chapel, Manchester, 55
Croxley Green Station, 281
Cullen, Mrs., 196
Curtis-Bennett, Sir H., 186, 188–90, 294
Curzon, Marquis, of Keddleston, 32,
215, 247
Cuvier, Baron, 69
Cycle Touring Club, 159

Daily Chronicle, 108, 157, 191, 301
Daily Express, 193, 239, 274, 282
Daily Herald, 241, 286
Daily Mail, 139, 239
Daily Mirror, 143
Daily News, 51, 210

Darling, Mr. Justice, 251
Darlington, 94
Darwin, Charles, 55, 77
Davenport-Hill, Florence, 51, 61
Davenport-Hill, R., 61
Davidson, Randall, Archbishop of Canterbury, 225, 241, 295
Davies, Emily, 48, 49, 140, 180
Dawson, Sir D., 297
D'Ewes, Sir Simonds, 21
Deborah, 279
Deceased Wife's Sister's Bill, 76
Dell, Ethel M., 231
Denman, George, 58
Derby, fourteenth Lord, 46
Derby, The, 284–5
Despard, Mrs., early years, 145; social work in London, 145; member I.L.P., 145; joins W.S.P.U., 146; candidate in 1918 election, 146, 305; later life and death, 146; on 'mud' march, 156–7, 158; resigns from W.S.P.U., 165; forms W.F.L., 166–8; 190–200, 224, 244, 259, 265, 273, 305
Devon, mid, 161, 163
Devonshire, sixth Duke of, 39
Dickens, Charles, 47–8, 71
Dickinson, W. H., 157–8, 175, 217, 275
Dickson-Poynder, Lady, 99
Dilke, Sir C., 66, 74
Disraeli, B. (afterwards Lord Beaconsfield), 26; supports woman's franchise, 48–9, 58
Donaldson, Reverend F. L., 295
Dorrington, Sir J., 74
Dorset, Anne, Countess of, 20
Downing Street, 140, 174, 186, 200, 248, 295
Drummond, Flora, 'The General', 129–30, 136, 139, 174, 176, 181; and trial, 1908, 186–92; 203, 224, 237, 282, 293–4
Dublin, 271
Dudley, 281
Duval, Una, 245
Duval, Victor, 245

Earle, Mrs. C. W., 202
Edinburgh Suffrage Committee, 61
Edward VII, 172–3, 174, 221
Edwards, Amelia, 50
Edwardians, The, 107
Egoist, The, 40
Electoral Reform Bill, 1917, 304

Ellis, Sarah, 36
Elizabeth I, 180
Emmerson and Co., 113
Encyclopedia Britannica, 26
Englishwoman's Journal, 41, 64
Englishwoman's Review, 41
Ensor, Sir Robert, 14, 137, 167, 255
Ervine, St. John, 161
Esperance Girls Club, 137–8, 202–3
Euston Station, 270
Evening News, 143
Exeter Hall, 156
Eye Division, 139

Fabian Society, 109
Farquharson, J., 269–70
Fawcett, H., 60, 74, 90
Fawcett, Millicent Garrett, 6; speaks at 1869 meeting, 74; 88, 133, 134, 150, 151, 180, 247, 303
Featherstone Riots, 141–2
Ferguson, Rachel, 303
Fitzgerald, Edward, 303
Fitzherbert, Maud, 212
First Division Treatment, *see* Prison
'Flapper' Vote, 305
Fletcher-Vane, Sir F., 300
Fonblanque, Mrs. R., 266
Forcible Feeding, 204–8, 210–14, 283
Ford, Isabella, 153, 184
Forsyth, W., 84
Fortnightly Review, 67
Forster, K. W., 220
Fox, C. J., 23
Fox, Mrs. Dacre, 296, 305
Fox, Helen, 191
Franchise and Registration Bill, 1912, 272–3, 275, 281
Franklin, Hugh, 232
Fraser, Helen, 182
Fraser's Magazine, 90
Free Church League, 241
Free Trade, 125
Free Trade Hall, Manchester, 73, 127–9
French, Sir J. (afterwards first Lord Ypres), 145–6, 224
Fry, Mrs. T., 94
Furniss, Harry, 191

Gardenia Restaurant, 253
Gardiner, A. G., 146, 215
Garland, Alison, 305
Garnett, Theresa, 195
Garrett, Millicent, *see* Fawcett

Gateshead, 90
Gawthorpe, Mary, 147, 148, 160
General Elections:
  1865, 43, 48
  1868, 67, 85
  1895, 110
  1906, 108, 120, 125, 126, 132
  1910 (January), 193, 195, 215, 218–19
  1910 (December), 219, 230, 233–4,
    235, 236
  1918, 4, 157, 305
  1929, 306
George V, 236, 271, 284, 290, 286–7
Gerald, 'Queenie', 288–9
'Girl of the Period', 71
Girls Public Day School Company, 51
Girton College, 19, 41
Gladstone, Herbert (afterwards first
  Lord), 143–4, 151, 159, 179, 186,
  187–8, 195, 207, 211, 212, 228, 231,
  262
Gladstone, W. E., 43, 44, 45, 49, 51, 60,
  84, 91, 92–3
Glandore, 25, 30
Glasgow, 186
Glasier, Bruce, 111
Glasier, Mrs. Bruce, 115
Globe, The, 289
Gloyne, Mrs., 55
Glyn, Elinor, 216
Godwin, Mary, 23, 24
Goldsmid, Lady, 56
Gooch, Sir H., 162
Gore-Booth, Constance, *see* Markievicz
Gore-Booth, Eva, 102–7; friendship
  with Sylvia and Christabel Pankhurst,
  115–16; 119, 140, 162
Gore-Langton, Lady Anna, 53, 61
Gore-Langton, W., 60, 61
Gorton Division, 110
Goulden, R., 111
Goulding, Edward (afterwards first Lord
  Wargrave), 277
Grant, J. A., 278
Gray, Thomas, 111
Grantham, Mr. Justice, 112, 169
Great Scourge, The, 289
Gregory, William, 44
Green, Captain P., 207
Green Lady Hostel, Littlehampton, 138
Greig, Mrs., *see* Billington
Grey, second Lord, 23
Grey, Sir E. (afterwards Lord Grey of
  Fallodon), 127, 133, 236, 275–6, 278

Grey, Lady, 128
Grey, Mrs. William, 51
Gribble, Councillor, 123
Grosvenor Chapel, 64
Grote, Mrs., 74
Gurney, Russell, 60
Gymnastic Teachers Suffrage Associa-
  tion, 241

Hoggan, Mrs., 88
Haig, Florence, 175
Haldane, R. B. (afterwards Lord), 133,
  172
Hall, Mrs. S. C., 52
Hallam, Arthur, 56
Hammersmith, 168
Hampden in the Nineteenth Century, A, 29
Hampstead, 103
Hampton, 293
Hanover Square Rooms, 74
Harberton, Lady, 158–9
Harberton, sixth Lord, 158–9
Harcourt, Lewis (afterwards first Lord),
  248, 252, 271, 276–7
Hardie, Keir, elected for West Ham,
  1892, 98; 113, 123, 126; advises
  W.S.P.U., 128–30, 137; disagrees with
  Labour Party over woman's suffrage,
  134, 140; criticizes sentences on
  W.S.P.U. members, 143, 158; on
  'mother element' in politics, 171; 187,
  212, 228, 243; on forcible feeding,
  263; friendship with Sylvia Pankhurst,
  274; 303
Hare, T., 73
Harraden, Beatrice, 152, 180
Harries, T. J., 254
Hautboy Hotel, Oakham, 158–9
Haverfield, Mrs., 224
Hay, Lord J., 60
Hay, Lord W., 60
Healy, Tim, 200
Heitland, Mrs., 134
Helby, Dr. E., 207
Henderson, Arthur, 242, 275
Hereford, 89
Herkomer, Sir H. von, 294
Hewitt, Harold, 286
Hibbert, J., 85
Hicks, E. L., Bishop of Lincoln, 295
Higginsbottom, Abijah, 39
Hill, M. D., 61–2
Hill, Octavia, 49
Hill, Rosamund, 49

Hobhouse, Sir C., 252, 304
Holloway Gaol, 143, 148, 205, 206, 262, 270
Home Rule, 94, 109, 110, 175
Horsley, Sir V., 206
Hornsey, 233
Houghton, Lord, 74
House of Commons, 23; Reform Bill, 1832, 32–6; Reform Bill, 1866, 42–53; J. S. Mill's Amendment, 1867, 57–60; 79, 80, 82–90, 91–6, 97, 106, 121–4, 136; and imprisonment of militants, 143; 147, 157–8, 175, 176, 177–8, 187, 188, 189, 191, 193, 198, 203, 211; suffrage committee of, 221; progress of Conciliation Bill, 225; 274, 275–9, 280, 282–3, 288; passing of woman's suffrage, 304–5
House of Lords, 194, 209, 218, 225; Reform of, 230, 233, 236
Housman, Clemence, 265
Housman, Laurence, 198, 225
How-Martyn, Mrs., 165, 173, 305
Howard, Geoffrey, 217, 220
Howey, Elsie, 197, 224
Huddleston, Baron, 86
Hughes, Tom, 60
Hunger Strike, 204–8, 250, 282, 283
Hunslett Moor, 176
Hunt, Henry, 33, 34, 35
Huxley, T. H., 77
Hyde Park, meeting, 1867, 45–6; 108, 156, 181, 183, 300

Illingworth, Percy, 262
Independent Labour Party, 109, 110, 113, 114, 129, 131, 196
India Office, 269
Industry, women in, 101, 104, 106–7
International Suffrage Society, 197
Irby, Adeline, 93
Irish Party, 109, 132, 160, 235

Jackson, Reverend F., 270
Jacob's Well, Bristol, 51
James, Sir H., 89
James, Henry, 294
Jameson, Dr., 149, 264
Jameson, Mrs., 37
Jarvis, Miss, 196
Jersey, Lady (wife of 7th Lord), 216
Jewish League, 241
Jex-Blake, Sophia, 93
Joachim, Maud, 175

Joan of Arc, 180, 197, 241
Joicey, Mrs., 79
Joynson-Hicks, W. (afterwards first Lord Brentford), 130, 162–3, 236

Keary, Annie, 51
Keating, Mr. Justice, 68
Kemp, Sir G., 236
Kendal Milne, 111
Kenney, Annie, joins W.S.P.U., 120; and Churchill's meeting in Manchester, 127–9; 136, 140, 142–3, 167, 203, 255; leads W.S.P.U., 255–6; 257, 292, 303
Kensington, 248
Kew Gardens, 281, 291
Kilmarnock, 84
King, Joseph, 262
King's Cross, 284
Kingsley, Charles, 74
Kinnear, Boyd, 74
Kipling, Rudyard, 240
Kitchener of Khartoum, first Lord, 224
Knatchbull-Huggessen, E., 87
Knight, Anne, 37, 38, 39
Knight, Holford, 238–9
Knowsley, 290
Kyllman, Max, 55

Labouchere, H., vote in 1867 amendment, 60; opposes woman's suffrage, 60, 95–6, 100, 121, 122, 126
Labour Movement, women and trade unions, 100–1; the Wigan by-election, 104–6; its early strength, 107–8; attitude to woman's vote, 120, 125–6, 132; preference for adult suffrage, 134; sympathies for W.S.P.U., 137, 147, 153; difficulties with Liberals, 160; diminishing support for W.S.P.U., 170–1, 203; position in 1910 Parliament, 219, 235, 243; vote in favour of woman's suffrage at Labour Party Conference, 1912, 273–4; 289
Labour Party, *see above*
Labour Representation Committee, 114
Ladies Gallery, House of Commons, 96
Laing, S., 59
Lambeth Palace, 295
Lancashire and Cheshire Woman's Suffrage Society, 102
Lang, Anton, 222
Lansbury, G., 274–5, 276
Law, Hugh, 212

Laws, Harriet, 46
Lawson, Sir W., 80
Lee, Lord Chief Justice, 21, 22, 32
Leeds (South), 176
Leigh, Mrs., 186, 194; first victim of forcible feeding, 206; 224, 230, 271
Lever, Sir W. (afterwards Lord Leverhulme), 290
Lewen, Octavia, 168
Liberal Party, 43, 68; reasons for indifference to woman's suffrage, 91, 92, 96; 98, 125, 127, 235; triumph of 1906, 130, 132; and militant by-election strategy, 159–64; improved position after, 1908, 193, 203; forms exclusively Liberal suffrage committee in House of Commons, 217; reverse in 1910, 219; intentions on woman's suffrage in 1910, 220–1; 272
Licensing Bill, 1908, 162, 191
Lime Street, Liverpool, 290
Limehouse, 194–5
Lincoln's Inn, 66
Lincoln's Inn House, 256
Linton, Mrs. Lynn, 71–2, 94
Lissadell, 102, 103, 116
Littlehampton, 203
Liverpool Exchange Buildings, 290
Llewellyn Davies, Miss, 242
Lloyd George, David (afterwards first Lord), 121, 122, 133, 140–1, 157, 159, 186; gives evidence at Bow Street, 187–90, 191; and budget of 1909, 193–4; attacks on by militants, 194–5; Limehouse speech, 194; speech in Albert Hall, 195, 247; and at Newcastle, 209–10; attacks Conciliation Bill, 227–8, 243; speech at Bath, 244–5; 262, 269–70, 276, 281–2, 287–8, 301
Lloyd George, Lady M., 187
Local Government and women, 85–7, 102, 248
London Committee for Woman's Suffrage, 56–7, 61
London County Council, 86–7
London Dialectical Society, 70
London Pavilion, 292
London University, 66
Louise, Queen of Prussia, 279
Louth, 195
Lowndes, Mrs. Belloc, 41
Lowe, Robert, 45
Lucas, Mrs. Samuel, 52

Lucas, Mrs., 305
Lupton, Arnold, 212
Lush, Mr. Justice, 287–8
Lyttelton, Alfred, 228, 275, 276
Lytton, Bulwer, 26, 201
Lytton, Lady Constance, 25; joins W.S.P.U., 201; joins Esperance Club, 202–3; and militant tactics, 203–4; first arrest, 204; and her stone at Newcastle, 209–10; imprisonment and release, 210; sentenced to imprisonment in Walton Gaol, 213–14; disguised as 'Jane Warton', 213–14; 222, 223, 224, 238–9
Lytton, Rosina, Lady, 26
Lytton, second Lord, 221, 222, 227, 236, 302–3, 306

Macarthur, Mary, 242, 305
Macdona, John, 95
MacDonald, Ramsay, 245–6, 278
McEwan, Mrs. J., 305
McGregor, O. R., 15, 16
McKenna, Reginald, 133, 261–4, 283–4, 288, 291, 292–3, 301
MacKenzie, Mrs., 305
McLaren, Sir Charles (afterwards first Lord Aberconway), 152
McLaren, Duncan, 52
McLaren, Mrs. Duncan, 53, 61, 88, 140
MacNeill, Swift, 191
Macmillan, Chrystal, 134
Mackworth, Margaret (afterwards Lady Rhondda), 233–4
Malone, Miss, 168
Manchester, 109; Victoria Park, 110; Brookwood cemetery, 110; Nelson Street, 119; W.S.P.U. in, 120; by-election in N.W. Manchester, 127–31; Chief Constable of, 127; Art Gallery, 301; see also Becker, Lydia and Pankhurst, Richard and Emmeline, and Manchester and Women's Franchise
Manchester Barmaids Association, 163
Manchester Courier, 112
Manchester Guardian, 62, 95, 118, 161, 220, 265
Manchester, North-west Division, 130–1, 162–3, 236
Manchester and Women's Franchise, 38–9, 40; start of suffrage movement in, 54; formation of provincial committee in, 55; formation of permanent committee in, 61; by-election, 1867,

63–5; Fenian executions in, 65; Republican Club, 66; University, 66; first public meeting in support of women's franchise held in, 73; municipal election in, 87, 102; formation of W.S.P.U. in, 119–24; W.S.P.U. tactics in during 1906 election, 125–31

Manchester and Salford Women's Trade Council, 115

Manchester Women's Suffrage Committee, 55–6, 78

Manning, Anne, 56

Mansfield House Settlement, 138, 245

Marion, Kitty, 185, 272

Markham, Violet, 216, 248, 305

Markievicz, Countess, 103, 162–3, 305

Marks, Sidney, 249

Marlborough, Duchess of, wife of 9th Duke, 247

Married Women's Property Act, 76

Marsden, R., 66

Marsh, Charlotte, 194

Marshall, Mrs. Arthur, 248

Martel, Mrs., 182

Martin, Sir T., 75

Martineau, Harriet, 36–7, 51, 62

Marylebone Police Court, 142

Marx, Karl, 111

Mary, Queen, 284, 290, 296

Masefield, John, 303

Mason, Hugh, 84

Masson, Professor, 74

Masterman, C. F. G., 138, 211, 282

Matters, Miss, 173, 191, 199

Maxwell, Lily, 63–5

Mayne, Sir R., 46

Melford, Jackiedawra, 281

Meredith, George, 40, 154

Merrington, Martha, 51

Merthyr Tydfil, 130

Metcalfe, A. E., 15, 222, 291

Middleton, J. S., 242

Militant action, start of, 123–4, 273, 300; and throughout; *see also* W.S.P.U., *and* W.F.L.

Mill, James, 26, 27, 29, 34, 47, 59

Mill, J. S., autobiography, 25, 88; *Subjection of Women*, 28, 69; supports women's cause in Parliament, 47–62; and Westminster election, 48, 49; presents petition to Parliament, 50–3; introduces woman's suffrage amendment to Reform Bill, 1867, 57–60;

speech, 58–60, 65, 70; defeated for Westminster, 68; 71, 73, 74, 83, 87, 90, 96, 133, 178, 279

Mill, Mrs. J. S., 28, 47, 48, 59

Mond, Sir A., 257

Montagu, Edwin, 216–17

Montefiore, Mrs., 121, 147, 168

Moore, George, 204

Morgan, Lady, 37

Morley, John (afterwards Lord), 67, 77, 133, 262

Morning Post, 282

Morpeth, 285

'Mud' March, 156

Municipal Franchise and Women, 85–7

Munshi, The, 113

Murray, Colonel, 186, 189

Murray, Mrs. E., 305

Myers, F. W. H., 73

Nation, The, 246, 258, 261

National Association for Advancement of Social Science, 54, 109

National Gallery, 294

National Liberal Club, 236

National Review, 94

National Society for Women's Suffrage, 61, 78, 94, 134, 174, 299–300

National Union of Women's Suffrage Societies, *see above*

Naylor, Marie, 175

Neal, Mary, 137, 167, 202

Neilans, Miss, 169

Neligan, A., 198

Nevinson, H. W., 183, 195

Nevinson, Mrs. H. W., 209–10

New, Edith, 174, 186

Newbold, Sir H., 156

Newcastle-on-Tyne, 209, 211

Newdigate-Newdegate, Sir F., 88

Newman, Cardinal, 61–2

Newman, F. W., 61–2, 63, 65

News of the World, 281

Newton Abbot, 161

Newton Park, 61

Nichol, Mrs. Pease, 52

Nightingale, Florence, 19, 41, 50, 61, 89

Northampton, 96, 113, 141, 270

Northcote, Sir Stafford (afterwards Lord Iddesleigh), 147

Norwegian Amendment, 272

Nottingham Castle, 252

Nuneham House, 271

Index

Observer, The, 277
O'Donoghue, The, 60
Old Bailey, 200, 251, 255, 293, 300
Oldham, 85
Oliphant, L., 60
Osborne, Bernal, 221
Oxford Street, 248, 250
Oxted Railway Station, 290, 300

Page, Sir Francis, 21
Paine, Tom, 23
Palmerston, third Lord, 43, 65, 98
Pankhurst, Adela, 119
Pankhurst, Christabel, helps to found W.S.P.U., 114; studies law, 115; influence over Mrs. Pankhurst, 115; and Churchill's meeting in Free Trade Hall, 127–9, 135; and 'seize the mace, 159; appointed secretary, W.S.P.U., 167; 172, 182; and trial at Bow Street, 186–92; 196, 203, 213, 219; conservative influence and, 243, 244; flees to France, 251; conspiratorial methods, 253, 255–6, 259; relations with Labour, 273–4, 280; and sex warfare, 289, 304, 305, 306
Pankhurst, Emmeline, 29; and Wigan election, 105–6; Manchester origins, 111; upbringing and marriage, 111–12; opens shop, 113; life in London in 1890's, 113; takes work in Manchester, 113; decision to form Labour Party women's organization, 114; founds W.S.P.U., 114; and 'political action', 119, 121; 122, 123, 127, 129, 136, 139; on deputation to Prime Minister, 1906, 140; 141, 142, 144, 146; in scene at House of Commons, 147–8; on 'mud' march, 156–7, 159; and by-elections, 160–3, 176; and split in W.S.P.U., 164–70, 172; arrest and first imprisonment, 176–7, 180–2; and trial after Trafalgar Square speech, 186–92; 196, 198, 201, 203, 204, 213; and general election, January 1910, 219–20; 222, 223, 224, 230, 236, 238, 241, 243; conservative influences and, 243, 245; returns from U.S.A., 1912, 246; and stone throwing, 246–54; in prison, 250; speech at Old Bailey, 1912, 253; 256, 262, 280, 282, 285; Old Bailey trial, 1913, 287–8, 291–4; her personal following, 300–1; 303, 304

Pankhurst, H., 119
Pankhurst, Richard (1836–98), Manchester origins, 66; violence of opinions, 66, 67; appears in *Chorlton* v. *Lings*, 68, 86, 108, 109; attempts to enter Parliament 109–10; death and funeral, 110–11; speech in Manchester Town Hall, 112; supposed atheism, 112; 170
Pankhurst, Richard (grandson of above), 17
Pankhurst, Sylvia, 15; studies art, 115; 136, 137; following in East End, 147; prison sentence, 1906, 148, 149; 181–2, 253, 267; Labour sympathies, 274–5, 291, 301, 302
Parker, Louis N., 179–80
Parkes, Bessie (afterwards Madame Belloc), 41, 48, 226, 279
Parliament Square, 156
Parnell, C. S., 160, 170, 301
Parry, Judge, 208
Parry, L. J., 79–80
Paterson, Mrs., 101–2
Pease, J. W., 60
Peckham By-election, 161–2, 168
Pembroke, first Lord, 20
People's Suffrage Federation, 242–3
Percy, Lord (afterwards seventh Duke of Northumberland), 89
Pethick, Dorothy, 209
Pethick-Lawrence, Emmeline, meets Mrs. Pankhurst, 137; marriage, 138; treasurer, W.S.P.U., 138–9, 140; writes article for *Evening News*, 143; 144, 146; prison sentence, 1906, 148; 152, 165, 166, 167, 177, 182; speech at Caxton Hall, 1908, 187; 196; celebrations on her release from prison, 197–8; 202; influence with Lady C. Lytton, 203–4; 213–14, 219, 229, 245; in Holloway, 250; Old Bailey Trial, 1913, 252; breaks with Mrs. Pankhurst, 256; 274, 300, 305
Pethick - Lawrence, F. (now Lord Pethick-Lawrence), early years, 138; makes gift to W.S.P.U. during wife's imprisonment, 151–2; 164, 166, 167; and Bow Street trial, 190, 205–6; 219, 251, 252; conducts own defence at Old Bailey, 251–4; 274, 300, 306
Petition to Parliament, 1866, 50–3
Peto, Sir S., 60
Phipps, Mrs. E., 305

Piccadilly Circus, 248
Piccadilly Flat Case, 288
Piggott, John, 240
Pinner, 250
Pleydell-Bouverie, Edward, 17, 84–5, 87
Pochin, Davis, 73
Police and militants, 157, 159, 230–4
Ponsonby, Arthur (later first Lord of Shulbrede), 203–4
Poor Man's House, A, 117
Potter, F. B., 73
Potter, Richard, 74
Powell, Sir F., 104–5
Priestman, Anne, 165
Priestman, Mary, 168
Primrose League, 93–4
Prince's Skating Rink, 198, 265
Prison, First and Second Division Treatment in, 149–50, 190–1, 203, 205, 262–4
Prison Reform Act, 1898, 150
Prisoners Temporary Discharge Bill, 283–4
Pritchett, V. S., 14
Proctor, Adelaide, 41
Proudhon, 30
Punch, 89, 106, 240, 262

Quakers, 37, 52, 94
Queen Anne's Gate, 269
Queen's Hall, 203
Quickswood, Lord, *see* Cecil, Lord Hugh
Qui Vive Corps, 266

Rathbone, Eleanor, 134
Rea, Walter, 242
Redmond, W., 271
Rees, Sir J., 178
Referendum on Woman's Suffrage, 247
Reform Bills, 1832, 32, 43, 108; 1866, 43–5; 1867, 57–8; 1884, 92–3, 132
Reform Club, 64, 254, 281
Regent Street, 248
Reynolds, Stephen, 117
Richardson, Mary, 294–5
Riddell, Sir J. (afterwards first Lord), 281
Rigby, Mrs., 290
Robert Street, Strand, 166
Roberts, Charles, 257
Roberts, first Lord, 224
Roberts, George, 242
Robins, Elizabeth, 153, 167, 180
Robinson and Cleaver, 254

Robinson, Rona, 211
Rochdale, 83, 236
Rochester Row Police Court, 148
Roehampton Croquet Pavilion, 290
Rokeby Venus, 294
Rolls, C. S., 221
Romilly's Act, 1850, 58
Roper, Esther, 102–7, 115, 119, 162
Rosebery, 5th Lord, 107, 141, 186
Rossendale, 276
Rotherhithe, 95, 109, 112
Royal Family, Republican attacks on, 66
Royal Statistical Society, 109
Royden, Maude, 134
Runciman, Sir W., 209–10
Runciman, Walter (afterwards Lord), 133, 206, 262
Ruskin, John, 275
Russell, Lord Arthur, 91
Russell, Bertrand (afterwards third Lord), 164
Russell, Frances (wife of first Lord), 74
Russell, Lord John (afterwards first Lord), 43, 53
Russell, Marion (wife of second Lord), 225
Russell, second Lord, 150, 225
Russell Square, 113

Sackville-West, Victoria, 107
St. Albans, Duchess of, wife of 10th Duke, 247
St. Andrews, 234
St. Bartolph Without Bishopsgate, 21
St. Catherine's, Hatcham, 290
St. George's, Bloomsbury, 285
St. George's, Hanover Square, 290
St. Mary Abbot's, Kensington, 207
St. Pancras, 233
St. Paul's Cathedral, 294
Saintsbury, Professor, 136
Salford (South), 218–19
Samuel, Herbert (afterwards first Lord), 133, 232–3, 262
Sandford, Archdeacon, 73
Sandhurst, Lady, 86
Sandow, Eugene, 227
Sargent, J. S., 294
Saturday Review, 71
Saunderton Station, 281
Savoy Hotel, 152
Sayers and Wesson, 167
Scantlebury, Inspector, 181
Scatcherd, Mrs. Cliff, 111

Index

Schreiner, Olive, 201
Scott, C. P., 62
Scottish Churches League, 241
Scottish Liberal Council, 172
Second Division, see Prison
Selborne, Lady (wife of second Lord), 238-9
Selden (quoted), 68
Shackleton, David, 104, 226
Sharp, Cecil, 202
Sharp, Evelyn, 177, 180, 188
Shaw, G. B., 101, 152, 225, 266
Shaw, Mrs. G. B., 152, 225
Sheffield Association for Female Franchise, 39-40
Shirreff, Emily, 51
Sidney Street, 240
Silver King, The, 296
Simon, Sir J. (afterwards first Lord), 277
Sinclair, May, 153, 176-7
Sitwell, Sir J., 299
Sitwell, Sir O., 14, 202
Smallman, Mr., 86
Smith, F. E., afterwards first Lord Birkenhead, 226, 247, 279, 305-6
Smith, Harold, 283
Smith, Horace, 148, 150, 188, 189
Smith, Mary, 34-6
Smith, Sydney, 36
Smith, Lady Sybil, 245
Smith, Thorley, 105
Smith, W. H. (afterwards Lord Hambledon), 68-9
Smollet, P. B., 88-9
Smythe, Dr. E., 249, 251-2, 272
Snowden, Philip (afterwards first Lord), 56, 152, 158, 173-4, 178, 212, 217, 228, 243
Snowden, Mrs. P., 247
Social Service, Association for Advancement of, 54-5
Solomon, Mrs. S., 198, 231
Socialism, 108, 110-11
Social Democratic Federation, 145
Somerville, Mary, 51
Standard, The, 128, 239
Stanger, H., 175, 177-8, 217
Stanhope, P. (afterwards Lord Weardale), 270
Stanley, Dean, 62
Stead, W. T., 149-50, 264
Steinthal, Reverend J. A., 55
Stedhall's, 250
Stephen, Leslie, 25

Sterling, Antoinette, 113
Stewart, Lady H., 89
Stirling, 203
Stobart, Mrs. St. Clair, 267
Stockport, 300
Strachey, Lady, 237
Strachey, Mrs. Oliver, 16, 305
Strangeways Gaol, 128, 206-7
Speaker's Conference, 1916, 304
Spedding, James, 56
Spencer, Captain, 173
Spencer, Herbert, 74
Spencer, sixth Lord, 270
Spiritual Militant League, 240-1
Spring, Howard, 171, 205
Stroud Mechanics Institute, 74
Suffrage Atelia, 241
Suffragette, The, 256, 291
Suffragists, see Constitutional Societies
Swan and Edgar, 254
Swanson School Case, 263
Swannick, Anna, 51
Swannick, Mrs., 246
Swears and Wells, 254
Symons, Mrs. Travers, 187, 189

Talleyrand, 13
Tariff Reform, 125, 127, 227
Taylor, Helen, 47, 69, 74, 75
Taylor, John, 47
Taylor, Paul, 142
Taylor, P. A., 52, 60, 74
Taxes, refusal to pay, 168
Temperance Movement, 140
Temple, William (afterwards Archbishop of Canterbury), 295
Tennyson, Lord, 51, 56
Terreno, Mrs., 250
Thames Lightermen, 95
The Times, 67, 70, 93, 151, 182, 210, 238, 239, 249, 258, 260, 261
Thompson, William, 24; forerunner of Marx, 24; plea for female franchise, 24; attends debates of Co-operative Society, 25; friendship with Mrs. Wheeler, 25-31; reply to James Mill's article, 27-8; death and will, 30-1; 47, 306
Thorne, George, 304
Three Guineas, 116
Tillard, Miss, 191
Tod, Miss, 88
Trades Union Congress, 101
Trafalgar Square, 46, 140, 186

Trench, Sir F., 35
Trevelyan, G. M., 242
Trevelyan, Mrs. G. M., 242
Trollope, A., 59
Tuke, Mabel, 170, 248, 250
Truth, 70

Unitarians, 52
University Franchise, 272
Uppingham, 160

Valentia, eleventh Lord, 227
Verney, Sir E., 86
Victoria, Queen, 43, 75, 130, 271
Victoria Station, 284
Victoria Street, 281
Vote, The, 248, 257
Votes for Women, 167, 256

Wallace-Dunlop, Marion, 204-5
Walpole, Horace, 21, 23, 81
Walsall, 85
Walton Gaol, Liverpool, 213, 214
Walton Heath, 281
War of 1914-18, 298, 304, 306
Warburton, Bishop, 36
Ward, Mrs. Humphrey, 216, 223, 261, 299
Ward, John, 264
Wargrave Church, 290
Warton, Jane, 213
Watts, G. F., 53
Webb, Beatrice, 110, 135
Webb, Sidney, 110
Webbe, A. J., 225
Webster, Augusta, 51
Webster, Daniel, 79
Wedgwood, Mrs. Hensleigh, 56
Wellington, fourth Duke of, 294
Wells, H. G., 99, 100, 177, 186, 199
West Ham, 98
West London Mission, 137
West, Rebecca, 289
Westminster Abbey, 175, 290-1, 295
Westminster Hall, 49
Wetherell, Sir C., 33
Wharry, Olive, 281
Wheeler, Francis, 27
Wheeler, Mrs., wife of above, 25-31, 201
Wigan, 104-6, 126, 130
White House Linen Specialists, 254
White's Club, 236
Whig Party, 43
Wilberforce, William, 36

Wilde, Oscar, 239
Wilde, Percy, 263
Wilding-Davison, Emily, 206-7, 208, 270-1, 284-6, 287
Wilks, Dr., 265-6
Wilks, Mark, 265
Willes, Sir J., 68
Wilson, P. W., 138, 244
Wimbledon, 164
Winkworth, Emily, 42
Winkworth, Susannah, 51
Winning Post, The, 289
Winterton, sixth Lord, 277, 301
Wise v. *Dunning*, 190
Wolmer, Lord (afterwards second Lord Selborne), 84
Wolstenholme, *see next entry*
Wolstenholme-Elmy, Mrs., 55-6, 123, 140, 167, 181
Women's Convoy Corps, 267
W.F.L., *see* Women's Freedom League
Women's Franchise League, 113, 168, 173, 232
Women's Freedom League, formation, 164-71; 180-1, 191, 199; lenient treatment of, 200, 210; suspends militancy, 222, 224; and modified militancy, 240-1, 265, 273
Women's Liberal Federation, 93-4, 125, 174
Women's Right to Vote, historical arguments, 20-4; and the Reform Bill, 1832, 32-6; petition to Parliament, 1832, in favour of, 34-6; inclusion in the Charter, 38; and Reform Bill, 1867, 42-62; confused state of law, 63-8; right to be admitted to Register, 65-9; objection to on grounds of decorum, 70-2; lack of progress after 1870, 76; strength of prejudice against, 77-8; discussions in House of Commons, 82-96; uncertain effect on parties, 91-2; indifference to in Parliament in 1890's, 99; petition in favour of, 99; and Wigan election, 104-7; support for in 1906 Parliament, 132; difficulties in Parliament, 147, 154-5; analysis of voting on 1908 bill, 178; deadlock in House of Commons, 216-20; changed position after 1910 election, 220; and service in 1914 war, 298-9
W.S.P.U., *see next entry*
Women's Social and Political Union, formation in Manchester, 114-15;

inaugural meeting, 119; connections with Labour Party, 119, 170–1; its speakers, 119; 121, 122; differences with Labour leaders, 126; work at General Election, 1906, 127–31, 196, 210; affinity with I.L.P., 129, 133; attempts to coerce Parliament, 136–7; influence on of Pethick-Lawrences, 138–9; 140, 150, 151; parliamentary objective, 155; and by-elections, 159–63; split with W.F.L., 164–70; and London, 169–70; 174, 180–3; increasing hostility to Liberals, 184–5; organizes meeting to 'rush the House of Commons', 186, 192; 'Ignorance of Parliamentary Life', 216–17; suspension of militancy, 222; support for Conciliation Bill, 223; and London procession, 1910, 224–6; resumption of militancy, 229–30, 232; and London procession, 1911, 237, 237–8; and newspaper publicity, 239–40, 243; and sex loyalty, 246, 250; arrest of leaders, 250–1; trial at Old Bailey, 251–4; criticism of leadership and split, 255–9, 300–1; relations with Labour Party in 1912, 273–4; in the East End, 274–5; 280, 285, 286; and sex warfare, 287–9, 291, 292; headquarters raided, 293; its funds, 293; sponsors' attacks on Royalty and disturbances in churchs, 296–7

Woman's Suffrage Bills, in nineteenth century, 82–90; 1904, 121; 1905, 121–2; Dickinson's Bill, 157–8; 1909, 217; 1910, 233; 1913, 278–81; *see also* Conciliation Bill

Women's Suffrage Journal, 79–81
Women Trades Union League, 101
Wood, Mrs. Henry, 50
Woodall, William, 84
Woods, Colonel W., 106
Woolf, Virginia, 15, 117
Wordsworth, C., 56
Wordsworth, William, 36
Working-man and the Vote, 43, 106
Worms, Baron de, 84
Wormwood Scrubs, 149
Wospola, 167
Wright, Sir Almroth, 260–1, 287
Wyndham, George, 84
Wyndham, Percy, 60

Yarmouth Pier, 290
Yeats, W. B., 103
York, 94
Yonge, C. M., 50

Zangwill, Israel, 152, 169